BROTHERS
and
STRANGERS

STEVEN E. ASCHHEIM

BROTHERS
and

THE EAST EUROPEAN JEW IN GERMAN AND GERMAN JEWISH CONSCIOUSNESS, 1800–1923

STRANGERS

THE UNIVERSITY OF WISCONSIN PRESS

Published 1982

The University of Wisconsin Press
114 North Murray Street
Madison, Wisconsin 53715

The University of Wisconsin Press, Ltd.
1 Gower Street
London WC1E 6HA, England

Copyright © 1982
The Board of Regents of the University of Wisconsin System
All rights reserved

First printing

Printed in the United States of America

For LC CIP information see the colophon

ISBN 0-299-09110-4

The chapter "Caftan and Cravat" is published
by permission of Transaction, Inc.,
from Political Symbolism in Modern Europe,
by Drescher and Sharlin,
copyright © 1982 by Transaction Books.

TO MY MOTHER
AND TO THE MEMORY OF MY FATHER ז"ל

And if thy brother be waxen poor, and fallen in decay with thee; then thou shalt relieve him: yea, though he be a stranger, or a sojourner; that he may live with thee.

Leviticus   25:35

CONTENTS

ILLUSTRATIONS

PREFACE

THIS work examines the place of East European Jews in German and German Jewish consciousness. On a more general level, it attempts to delineate the fateful and complex role of "the ghetto" in modern self-understanding. The analysis is not primarily socio-economic, demographic, or institutional, nor is the central focus upon the migration and absorption of East European Jews into Germany. These aspects have been covered by S. Adler-Rudel in *Ostjuden in Deutschland 1880–1940*, and more definitively, by Jack L. Wertheimer in his "Germany Policy and Jewish Politics: The Absorption of East European Jews in Germany (1868–1914)."* I include such data where appropriate, but my central goal has been to write a cultural and intellectual history. I have attempted to discover the nature of discourse concerning the East European Jews and to pinpoint its major changes and continuities. This will, I hope, help to fill a significant gap in the literature.

Although the study is basically about Germany, I have included the experience of other areas of the German *Kulturbereich* (Austria and Czechoslovakia) where this has directly influenced German attitudes or is of comparative value.

*Both works are listed in the bibliography at the back of this book. Wertheimer's thesis, which became available to me only after I had completed the original version of my book, contains much of importance. Given its different emphases and approach, it should be regarded as complementary to my own.

It is a pleasure to record my debt to George L. Mosse. He has had a profound personal as well as intellectual influence on my life. His guidance and acute criticism have always been constructive, his interest and support unfailing. Without him I would never have begun, let alone completed, this work.

Sterling Fishman has been the source of constant encouragement and warmth, his friendship deeply valued. Stanley Payne has always gone out of his way to help and encourage me. I must make special mention of Klaus Berghahn. His unflagging interest, numerous suggestions, and bibliographic references have all been incorporated in this work. I also thank Jehuda Reinharz and Alexander Orbach for their useful suggestions.

For their generous assistance, I am indebted to the staffs of the Memorial Library of the University of Wisconsin in Madison, the Library of Congress, Washington, D.C., and the Jewish National and University Library in Jerusalem. The archivists at the Leo Baeck Institute in New York, the Central Zionist Archives, the Martin Buber Archives, and the Central Archives for the History of the Jewish People (all in Jerusalem) were unfailingly helpful and courteous. I also wish to express my appreciation to the Memorial Foundation for Jewish Culture, whose grants partly supported the conception and completion of this work. I am grateful to Mary Maraniss and to those on the editorial and production staffs of the University of Wisconsin Press who helped transform my manuscript into a book. I thank Deborah Goldberg for her bibliographical and technical assistance.

Last, but far from least, my beautiful wife, Hanna, and my lovely children, Ariella and Yoni, made sure that I never lost my sense of perspective. They made this worth writing.

BROTHERS
and
STRANGERS

1

GERMAN JEWRY AND THE MAKING OF THE OSTJUDE, 1800—1880

THE idea of the *Ostjude* ("Eastern" Jew) was developed, in its essentials, over the course of the first half of the nineteenth century. To be sure, the generic term *Ostjude* did not gain popular currency until the early twentieth century.[1] Nevertheless, a generalized negative thinking prevailed much earlier. East European Jews were held to be dirty, loud, and coarse. They were regarded as immoral, culturally backward creatures of ugly and anachronistic ghettoes. In large part this was a view formulated and propagated by West European and especially German Jews, serving as a symbolic construct by which they could distinguish themselves from their less fortunate, unemancipated East European brethren. In this sense, the very notion "Ostjude" was the product of the modernization of Jewish life and consciousness, for before the penetration of Enlightenment thinking, Jews did not divide themselves into radically antithetical "Eastern" and "Western" components. Local differences had always existed, but in the preemancipation era they were of little significance when compared with the overall similarities. Jews everywhere lived in what Jacob Katz has called "traditional" society,[2] and were bound by a common sociopolitical situation and linked by a shared system of beliefs and attachments.

Within that traditional social context there was a strong sense of Jewish solidarity. Before the era of emancipation East European Jews who moved to Western Europe underwent a very different experience from the one that awaited their counterparts in the nineteenth century. Between 1600 and 1800 wave after wave of Eastern Jews made their way to Western Europe. The reception given them was generally cordial. Local Jews did everything they could to help, and despite some natural initial tensions, integrated these Jews into their own communities. It was only in the late eighteenth century that the attitude changed and a generalized antagonism began to develop.[3] It is not difficult to see why this should have been the case: the new antipathy went hand in hand with the attempt to modernize Jewish life and thinking. The overwhelming concern for enlightenment and emancipation gradually effaced the older, more traditional sentiments.

Nineteenth-century Jewish emancipation in Western Europe destroyed both the assumptions and bases of traditional Jewish society. Inevitably, it also transformed older patterns of Jewish national solidarity, for at least in theory, political equality demanded a new kind of Jew whose identity was so closely interwoven with the modes of his particular society that he would be recognizable only within that specific society. This marks the birth of the *German* or *English* or *French* Jew.[4]

A novel situation had been created. Jewish historical development was now characterized by a profound disjunction. On the one hand, emancipation and enlightenment in the West; on the other, the continuation of political disenfranchisement and traditional Jewish culture in Eastern Europe. The new polarity introduced an unprecedented dialectical tension into Jewish life.

Many West European Jews expressed their disdain for Eastern Jews, but it was in Germany that such notions were given their most radical formulation. This was so because German Jews felt the rift most acutely. Germany, after all, bordered Poland, a geographical factor of great importance. The physical accessibility of Germany from Poland had for centuries made it the historical gateway for Jews migrating from East to West.[5] Moreover, Prussia's acquisition of Poland's western provinces in 1772 and of Posen in 1793 and 1795 brought the problem literally closer to home.

When Jewish emancipation became the center of public discussion in Germany, this proximity became a potent argument against emancipation. Critics asserted that granting political freedom would lead to an invasion of Jews from Eastern Europe.[6] The concern was a continuing one; in fact, the Jews of Posen were not granted the same rights as Jews of the other Prussian provinces until 1847, and caught between Poles and Germans, maintained an "Eastern" image into the twentieth century. While the geographical dimension was absent in other West European countries, German Jews were never able to forget that they shared a common border with the unemancipated Eastern ghetto masses. Throughout the nineteenth century and into the twentieth, German Jewish history was conditioned by this presence, as both myth and reality.[7] Elsewhere in Western Europe the East European Jew was an irritant; in Germany, for both Jew and non-Jew, he became a major preoccupation and at times even an obsession.

The story of German Jewish assimilation would therefore be incomplete without taking this factor into account. For assimilation was not merely the conscious attempt to *blend* into new social and cultural environments but was also purposeful, even programmatic, *dissociation* from traditional Jewish cultural and national moorings. Such dissociation was of course part of the general Emancipation agreement and was not limited to Germany. It must be remembered that the path to German Jewish emancipation, unlike the French, was extremely rocky and was not fully achieved until 1871. In this tortuous process, marked by constant pressure to prove their fitness for equal rights, German Jews provided assimilation with its most systematic ideological articulation.[8]

An examination of the ways in which this ideology operated may help to reveal the "underside" of Jewish assimilation. For when that ideology had matured and was broadly diffused throughout German Jewry, it was not just the modern "German Jew" who had emerged as a new and distinctive creation, there was also his mirror opposite, his antithesis—the "Eastern Jew," embodiment of all those negative traditional traits German Jews had purportedly overcome. The emergent stereotype of the Ostjude was as much the product of the acceptance of Enlightenment thinking as was German Jewry's own new self-image. Both had their origins in the drive to modernity; both were the outcome of the breakdown of traditional Jewish self-understanding and signalled the rise of new modes of cultural perception. One fashioned the other.

By the second half of the nineteenth century, the expression *ghetto Jew* had become virtually synonymous with *Ostjude*, but this exclusive identification was relatively new. At the beginning of the century, German Jews had also been considered ghetto Jews. In Germany, discussions about the ghetto and ghetto Jews did not refer merely to areas in which Jews were forced to live by law. The conception was far broader than that. *The ghetto* referred to the simple fact of Jewish physical concentration regardless of its coercive or voluntary origins, and even more crucially, to the perception of the separatist culture generated by such concentration. *Ghetto* increasingly came to connote a state of mind. It was not necessary for Germans of the eighteenth and early nineteenth centuries to cross the border to get a view of Jewish ghetto life thus understood. Goethe's classic description of the ghetto as he remembered it from his youth in the 1750s referred to the Jewish quarter in Frankfurt and not to Eastern Europe, and there was nothing agreeable about his experience. In the narrow streets he encountered dirt, throngs of people, the accent of an "unpleasing language," and ceaseless haggling.[9] For Goethe and many others, the ghetto seemed to concentrate all the negative aspects of Jewish life within its boundaries. Jews like Heinrich Heine shared this viewpoint. Heine concluded his description of the same ugly Frankfurt ghetto by calling it "a dreadful monument of the Middle Ages."[10]

The ghetto, Enlighteners argued, had produced an essentially unacceptable culture. Jews were utter strangers to Europe. Social isolation had created traits in need of drastic transformation: Jews harbored within them hatred of the Christian nurtured by centuries of Talmudic and rabbinic indoctrination, they were religious fanatics, parasitic in their economics and dishonest in their dealings.[11]

Christian Wilhelm Dohm's classic tract *Concerning the Amelioration of the Civil Status of the Jews* (*Ueber die bürgerliche Verbesserung der Juden*, 1781) was typical of the Enlightenment approach. Dohm grasped the sociological nature of the problem and attributed Jewish defects to Christian maltreatment, but like most other Enlighteners, he never doubted the existence of the defects themselves. Jewish habits and superstitions, products of the long historical experience in the ghetto, would have to be overcome. Emancipation was conditional upon the successful transcendence of the inheritance of the ghetto.

This identification of the ghetto with social pathology was to become the norm in almost all modern discourse concerning the Jews. To the outside observer, ghetto culture appeared morally and physically degenerate. It conjured up images of medieval separatism and religious obscurantism. Already at the beginning of the nineteenth century the ghetto symbolized the distinction between enlightenment and superstition, progress and reaction, even beauty and ugliness.

The German Jew's attack upon his own and later upon the East European ghetto was made easier by the fact that the attack was in the mainstream of Enlightenment humanism. Jewish reformers quickly agreed that integration required emphatic rejection of ghetto traits, traits which Goethe in his discussion of the traditional rabbi had summed up as "fanatic zeal . . . repulsive enthusiasm . . . wild gesticulations . . . confused murmurings . . . piercing outcries . . . effeminate movements . . . the queerness of an ancient nonsense."[12]

From 1800 to 1850 German Jews applied the critique of the ghetto to themselves as well as to other Jews; only when German Jewry was sufficiently confident that its own ghetto inheritance had been overcome did the stereotype of the Ostjude assume its full meaning. The Eastern European Jew became exclusively identified as the ghetto Jew toward the middle of the nineteenth century, when most German Jews began to regard their own project of cultural assimilation as relatively complete.

This was so at least for the urban centers of Germany. It was in the cities that the "new Jewry" was created and its journals and salons set the tone. Urban intellectuals articulated the premises of cultural assimilation. We know less about the inarticulate Jews—the peddlers, cattle-dealers, small businessmen—who lived in the villages and small towns. In the mid-nineteenth century they were still the majority of German Jews; even in the villages the Jews were the "middle class." But rapid urbanization coupled with the political and economic importance of the cities meant that the larger Jewish communities set the tone, while the voice of village Jews remained muted. We need therefore to turn to the experience of cultural assimilation in the cities. (It goes without saying that the rates of assimilation varied from place to place. The process was never a uniform one.)

What was the substance of Jewish assimilation? In practice it was linked to the process of *embourgeoisement*. German Jewry never had a wide social base. Jews did not integrate into some abstract *Volk* but into the middle class,[13] and they spent much of the nineteenth century internalizing the economic, ethical, and aesthetic standards of that class. Yet they interpreted these standards in a particular way. As George Mosse has demonstrated, the Jewish struggle for emancipation occurred when the Enlightenment ideal of *Bildung* was at its height.[14] Jews enthusiastically accepted the ideal, and long after the non-Jewish German middle class had deserted its tenets of rationality, tenaciously clung to it. What was the ideal of *Bildung*? As enunciated variously by Goethe, Schiller, Humboldt, and Herder, it centered on the theme of self-improvement and referred to an integrated conception of "rationality" and "refinement." The person of *Bildung* was one who showed breeding, who had developed his higher spiritual faculties. Most simply, *Bildung* implied the self-cultivation of a "cultured" personality.[15] German Jews never lost sight of these Enlightenment ideals. Their belief in the primacy of culture, which to them meant faith in reason and the regenerative power of ideas and education, remained a central if illusory element in their view of life.

Assimilation legitimated itself according to the perceived dictates of the *Bildung* ideal. That ideal determined the pattern of German acculturation and became the criterion by which traditional Jewish culture was judged. More often than not, *Bildung* seemed to require that old Jewish habits be discarded and traditional modes of Jewish solidarity disbanded.

Little illustrates this better than the attitude of the early reformers towards *jüdisch-deutsch* (Yiddish). This, of course, was the pre-Emancipation language of both German and East European Jewry. Enlighteners everywhere opposed the *Jargon*, seeing it as an impediment to local linguistic integration and assuming that feelings of Jewish national unity would weaken if there were no common language. But the attack was particularly marked in Germany, for there the situation was doubly embarrassing. The *Jargon*, after all, was widely regarded as a corrupt and lowly derivation of German itself. Elsewhere Yiddish sounded merely strange, but in Germany it was precisely its familiarity that bred contempt. Because of this, German Jewish modernizers invested the language with almost demonic powers. In 1782, Moses Mendelssohn, who had used the language himself as a youth, declared that Yiddish had "contributed not a little to the immorality of the common man; and I expect a very good effect on my brothers from the increasing use of the pure German idiom."[16] The *Jargon* seemed to embody all the negative Jewish qualities of the past. Its association with coarse Jewish behavior made it the very antithesis of *Bildung*. More and more the traditional ghetto Jew—the language he spoke, the habits he retained—became synonymous with *Unbildung*, counter-example of what the new German Jew had to become. It was typical that faith in culture led to the belief that immorality could be countered by the correct use of language, that purity of expression would somehow create an ethically upright personality.

Such a transformation, it was argued, could be accomplished only by education. It was an urgent task, for as Tobias Feder wrote at the beginning of the nineteenth century, Yiddish sounded to the modern ear like the "cackling of hens or the snorting of cattle."[17] Reformers held that only a systematic educational campaign to suppress "that corrupted dialect" and replace it with "pure" German would have any effect,[18] but the problem was not easy to solve and as late as 1841 one finds complaints about the prevalence of the *Jargon*. This was an impossible situation, one educational theorist proclaimed, for real *Bildung* was attainable only through the use of an uncorrupted German.[19] All sections of the German Jewish community were influenced to distance themselves from their own language. The "new" Orthodox community under the leadership of S. R. Hirsch held essentially the same opinions as the most extreme Reformers. Jüdisch-deutsch, their journal reported, was like a "caricature," incomprehensible to German ears and a "profanation" of the beautiful German language.[20]

Self-rejection was not limited to the linguistic realm; a generalized middle-class gentility became the norm for Jewish behavior.[21] Jewish reformers stressed manners, politeness, and refinement and contrasted these modes with the crudity and boorishness of traditional Jewish life. What distinguished the ethical and noble person from the common man? The editor of *Sulamith* had no hesitation in answering the question: a feeling for the aesthetic, a sense of the beautiful in art and nature.[22] His choice was not a random one, for it stressed precisely those qualities which were lacking in the ghetto Jew. The "new" Jew was defined in terms of what the old Jew was not. Only when a portrait of the Madonna could inspire the Jew, proclaimed the author, would the transition be successfully accomplished. Others stressed "industriousness" and greeted the disappearance of the West European *Yeschiwoth* (Talmud schools) as a form of liberation. Jews could now enter into "useful" occupations and joyously apply their newly acquired worldly knowledge to "productive" work.[23] Traditional rabbinic endeavors were labelled obscurantist. *Bildung*, not Talmudic study, was the route to the modern work ethic. It was the vehicle for transmitting the predilections of middle-class morality. Embourgeoisement came suitably camouflaged in Enlightenment dress.

These were some of the ways in which German Jews attempted to transcend their ghetto past and erase its influence from their personal and collective Jewish lives. But to be modern was also to be perceived as such. Jewish modernization meant more than the acquisition of new rights and work habits. It also entailed a change of dress, a modulation of tone, a lowering of the decibel level. Assimilation demanded the disappearance of the conspicuous ghetto Jew. Traditional external badges of distinction had to be removed. That is why the dress of the Ostjuden, the caftan and sidelocks, was regarded in later times as a source of embarrassment, a deliberate provocation to the non-Jew. German Jews, Orthodox as well as others, increasingly stressed the need for social blending. The absence of a hat is conspicuous in an 1835 rabbinical portrait of Samson Raphael Hirsch. The wig that he wore was deliberately intended to simultaneously satisfy Jewish religious requirements and conform with the general fashion of the day.[24]

One worried Jewish commentator, Anton Rée, wrote in 1844 that political freedoms and religious reform had not led to any real emancipation.[25] The gap that divided Jew from non-Jew, he argued, was really *social* in nature: it could be bridged only by a radical reshaping of Jewish manners and mannerisms. Proving one's worthiness of emancipation was no easy task. For Rée, unless Jews ceased to act in ways that immediately betrayed their Jewishness, civil equality would never be realized. His work is a sustained plea to German Jews to once and for all remove all traces of the cramped ghetto past from their language and gestures. Only this would render them *salonfähig* (socially respectable). Rée explicitly incorporated "gentility" as an official Jewish aim. ("Es is doch gar zu ungentil, ein Jude zu sein!")[26] In polite (that is, non-Jewish) company, Jewish characteristics were a source of shame.

Rée's diagnosis of and solution to the problem is a marvelous illustration of nineteenth-century assimilationist assumptions.[27] He perceived the problem largely in terms of etiquette, almost as an exercise in impression management. Manner of speech became a key to social acceptance. By "dialect" Rée meant not only the *Jargon* but also the tone and manner and the particular gesticulations Jews used, even when speaking German. It was to these particularly "Jewish" elements that he referred when he proposed setting up special schools to be run by teachers committed to the correct use of German and who knew how to combat the Jewish dialect in the proper manner. For Rée the problem could be solved only by treating the entire *Gestalt* of the ghetto Jew. Only then would the dialect disappear.

Assimilationists were not merely being ultrasensitive; Jewish speech was the subject of much caustic non-Jewish discussion. The dialect became a favorite means for German playwrights to ridicule Jewish attempts at acculturation. One actor, Albert Aloys Ferdinand Wurm, won special popularity with his imitations of Jews lapsing uncontrollably into the *Jargon*, despite the fiercest efforts to sustain a conversation in correct German.[28] There was a long tradition of identifying Jews according to their manner of speech. The words *judeln* and *mauscheln*—from Mausche, Mosche (Moses)—had entered the German language long before as pejorative terms denoting Jewish ways of talking. Significantly, they also referred to Jewish ways of thinking and economic dealing.[29] Both terms retained currency through the Nazi period.

Nineteenth-century German Jews, then, shared the general distaste for the ghetto and what it symbolized, but because they themselves were products of the ghetto they internalized the distaste in a particularly intense and urgent way. Certainly by the time the westward mass migrations of East European Jews began in the 1880s, German Jews believed that they had succeeded in their project of deghettoization. By then it seemed that only the unemancipated Eastern Jew rightfully fitted the description "ghetto Jew." Ostjuden retained precisely those characteristics which German *Bildungsjuden* had sought so mightily to overcome: locked in narrow Talmudic worlds, unproductive itinerants, boorish and dirty, still speaking the despised *Jargon*, they were identical with *Unbildung*, the incarnation of the Jewish past which German Jews had rejected and transcended.

It must be noted that we are talking here of images and stereotypes. East European Jews were usually perceived as an undifferentiated mass and this, of course, was misleading. The Jews of Warsaw and Vilna were different in many ways from those living in obscure Galician ghettoes, for instance. Regional differences and varying modes of religious identification were compounded by the fact that amongst a small but visible minority, *Haskalah* (Jewish Enlightenment) had penetrated quite deeply. There was no single way of life and thinking that characterized all these Jews. But stereotypes are never constructed as refined instruments of social understanding. They serve other, less disinterested, purposes. Yet all myths possess a core of reality. The notorious Pale of Settlement, after all, was no figment of the imagination. The masses of Russian, Polish, and Austro-Hungarian Jewry *did* live in conditions of desperate poverty. There *were* dark, dirty, and overcrowded ghettoes. The language of discourse *was* overwhelmingly Yiddish—as late as 1897, 96.9 percent of Russian Jewry declared this to be their mother tongue—and the vast majority of East European Jews continued to live in recognizably traditional and "Jewish" ways.[30] There was enough substance to give the stereotype plausibility.

Increasingly, East European Jewry, bordering Germany and constantly infiltrating her space and consciousness, became the living reminder to German Jewry of its own recently rejected past. The Eastern Jew was the bad memory of German Jewry come alive and an ever-present threat to assimilationist aspirations. At the same time he was a convenient foil upon which German Jews could externalize and displace what were regarded as negative Jewish characteristics. Precisely because he was perceived as a threatening remnant of a bygone age, the Ostjude could also become a psychological repository into which German Jews could deflect anti-Jewish sentiments. This dual function of the ghetto Jew—threat and foil—came into its own when, in the wake of persecution and poverty, masses of East European Jews streamed into Western Europe in the 1880s.

By that time, two radically juxtaposed Jewish cultures appeared to confront each other. The distance between the Enlightened, Western Jew and the unemancipated Ostjude of the ghetto seemed almost unbridgeable. The ghetto was described as a kind of anthropological curiosity: "Whoever desires to experience an ethnological sensation need not venture to the far corners of the world. For that, a day's journey from Berlin will suffice. One need only cross the Russian border to find an almost unknown human type full of mystery and wonder . . . to look with astonishment at these people with their dirty caftans, the exotic faces which, like ghostly apparitions from times long lost, still haunt the modern present. . . ."[31]

The nineteenth-century transformation of the German Jew into the *Bildungsjude* was complete. It was across the border, in the Eastern ghettoes, that Jewish *Unbildung* was to be found.

The transformation was not completed until the second half of the nineteenth century. Yet it should be clear that while German Jewry applied the rationalist critique of the ghetto to itself, it always reserved a special animus for the Jews of Eastern Europe and especially Poland.

As we have seen, assimilationists emphasized pedagogic reform as a major instrument for the cultural reconstruction of the Jewish self. As a result of their migrations over the years 1600–1800, Polish Jews had come to dominate the institutions of German Jewish education. These Polish teachers were consistently accused of "infecting" the language of German youth with their despicable *Jargon*.[32] Heinrich Grätz, for instance, attributed the entire "degeneration" of West European Jewry directly to this early "Polonization," and argued that Polish Talmudists had reduced the "language of the German Jews . . . to a repulsive stammer."[33]

The criticism was not limited to language. It was based, after all, upon the newly acquired criteria of the Enlightenment: all of traditional Jewish culture was judged through these new spectacles. Thus as early as 1812, educational thinkers were stressing that Polish Jewish teachers were importing more than bad grammar into Germany and were the quintessential embodiments of a flawed and backward culture. Unlike German Jews, who were straining towards genuine science and rationality (*wahre Wissenschaft*), these Polish teachers were purveyors of Talmudic sophistry, or worse yet, the superstitious aberrations of Kabbalah.[34]

In this manner, from the beginning of the Enlightenment, Polish Jews were made to bear a special burden. If assimilation did not proceed apace, it was their defects that could be blamed. Accepted educated opinion held that these Polish Jews had nothing in common with the more civilized modes of "quiet and straight" thinking characteristic of Enlightened men. German *Bildung* was explicitly juxtaposed to Polish Talmudic barbarism. At times the attack was so extreme that avowed Enlightenment environmentalists doubted whether Polish Jews had the capacity to progress: they suffered from "psychic deafness" and assimilated everything in an undifferentiated manner according to their inherited conceptual habits.[35]

Certain elements of East European Jewish life appeared especially unattractive to the proponents of the new rationalism. Poland, after all, was the home of Hasidism, the late-eighteenth-century mystical movement that spread rapidly across most of Eastern Europe. This "revolutionary" movement seemed profoundly antithetical to the fashionable German Jewish idea of "the religion of Reason" and was roundly condemned for its irrationalist and superstitious character.

Early assimilationists like David Friedländer, an avowed advocate of universalist Enlightenment principles, obviously found this movement extremely unpleasing, categorizing it as "an incomprehensible mixture of cabalistic, mystical and neo-platonic ideas."[36] Perhaps more surprising were the attitudes of leading figures of the *Wissenschaft des Judentums* (Science of Judaism), which had its origins in the first two decades of the nineteenth century. Their view of Jewish irrationalism in general, and Hasidism in particular, was equally antagonistic. This appeared to contradict their early goals. After all, the *Wissenschaft des Judentums* developed under the influence of German romantic historiography, which stressed the unique qualities of different nations and cultures as part of a conscious reaction to abstract Enlightenment universalism.[37] Leopold Zunz's formulation of the goals of the new *Wissenschaft* explicitly applied this cultural historicism to an open-ended investigation of all Jewish sources. The study of Judaism was to be nondogmatic in approach, all-inclusive in focus. Consequently one would have expected a serious, perhaps even sympathetic, study of "nonrational" Jewish phenomena. This was not to be the case, for as we have seen, German Jews were still engaged in an immediate political task: they still had to prove their worthiness of Emancipation, an impulse that tended to express itself in distinctly apologetic scholarship. The drive for acceptance on the basis of *Bildung* muted the formal romanticist principles. On this point Wissenschaft Jews differed little from their Enlightenment predecessors: despite the nineteenth-century historicist rhetoric, they remained wedded to eighteenth-century rationalist and universalist principles. *Bildung* and reason were the keys to social and political acceptance. It was typical that Zunz, upon touring Leipzig in 1820, would write that the aesthetic dimension of the city was marred for him when he came across some Hasidim from Sklow who "screamed and raved and sang like the savages of New Zealand."[38] Abraham Geiger, the great theoretician of modern Reform Judaism, regarded Hasidism as an expression of ignorance and laziness of thought (*Denkfaulheit*). For him, mysticism was a symptom of the decline of *Bildung:* the only antidote, more rationalism. This classical Reform Jew freely admitted that he had never been able to read the *Zohar.*[39]

One journal summed up what can be regarded as the prevailing mid-nineteenth-century German Jewish attitude to Hasidism. It was a movement which, even if some of its original ideas were acceptable, had totally degenerated. Here was a fanaticism based upon the darkest mysticism. The Hasidic leaders, the *Wunderrabbis*, who were revered as infallible by their naïve followers, opposed all modern science and purposely kept the masses in a state of utter ignorance.[40] For the historian Markus Jost such men were simply materialist charlatans.[41] This attitude was not limited to liberal and Reform Jews; German Orthodoxy expressed exactly the same opinions.[42]

Perhaps the new rationalism made their position entirely predictable, but the attack was not limited to manifestations of Polish mysticism and irrationalism. It was equally vehement against traditional Talmudic modes of discourse, this time on the grounds of their exaggerated scholasticism. The non-Jewish perception of the Talmud rapidly came to be accepted by Jewish reformers, and the Talmudists, especially the Polish variety, were said to be sharp but captious; their wit and shrewdness were emphasized at the cost of all other spiritual qualities.[43] No one enunciated this theme with greater venom than Heinrich Grätz, who despite his incipient nationalism was in the mainstream of nineteenth-century German Jewish antipathy to the Ostjuden. Over the years, he wrote, Polish Jews had lost all sense of simplicity and truth and delighted in deception and cheating. "Against members of their own race cunning could not be well employed, because they were sharp-witted; but the non-Jewish world with which they came into contact experienced to its disadvantage the superiority of the Talmudical spirit of the Polish Jews." They had a love of "twisting, distorting, ingenious quibbling, and a foregone antipathy to what did not lie within their field of vision." Their manner of thinking led to a "crabbed dogmatism that defied all logic."[44]

To Enlightenment eyes the passionate internal differences that divided the "irrational" Hasid from the "superrational" Talmudist seemed irrelevant. Both were exemplifications of the ghetto and the parochial spirit. Neither even approximated the ideal of *Bildung*. Both lacked "breeding" and a feeling for the aesthetic. Most Jews, wrote one reformer in 1806, lacked the sense of beauty, but amongst Polish Jews the feeling had completely died out and in relation to their German brothers they had much to learn.[45]

This aesthetic dimension was important because, amongst other things, it determined nineteenth-century German Jewish modes of worship. The way in which one prayed now became a crucial way of distinguishing civilized from uncivilized Jews. Hasidism was often offered as the negative model, while at least implicitly, Protestant forms of worship became those to be followed. The Hasidic way, it was held, lacked "inner" devotion and true surrender to the highest Will; it consisted of demonstrative and noisy physical movement, restless shuffling, accompanied by a fearful screaming. To the uninitiated it conjured up images of agitation, not piety.[46] True piety demanded the introduction of dignity and decorum in the synagogue.

Dignity and decorum extended also to questions of appearance. But for German Jews, clothing became more than an aesthetic problem. The Polish Jewish caftan symbolized their own recently rejected past and was perceived as an obvious obstacle to integration. When Eastern Jews entered Germany wearing these accoutrements, German Jews were infuriated. They sought to persuade the Easterners to discard the caftan on the grounds that it had nothing to do with Jewish ritual or legal observance but was merely a late Jewish adoption of discarded Polish aristocratic dress.[47] They were of course quite correct as a matter of historical fact, but their admonitions did not touch the real issue. Most Polish Jews continued to wear traditional clothing precisely because they wanted to emphasize their separate identity and maintain the line of demarcation that German Jews longed to remove.

By the mid-nineteenth century most German Jews would have agreed with *Der Israelit's* appraisal of Galician Jewry[48] and have generalized it to all of pre-Enlightened Eastern Jewry—that they were sunk in the lowest ethical and spiritual depths, lived in terrible filth and poverty, and were ruled by ignorance and superstition. Their immorality, helplessness, and servility were highlighted by the contrast with German Jewry, who were making steady progress and advancing towards the light.

Comparisons like these were made constantly. They served as a kind of reassurance to German Jews that they had progressed to a point where little connected them with their unenlightened ghetto brethren across the border. The prospect was pleasing but was accompanied by another, more ominous aspect of the East-West disjunction, for the Eastern Jewish masses loomed threateningly as an obvious impediment to the successful integration of German Jews. The requirement that Jews dissolve older notions of national solidarity and become loyal citizens of their home country was of course part of the general Emancipation agreement. But given the particular geographical circumstances surrounding the German situation, the "denationalization" of Jewish identity acquired special urgency. Perhaps this partly explains why Germany spearheaded the movement to dismiss the ethnic component of Jewish faith and to radically "spiritualize" it. The general German preoccupation with *Geist* was employed to denationalize Judaism and sublimate it in purely religious expressions.

Those most closely associated with this spiritualization challenged traditional notions of Jewish solidarity radically. In 1840 when he was thirty years old, the young reformer Abraham Geiger spelled out the political ramifications of this conception. (He was writing about the notorious Damascus blood libel of the same year, but his ideas were equally applicable to East European Jewry.) Concern for what had happened in Damascus, he argued, did not flow from a genuine understanding of Judaism. Those Jews who tried to help were not doing so on the basis of Judaism but rather on the

> purely traditional, half-national and half-ordinary content of that wholly abstract concept of "being a Jew," without any deeper permeation with the content of Judaism. . . . We can term as "of

universal Jewish concern" only whatever goes on among those Jews who reside among the civilized nations, particularly in Germany, and who will later be emulated and followed by those who now are still among the uneducated. That which goes on among the Jews living in the uncivilized countries, on the other hand, is of trifling importance only, even if it were to be of general import in these particular lands. But it is not even that. . . . Of course it is a fine humanitarian deed to take up the cause of individuals who are victims of oppression; but it is not a specifically Jewish problem, and if we make it so, we disturb the outlook and confuse the gradually developing good sense of the Jews. . . .[49]

The spiritualization of Judaism was at least in part a consequence of the politics of assimilation. For Geiger it could work only through the rigid division of Jews belonging to the "civilized" and "uncivilized" nations. Once again, *Bildung* legitimized Jewish denationalization, and the implicit hope remained that Jews from less fortunate countries would somehow have the good sense to maintain a low profile. For all that, Geiger's attempt to challenge centuries of the experience of Jewish solidarity never wholly triumphed. Ideology and practice did not coincide, for the fact remains that a stubborn sense of Jewish collective responsibility persisted albeit under a changed rationale. Beneath the rhetoric, traditional forms of mutual aid operated as a real social force. The dissociation from East European Jewry, strong as it was, was never total.

But how could this ancient reflex of national solidarity be justified in an age when Jews were to be granted German or French or English citizenship? The same Enlightenment philosophy that had provided the grounds for Jewish denationalization could be invoked, since Enlightenment notions and emancipationist aspirations were grounded in universalist claims. Surely German Jews could apply the same goals of Enlightenment to their Eastern brethren as to themselves? *Aufklärung* was at the same time a base for dissociation and a justification for mutual aid! Old habits could realize new ends: bringing Jews everywhere the same rights would ensure one's own emancipation and assimilation and in this manner reduce the significance of Jewish national definitions. These goals seemed to satisfy the imperatives of integration as well as of Jewish conscience and were shared consistently by all streams of German Jewry, including Orthodox Jews.[50]

The two tendencies coexisted at the outset. David Friedländer's classic *Ueber die Verbesserung der Israeliten im Königreich Pohlen*

(1819) already reflected this dualism—an important fact, for his analysis of the Polish Jewish problem became the accepted approach of German Jewry. Exactly a century after the work appeared, the German Jewish journal *Ost und West* protested that despite the enormous changes that had taken place within Eastern Europe, Western Jews still insisted on giving exactly the same mistaken counsel as had Friedländer.[51] Friedländer, they argued, had confused cause with effect. He had been too concerned with remedying Jewish *Unbildung* and had never seen that the real problem was not religious and cultural in origin but political and economic.

Such criticism had some validity, but it also misstated Friedländer's position. As an Enlightenment man, Friedländer understood that behavior derived from institutional settings and that appropriate political change could transform behavior quite radically. Political environmentalism was always present in his work. Yet his presentation of the Polish Jewish problem did seem to place the burden of blame very largely on the Jews themselves. He never forsook the belief in perfectibility, but he also made it clear that Polish Jews were particularly far removed from any such elevated state. They belonged to the most uncouth and uneducated classes of humankind, and their fanatic rabbis were at the heart of the corruption and the immorality.[52] Friedländer's dissociation from these Jews is quite clear, but so too is his concern, his desire to help them through radical reform. As a *Bildungsjude* he believed that progress was possible only through educational transformation (*Umbildung*). Here lay the dualism. Polish Jews were explicitly placed on a rung far lower than that occupied by Western Jews. Nevertheless, given steady support and encouragement, they would eventually be worthy of emancipation and become loyal citizens of Poland.[53]

Friedländer made his proposals on the basis of an already established distance: he could become the modern champion of the Polish Jews precisely because he had so little in common with them. His ideology, of course, suited assimilationist purposes admirably. Gradual emancipation in Poland and elsewhere in Eastern Europe would remove a potentially explosive force across the border that threatened German Jewish assimilation. It satisfied the nagging sense of Jewish responsibility at the same time.

That sense of responsibility had much to do with the fact that Geiger's early program never became normative. Beneath acculturation the "purely traditional, half-national and half-ordinary content" did indeed prevail. Such sentiments were the emotional stimulus for the increasing aid given the Ostjuden. A degree of sanitized nostalgia and sentimentality, what one commentator has termed *Schmalz* Judaism,[54] was never entirely wiped out and always coexisted with the disdain.

In this manner old traditions of Jewish welfare and mutual help were directed to new, antitraditional ends. All Jews were to be remade in the image of German *Bildung*—this was the new Jewish mission. The older Geiger himself realized that his previous isolationism was unworkable and that one had to engage actively in "spiritualization." The most important challenge in the East, he wrote in 1865, was schools. Teachers should be recruited from local communities and German Jews should limit their role to advising. But German literature was to be central to the new educational enterprise. This should penetrate everywhere, for even if the language was not universally accessible, its insights were. The diffusion of German literature was to be the major goal of any educational effort.[55] Once again, as George Mosse has argued in another context,[56] the emphasis on *Bildung*, the faith in education, led men like Friedländer, Geiger, and many others to confuse the realms of culture and politics.

Education was perhaps the major way that Jews from civilized countries proposed to take care of their unemancipated brethren during most of the nineteenth century. Max Lilienthal's famous attempt in the 1840s to modernize Russian Jewish schools and transform Jews into "useful citizens" by means of "*allgemeine Bildung*" is the classic example.[57] Commentators constantly argued that only with the total reform of the traditional Jewish school, the heder, was progress conceivable. This institution, above all others, was held to be at the root of the "distortions" of Eastern Jewry. Dark, dank, overcrowded, chaotic, as indeed it was, it was here that the seeds of spiritual and physical degeneration were sown.[58] Barbarism had to be combatted by enlightenment, and there was no better version of this than the German model.[59]

This advocacy of German culture was not simply a form of German nationalism in the guise of Enlightenment. The idea of *Bildung*, after all, was always tied to liberal humanism; German Jews were not indulging in a crude cognitive colonialism. The problem must be seen in its proper historical context: when they made these arguments, German cultural superiority seemed self-evident. The passion for assimilation was part of this perception. Jews enthusiastically embraced the tenets of German culture. The proclaimed synthesis between Germanism (*Deutschtum*) and Judaism (*Judentum*) was made easy even for the most committed of modern German Jews, because they fully acknowledged the excellence of German culture. This, in fact, was a major defining difference between German and East European Jewry of the period. German Jews had a culture into which they were proud to assimilate. Eastern Jews did not. They were highly unlikely to express for their own countries the sentiments that the freedom fighter Johann Jacoby proclaimed in 1837: "I am inextricably Jewish and German and could as little separate the Jewish from the German and the German from the Jewish part as I could split myself."[60] To be a "German" Jew meant something very specific, as Jacoby later explained: to be a German Jew was to be a Jew of the European, not the Asian, variety. Unlike Asian Jews, German Jews desired to be "useful citizens."[61]

Few doubted that it was the Ostjuden who most exemplified the "Asian" form of Judaism. This perception fitted the German tendency to view the whole of Eastern Europe as a cradle of barbarism,[62] a perspective that Jews shared. In a letter of 1870, Zunz enunciated a growing German *Kulturpessimismus* about Germany's Eastern neighbors. It was merely a matter of time, he mused, before the civilized nations would be overrun. By the year 2170 Russia would have conquered Germany and everyone would be speaking Russian.[63] The general attitude to Eastern Europe provided a certain legitimacy to the German Jewish attempt to bring to Eastern Jews the fruits of German culture, but at the same time it reinforced their negative image. At any rate, before mid-century, German Jews had already taken to describing their fellow Jews as *Asiaten*,[64] expressing the same dualism: Eastern Jews were utterly different from their Western counterparts, who in turn now assumed the responsibility of civilizing their brethren and taking them out of their misery.

These were the elements of the new relationship. Western Jews looked with distaste upon the habits of their "Asian" cousins and worked towards their reformation within their own newly acquired *Bildung*. Despite occasional nostalgic backward glances, this was a relationship characterized by an increasing sense of cultural distance. When Eastern Jewish refugees streamed into the cities of Western Europe, the gap was so large that only the philanthropic and the paternalist modes seemed possible. The major expression of Jewish commonality resided no longer in the sharing of a great historical tradition but in the provision of social welfare. Middle-class German Jews related to Ostjuden on the basis of responsibility rather than of genuine feelings of solidarity, more out of compassion than out of a sense of identification. The breakdown of traditional

Jewish society and values had led to the collapse of even the pretense of equality in Jewish relationships.

The inequality was not only cultural. Even before the migrations of the 1880s, Ostjuden were an embarrassment for upwardly mobile German Jews. More often than not, the problem assumed an obvious class character. The history of the famous Jewish folk figure, the schnorrer, illustrates this well.

Before the 1800s when the institutions of Jewish society were still relatively intact, German Jews did everything they could to help the hordes of that subterranean Jewish class, the *Betteljuden*—wandering, begging Jews—who from 1600 to 1800 swept through Western Europe in waves. Jews were supportive of the itinerants, despite regular official attempts to drive away these people who often turned to crime and became part of the local underworld. Some authorities even attributed the influx of the Betteljuden to local Jewish charitableness, and it is true that this bizarre Jewish subculture could not have survived in Germany without local Jewish support. Emancipation eventually made it possible for the vagrants to become citizens of their various cities and states, by which time they had become integral parts of the German Jewish community.[65]

Precisely the opposite attitude prevailed in the nineteenth century, and Jews did everything they could to remove the renewed *lumpen* presence. Embourgeoisement was so rapid for German Jews that by 1840 the schnorrer was almost exclusively Eastern Jewish and designated as *Fremder* (alien). Class distinctions and geocultural differences meshed, and the class distinctions were often decisive, as they had not been in previous centuries. In 1849 in Braunschweig, for instance, the Jewish community, unable or unwilling to deal with the matter themselves, placed the question of Betteljuden entirely in the hands of the police.[66]

German Jewry's exhortations to Eastern European Jewry to become productive, law-abiding, and loyal subjects was related to the fear that the flood of these beggars would continue to inundate local German Jewish communities and undermine their position. The Deutsch-Israelitischer Gemeindebund (D.I.G.B.) typified these anxieties. Founded in 1869, it was the first successful German Jewish attempt to create a national organization. Characteristically, one reason for this unity was a determination to stem the flow of impoverished Ostjuden into Germany.[67] "From now on," it was agreed at their assembly in 1869, "the highways of Europe will be cleared of the already proverbial Jewish schnorrers." Such beggars were not only demoralizing themselves but were also shaming the more respectable Jewish classes. Those capable of working should be made to do so and those in genuine need should be helped, but only the creation of a rational welfare and emigration system could solve the problem.[68] Efforts to create such a system were clearly not successful, for in 1871 the central board of the D.I.G.B. sent an urgent and official appeal to the leading rabbis and notables of Russian and Polish Jewry requesting that the flood be controlled. German Jews gave these people money, said the appeal, but this merely reinforced their indolence and perpetuated the problem. Even more serious, the complaint continued, was the effect that such elements were having on the indigenous communities. They were a constant source of serious embarrassment to respectable Jews: one look at the prisons would show how few German Jews and how many Polish and Russian Jews were to be found there. The "flood" of Betteljuden was doing nothing less than rekindling the old flames of Jew-hatred, and to make matters worse, all Jews were being held accountable.[69]

This was not the last time that German Jews would attribute anti-Semitism to the presence of destitute Eastern refugees. Over the years, the feeling grew that the German *Judenfrage*, "Jewish question," was an import from the East, and that with the elimination of Jewish immigration from those areas it would be rapidly solved. Stop exporting your poor Jews to Germany, the D.I.G.B. told the Russian rabbis. Instead, train them to lead "a useful, civic existence." Only a solid Jewish middle class in Eastern Europe, it seems, would give German Jews the confidence that their own tenuous middle-class status would remain intact.

These pleas were obviously ineffective, for in the following year the organization explicitly linked the provision of aid to Russian Jewish communities with the cessation of *Wanderbettlerei*.[70] Bourgeois philanthropy was conditional upon keeping its own foundations secure. By 1879 the warnings and a centralized welfare system seemed to have been effective. The D.I.G.B. confidently reported a significant decline in the number of itinerants. Genuine cases of need had been distinguished from unworthy ones.[71] The "success" was ironic, for in reality the problem of the schnorrer was never really solved and continued well into the twentieth century. Moreover, the "accomplishment" came on the very eve of the great migrations that presented the acculturated German Jews, deeply set within middle-class modes, with an even graver threat.

The Jews who were about to come to Germany seemed almost a race apart, strange figures from a no longer comprehensible past.

During the second half of the nineteenth century, German Jewish organs simultaneously reinforced and attempted to mediate this sense of strangeness. Cultural distance had become so great that the relationship had to be maintained through "interpretation," but the very need for such interpretation served to accent the distance. Increasingly, the world of the Eastern Jews was filtered to German Jewry through such mediated images. Ostjuden became the objects of a kind of "anthropological" interest. This was equally true of accounts that stressed some of their sympathetic and positive qualities.

A constant stream of articles, travel accounts, and novels were to give the stereotype its specific shape. The content of the stereotype was often formulated in supposedly scientific and objective journals. Thus the 1867 *Monatsschrift für Geschichte und Wissenschaft des Judentums* took it for granted that its readers were radically alienated from their Polish and Galician counterparts and that the behavior of such Jews was in need of basic explanation. German Jews simply could not comprehend their customs and thinking. Part of the problem, the writer I. Horowitz noted, lay in the very nature of the Polish Jew, for there was a fundamental lack of correspondence between his external appearance and his inner being, a dichotomy that made it difficult for the observer to really understand him. The key to the riddle, however, lay in the conscious dualism with which he operated: the Polish Jew "holds himself to be worth more than he actually is, but presents himself as lower than he is worth." Eastern Jews, at least according to this analysis, were masters of role-play. Why, asked Horowitz, did Polish Jews indulge in these pretenses? This was less a matter of intentional hypocrisy than a deeply rooted element of their historical being. The disharmony between inner and outer, body and spirit, was at the basis of their existence and was a direct outcome of ghetto life. The Polish Jews of the ghetto were filled with contempt for everything outside their narrow world. Their servile, craven exterior simply masked their real sense of Talmudic superiority. Beneath the helpless aspect lay a cynical, arrogant view of the non-Jew; Jews had shut themselves off and created states within states. The ghetto, originally born of compulsion, had become second nature, an inner necessity.[72]

Scholarly journals were important articulators of the image of the ghetto, but for the diffusion of the stereotype we must turn to popular literature, for this was much more widely read. From the historical perspective these sources are important, because they reveal the assumptions of the authors and their readers far more sharply than they uncover the subjects about which they wrote. Such literature both reflected and shaped attitudes. In its pages the stereotype was most clearly delineated and transmitted.

It is important to note that early German Jewish writers like Berthold Auerbach (1812–64), author of famous German "village" tales, did not write ghetto novels. On the contrary, Auerbach was an intense proponent of Jewish integration; describing the German ghetto and its life hardly suited his purposes. Leopold Kompert (1822–66), on the other hand, wrote extensively about the Bohemian ghetto of his youth, but although he treated his ghetto past with sympathy, his is clearly memoir literature, reminiscence of a life securely transcended. The very nature of his ghetto life was different from the harsher experience of the East: Jews were portrayed as having good relations with Czech workers and peasants, spoke pure German, and had very few Talmudic scholars. The happy and light-hearted accounts of life in the Posen ghetto written by Aaron Bernstein (1812–44) were much the same. This was essentially a literature of *Gemütlichkeit*, one that attributed warmth and quaintness to a past that, because it was the past, invited a certain nostalgia.[73] The ghettoes of Eastern Europe, however, were not merely literary memories but were gross realities, and it was onto them that most of the evils of ghetto life were deflected. It was this contemporary dimension that gave German Jewish literature a peculiarly didactic and sometimes shrill tone when it dealt with the Eastern ghettoes.

This does not mean that all such writings were devoid of sympathy for Eastern Jews. On the contrary, these authors were all fervent advocates of East European Jewish emancipation. Beginning in the mid-eighteenth century, they even had non-Jewish models that portrayed Polish Jews rather positively. As part of the Enlightenment drive to persuade a sceptical public that individual Jews were capable of ethical behavior, Christian Gellert, in his *Leben der Schwedischen Gräfin von G.* (1746), pointedly made a clearly recognizable "Polish Jew" typify the required nobility of character.[74] This stood in marked contrast to Gotthold Ephraim Lessing's play *Die Juden* (1749), which portrayed Jews, quite unrealistically, as entirely indistinguishable from their gentile counterparts. But it was precisely the perception of difference that encouraged notions of positive Polish Jewish exoticism. Goethe exemplified this tendency in his review of the much-heralded *Poems of a Polish Jew* (1772) by Isachar Falkensohn Behr. Goethe wrote that he had expected to find something new, a wisdom that went beyond convention, from a poet who had spent his years under a "strange and bleak sky."

Needless to say, his expectations for the exotic were disappointed. There was no secret wisdom here, he wrote, but merely imitative and mediocre contemporary poetry.[75] To be sure, Polish Jewish exoticism seemed confirmed by the occasional eccentric appearance on the German cultural scene of characters like the boorish but brilliant philosopher Solomon Maimon; and some years later, of the talented xylophonist Mikhail Gusikow, who on his extensive concert tours of Europe made a point of performing to high society in full Orthodox garb. [76]

Polish Jewish women also became a part of the broader literary myth of the exotic Jewish woman.[77] In the works of the non-Jewish Galician-Austrian writer Leopold von Sacher-Masoch (1836–95)[78] the fascination with the dark, sensuous (even semidemonic) woman of the Eastern ghetto is most developed.[79] Sacher-Masoch, most remembered not for his ghetto tales but for his sado-masochistic literature laden with erotic undercurrents, gave women a central role in his Jewish stories, where they often possess a power far greater than the men of the ghetto within or the anti-Semites without. Ironically, Sacher-Masoch's emphasis on feminine domination and his eroticizing of Jewish life was based upon his desire to promote the emancipation of Eastern Jewish women. Their strength and beauty, he implied, made them worthy of it. As a Galician, he was directly exposed to Jewish life and in many of his stories demonstrated an accurate knowledge of Jewish custom and vernacular. This strange philosemite (who may have ended his life in an insane asylum) was also able to view the Talmud and Hasidism far more favorably than many of the German Jewish ghetto writers.

This is not to say that these Jewish storytellers found all Eastern Jews equally distasteful but rather that their predilections were usually ideologically determined. Their sympathy would typically go to youth struggling to escape the rigid confines of ghetto life and to those attempting to acquire Enlightenment knowledge. Like Sacher-Masoch, they would often create sympathetic female characters, for the status of women clearly symbolized the oppressive effects of traditional life. It was upon the institutions of the ghetto—the heder, rabbinical authority, early marriage—and their debilitating consequences that these writers poured their wrath. The overall effect of their work, however, was to emphasize the strangeness and ugliness of ghetto life, and it crucially affected the general stereotype of the Eastern Jew.

Perhaps the earliest German Jewish writer to explore the Eastern ghettoes in literary form was Hermann Schiff (1801–67). Schiff was sympathetic to Zunz's call to reawaken interest in all aspects of the Jewish cultural heritage. His *Hundert und ein Sabbath* (1842) was a collection of legends and tales probably based upon the fictive oral tradition of the *Decamerone*. Yet despite his purportedly nondogmatic interest in things Jewish, his *Schief Levinche mit seiner Kalle oder Polnische Wirtschaft* (1848) set the tone for much of the century's German Jewish literature on Eastern Jewry. Supposedly a comic novel, it borders on the grotesque and hardly manages to conceal its bitter undertones. Much of it becomes mere caricature. Levinche is portrayed as physically and spiritually misshapen, as is the entire milieu of the ghetto.[80]

With minor variations this was the kind of picture that German Jewish writers generally painted for their German readers. In his *Polnische Juden* (1866) Leo Herzberg-Fränkel (1827–1915) blamed economic and political conditions for the horrors of the ghettoes. But again the emphasis seemed to turn around the wretchedness of the Jews themselves; the misery and filth are in abundant display. His stories sum up the familiar themes of ghetto life—the grim heder, the rabbinical fanaticism, the abuses of early marriage, and so on.

In a highly perceptive but atypical review of *Polnische Juden* (a review whose sensibility was too much in advance of its time to have any noticeable impact), one critic sharply identified some of Herzberg's implicit assumptions.[81] The critic began with the recognition that the world of Polish Jewry, in concept and experience, was alien to German Jews. What then, he asked, were the responsibilities of the writer in clarifying an unknown world? What, in other words, was the best way to make an alien culture comprehensible? Such an exercise, the reviewer warned, was difficult and knife-edged. On the one hand, there had to be a relation between the writer and the life he was describing—otherwise the account would merely render "a skeleton" and leave readers untouched "by the life that pulsated through the body of the nation [*Volkskörper*]." In a manner far removed from the usual tone of the *Wissenschaft* journal in which the article appeared, the reviewer stressed national and existential elements: truth was possible only when the life described was seen from within. At the same time the writer had to view his subject from a broader human perspective—epistemological universalism was the other key to grasping any particular nationality. The balance was difficult to achieve, but the writer with insight was the one who used both wisely and did not let one dominate the other. Herzberg's

Polnische Juden did not satisfy these ground rules. His cursory dismissal of the Talmud as "labyrinthine," for instance, displayed ignorance and lack of cultural-historical depth. The real problem, the reviewer concluded, was that Herzberg-Fränkel was caught in his own cultural web and saw Polish Jews through the muddy spectacles and the dominant myths of his society. As a result he missed the vital elements, the core of the living culture that was Polish Jewry. Readers learned much about the pathology of ghetto life but were given no inkling of the positive elements of the Polish Jew as a specific historical type.

These were telling points and anticipated a later (minority), twentieth-century sensibility in which German Jews would write about the ghettoes in radically different ways. The reviewer could comfortably have added many other nineteenth-century writers to his critique, for at least in that century, German Jewish literature on Eastern Jewry never lost its didactic, tendentious character. After *Polnische Juden*, "art" seldom overcame programmatic intentions. It was only after Herzberg-Fränkel, in fact, that the stereotype was given its definitive literary and cultural form.

This was to be accomplished in the works of Karl Emil Franzos (1848–1904). Although forgotten today, his writing was extremely influential and widely translated in his own time. Actually, he did little more than articulate in literary form the post-Enlightenment perception of the ghetto. His works were less the creation than they were the crystallization of this image. But the particular shape Franzos imposed on the material was tremendously popular. His works found an echo because he gave form to inchoate popular notions and sentiments.

Franzos perhaps more than anybody else was the embodiment of German Jewish Enlightenment, vehemently restating its postulates at the very moment political events, intellectual developments, and literary fashions seemed to render his brand of *Bildung* didacticism out of date. Perhaps his particular fervor was linked to the fact that he himself was an Eastern Jew, though one of a very specific kind. Born in Chortow, Eastern Galicia, he was raised by a Germanophile father who sent him to a Dominican school where he learned Polish and Latin.[82] This was hardly a typical shtetl upbringing, and Franzos was always an outsider in relation to the ghetto. In the drive to dissociate himself from the Ostjuden, he stressed his father's aristocratic pre-Inquisition, Sephardic background.[83] This was not unusual; Jews often sought to construct a counter-myth about more respectable origins, and Spanish Jewry was viewed by many as a suitable antidote to a suspected East European background. (Theodor Herzl also, quite falsely, claimed such a heritage.)[84]

Franzos was not the first or last transplanted Ostjude to diffuse the stereotype in the West; East European Jews were very much in the forefront of this work. Solomon Maimon (1754–1800), the Enlightenment prodigy who made his way to philosophical heights in Berlin, was the first Polish Jew to leave a scathing account of the ghetto in his *Lebensgeschichte* (1793). Jacob Fromer, who much later edited Maimon's biography, followed a similar path and recorded his experiences in his 1906 work, *Vom Ghetto zur modernen Kultur.* Fromer not only rejected the ghetto but regarded Judaism, as such, to be inappropriate to the modern world. Yet these two writers had really emerged from the ghetto. Franzos had never been part of that experience. It was easier for readers to respond to him, since his viewpoint had more in common with their own. Franzos, even when he lived in Galicia, had always been a "German," not a Polish, Jew.

Circumstances and inclination thus combined to make Franzos an inveterate Enlightener. Although he looked upon the Jews of the ghetto with a mixture of sympathy and distaste—with clearly no possibility of an equal relationship—there was an obvious Jewish commitment: to elevate the pitiful creatures of the ghetto to a condition of *Bildung.* All the familiar themes of ghetto literature are to be found in his stories. Like many other German Jews, Franzos saw the Jewish question in the East as a *Kulturfrage.* German culture, specifically, was the obvious instrument for solving the problem. Franzos did not refer to political hegemony when he talked about Germanization but to a cultural ideal. *Deutschtum* was the humane standard by which other nations should measure their own particular cultural progress.[85]

The Jews of fictional Barnow (probably based on Franzos's home town, Chortow) were clearly backward, but this was merely a reflection of the greater backwardness, even barbarousness, of their hosts. It is in this context that we must understand Franzos's famous formulation *half-Asia.* Franzos referred to the cultural condition of all peoples in the area of Galicia, Rumania, Southern Russia, and Bukovina. Half-Asia was not merely a geographical designation, it was also a condition of the mind. It referred to a strange amalgam of European culture and Asian barbarism, Western industriousness and Eastern indolence. In forms borrowed from the West, the East remained rooted in fundamentally Asian modes and customs. Sometimes, Franzos noted in what may have been an autobiographical remark, real culture and *Unkultur* existed side by side; more often, however, it was an unsettling mixture that prevailed. In this twilight zone half-Asia was to be found.[86]

The Jews of Eastern Europe were "half-Asian" because they lived within its cultural and political boundaries. Their oppressors were therefore to blame for their deplorable condition. If Polish Jews were not on the level of German Jews, this was not entirely of their own doing: the fault lay also with Polish Christians. It was as part of this analysis that Franzos formulated his much-quoted, deliciously ambivalent dictum, "Every country gets the Jews it deserves" ("Denn—jedes Land hat die Juden, die es verdient").[87] This was an apologetic in the back-handed mode, full of ambiguity. If his readers were more likely to dwell on Jewish defects than their purported causes, Franzos could not go blameless.

Defects there certainly were, and Franzos did not hesitate to catalogue them. Jews who had redeeming qualities were those who shared his values. "Good" Jews were those who sought *Kultur* and who were locked in struggle with their repressive Orthodox elders. This, of course, referred to a real generational conflict. Martin Buber's grandmother, for instance, set up a secret library in which, among other things, stood volumes of Schiller's periodical *Die Horen*. Franzos story "Schiller in Barnow" was therefore not purely fictitious and typified a whole genre of literature. It depicted the strivings of a young generation to acquire *Bildung*; a copy of Schiller becomes the new Bible, measure of reason pitted against ignorance. (Years later the Zionist satirist Sammy Gronemann caricatured this story by titling the first chapter of his hilarious 1920 novel *Tohuwabohu* "Goethe in Borytschew.")

As Miriam Roshwald has pointed out, Franzos wrote in a fundamentally different mode from novelists who had been raised in the ghetto.[88] Her comparison of these modes may help us understand the universe of discourse that informed Franzos's (as well as his readers') view of the ghetto. The major difference is not between a critical and an apologetic approach. On the contrary, shtetl writers from Mendele to Agnon were often uncompromising and sometimes vitriolic critics of the ghetto. The divergence is to be found in the point of view: indigenous writers, however critical, were thoroughly identified with their subject. For Franzos, the "half-Asian" Jews of Barnow—narrow, repressed, dirty—were objects of observation. Even in his most compassionate moments he wrote as an outsider looking in and seemed to identify with his readers more than with his subjects (whom he often referred to as "these people"). A massive cultural gap divided him from his material. Clearly a writer like Shmuel Agnon (1888–1970) approached his subject in an entirely different way. What to Agnon represented spirit and culture was to Franzos a symptom of backwardness and degeneration. Their ghettoes appear as almost entirely different universes because they were bound to radically antithetical conceptions of Jewish existence. For Franzos, Jewish salvation lay in Enlightenment. Agnon, writing some years later, acknowledged the victory of Enlightenment but viewed the destruction of traditional Jewish culture as a tragic, irreparable loss. While Franzos judged the ghetto in terms of secular standards, Agnon conceived of it in terms of criteria intrinsic to the culture itself. What for Franzos represented regeneration appeared to Agnon as a sad parade of Jews in borrowed and ill-fitting clothes. Even Schiller in Barnow could not measure up to those books which made up the great historical tradition of Judaism. For Franzos, however, Schiller was the epitome of the desired cultural regeneration, and right until his death he worked tirelessly towards this goal. He remained an Enlightenment moralizer to the end.

Seven years after Franzos's death it was precisely this element of didacticism that prompted the Zionist critique of his work.[89] Critics argued that his didacticism had strangled his vision. This exemplar of modernity had simply never become a "modern" writer, for he was incapable of penetrating inner psychological conflicts and depths. There was no complexity in his work; types, not real characters, inhabited his stories. He was a Sisyphus who never lost the eighteenth-century faith and tirelessly pushed the doomed Enlightenment rock up the mountain. Apart from the criticism of some Zionists, however, the only voices raised were those of a few Westernized East European Jews. One bitterly complained that Franzos had transmitted a picture of the ghetto that was completely false and based upon utter ignorance of Jewish matters.[90]

But these were relatively isolated, minority voices. For the majority of German Jews Franzos remained the authoritative guide to the Eastern ghetto.[91] This was certainly true for liberal and Reform Jews. Even more revealing was the attitude of German Orthodoxy. Franzos, after all, had bitterly attacked the religious obscurantism of the East, but despite this, German Orthodox Jews invoked him as the most knowledgeable and impartial guide to all the complex problems associated with the Eastern Jewish question, the *Ostjudenfrage*.[92]

More than anyone else Franzos mediated the German understanding of the Eastern ghetto. His influence extended far beyond the

Jewish community. Written in popular and accessible form, his version was to prevail. His works began appearing on the very eve of the great move of the Ostjuden into the West and just before this question became a burning political question, and as a result, his concepts and his very terminology partially determined the categories in which the Ostjuden debate proceeded. *Halb-Asien* became a political code-word to both Jew and non-Jew. Assimilationist Jews used it as shorthand for the general Jewish condition in Eastern Europe. The liberal journal *Allgemeine Zeitung des Judentums* castigated German Jewish treatment of Eastern Jews in 1906 by saying, "For us, Polish Jews are Jews who come from 'half-Asia,' even those who have never seen Poland."[93] *Nationaldeutsche* Jews like Max Naumann gave the notion a practical application: "Whoever comes from 'half-Asia' to Germany is a dangerous guest. . . ."[94]

Franzos's work was used by circles whose purposes went directly contrary to his humanist intentions. Anti-Semites regularly annexed the language and descriptions of half-Asia to buttress their case.[95] (To make matters worse, they often invoked Franzos as proof that the German Jews opposed the Ostjuden as much as they themselves.) Some politicians in the Weimar period defended German Jews by deflecting negative Jewish characteristics onto the Ostjuden in specifically Franzosian terms. On the eve of the rise of Nazism, one conservative proposed a full integration of German Jews to be combined with a complete sealing off of "the German cultural community against half-Asia."[96] Franzos even became a part of parliamentary debate. Replying to critics who quoted Franzos in their arguments advocating the cessation of Eastern Jewish immigration into Germany, Prussian minister of the interior Carl Severing invoked "someone far greater: Lessing."[97] That Franzos saw himself not in opposition to but in direct line with Lessing does not diminish the ironic reality that within the realm of German discourse about the Ostjuden, Franzos had systematized a stereotype more than he had contributed to Enlightenment.

With the appearance in 1876 of *Aus Halbasien*, all the contours of the stereotype were clearly defined. A thoroughly acculturated German Jewry had created the stereotype of the Eastern Jew as its mirror opposite. Both the "German" Jew and the "Ostjude" were products of a "modernized" perspective: their polarity formed part of the same dialectic. The great post-1880 migrations were about to test and transform the nature of this dialectic.

2

THE AMBIVALENT HERITAGE
Liberal Jews and the Ostjuden, 1880–1914

THE year 1881 marked a crucial turning point in modern Jewish history; it was the year that heralded the great demographic redistribution of the Jewish People from East to West.[1] Between 1881 and 1914, in the wake of successive pogroms and systemic poverty, millions of East European Jews made their way westward in search of better, more secure lives.[2] Although America would be the final destination for the overwhelming majority, it was Germany, once again, that served as the vital gateway, the passage to the West. The task of coping with the physical reality of the exodus fell most acutely upon German (and Austrian) Jews, because it was through their borders that the Ostjuden had to pass. This unprecedented exercise was, moreover, complicated by the fact that the great migrations coincided with, and some claimed had precipitated, the rise of organized political anti-Semitism in Germany and Austria. Under these historical circumstances the problem of East-West Jewish relations became more real than ever before. The ghetto was moving West.

The first pogrom occurred on April 15, 1881—Easter time—in the Russian town of Elizavetgrad. From then until the summer of 1884 there were literally hundreds of attacks visited upon Jews in White Russia, the Ukraine, some parts of Bessarabia, and even the city of Warsaw. To Westerners these events were particularly shocking, for the violence appeared to be officially sanctioned. Respectable opin-

ion in Germany, Jewish and non-Jewish, was unanimous: the outbursts were nothing less than barbaric. They were condemned even
by many like the philosopher Fritz Mauthner who later publicly voiced
their distaste for the Eastern ghetto presence *within* Germany.[3]

The compassion that German Jews felt for their Russian brothers
was not feigned. Their outrage fitted the general Franzosian perception that such atrocities were possible and even to be expected in a
"half-Asian" environment. From this point of view, social distance,
cultural disparity, and political disenfranchisement served to reinforce rather than diminish the German Jewish sense of responsibility for the Ostjuden: German Jews would do all they could to fight
for the political and human rights of their Eastern counterparts. But
at the same time the pogroms seemed to widen the gulf between
German and Eastern Jew even further. Persecution reinforced
patronizing German Jewish attitudes. More than ever the relationship was defined in philanthropic, "welfare" terms.

The German Jewish response to the problem of Eastern Jewish
persecution and mass migration was, then, grounded in an old
ambivalence. German Jews approached the problem on the basis of
categories inherited from their nineteenth-century experience. Pro-
tective and dissociative modes operated side by side in uneasy
alliance. German Jews undertook massive charitable work on behalf
of the persecuted East European Jews at the same time that they
sought the most efficacious means to prevent their mass settlement in
Germany. This dialectical tension between responsibility and dissociation was built into the German Jewish liberal approach to the
Ostjuden and underlay the way in which German Jews responded to
the challenge of the great move West.

Four days after the first pogrom broke out in Russia, the main
organ of liberal German Jewry, the *Allgemeine Zeitung des Judentums,* published an editorial entitled "What Our Russian Brothers
Have to Do."[4] In a sermon dedicated to political instruction, Russian
Jews were advised at all costs to stand "on the side of the law and the
forces of order." Under no conditions were they to participate in
"secret conspiracies or subversive activities." But this was a pre-
sumptuous misjudgement of Russian anti-Semitic motivation. At
best, radical Jewish activity was the pretext for, not the cause of, the
outbursts. Like David Friedländer sixty years before, the editorial
indiscriminately projected middle-class West European standards
onto a situation where they seemed hopelessly irrelevant.

The editorial did not envisage the mass exodus. Until the 1880s,
migration seldom had been suggested as a solution to the continuing

problem of East European Jewry. Ludwig Philippson's 1846 proposal was both atypical and highly prophetic. The only way German
Jews could help their oppressed brothers in Eastern Europe, he had
argued, was to organize their mass migration. Political conditions
had made life in Russia intolerable for the Jews, and since there was
"no room" for them in Europe they should be sent to "Texas . . . and
New Holland," for there was plenty of space in the New World.[5]
Decades later his scheme became reality. Until then, however,
German Jewry proposed political emancipation, becoming economically productive, and cultural regeneration for Russian Jewry. Not
migration, but the transformation into "loyal and useful citizens"
was the aim.

Western Jewry was taken by surprise when the mass migrations
began, and German Jews were not the only ones who would have
liked to prevent the whole movement from taking effect. It soon
became apparent, however, that the problem was not going to
disappear and that the floodgates would be unleashed. This created
an unprecedented dilemma for all emancipated Jewry. Symptomatic
of the crisis was the serious split amongst the various national
organizations whose job it was to manage and channel the emigration. Everybody—European and American Jewry—wanted to help
the East European Jews and alleviate their plight. Nobody wanted
them in his own country.[6] It was not just German Jews who feared
that the mass presence of destitute Jewish refugees would threaten
the fragile fabric of local Jewish integration, but in Germany the fear
was particularly acute, and not only because the refugees were just
across the border. More ominously, the feared "invasion" from the
East occurred at exactly the same time that popular outbursts against
Jews erupted within Germany itself. The mass migrations began
when German Jews themselves felt under attack. The late 1870s,
after all, marked the beginnings of organized political anti-Semitism. The early ideologues of the movement, Otto Glagau, Wilhelm
Marr, and Adolf Stoecker, had already formulated its basic principles.[7]

The ambivalence thus had added grounds and is well illustrated by
the activities of the various German Jewish committees formed to
deal with the crisis. At first the refugees concentrated in Brody on
the Russian-Austrian border. For the short period from May to
September of 1882 the German Jewish Central Committee spent a
phenomenally generous 642, 274 marks aiding these refugees.[8] Yet of
that amount, large portions were used to speed them off to the
United States and to finance their repatriation. Liberal Jews were

generous, but their charity was directed to spheres which would preclude East-West Jewish contact of a more permanent sort. Conscious of anti-Semitic pressure (Heinrich Graetz declined to work with the Alliance Israelite Universelle for fear that such cooperation would be portrayed as evidence of an international Jewish conspiracy),[9] Jewish organizations did all they could to facilitate the speedy departure of Ostjuden from German shores. So great was the sensitivity that at one point, the Berlin Jewish community officially warned the Alliance that all collaboration would cease if it continued to send Russian Jews through the German capital.[10] All agreed that Germany should not become a settling point.

For all that, the flood continued. The conflict between the self-defined imperatives of liberal Jewish conscience and perceived self-interest was a continuing one. Both could be satisfied only if the emigration process operated smoothly. A relieved Central Committee reported, in a confidential memorandum of 1891, that the post-1881 immigration had increased to an alarming extent and had threatened to create almost total chaos, but that reorganization and centralization had brought the process under control and the primary goal—that the migrants spend as little time as possible within the Reich—had been achieved.[11]

Anxiety in the German Jewish community was in large measure linked to the nervous and at times hostile attitude of the German authorities. Such hostility was not always the result of anti-Semitic prejudice; the threat of being overrun by immigrants must have seemed very real. Germany had never been a country of immigration, and unlike the United States, it lacked an ideology of ethnic and political pluralism. Where economics dictated, migrant seasonal workers could be brought in, but no tradition receptive to mass settlement of immigrants existed.

Regardless of what motivated it, the hostility did not make the passage of Jewish migrants through Germany any easier. German Jewish organizations tried simultaneously to soften their paths and to comply with the order of the authorities to expedite their departure. The tension became acute after the cholera outbreak of 1892. The Prussian authorities attempted to seal off the eastern borders, and it was only through the efforts of the Central Committee for Russian Jews—and the German shipping lines who stood to lose money with the cessation of transmigrant traffic—that the refugees were allowed once again to come through. Disinfecting stations were established at the borders, and medical control was made extremely stringent both at the frontier and at the ports. In effect, before sailing, refugees in

Germany spent their time in quarantine. German Jews were caught in the middle. Special protection committees for "in-transit Jews" were formed to shield the refugees from unnecessary hardships and indignities during the stopover. The work was helpful, but once again, its main purpose was to comply with official directives to provide relief on the frontier and thus cut down on the transit time spent within Germany.[12]

Delousing stations, cleansing procedures, quarantines; destitute, tired refugees hungrily devouring the offerings of Jewish charitable soup kitchens—all of this reinforced the traditional image of the Eastern Jew. The stereotype of dirt, disease, and degeneration seemed to be confirmed. This did not necessarily contradict the compassion many felt, but it was seldom possible to feel genuine empathy in the face of such powerlessness and vulnerability. Perhaps careful observation and close contact would have helped to dispel the image; an emissary at Brody was surprised to see that "the men wear neither *pe'ot* (sidelocks) nor caftans; they are handsome, tall, clean, intelligent. . . ."[13] But his observation was made during the early migrations, before the exodus had become a flood.

In any case, the very treatment meted out to the refugees perpetuated, even worsened, their ragged condition. One traveller has left an account of this experience which grotesquely foreshadows later German bureaucratic methods when Jews were shipped towards, instead of away from, the East: "We emigrants were herded at the stations, packed in the cars, and driven from place to place like cattle. . . . those white-clad Germans shouting commands, always accompanied with 'Quick! Quick!'—the confused passengers obeying all orders like meek children, only questioning now and then what was going to be done with them. . . ."[14] The delousing is described thus: "Here we had been taken to a lonely place . . . our things were taken away, our friends separated from us; a man came to inspect us, as if to ascertain our full value; strange-looking people driving us about like dumb animals, helpless and unresisting; children we could not see crying in a way that suggested terrible things; ourselves driven into a little room. . . . Those gendarmes and nurses always shouted their commands at us from a distance, as fearful of our touch as if we had been lepers."[15]

Such dehumanization was almost routine. Jews from the Ukraine on their way to Rotterdam, for instance, were transported through Germany in sealed railroad cars and were not allowed to leave them for a period of days, not even for drinks or replenishment. The refugees were always handled en masse, supervised by the trainload and lodged in special, impersonal halls; their very isolation and segregation reinforced traditional perceptions.[16]

For all that, as Karl Emil Franzos pointed out, the sheer magnitude of the German Jewish effort to help the East European Jews was impressive. Germany's geographical location had given it the most central role in dealing with this problem. German Jewry's effort was unique. Most mass migrations in history had been undertaken, he observed, by states and governments possessed of vast resources. But the present operation was conducted on an entirely private and voluntary basis.[17]

The figures were indeed spectacular. Between 1905 and 1914 alone, approximately 700,000 East European Jews passed through Germany to embark at Hamburg or Bremen or other West European ports bound for the United States.[18] Although statistics are not complete, we know that a large proportion of the total of 2,750,000 Eastern Jewish immigrants who left Europe for overseas lands between 1880 and 1914 passed through Germany.[19]

The most important of the relief agencies, the Hilfsverein der deutschen Juden, was instrumental in facilitating and rationalizing the process of emigration. The Hilfsverein was founded in May 1901 under the inspiration and leadership of Paul Nathan (1857–1927) and his friend, the Berlin philanthropist James Simon (1850–1932). It arose partly as a reaction to the domination of the French Alliance and represented a specifically *German* Jewish attempt to deal with the problems of Jewish welfare.[20] The constitution of the Hilfsverein defined its welfare concerns in terms of a German liberal patriotism, a strong sense of Jewish denationalization, and the belief in the humanizing effe s of German *Bildung* and commerce. Although the organization played a major role in the transmigrations—by 1905 it was recognized by the Prussian minister of the interior as the official agent overseeing the operation—it stressed the primacy of "culture" as a political instrument. Paul Nathan was a tireless exponent of this approach. The only way to liberate unemancipated Jewry, stated the constitution of the Hilfsverein, was through German *Bildung*. Only its diffusion would raise external political and internal cultural standards sufficiently to ensure that Jews would remain secure and rooted in their countries of residence.[21] Leaders of the Hilfsverein did not consider Jewish philanthropic concerns to be opposed to German trade or progressive foreign policy interests; indeed, they often regarded them as identical.[22] In effect, the Hilfsverein institutionalized German Jewish liberalism as it related to the unemancipated Jews of Eastern Europe and Asia.

In keeping with its emphasis on *Bildung*, the Hilfsverein, like the Alliance before it, established a network of modern schools in Eastern Europe and elsewhere.[23] This was an especially urgent task, because the continuing influence of the traditional Jewish school, the heder, was still widely regarded by German Jews as morally and physically debilitating.[24] Equally serious was the lack of education for women, which related to another more depressing and more embarrassing issue, one which middle-class German Jews very much wanted to avoid and yet were forced to confront: the question of East European Jewish prostitution.

During World War I and after, the Jewish "sexual danger" became a central part of the anti-Semitic armory. Hitler explicitly linked this "danger" with East European Jewish prostitution and involvement in the white-slave trade.[25] It was not pure myth. The problem went back many years. Before 1880 it was not widespread, but with the onset of persecutions and a worsening of economic conditions it became more widespread. East European Jewish women (and girls) could be found in brothels throughout the world as well as in the white-slave trade, which was itself operated heavily by Jews.[26] Prostitution was obviously related to the extreme poverty of the ghetto, but as the German Jewish feminist Bertha Pappenheim and her *Frauenbund* pointed out, it was also linked to Orthodox neglect of education for women in Eastern Europe.

What must concern us here, however, is not the fact or origins of Eastern Jewish prostitution but the German Jewish response to it. The initial reflex was predictable: such a sensitive matter could only be discussed, if at all, behind closed doors. Too open an approach, it was feared, would provide ammunition to the anti-Semites. Early efforts to investigate and curtail Jewish prostitution were thus shrouded in semisecrecy and were predominantly in the hands of male organizations like the Hilfsverein and the Hamburg B'nai Brith. This approach did not prevail, however, primarily because of the feminist tenacity of Bertha Pappenheim. She argued that the fact of Eastern Jewish prostitution in the East was already well known and thus could not be hidden. The Jewish community would therefore be guilty of complicity if it did not seek to combat the evil openly and aggressively.[27] Pappenheim and her Frauenbund, with the help of other Jewish bodies, aggressively threw themselves into the task and tried to address the problem through various political, material, and educational means.[28]

For all the pity and compassion which this problem evoked, it too could not but magnify the perceived differences between Eastern and Western Jewish life. German Jews constantly stressed the "half-Asian" context of Jewish prostitution, and their committees made a special point of noting that almost no German Jews were involved in such activities. Some proposals even made East-West Jewish class distinctions the very basis for the solution to the problem. As one commentator noted in 1903, the "servant problem," for example, was a common topic around German Jewish coffee-tables.[29] It was getting more and more difficult for German Jews to obtain reliable help, especially since Christian girls were increasingly reluctant to serve in Jewish houses. The servant problem could be solved by importing East European Jewish girls. At the same time, this would radically improve the lot of these unfortunate people. Special schools would have to be set up in Galicia to teach the girls the arts of cooking and sewing as well as to provide them with a sense of "order and beauty." Even the feminist Frauenbund advocated this as one solution and set up special home economics schools to train domestics. As the historian of the Frauenbund comments, it was a "particularly thorny problem" because members of the organization themselves employed domestics.[30] Clearly the solution, like that of the wealthy Jewish society women who handed out soup to tired refugees in the Berlin railway station, only amplified cultural and economic distance and demonstrated that the bond which the givers felt was predicated upon compassion, not identification.

Despite the gulf, perhaps because of it, German Jewish philanthropy persisted. Indeed, the reflex of responsibility was so great, the material aid so large, that it seemed to require special legitimation and justification. The way in which Franzos couched the rationale for continuing welfare to Eastern Jews in 1891 typified the liberal German Jewish approach. There *was* a special relationship between Eastern and Western Jews but, Franzos insisted, it flowed from an essentially "denationalized" Judaism: "We are no longer a uniform People [*Volk*]. . . . the Jew who lives in the civilized countries is today a German, a Frenchman of the Jewish faith, and thank God that this is so! We are now only a community of faith [*Glaubensgenossenschaft*] dispersed in all lands of the World! We feel Jewish only through our faith, not our nationality: we sacrifice our money, our energy to save our unfortunate brothers in-faith. . . ."[31] This, of course, was the classical liberal formulation designed to answer the bothersome question regarding the persistence of Jewish commonality within the modern world. It was infinitely preferable to a national perspective, which Franzos regarded as "really dangerous." Jewish national solidarity, he argued, existed only in the minds of anti-Semites.

But there were obvious problems with a purely "religious" justification. For one thing, many liberal Jews, like Franzos, were quite indifferent to questions of faith and remained obstinately attached to the anticlericalism of the Enlightenment. The notion of a common faith was clearly more a legitimizing slogan than a reflection of the actual behavior and beliefs of most liberal German Jews. These Jews were impelled more by Geiger's "purely traditional, half-national and half-ordinary" idea of being a Jew than they were by faith. Under new slogans, older habits and traditional expressions of mutual concern remained intact.

The family was a more accurate if less invoked model for justifying the East-West Jewish relationship. This at least captured the emotional and existential dimension. At the same time it did not threaten the sense of *Deutschtum*, for as Dr. Hugo Ganz argued, members of the same family could belong to different nations. But there was a more profound element to which Ganz alluded and which perhaps pointed to the unconscious source of the Western Jewish tie to the Ostjude: the caftan Jews, he said, were simply "the images of our own fathers." This was less a formulation of ideological relationship than an admission of a (not particularly desired) psychological fact. Families, Ganz pointed out, often contained inequalities in which some members had "worked themselves into the brightness, while others had to remain in the shadows of wretchedness." Western members had to help their Eastern brothers become more like themselves. This could be achieved by unloosening their political shackles and overcoming their inner ghetto culture. Ahasver would be replaced by a proud and upright figure.[32]

The analogy of the family did, in effect, most faithfully reflect German Jewish sentiments for their oppressed Eastern brothers. A common "father" accounted for inherited responsibilities and explained the ambivalence. At the same time it did not threaten the structure of Jewish denationalization or undermine the basic sense of Western superiority. The condition for equal family membership was the overcoming of a common, debilitating past. Ostjuden replicated German Jewry's own physical and psychological history. This was the source of both the rejection and the responsibility.

For all that, liberal Jews seldom attempted to define systematically the exact nature of the ties that bound them to the Ostjuden. "Faith" and "family" seemed sufficient indices of commonality. In any case the need for such special definitions would disappear, many hoped, with the modernization of Polish Jews. It was amazing, they stressed, how rapidly Polish Jews shed their distinguishing characteristics once they were given the opportunity.[33] Cultural levelling of the Jewish condition, so went the hope, would dispel the problem.

But in these hopes lay an irony. The very attempts to help the Ostjuden and make them culturally assimilable had slowed down German Jewry's own project of assimilation. This at least was the view expressed by some alarmed liberals in the years preceding World War I. These men were less concerned with justifying the East-West relationship than they were with explaining the unexpected persistence of the bond. Confronted with anti-Semitism on the one hand and Zionism on the other, they found it necessary to inquire into the failure of the Emancipationist dream. Why had the goal of assimilation not been reached and how could the process be corrected?

It was significant that many of these questions were posed in the general scholarly and popular press and found an audience well beyond the confines of the Jewish community. Eastern Jews were to become a major explanation for the increasing failure of the German-Jewish dialogue. Adolf Grabowsky's *Zeitschrift für Politik*, a leading journal of political science, regularly carried articles which, though dressed in scientific garb, espoused extreme assimilationist positions. Moritz Friedländer (1844–1919), author of Eastern ghetto novels written in the typical Enlightenment mould[34] and a man active in Jewish charitable work, typified this trend. In a 1911 *Zeitschrift* article Friedländer attempted to explain the ironic dialectics of assimilation.[35] Why, he asked, had international Jewish solidarity persisted so unexpectedly? The answer was to be found in the Hegelian law of antithesis. German Jews had been so determined to realize the promise of emancipation that they had tried to carry the same dream to their East European and Oriental counterparts—a sound aim, but the project had ricocheted against its authors. German Jewish institutions that had been created to spread freedom and equality amongst less fortunate Jews had engendered an opposite effect. They had aroused the antagonism of the anti-Semites and the resentment of the recipients of the philanthropy. Liberal rationalism, Friedländer claimed, had overlooked how deeply tradition-bound the Eastern masses were. Moreover, the new philanthropy had assumed that there would be a passive response from its beneficiaries, but this did not happen—the recipients, in fact, had developed pretensions to leadership. This all added up to an astounding phenomenon: the hand that the *Kulturjuden* had extended to their Eastern brothers had been gripped, but not to receive salvation. Those who were offered help had tried to pull their helpers down with them, had attempted to provide them with new Jewish goals. The liberator was caught in the chains of the victim he sought to liberate. Assimilation had produced its own reaction.

This mistake had been made, argued Friedländer, because German Jews had not realized that successful assimilation was possible only under very specific circumstances. Genuine assimilation could take place only in those situations where Jews could be rooted within the home culture. It was possible in Germany but not in Eastern Europe. Few Ostjuden were looked upon, or regarded themselves, as "loyal citizens" of their society. In Germany, however, assimilation had proceeded very smoothly until the pogroms of the 1880s had erupted. The mass migration and concomitant Western Jewish efforts to organize and aid it had badly ruptured the process. Western Jewish consciousness was increasingly being penetrated by old Jewish forms at a time when cultural assimilation had reached its highest point. Assimilation had planted the seeds of its own supersession when it so carelessly set in motion the dialectical forces of change in the East. Of course, Friedländer added, the failure of assimilation could not be blamed primarily on the Jews. All these developments would not have taken place without the rise of political anti-Semitism. Still, he left little doubt that the Eastern Jews had created ripples on the surface of a previously smooth cultural pond.

What Friedländer termed the penetration of "old Jewish forms" referred not merely to traditional cultural habits but also to the growing physical presence of Eastern Jews within Germany itself. As we have seen, the authorities did everything they could to prevent mass immigration.[36] They succeeded in averting anything comparable to the mass settlement that occurred in the United States or even England. Nevertheless, the resident foreign Jewish minority within Germany rose from 15,000 in 1880 to over 78,000 in 1910 (or 12.8 percent of the total German Jewish population of 615,021).[37] Of these, 70,000 were from the East.

This presence critically highlighted a dilemma already faced by German Jewish liberals, for anti-Semitic agitation over Eastern Jews had preceded the post-pogrom migrations. Beginning in 1879, a rash of publications appeared stating that Germany was being overrun by undesirable Jews from the East.[38] The attack was initiated by the eminent historian Heinrich von Treitschke, who thereby bestowed upon it an aura of respectability. He warned that the movement of

Eastern Jews into Germany constituted a fundamental threat to the country's national integrity.[39] (Treitschke was, in the main, drawing attention to the *internal* migration of Posen Jews into the major German cities. The fact that he regarded Jews from eastern Prussia as Ostjuden is significant. These Jews, however Germanized they were, never overcame their "Eastern" image.)

German Jews attempted to counteract these accusations,[40] but their tactics in doing so reflected their conflicting sentiments. They consistently denied that an "invasion" had taken place and dismissed it as an anti-Semitic "fable,"[41] yet at the same time, they made it clear that they themselves did not want an influx of Easterners. No one paused to defend Eastern Jews as positive or desirable elements but, rather, stressed that no such unwanted immigration was underway.

There can be no doubt that middle-class German Jews found the presence of the new arrivals embarrassing and not a little threatening to their own security. Thus when the Prussian government ordered the expulsion of Russian-Polish Jews from Berlin in the summer of 1884, the *Allgemeine Zeitung des Judentums* passed over the incident in silence.[42] Similarly, the paper did not resist the mass expulsion of all Russian Poles from Prussia in 1885–86. It stressed that Polish Jews were expelled not because they were Jews, but because they came from Poland.[43] It is true that the order applied to all Poles and that in addition to the 10,000 Jews affected, 20,000 Polish Catholics were expelled. But there was also an element of selective assimilationist political perception at work. The majority of liberal newspapers—also Jewish-owned but not representing the Jewish community—saw quite clearly what the *Allgemeine Zeitung des Judentums* refused to acknowledge, that the expulsions were linked to anti-Jewish motives and were the "first tangible success" of the popular anti-Semitic movement.[44]

Yet the *Allgemeine Zeitung* did gradually modify its position. It later acknowledged the anti-Semitism behind the expulsions and occasionally even defended the positive, conservative qualities of Eastern Jews. One historian, Jack L. Wertheimer, has related this change to the growing resolve of German Jews to confront anti-Semitic issues.[45] By 1893, the major representative defense organization of liberal German Jewry, the Centralverein deutscher Staatsbürger jüdischen Glaubens (Central Union of German Citizens of the Jewish Persuasion, C.V.), had been formed.

But the new resolve never overcame the old ambivalence, and in the first few years of the organization's existence an almost wholly dismissive attitude to Eastern Jews prevailed. In 1894 when representatives of the C.V. met with the German Foreign Secretary, they not only agreed that Russian Jews were an unwanted element but also questioned whether safeguards against their entry into Germany were sufficiently strong.[46] It is true that an awareness gradually developed that the mistreatment of foreign Jews could not always be severed from the fate of German Jewry itself, and the C.V., together with the other major defense organization, the Verband der deutschen Juden, protested discriminatory actions against Ostjuden as a provocation against all Jews. It was a fitful realization and yet another theory that liberal Jews never espoused consistently; nevertheless the official journal of the C.V., *Im deutschen Reich*, often condemned expulsions and unfair naturalization and residence policies. Apart from these essentially defensive issues, however, its pages were peculiarly devoid of the Eastern Jewish presence. Wherever possible the dissociative mode prevailed. We should not forget that the C.V. was established in the name of an uncompromising commitment to *Deutschtum*. Its statutes demanded "German-mindedness" (*deutsche Gesinnung*) from all its members. Before World War I, as Jehuda Reinharz has pointed out, the C.V. clearly advocated *Deutschtum* as the primary loyalty above all others, including *Judentum*.[47] It never admitted foreign Jews as members. It always stressed that it was a German organization defending the rights of German citizens. The sense of personal and cultural estrangement from Eastern Jews remained intact.

Although the number of Eastern Jews within Berlin was small in comparison with London or New York, there were sufficient by 1910—over 13,000, or 20 percent of Berlin Jewry[48]—to conjure up for many the old specter of the ghetto. Eastern Jews congregated in Berlin's Scheunenviertel, close to the center of the city. Unlike the immigrants of New York, London, and Paris, many did not stay in the ghetto for very long, but upon obtaining employment moved to other areas of the capital and thereby minimized the concentration that characterized Eastern Jewish settlement in other parts of the Western world.[49] But this did not prevent some Jews from regarding "the ghetto" with a mixture of fear and repulsion. Adolf Grabowsky's 1910 description of his *Ghettowanderung* for *Die Schaubühne*[50] referred not to travels in Galicia but to a visit to the Scheunenviertel. His account was not too far removed from similar pieces that appeared in the anti-Semitic press. "As one moves further along the Kaiser Wilhelm Street," he wrote, "one goes ever deeper into the East of the world. . . . These figures! Is this Berlin? Wearers of caftans and stout women . . . ragged children with expectant eyes, sneaky men . . . incomprehensible words. . . ." The ghetto—strange and frightening—had arrived in Berlin and for many assimilated Jews represented a palpable threat. For middle-class Jews, products of a cultivated sensibility, this world *was* alien. The Berlin ghetto reinforced the Germanness of German Jews and strengthened the stereotype of the Ostjude.

Of course, the stereotype blurred a reality that was far more complex. Germany's Ostjuden were perceived as an undifferentiated mass, which was ironic, for in fact they were deeply fragmented and almost as isolated from each other as they were from both the general German and German Jewish communities. The fragmentation was not merely residential. It was also national in nature. Russian Jews hardly associated with Galician Jews, who in turn were divided from Rumanian Jews. Anti-Semites pictured a monolithic, single-minded group. The sad truth was quite the opposite—right into the years of the Weimar Republic, Germany's Ostjuden never succeeded in uniting effectively, even in the face of severe attack. Their occupational structure compounded the social and cultural differences. There were, of course, the various itinerant schnorrers. Yet contrary to the received wisdom, the majority of Germany's Ostjuden were industrious and earned their living in a variety of ways.[51] There were artisans and manual workers, peddlers, tradesmen, salesmen, and small businessmen. Some even became successful entrepreneurs in the fur and grain trades. Another important sub-group acted as communal functionaries for the German Jewish community—rabbis, teachers, cantors, librarians, ritual slaughterers, and the like.

In a different category were the intellectuals and students. They were, in the main, secularized and politically minded Russian Jews who in the words of one famous student, Chaim Weizmann, "were vastly impressed by German achievement, German discipline and German power."[52] These students and intellectuals formed their own coteries. Zionist, Socialist, and revolutionary circles lived intense but separate lives, isolated from each other as well as from the general student and German Jewish student body.[53] Certain East European Jewish intellectuals—such as Ephraim Frisch (1873–1942), who became editor of *Der Neue Merkur*—did make their mark within the wider world of German letters. Others, like Fabius Schach, Leo Wintz, and Binjamin Segel, became central figures in German Jewish journalism. As we shall see, some East European Jewish thinkers and writers would crucially influence the second generation of German Zionist youth. But the majority of the intelligentsia remained isolated from the organized German Jewish community.[54] Many of the students were radicals, a fact that lent credence to yet another component of the stereotype: Eastern Jewish "nihilism."[55] Little connected the social and intellectual world of these students with that of middle-class German Jewry, whose sense of distance increased with the growing public sentiment that they were, in the words of Chancellor von Bülow, "schnorrers and conspirators."[56] The agitation of the German student body against the presence of these "Eastern" elements at times received a sympathetic echo even amongst certain German Jewish student organizations. In 1912, when agitation was particularly heated, the Munich Jewish student body, for instance, passed a resolution opposing the presence of Russian students at German universities. They knew, as their Zionist critics pointed out, that in this context the terms "Russian" and "Jewish" were practically synonymous.[57]

Few German Jews, then, bothered to see the distinctions within the Eastern Jewish community of Germany. It was easier to compress a complex reality into an undifferentiated, simplistic perception. In one sense, the German Jewish stereotype of the Ostjude represented the end-point, the limits of Jewish liberal-rationalist consciousness. *Bildungsjuden*, Peter Gay points out, energetically rejected collective verdicts, which were clearly anathema to their liberal and individualistic impulses. Many consequently eliminated distasteful and prejudicial expressions like *goy* from their vocabulary. They were extremely sensitive to any slighting of their own Jewish identity. Yet with regard to the Ostjuden this standard collapsed, and their sweeping dislike represented "the triumph of uninterpreted experience over cherished principles."[58]

What lay behind this double standard, of course, was the German Jewish rejection of the ghetto past. The Ostjuden who settled in Germany were regarded as being in the process of recreating that very past. The need to distance oneself from this was often more important than self-proclaimed humanist principles. An important element of the specifically *German* Jewish sense of identity, in fact, was based upon differentiating comparisons with Ostjuden. The German Jew was to be understood in terms of the explicit differences that divided him from the East European Jew.

At times this dissociation assumed even racial terms. Thus the legal scholar Eugen Ehrlich recalled Ernst Renan's theory—which Arthur Koestler has recently tried to revive—that the Ostjuden were descended, in the main, not from the original Jews but from the Khazars, and converted to Judaism only in the fourteenth and fifteenth centuries. Ehrlich argued that even if Renan was wrong and there were no differences in origin, Ostjuden were nevertheless physically distinguishable from Western Jews—both facial and body structure differed.[59]

This was an extreme view; usually the distinction was made on the social and cultural levels. But regardless of the ways in which it was defined, the distance appeared to be enormous. For Ernst Lissauer (1882–1937), author of the famous "Hate Song against England" in World War I, the juxtaposition was central to his own (very minimal) Jewish self-understanding. "Once," he relates, "as I stood with some fellow Jewish students outside my Berlin school, a man with a Jewish caftan and side-locks came from Friedrich Street station and asked us, 'Are there no Jews in Berlin?' And instinctively I answered to myself, 'No,' for he meant something else by the word than I did."[60] For Lissauer the confrontation did not entail a denial of Jewishness as much as it demanded a new differentiation and a redefinition— the world was divided into cultured German and uncultured Eastern Jews. Sometimes, however, the meeting did lead to total denial. When Theodor Lessing, who was raised without knowledge of his Jewish origins, was told by his classmates that he was a Jew, he was deeply shocked. He returned home and asked his mother what a Jew "really" was. Her answer, as Lessing reports it, revealed the Ostjude's symbolic role for certain assimilationist Jews: "Once, on the street, my mother pointed to a man in a caftan and said, 'There goes a Jew.' I then concluded that we were not really Jews."[61]

In this way Ostjuden helped to delineate more sharply the distinctive German sense of self among German Jews. At the same time their presence was perceived as a radical threat to the already insecure political status of native Jewry. Some assimilationists explicitly maintained that the Ostjuden were responsible for the rise of anti-Semitism. There was indeed a real, objectively grounded Jewish problem in Eastern Europe, one analyst stated in 1909, but this did not apply to Western Europe. The trouble was that East Europeans were continually importing the issue into the West. If the Ostjuden did not "at every moment carry a new, uncomfortable problem into the West, no one would be thinking any more about the Jewish problem."[62] In the years preceding World War I this conviction, while sometimes articulated in more or less muted tones, was shared by many German Jews.

Although the sentiment prevailed, it was less widely circulated in public than the notion that the influx of East European Jews seriously impeded assimilation. Some non-Jews even made the cessation of such immigration the explicit condition for the successful continuation of the German-Jewish dialogue. The Eastern Jewish problem, they argued, had to be solved, and it was acceptable for German Jews to help their distressed ghetto brethren, but it was an entirely different matter to allow them entrance into the borders of the Reich.

This was a prominent theme of the Jewish-German symposium organized by Werner Sombart in 1912.[63] There was almost unanimous agreement that the Ostjuden were a dangerous hindrance to German Jewish integration. In his earlier *The Jews and Modern Capitalism* (1911) Sombart not only bemoaned the effects of the ghetto but suggested that "perhaps a section of the Jews lived the Ghetto life because they were by nature inclined that way."[64] In the symposium, Sombart gave practical expression to this conviction. He clearly differentiated between Eastern and Western Jews, and in a disquieting and regularly employed phrase, warned German Jews "in their own interests" to discourage the entrance of Ostjuden into Germany.[65] He argued that if the Jewish population of Germany did not exceed one percent of the total population, amicable relationships could be achieved. Hermann Bahr was even more sceptical about the prospects for assimilation, he said, largely because of the continuing presence and influence of Eastern Jews, who maintained a stubborn, separatist will to Jewish survival. Only a small minority of German Jews were capable of that "spiritual transformation which would ultimately affect their blood."[66] Not all non-Jews denied the possibility of assimilation with such vehemence. Hanns Heinz Ewers, for instance, argued that it was quite feasible—if the Jewish flow from the East was stemmed.[67]

This does not mean that all the non-Jewish contributors were unsympathetic to the sufferings and political problems of the Eastern Jews, but they made it clear that in their opinion Germany was not the arena in which these problems could be solved. Thus Matthias Erzberger advocated a "philanthropic" Zionism purely for the needy Ostjuden, and maintained that Zionism, apart from solving the Eastern Jewish problem, could act as a safety mechanism for assimilated and wealthy Western Jewry.[68]

Similar sentiments were voiced by most of the Jewish contributors to the symposium.[69] Fritz Mauthner, the philosopher and critic of language, exemplified the assimilationist tone of the Jewish contributors. German Jews, he argued, were entirely German in their cultural heritage—Kant, Goethe, and Beethoven were the best parts of their existence. Zionism to him was "incomprehensible." Perhaps it was necessary for Eastern Jews, whose situation and sufferings still seemed medieval. At any rate, it was clear that the German borders needed to be sealed from the Ostjuden: "Western Jews and the Western anti-Semites should both desire such a sealing: the Jews because it would create a sharp dividing line between the cultivated elements and a mass with whom the educated German Jew no longer has anything in common."[70] These intellectuals had little doubt that the precondition for the successful maintenance of the German-Jewish symbiosis was the exclusion of Jews without *Bildung* from any aspect of their dialogue.

By 1910, under the combined impact of the Eastern migrations, political anti-Semitism, and an increasingly militant Zionism, many assimilationists were alarmed. The Zionist Leo Rosenberg was not incorrect when he noted that, at least for the more extreme cases, German Jewish assimilation required geocultural isolation. Severing the physical link with Eastern Jews, he asserted, was vital to the assimilationist program of "self-extermination" (*Selbstvernichtung*).[71] At least one such assimilationist, Friedrich Blach, would not have taken exception to the expression *Selbstvernichtung*. "Well then," he wrote, "so be it, free and joyful suicide. For I no longer want to be the self that I was, I want to belong to that magnificent people in whose midst I was born. 'Die at the right time: thus spoke Zarathustra.' We have endured too long."[72] But the transmutation of assimilation into a life-affirming Nietzschean act was dependent, of course, upon radical dissociation from the Eastern Jews: "We must finally end our involvement with our overseas *Glaubensgenossen*. As long as they are in need, we will certainly help them. That is our human duty. But to ask them to make their homes in our country, that is against duty and reason. Duty towards Germany: We really cannot use these 'East European' elements here. . . . Against reason: For over fifty years our most passionate goal has been the extinction of all traces of our centuries-old ghetto life and to efface all cultural distinctions between us and the majority." The notion that Ostjuden should replenish German Jewish "losses" through baptism and conversion, as some suggested, was "sheer madness."[73]

For some intellectuals, concern reached almost hysterical proportions and fear of the East European presence bordered on the paranoiac. This was voiced regularly in the public realm. Thus Max Marcuse's 1912 attack on the Ostjuden appeared, significantly, in *The Journal of Sexual Science*, where it was fitted into a broader analysis of German Jewish–Christian intermarriage. Like other German Jews, Marcuse argued from a fundamentally liberal viewpoint and dismissed all racial claims against intermarriage. Racism was a bogus ideology, and the disappearance of German Jewry through intermarriage was to be welcomed. Yet once again, in his treatment of the Ostjuden, Marcuse belied his own purported liberalism. Eastern Jews were dealt with in terms not far removed from the vocabulary of the Volkish anti-Semites. Ostjuden conducted themselves in ways that were entirely unsuited to Western *Kulturstaaten.* Moreover, they lacked all desire to change their ways: "These Jews are a disaster for us. . . . they constantly create new barriers, bring in old ghetto air, and are the greatest danger to the prosperity and harmony of the nations."[74] Oblivious of the double standard of his analysis, Marcuse bemoaned the fact that liberals associated the attack on Ostjuden with a politically reactionary position when it came to the question of allowing the Ostjuden into the Reich. This, he argued, was quite wrong, for the demand to close Germany's borders (*Grenzsperrung*) was not an anti-Semitic act but a "German cultural imperative." It would allow the process of intermarriage to reach completion, and the Jewish question would be finally solved through the combination of opposites into a higher synthesis.

The attitudes of people like Marcuse, Mauthner, and Blach advocating total Jewish assimilation were extreme. For them the disappearance of Germany Jewry itself was a desideratum, and the Jewish press roundly condemned their positions. The majority of German Jews sought ways, however minimal, of combining their Jewish heritage with their Germanness. It is this fact of acceptance of Jewishness, however diluted its cultural or religious expressions, that lies at the heart of the continuing liberal German Jewish sense of responsibility for the Ostjuden. If there was a strong sense of disdain, for many it coexisted with a nagging sense of commitment.

Moreover, the rougher edges of the disdain were softened, humanized by a recognition of the Eastern Jewish sense of humor. Admiration for their wit, gall (*hutzpah*), and spirit in adversity was always a kind of hidden counter-theme in the Western Jews' regard for their Eastern brothers. It is instructive that an altogether disproportionate number of Freud's examples in his *Jokes and Their Relation to the Unconscious* (1905) were East European (especially Galician) Jewish jokes. Freud identified their major quality as self-criticism. He tellingly contrasted this Jewish propensity for self-mockery with anti-Semitic stories. Jewish self-criticism had grown up on the soil of Jewish popular life. "They [the jokes] are stories created by Jews and directed against Jewish characteristics. The jokes made about Jews by foreigners are for the most part brutal comic stories in which a joke is made unnecessary by the fact that Jews are regarded by foreigners as comic figures. The Jewish jokes which originate from Jews admit this too; but they know their real faults as well as the connection between them and their good qualities. . . ."[75] This, quite apart from the rebuff to anti-Jewish bigotry, provided the Eastern Jews with a complex, genuinely human face.*

At times the dissociative sense would even be accompanied by feelings of secret pride. Small towns and villages would often warmly receive itinerant Eastern Jews. In his memoirs, Sammy Gronemann relates the establishment of a "hotel" for schnorrers in his native Pomeranian town. Hospitality was provided in exchange for a few pious homilies.[76] The poet Jakob Loewenberg (1856–1929) wrote of those Polish *Betteljuden* who came to his village when he was a youth: "We were a little ashamed in the presence of our Christian playmates that these dirty, shabbily dressed beggars were also Jews. . . ." Yet on the Sabbath his father would invite them for a meal and they would discuss Talmud. Then it would become apparent that it was the Polish Jews who possessed the real spiritual treasures.[77]

But Loewenberg was a *Dorfjude*, a village Jew, whose formative years came before 1880 and who always regarded himself, even in his adult years, as a "Westphalian village boy."[78] Although the question needs more careful research, it may very well be that for small town and village Jews the rhythms of life were more relaxed than in the urban centers. Relations with one's Christian neighbors may have been less ambiguous, for there was little possibility of "hiding" one's identity. Perhaps consciousness and acceptance of differences made for more cordial Jewish-Christian relationships and thus contributed to a greater sense of Jewish security.[79]

For urban Jews the tensions may well have been greater. Jewish ambivalence may have been more acute because the social lines seemed fluid and unclear. Certainly for the post-1880 period, few urban middle-class German Jews felt much pride in the schnorrer.

---

*Freud particularly liked the following joke: " 'A Galician Jew was travelling in a train. He had made himself really comfortable, had unbuttoned his coat and put his feet up on the seat. Just then a gentleman in modern dress entered the compartment. The Jew promptly pulled himself together and took up a proper pose. The stranger fingered through the pages of a notebook, made some calculations, reflected for a moment and then suddenly asked the Jew, "Excuse me, when is Yom Kippur [the Day of Atonement]?" 'Oho!' said the Jew, and put his feet up on the seat again before answering." (From Sigmund Freud, *Jokes and Their Relation to the Unconscious*, trans. James Strachey [New York, 1963], pp. 80–81.) Apart from the *hutzpah*, this tells us much about the Eastern Jewish perception of Western Jews.

In the cities he was far more likely to receive his money at the back door than to get an invitation for the Sabbath meal. But the matter went further than this. Concerted efforts were made to rationalize and centralize Jewish charity. As the *Allgemeine Zeitung des Judentums* put it, welfare organizations should remove the schnorrer entirely from "house-begging," the worst manifestation of an already immoral activity. Perhaps it had once been necessary when poor Jews wandered on foot from town to town, but now they simply took the train. The only answer was a uniform system of Jewish charity.[80]

The attempt to remove the Ostjude from the doorstep was related to the post-Enlightenment Jewish aversion to being conspicuous. Jewishness was defined as a denominational and private affair. In the public and cultural spheres there were to be no divisive or separatist customs or symbols. This was a general matter and did not apply merely to the problem of Eastern Jews. Orthodox German Jewish children were admonished by their parents not to wear yarmulkes (skull-caps) in public.[81] But clearly, it was the appearance of the Eastern Jew that made the German Jews acutely sensitive. He was a potent challenge to and a symbolic refutation of the doctrine of Jewish inconspicuousness.

The shame—the feeling of being trapped by the image of a rejected self—was particularly painful in the company of non-Jews. Kurt Blumenfeld, later to become the leader of a radicalized German Zionism, relates how as a deeply assimilated youth he went for a walk with a Christian singer in Insterburg, Eastern Prussia. There he was stopped by an Ostjude, who asked him a question in Yiddish. Blumenfeld, although unfamiliar with the language, understood the question but pretended not to and did not answer the man. The singer turned to Blumenfeld and asked him why he did not answer. "Are you ashamed?" she asked. Blumenfeld felt "destroyed," and deeply embarrassed, answered the Ostjude and hurried on.[82]

Sometimes the embarrassment occurred in more intimate and therefore more threatening circumstances. Eastern Jews frequented the various health spas of Germany. Upon going to one such resort in Marienbad in 1888, Ernst Lissauer was given strict instructions by his grandmother, daughter of a Posen rabbi, not to go anywhere near the Ostjuden, for they were "too dirty."[83] There is little doubt that both the myth and the reality of the "dirty" ghetto Jew clashed with the strict German bourgeois emphasis on cleanliness and tidiness. This made the Ostjude a highly suitable physical and symbolic target for anti-Semites who wanted to brand the Jew as a "polluting" presence. But for German Jews the presence of Ostjuden at the spas—public places where Jew and Christian intermingled and where protocol was important—was simply embarrassing. As the *Allgemeine Zeitung des Judentums* complained, the pushy, loud, indiscrete manners of the East European Jews were making life extremely uncomfortable for the German Jews at such resorts.[84]

A good mirror of the role of the Ostjude as irritant and threat to middle-class respectability is to be found in German Jewish Wilhelmine novels. This literature is even more revealing of liberal Jewish attitudes than the ghetto novels of Herzberg-Fränkel and Franzos, for the latter were consciously didactic, reformist works. The authors were outsiders looking in at the ghetto. In German Jewish novels it is the Ostjude who is the stranger, the outsider. Perhaps because he is *not* at the center and because he enters into German Jewish life only obliquely do we get a less contrived, unselfconscious representation.

Georg Hermann's *Jettchen Gebert* (1907) is perhaps the best illustration of this genre. The work deals with pre-1848 Berlin Jewish attitudes. Hermann's Jewish bourgeoisie is almost indistinguishable from its Prussian Christian neighbors. Here was a class characterized by *Bildung* and great delicacy. It is the Gebert's Eastern cousins, the Jacobys, who epitomize *Unbildung* and indelicacy. The Jacobys provide a measure of the cultural distance German Jews had travelled, a reassurance that they had overcome their miserable ghetto past. Nothing connects Jettchen with her provincial cousin Julius: "But what concern was he of hers, this cousin Julius Jacoby . . . who after all was no cousin at all." When they shake hands, Jettchen has the sensation of touching "a glassy creature, a frog or a caterpillar." Yet if the Gebert's are obviously superior in culture to the Jacobys, the Jacobys are nevertheless an obvious and palpable threat. Julius not only lacks sensitivity, he is also unscrupulous. This, in combination with his tactlessness, is a source of discomfort for the established Jewish bourgeoisie, an embarrassing reminder of common origins. Hermann presents Julius as the type who would make money, marry, and five years later proclaim that "he is from Posen, but came to Berlin as quite a little chap, so could only dimly remember his native place . . . ten years hence . . . he is a native of Berlin. . . . By then he will be quite unable to imagine the possibility of anyone being born out of Berlin."[85]

Hermann's prediction for Julius was based on reality. Transplanted Ostjuden very often did try to camouflage their origins, which in itself is a measure of the derision in which Eastern Jews were held. At times the matter went beyond a denial of Eastern background to an active contempt for later Eastern Jewish arrivals. This was common enough for the German Zionist newspaper *Jüdische Rundschau* to brand it "the Russian disease."[86] Fritz Mauthner and Eugen Ehrlich, for instance, themselves of "Eastern" origin, were not only ashamed of their background but vehemently opposed the entrance of Ostjuden into Germany on "national" and "cultural" grounds.[87] Hermann's point, then, had some validity, but it obscured the fact that very large numbers of "established" German Jews had emerged from similar ghetto backgrounds. At a meeting with Berlin's liberal Jewish representatives who were inveighing against Eastern Jewish infiltration, the Zionist leader Alfred Klee went round the room and demonstrated that without exception those present were themselves from Posen, Breslau, or Poland, or at the very least had forefathers from that part of the world.[88] As a matter of historical fact the question of origins was a generationally relative matter.

Perhaps it was precisely this proximity, the thin line that separated the German Jew from his Eastern cousin, that explained the extraordinary sensitivity. The theme of the shame of Jewish origins was most starkly portrayed in the work of Ludwig Jacobowski (1868–1900). Jacobowski was himself born in Posen, symbolic and geographical mid-point between the ghetto and *Deutschtum*. His 1898 novel *Werther der Jude* was almost maudlin in its praise of German culture but pessimistic about the possibility of Jewish integration within it. The protagonist, Leo Wolff, is a sensitive youth obsessed, even paralyzed, by the shame of his Jewishness. He attributes to Jews all the stereotypical qualities. His speculator father and his boorish cousin from the Polish shtetl are ruthless and bring shame to the more idealistic, refined Jews. Wolff does not want to cast off his Jewishness entirely, but he does try to redefine it radically so that he can be "a Jew, noble, helpful, and good."[89] Traditional Jewish behavior, for Leo, is indeed as the anti-Semites portray it—"we know how much Jew-hatred is justified"[90]—and this constitutes what he calls his "tragicomic" reality. For despite the enormous gulf which separates the idealistic Jewish youth of Leo's generation from the older and traditional Jews, it is the innocent young who must pay the price for the unscrupulous ways of the ghetto. Shamed and despairing, estranged from his family and his Jewish origins, Leo commits suicide and dies in the arms of his "Aryan" friend, Richard.

But this, of course, like the nonfictional suicide of Otto Weininger which also had its roots in radical Jewish self-hatred, was the most extreme expression of shame and disdain. It does not tell us much about the larger body of liberal German Jews and their communal ambivalence toward the Ostjuden. Their attitudes were revealed more accurately in the wake of the post-1910 struggles within the German Jewish community.

During this period, both the Zionists and the Orthodox—internal minority opponents of the "liberal" German Jewish consensus—attempted to wrest control of the Jewish community from the dominant liberal bloc.[91] When it became clear that resident Ostjuden were being mobilized and would support the movement, over a dozen communities—Hamburg, Altona, Danzig, and Wandsbek amongst them—attempted to either limit or abolish entirely the right of Ostjuden to vote in community elections (*Wahlrecht*). We should not forget that most states legally obliged all Jews, whether resident aliens or German citizens, to become members of their local communities (*Gemeinden*). Membership included the right to vote in *Gemeinde* elections. Most communities—with the exception of Dresden and Leipzig, where Eastern Jews were a majority—had acceded to this requirement and extended the franchise to Ostjuden.

This was to change, however, as the challenge to liberal control grew. Liberals actively engaged in a campaign, at times characterized by blackmail and defamatory methods, to disenfranchise all alien Jews. Highly technical legal arguments were put forward to justify the move.[92] What they all boiled down to was the proposition, at least in the Prussian case, that state law disallowed voting rights for non-nationals in local elections. In reality, the laws were obsolete and were ignored wherever possible. Indeed, when such issues were brought to the state authorities they concluded that state citizenship had no bearing on the matter of community elections.[93]

The legal arguments, of course, were designed to protect German Jews from the influence of an undesirable element which, as one liberal lawyer prominent in the disenfranchisement campaign stated, possessed "alien and unsympathetic views and habits."[94] The movement against aliens climaxed in late 1912 in what became widely known as "the shame of Duisburg," when liberals, after legally being voted out of office, arbitrarily disenfranchised the Ostjuden. They moreover claimed before government officials that Eastern Jews had voted fraudulently. The C.V.—officially "neutral" on the *Wahlrecht* question—defended its Duisburg constituents on the grounds that Jewish liberalism was being unfairly demeaned.

The Orthodox journal *Der Israelit* described liberal actions as "unjust, illiberal, and unprecedented."[95] The "scandalized" Zionists made this issue a *cause célèbre* of German Jewish politics.[96] Was there not a contradiction, they asked, at the very heart of German Jewish liberalism? German Jewish liberals were always in the forefront of opposition to measures that discriminated against particular national or religious groups. Yet here were Jews indulging in precisely those actions which they habitually condemned—on their own liberal grounds.

Of course, the liberal disagreement with Zionism extended further than the question of voting rights. Although the C.V. was unsympathetic to Zionism, it had maintained a public neutrality on the question until the post-1910 radicalization of the Zionist movement.[97] For all that, most liberal Jews identified Zionism with *Ostjudentum* in terms of both its clientele and its ideological spirit. Liberal Jews, in many cases hostile to the reassertion of Jewish "national" definitions, regarded Zionism and the Ostjuden as alien, undesirable imports. Ludwig Geiger, editor of the *Allgemeine Zeitung des Judentums*, typified this approach. There was no possibility for German Jews to actively participate in that movement, he wrote, for they knew only one *Volk*, the German *Volk*. A "welfare" Zionism was, perhaps, permissible for the persecuted Eastern Jewish masses, but support would be given on humanitarian, not national, grounds. Geiger emphasized that the compassion he felt for the hungry German laborer was as great as it was for the hounded Russian and Rumanian Jews.[98]

Liberal and C.V. Jews grew publicly more hostile to Zionism, however, as young German Zionists loudly proclaimed that German Jews would always be regarded as aliens. Instead of dominating German culture, Moritz Goldstein wrote in the prestigious journal *Der Kunstwart*, German Jews should migrate to Palestine, where they could openly express their Jewishness.[99]

Liberal Jews were outraged. Such assertions—that German Jews "controlled" German cultural life—provided Jewish confirmation of a thesis anti-Semites had been forwarding for years. Their responses did not really touch the essence of Goldstein's case but demonstrated the centrality, and uses, of the East-West Jewish distinction in German Jewish self-understanding. Perhaps, argued Ernst Lissauer, Goldstein's "national" Jew, socially segregated and culturally distinct, described the Ostjuden, but "we German Jews do not speak the *Jargon*, have laid down the caftan and *Peies*, and apart from an external confessional designation that has little internal reality, have nothing in common with them. We are not their *Volksgenossen*."[100] The official C.V. reply also regarded the basic fallacy of Goldstein's argument to be the lack of a distinction between Eastern and Western Jewry. The Zionist desire that Jews be nothing other than Jews applied to the Ostjude because "he lives in an environment which has no culture; consequently the Ostjude may be satisfied with the old and poor culture of the Middle Ages. We, the Jews of the West, are and can only be Germans, as far as any culture is concerned . . . not because of our desire to assimilate, but because our whole being is tied to Western cultural tradition with very strong bonds."[101]

Ultimately the difference between German Jews and Ostjuden, both in and out of Germany, was regarded as cultural in nature. Liberal German Jews viewed Eastern Jewish culture as "ghetto" culture which by definition was backward and underdeveloped.[102] The German historical experience had made it abundantly clear that Jewish modernization was conditional upon deghettoization, and this in turn left no room for *Kulturjuden* along the lines still maintained in Eastern Europe.

This point of view was perfectly understandable. German Jews felt like Germans and their culture *was* German culture. By the beginning of the twentieth century they possessed almost nothing akin to the "Jewish" culture that characterized life in the ghettoes of Eastern Europe. The distance they felt, the dissociation from Ostjuden was, then, predicated upon both an objective and a subjective reality. Even so, most German Jews never wanted to make the dissociation total and maintained an obstinate sense of responsibility for their Eastern brethren. But even had they attempted, as a minority did, to break the bonds entirely, the combined weight of anti-Semitism on the one hand and Zionism on the other would have prevented it. The liberal Jew found himself caught between these two movements, both of which became centrally implicated in Germany's relation to the Ostjuden. We must turn, now, to an examination of these forces.

3 CAFTAN AND CRAVAT
"Old" Jews, "New" Jews, and
Pre-World War I Anti-Semitism

Once, as I was strolling through the Inner City, I suddenly encountered an apparition in a black caftan and black hair locks. Is this a Jew? was my first thought.

For, to be sure, they had not looked like that in Linz. I observed the man furtively and cautiously, but the longer I stared at this foreign face, scrutinizing feature for feature, the more my first question assumed a new form:

Is this a German? . . . Wherever I went, I began to see Jews, and the more I saw, the more sharply they became distinguished in my eyes from the rest of humanity. Particularly the Inner City and the districts north of the Danube Canal swarmed with a people which even outwardly had lost all resemblance to Germans. . . . The cleanliness of this people, moral and otherwise, I must say, is a point in itself. By their very exterior you could tell that these were no lovers of water, and, to your distress, you often knew it with your eyes closed. Later I often grew sick to my stomach from the smell of these caftan-wearers.[1]

WHEN Hitler wrote the words above he was appealing to an established cultural tradition that was bound to have resonance for his German and Austrian readers. The historical memory of the "ghetto Jew" was never erased in Germany. Once German Jewry itself became modernized and no longer seemed to fit the traditional image, unemancipated East European Jewry served as a constant

58

reminder of the mysterious and brooding ghetto presence. Ostjuden, in reality and myth, kept the stereotype alive. They were increasingly regarded by many as the living embodiment of a fundamentally alien, even hostile, culture. In this sense the modern German perception of the Jew was profoundly affected by the disjunction between emancipated and unemancipated Jewry.

We should not forget that German progressives, Jews and anti-Semites alike, appeared to repudiate the physical and spiritual characteristics associated with the ghetto. For them, the ghetto Jew symbolized all that was wrong with the Jew of old. As George L. Mosse has pointed out, even those writers most responsible for the articulation of the nineteenth-century stereotype of the Jew were in favor of assimilation,[2] a view that was of course antithetical to racism, for it presupposed both the desirability and possibility of Jews escaping the ghetto and submerging themselves radically in Germanism. "Good" Jews were portrayed as assimilated Jews. The problem lay with the "old" Jews, Urjuden, intent on maintaining traditional, unethical ghetto practices and unwilling to change their national loyalties and dubious values. Gustav Freytag's famous rendition of Veitel Itzig, the quintessential Jew, in Soll und Haben (Debit and Credit, 1855) was based upon his observations of Eastern Jews who had penetrated into his city of Breslau. Wilhelm Raabe's Hungerpastor (1864) portrays Moses Freudenstein as a demonic Jew who has inherited the age-old ghetto hatred of the Christian and ruthlessly seeks self-aggrandizement.

The animus against Eastern ghetto Jews was not expressed in popular literature alone; agitation in the political arena, using similar imagery, began early. In 1852, long before the rise of organized political anti-Semitism, Polish Jews were identified to the Prussian Chamber as habitual thieves and criminals.[3] The subject of Russian and Polish Jewish refugees was, as we have seen, always a concern to the political authorities. Treitschke's famous 1879 warning on the dangers of an Eastern Jewish invasion was thus addressing an already familiar theme: while accepting the possibility of German Jewish assimilation, Treitschke argued that further influx from the East constituted a fundamental danger to German national integrity.[4] In his History of Germany in the Nineteenth Century, Treitschke enunciated the stereotype in classical form. He described early nineteenth century Posen as a "fermenting mass of Jewry . . . for here there had occurred a precipitation of all the filth in Polish history. There was nothing German about these people, with their stinking caftans and their obligatory lovelocks, except their detestable mongrel speech."[5]

A major demand of the famous 1881 Anti-Semites' Petition, signed by 250,000 German citizens and one of the high points of the early anti-Semitic movement, was for the cessation of immigration of alien Jews.[6] Many contemporaries did not regard this as fortuitous. The emergence of political anti-Semitism seemed to coincide with the westward mass movement of East-European Jews. Their entry into Western Europe lent plausibility to the stereotype of the ghetto Jew.

Physical cues were vital in this process. Even the most liberal non-Jewish descriptions of the Ostjuden, sympathetic to their plight and sufferings, stressed the filth of their surroundings. One such account dwelt upon the degenerate appearance of the children, the dirtiness of the women. The marketplace was described as a conglomeration of "stinking fish, rotten meat covered with swarms of flies, overripe vegetables, and rotting fruit."[7] Almost as unpleasing as the dirt was "the Jewish smell." Over the years "scientific" analyses pondered whether there was an inherent and racial Jewish smell or whether any smell was simply the product of unsanitary ghetto life or of the specific dietary habits of the East European Jews, who used garlic in their daily diets.[8] Typically, the anti-Semitic movement composed mock "hymns of praise" to the Jewish garlic smell, sung in pseudo-Yiddish *(Mauscheln)*.[9] All of this was easy to caricature, of course, but at times the ridicule was combined with a fear of contagion. German children at play would instantly recognize Polish Jewish children, taunt them with cries of "Itzig"—and refuse to sit on park benches after them.[10] This physical dimension, the obviously alien appearance of Eastern Jews, made them an easy target for the anti-Jewish animus. Yet it went further than that. As the quotation from Hitler indicates, anti-Semites regarded external appearance as proof of an equally degenerate inner life, sign of a twisted moral condition.

Even when the identification was merely on the symbolic level, the imagery remained stubbornly physical. Karl Marx's description of the Polish Jews as the "dirtiest of all races . . . they multiply like lice"[11] was not apt to provoke much disagreement amongst his peers. It was easy to make the Ostjude a yardstick for the unaesthetic; many people quite opposed to Volkish anti-Semitism did this. Thus Nietzsche, certainly no Volkish anti-Semite, could write, "We would no more choose the 'first Christians' to associate with than Polish Jews—not that one required any objection to them: they both do not smell good."[12]

This almost consensual distaste doubtless contributed in no small measure to the fact that the Ostjuden became the first victims of early anti-Semitic successes. The constant agitation against "alien"

Jews was connected to the 1884–87 series of official expulsions from Prussia of Polish nationals. While these orders applied to Jew and non-Jew alike, the evidence is clear that they contained an anti-Semitic element, one closely linked to the fears which the stereotype of the ghetto conjured up.[13] The importance of the expulsions lies in the fact that previously outlawed anti-Semitic demands were now incorporated in official state policy, and it was precisely on the question of the "alien" Jew that this change could occur in the first place. Of course, officials denied the anti-Jewish component, but the documents demonstrate that Bismarck himself (never an "ideological" anti-Semite; his political thinking was too fluid and subtle for that) shared the animus against the ghetto Jew. Certainly he viewed the threat of Jewish immigration from the East with grave concern, and at a cabinet meeting in May 1882 he urged that these "undesirable elements" be kept out of Germany. He also ordered that all Jews living off usury be expelled from Oppeln, an area of concentration for Jewish refugees. Thereafter, the cabinet initiated special patrols of the Russian border in order to keep out persons who—in obvious code language—"looked undesirable."[14]

These were not even the first expulsions. In Prussia's Polish provinces there was a considerable prior history, going back to the eighteenth century, of governmental measures against Polish Jews.[15] Still, the expulsions of the 1880s acquired a significance beyond the routine matter of dealing with a poor refugee community, for they coincided with and even seemed to mirror organized political anti-Semitic demands. It is important to note that thereafter, in every subsequent decade before World War I, there were various local expulsions of Ostjuden.[16] This official action was combined with heated agitation against East European Jewish students that resulted in the promulgation of stringent quota regulations by universities in Prussia, Bavaria, and Baden.[17]

The antipathy to the Ostjude permeated the highest levels of government. It was Bismarck's press secretary, Moritz Busch, who wrote one of the most vicious diatribes against East European Jews; some observers have even suggested that his writing reflected Bismarck's own ideas.[18] Busch's anonymously published *Israel und die Gojim* exploited to the fullest the fear of the ghetto Jew as radically alien and hostile.[19] The Eastern Jews, Busch claimed, were entering Germany in an unending stream. They were the "real" Jews, strange medieval Semitic types, bringing their criminal ways into Germany, maintaining their primeval hate for all Christians, and waiting to enrich themselves while impoverishing Germans. Like vampires they sucked the life blood out of the German national organism, in accordance with the ancient Talmudic injunction to hate the Christians (*"gojim"*). The only way to stop these "leeches" was to hermetically seal Germany's borders. Busch's language was extreme, but his 1880 political demand for such a border closing (*Grenzschluss*) received increasing, if never decisive, Jewish and non-Jewish support as the "invasion" continued.[20]

With regard to those East European Jews who had managed to settle in Germany, the anti-Semitic press effectively exploited the traditional fear and distaste of the ghetto. Ostjuden, they argued, had reintroduced the ghetto to Berlin.[21] Germany was once more confronted with its filth, backwardness, and criminality.

It should be clear from this review that the Ostjuden played a central role in the genesis, mythology, and disposition of pre–World War I German anti-Semitism. The East European Jews were symbolically and legally alien, a lethal combination. Visible and vulnerable, they made obvious and easy targets.

We need to spell out some of the implications and limits of this analysis, however, for it seems to lay the blame for the rise of German anti-Semitism almost exclusively upon the Ostjude. It accepts the assumption that to a large degree modern anti-Semitism was derived from an objectively based "clash of cultures."[22] It implies that only the fact that there was a continuing presence of unemancipated Eastern Jewry lapping the edges of civilized Europe, reinforcing the ghetto stereotype, and constantly infiltrating the "emancipated" West makes the rise of modern political anti-Semitism comprehensible.[23] Hitler's own juxtaposition of the "caftan" Jews of the East and what we shall term the "cravat" (acculturated) Jews of Linz seems to reinforce this point: while the assimilated Jew was becoming increasingly indistinguishable from other Germans, Ostjuden were keeping alive the cultural differences as well as the historical stereotype of the Jew. This is not only a question of historical analysis; many liberal Jews in the period under discussion quite openly insisted that the *Judenfrage*, the "Jewish question," was essentially a product of the influx of East European Jews.[24] Clearly such a view implies that an assimilationist strategy would have been successful had it not been for the continuing intrusions from the East.

There can be no doubt that the Ostjude played an important role in the development of German anti-Semitism. Yet such an analysis needs refinement and modification, for it sidesteps an equally

significant factor, the attack on the assimilating *and* the assimilated
Jew. We need, therefore, to make a more differentiated analysis that
will illuminate the dialectic and allow us to sort out the respective
places of the "caftan" and "cravat" Jews in the cultural mythology
and political practice of German anti-Semitism.

While the image of the ghetto Jew was inherited from centuries of
separate Jewish-Christian existence, a new, although related, stereotype of the emancipated Jew was created in the nineteenth century
and appeared in German popular culture almost simultaneously
with the attempt to assimilate. The stereotype at first employed old
notions of the ghetto Jew but in a new context. Because much of this
early critique was based upon the use of visual caricature and
contrast, the dramatic stage was an effective vehicle for it. In Julius
von Voss's 1807 play *Die Griechheit*, for instance, Rahel Joab
interests herself in "high culture," avoids all intonations of a Jewish
accent, but betrays her "Jewish being" when it comes to matters of
money.[25] This perception in von Voss was ominous, for he was not
opposed to assimilation but favored it.

The most biting attack on Jewish assimilation appeared in Karl
Alexander Sessa's satire *Unser Verkehr* (1814).[26] In this extremely
popular and controversial play Sessa mercilessly satirized the "new"
German Jews who were desperately denying their ghetto origins and
were seeking to make themselves culturally respectable (*salonfähig*).
The young hero of the play, Jacob, represents a new social type.
Unlike his father, an "old" Jew obsessed by money, Jacob regards
himself as a gifted intellectual, a man of *Bildung* who desires
nothing more than an escape from the bonds of his origins. But
Jacob's cultured intellectuality is patently spurious: after all, his
proclamation that he has transcended his Jewish "nature" is made in
unmistakable Yiddish! There was little artistic merit in the play, but
its vogue attested to the fact that it had captured the comic side of a
popular perception. Sessa's satire on the move from the ghetto to
Enlightened society was effective precisely because it concentrated
on the absurdity (and implied impossibility) of Jewish assimilation.
The locus of animosity now shifted to the Jew's spinelessness,
hopeless mimicry, lack of respect and character. If anything, the
new view despised the Jew because he wanted to leave the ghetto, not
because he was of it. The emancipated Jew presumed to leave his
allotted historical place, and it was precisely in the attempt to
assimilate, to lose his traditional colorings, that the threat was now
placed. The Jew who before was blamed for being a product of the
ghetto was now castigated for his pretensions to transcend it. German

Jews, of course, protested vociferously about their representation in *Unser Verkehr*.[27] To stereotype the ghetto was one matter, to caricature assimilation quite another.

Sessa was not even the first to try to popularize this theme. As early as 1791, C. W. F. Grattenauer published his tract *Concerning the Physical and Moral Characteristics of Contemporary Jews*, warning of the deeply rooted characteristics of Jewry which would resist the forces of assimilation. But the work came too early in the history of German Jewish acculturation to find an echo.[28] His *Wider die Juden* (1802) was more widely read, and here again the contempt for the old Jew was transferred to the rapacious Jewish urge for social integration. The "new" Jew was viewed as a vulgar upstart and not so new at all: the Jewish desire to discard Jewishness became itself an object of ridicule. In the early days of acculturation the Jew was increasingly identified as a philistine. Others, like Friedrich Bucholz, declared that baptism itself would not rid Jews of their corrupt qualities: "The Jew will not renounce *Schacher* on account of baptism, he will make the sacrament itself the object of commerce."[29]

As the century wore on, it grew more difficult to satirize cultural assimilation precisely because German Jews were acculturating so successfully. What had made Sessa's work effective was the hilarious contrast between "Jewish" characteristics and the genteel manners of the salon. When he wrote, Jews still retained mannerisms and speech patterns associated with the ghetto. Sessa combined these old characteristics with the new aspirations. In horribly deformed German, Jacob's father, Abraham, instructs his son on how to proceed in the world: "A new perzon you'll become! Away from Egypt. . . . You'll see der da promized lant of da rich goyim! Your inheritenz you'll take avay from dem however you can, if you'll be a true zon of the children of Izrael!"[30]

This despised *Jargon* was enough in evidence to provide additional work for the famous actor Albert Wurm. Wurm, who had a major role in *Unser Verkehr*, entertained audiences with imitations of Jewish arrivistes not only on the stage, but more significantly, in the houses of Berlin burghers.[31] In the mannerisms he was imitating there lay a genuinely comic side, but by mid-century most of these embarrassing vestiges had been removed from the language and gestures of German Jews. Certainly with the rise of the organized anti-Semitic movement of the 1880s the obviously distinguishing elements had disappeared. Even before this, however, when caricature was no longer appropriate, deadly "culture criticism" could take over.

Jacob Toury has pointed out that the very formulation of the term *Judenfrage* referred to the problem of assimilated Jews. As early as 1821, fears that Jews would dominate the cultural worlds of literature and journalism were voiced. By the 1830s anti-Jewish feelings were directed not so much against the *Betteljuden* and peddlers, or even against traditional Jewish economic activities, as against what was perceived as the "new" Jew.[32] This kind of Jew sought mightily to overcome his Jewish origins and dissociate himself from the mass of Jewry. Nothing exemplifies the trend better than the emergence of modern Jewish intellectuals during this period, thinkers and artists who would play a major role in shaping nineteenth-century German culture. From 1830 on, men like Heinrich Heine, Ludwig Börne, and Felix Mendelssohn were only the most famous amongst the many Jewish aspirants to cultural and intellectual fame. According to the estimate of Jacob Katz, about two-thirds of these intellectuals converted to Christianity,[33] but this did not prevent more and more critics from voicing concern over "destructive" Jewish influence. The works of Jewish intellectuals were dismissed as "arid" and "soulless." The Jewish "spirit" was equated with the modern forces of decomposition and juxtaposed to the deep, organic qualities of German culture. The critique of the new Jewish intellectual berated the Jew, in part, not for having his own organic tradition but for giving it up!

Thus in 1831, in a polemic directed mainly against Börne and Heine, Eduard Meyer portrayed the uprooted intellectual Jews in ways still familiar to us today. Estranged from their Jewish roots and certainly not part of the German people, such men "became unsavory interlopers (*Mitteldinger*). . . . they dissolve absolutely the bonds of piety. They do not belong to any state, to any community, they lack a definite sphere of activity, they roam about the world like adventurers."[34] Yet another critic put it succinctly: Jewry thrived in "mechanical" rather than "organic" situations. That is why they flocked to Berlin, where even spiritual exercise was the product of mechanical forces.[35]

The most influential and systematic comment on the nature of modern Jewish intellectuality was penned by Richard Wagner in his *Judaism in Music* (1850). The fundamental deficiency of the Jewish artist, wrote Wagner, lay in his inalienable status as an outsider. Genuine artistic creativity proceeded from the "inside": "only he who has unconsciously grown up within the bond of this community, takes also any share in its creations."[36] While Wagner's animus was directed specifically against the modern Jewish artist, he did not

sever the link between old and new Jews. Indeed, his essay begins
with the "need to explain to ourselves the *involuntary repellence*
possessed for us by the nature and personality of the Jews, so as to
vindicate that instinctive dislike which we plainly recognise as
stronger and more overpowering than our conscious zeal to rid
ourselves thereof."[37] Jews—all Jews—were by nature "disagreeably
foreign."

Yet Wagner gives to the new Jew a special emphasis, for he is
acutely aware of the novelty of the situation. The attack on the
Enlightened Jew combines venom with sharp social insight—the
position of the modern Jew in German society is linked to the
commercialization of culture and its concomitant vulgarization.
With their gold, Jews had bought their way into culture, which
under modern conditions is transformed into "a venal article of
luxury":

> Henceforward, then, the *cultured Jew* appears in our Society; his
> distinction from the uncultured, the common Jew, we now have
> closely to observe. The cultured Jew has taken the most indicible
> pains to strip off all the obvious tokens of his lower coreligionists:
> in many a case he has even held it wise to make a Christian baptism
> wash away the traces of his origin. This zeal, however, has never got
> so far as to let him reap the hoped-for fruits: it has conducted only
> to his utter isolation, and to making him the most heartless of all
> human beings; to such a pitch, that we have been bound to lose even
> our earlier sympathy for the tragic history of his stock. His
> connexion with the former comrades in his suffering, which he
> arrogantly tore asunder, it has stayed impossible for him to replace
> by a new connexion with that society whereto he has soared up. . . .
> Alien and apathetic stands the educated Jew in midst of a society he
> does not understand, with whose tastes and aspirations he does not
> sympathise, whose history and evolution have always been indiffer-
> ent to him. In such a situation have we seen the Jews given birth to
> Thinkers. . . . Completely shut from this community, by the very
> nature of his situation; entirely torn from all connexion with his
> native stock—to the genteeler Jew his learnt and payed-for culture
> could only seem a luxury, since at bottom he knew not what to be
> about with it.[38]

For Wagner, however, the problem of Jewish artistic creativity
remained insoluble. Even a return to the organic Jewish tradition
was no solution, for its sterile essence precluded such a possibility.
Like Bruno Bauer in his famous *Die Judenfrage* (1843), Wagner
attacked the modern Jew but also maintained his antipathy toward

"traditional" Jews and Judaism itself. The negative connection remained intact.

Later cultural criticism found some value in the "old" Jews and concentrated its animus entirely on "modern" Jews. Significantly, it was the "emancipated" German Jew whom Julius Langbehn, the important Volkish thinker obsessed with "aestheticizing" German life, viewed as the key obstacle to the successful accomplishment of his vision. The new Reformation, transforming German society from its mechanized, rationalistic, and soulless condition into a sensitive "work of art," was regarded by Langbehn as a matter of life and death. The future was depicted as dependent upon the extirpation of the—quintessentially modern—assimilated German Jew.

In Langbehn, the Volkish attack on assimilation as such reaches its most extreme pre–World War I expression. Langbehn explicitly distinguished the traditional from the modern Jew. The traditional Jew, he argued, was worthy of respect and indeed had something in common with a spiritual and moral aristocracy. This was the "genuine" Jew who wanted nothing else but to be a Jew, and as such, had character. "Modern" Jews were quite the opposite. They wanted so desperately to become Germans that they had lost all integrity and character. Nothing was worse than this characterlessness, for it betrayed the "holy spirit of individualism." The self-acknowledging Jew was the "authentic" Jew (*rechter Israelit*) and was acceptable; not so the inauthentic (*gefälschter*) Jew, for honor resided only in those who remained true to themselves. The "old" Jew at least possessed a spiritual homeland. The "Enlightened" Jew had nothing and was in constant restless flight. It was against such rootless Jews that Germans had to take a decisive stand.[39]

Langbehn typified one strain of Volkish and anti-Semitic thinking which feared the Jew precisely because he seemed to have lost all resemblance to the ghetto Jews of old and was realizing the promise of assimilation—according to those premises of liberal modernity which Langbehn and his colleagues were so vitriolically opposing.[40] Such thinking held that assimilated Jews were "poison" for Germany and would have to be treated as such.[41]

For those Volkish thinkers like Langbehn who confronted simultaneously the "modern" Jew and a radical uprooting of traditional values and structures, there was a certain bewilderment. The ghetto Jew might be distasteful but he was at least easily identified. The assimilated Jew, on the other hand, was slippery and elusive. No longer synonymous with a backward and unenlightened past, he embodied the ruthless drive for constant change. He became a metaphor for decomposition. This is significant, for if the rise of organized anti-Semitism coincided with the westward migration of the Eastern masses, it also dovetailed with the push to rapid industrialization in Germany and various financial scandals in the capitals of Europe.[42] The identification of modernity and capitalism with explicitly assimilated Jewry was to lead Volkish thinkers like Paul de Lagarde, who in the 1850s accepted the possibility of German Jewish assimilation, into radically hardened positions. From 1881 on, he lumped all Jews together and was at his most vitriolic when describing the machinations of the modern Jewish capitalists. It is in this context that he employed the horrifyingly prescient language of extermination: "With trichinae and bacilli one does not negotiate, nor are trichinae and bacilli subjected to education; they are exterminated as quickly and thoroughly as possible."[43]

Even for men like Freytag and Raabe, who appeared to distinguish "good" assimilated from "bad" ghetto Jews, the distinction was never clearcut; the one merged with the other. Indeed, the danger was located at the point where the Jew was uprooted from the ghetto and sought his fortune without. Veitel Itzig's parents, rooted in the ghetto, are portrayed as decent people.[44] Not the ghetto as such but the break from it represented much of the new Jewish threat.

Close examination reveals that even for Treitschke—who demanded that German Jews become Germans and who thereby accepted the possibility, indeed the necessity, of assimilation—the distinction between German and Eastern Jews was exceedingly thin. His fear centered on the continuity rather than the distinction between "old" and "new" Jewry. Jewish immigration was linked to the problem of *German* Jewry and its tendency towards domination of specific economic and cultural activities: "Our country is invaded year after year by multitudes of assiduous pants-selling youths from the inexhaustible cradle of Poland, whose children and grandchildren are to be the future rulers of Germany's exchanges and Germany's press. This immigration grows visibly in numbers and the question becomes more and more serious how this alien nation can be assimilated."[45] Even the possibility of German Jewish integration was seriously undermined by a quasi-racial analysis. While most West European Jews were assimilable because they came from the more elevated "Spanish" background, "we Germans have to deal with Jews of the Polish branch, which bears the deep scars of Christian tyranny. According to experience they are incomparably alien to the European, and especially to the German national character."[46] Treitschke's meaning was clear. An analysis made in terms of "stock" meant that even emancipated German Jewish citizens possessed "Polish Jewish characteristics." Behind his rhetoric of assimilable German and unassimilable Polish Jews, Treitschke regarded the Jewish problem as indivisible.

Certainly for political activists most closely associated with the drive for *Grenzschluss*, the distinction between old and new Jews was tenuous at best. One supporter of Treitschke asserted that German Jews would always remain essentially different from the Germans, even if they were superficially changed and had removed the caftan and shaved off their beards.[47] Ominously, Moritz Busch (who was one of the first to advocate the formation of political groups exclusively dedicated to fighting the Jewish menace) made a distinction between ghetto and assimilated Jews in which the latter were, if anything, more dangerous. German Jews, proclaimed Busch, made up "Semitic colonies in the West."[48] They were particularly insidious because they were coiffured and disguised. They had made themselves so "respectable" that it was hard to believe that they had any connection with their Polish or Lithuanian counterparts. But this was an illusion, for with a few exceptions acculturation had not removed the Jewish *Volksseele*. The assimilated Jew still felt the ancient ghetto hatred for the Christian. His "invisibility" made him more dangerous than the ghetto Jew, for it put him in an ideal position to achieve, from within and unrecognized, the aims of Jewish power and domination.

The attack on and fear of the assimilated Jew began with the attempt to assimilate, and Busch formed part of a continuing tradition.

Fear sometimes reached pathological proportions. Nowhere was it more starkly articulated than in the nightmarish short story "The Operated Jew" (1893). This demented tale by Oscar Panizza (1853–1921), himself a demented man who spent the last sixteen years of his life in an insane asylum, is at once burning indictment, biting satire, and unadorned expression of German intolerance and virulent anti-Semitism. It is the story of the desperate attempts of a stereotypical Jew, the culturally and physically deformed Itzig Faitel Stern, to become "modern" ("I observed with astonishment how this monster took terrible pains to adapt to our circumstances, our way of walking, thinking, our gesticulations, the expressions of our spiritual movements, our manner of speech"). Eventually radical surgery, an unprecedented operation on Faitel's entire "skeletal framework," is undertaken by the famous Professor Klotz as the only hope of bringing about the required metamorphosis. ("It is impossible for me to give the reader an account of all the garnishings, changes, injections and quackeries to which Itzig Faitel Stern submitted himself. He experienced the most excruciating pain and showed great heroism so he could become the equivalent of an occidental human being.") When this physiocultural transformation is at last achieved, a financial arrangement enables Faitel to marry a "blonde Germanic lass." He is now almost indistinguishable from other Germans. It is at his sumptuous wedding, the day that Faitel "entered Christian society for good," that his fatal regression to "Jewishness" occurs. Uncontrollably, the man who has undergone such painful operations, lapses into his real accent: "I done bought for me Chreesten blud! Waitererá, where is mine copulated Chresteen bride? . . . I want you shood know dat I'm jost a Chreesten human being like you all. Not wan drop of Jewish blud!" But the regression is not merely cultural. The return to pristine Jewish modes is palpably physical, the assimilationist project revealed in all its genetic absurdity: "Those people who remained behind watched with horror as Faitel's blond strands of hair began to curl during the past few scenes. Then the curly locks turned red, then dirty brown and finally blue-black. The entire glowing and sweaty head with tight gaunt features was once again covered with curly locks. . . . His arms and legs which had been stretched and bent in numerous operations could no longer perform the newly learned movements nor the old ones. . . . A terrible smell spread in the room which forced those people who were still hesitating at the exit to flee holding their noses. . . . Klotz's work of art lay before him crumpled and quivering, a convoluted Asiatic image in wedding dress, a counterfeit of human flesh, Itzig Faitel Stern."[49]

Der Stürmer's 1938 textbook for school children *The Poison Mushroom*[50] was merely restating an old theme in its didactic warnings to innocent Aryan youth. The modern Jew, the textbook warned its readers, resembled the mushroom. As one often confused the poisonous from the healthy mushroom, so, too, could one be confused when trying to identify the Jewish swindler. Jews seemed on the surface like everyone else. This sameness of appearance had caused many unwary Aryans to succumb to the illusion that Jews were not different from others. In this way they had fallen prey to *Judenschwindel.* One always had to keep one's eyes wide open, for then the disguise could be penetrated. Underneath, "the Jew always remained a Jew." This attack on the assimilated Jew, like that of

Illustration from *Der Stürmer's* textbook for school children *Der Giftpilz*. The caption reads, "To see the difference between edible and poisonous mushrooms is often as difficult as to recognize Jews as swindlers and criminals."

Illustration of a story in *Der Giftpilz* contrasting German cleanliness with East European Jewish filth. The picture is captioned "Look at those characters! Those lousy beards! Those dirty, protruding ears . . ."

The Jew as poisonous mushroom. Drawing from the title page of *Der Giftpilz*.

Busch, went side by side with hatred for the Ostjude. The dialectic continued, and the relationship was never fully severed. The same textbook, with suitably repellent illustrations, portrays the infiltration of three hideous, stereotypical Ostjuden into a spotlessly clean Aryan village. The contrast between Jew and Christian could not be more marked; here there are no problems of recognition. After describing the criminal natures of the Jews, the commentator asks, *"Und die wollen auch Menschen sein?"* ("And they also want to be people?").

From the outset, the Berlin anti-Semites of the 1880s, while they had to be more circumspect with their prescriptions for German Jewish citizens, concentrated their attack equally on assimilated Jews and sought to undo many of the successes of Jewish emancipation. The aforementioned Anti-Semitic Petition of 1881 was not only concerned with the problem of alien Jewish immigration but also outlined a program for excluding Jews from government posts and teaching jobs in primary schools, limiting their employment in higher education and restricting appointments of Jews as judges. It even contained the ominous demand for a special Jewish census.[51] These anti-Semites explicitly distinguished "old" from "new" Jews. Adolf Stoecker's first anti-Jewish speech was addressed specifically to the emancipated Jews of Germany. Entitled "What We Demand of Modern Jewry," it stressed that "the Berlin Jews are much richer, much more clever and influential than the Polish Israelites. They control the arteries of money, banking and trade; they dominate the press and they are flooding the institutions of higher learning." The center of the Jewish danger lay in the fact of emancipation. German Jews, rootless and devoid of genuine creative depth, had been provided with a license to dominate modern German culture.[52]

The strength of the attack on the modern emancipated Jew was mirrored in the structure of German Jewish self-hatred, which based itself largely upon the specific stereotype of the "modern" Jew. This may seem obvious, but the point has never been made explicit. The pre–World War I documents of German Jewish self-hatred echo Volkish perceptions of the German Jew more than of the East European Jew. Of course the writers were never enamored of caftan Jews, but more centrally, they shared the preoccupation of the Volkish critics of "Jewish modernism." Like Stoecker and Lang-behn, Walther Rathenau (1867–1922) regarded the restless, rootless parvenu spirit as the most distasteful aspect of contemporary German Jewish behavior. In his tract "Höre Israel" (1897) he stressed the offensive philistinism of German Jews. They tried to become pillars of culture, but not even eau de Cologne could wash away their alien natures. They were "loud and self-conscious in their dress, hot-blooded and restless in their manner."[53] Rathenau, like other Volkish thinkers, regarded modern restlessness as spiritually corroding, and modernity and spirituality as virtually antithetical qualities. This was profoundly paradoxical: Rathenau, the industrialist, was himself an exemplar of the very modernity he so despised, a capitalist who despised capitalism.[54] Perhaps Rathenau's Jewish problem lay in this profound ambivalence towards modernity and was rooted in his acceptance of the Volkish analysis of the Jewish role within modernity. It is instructive that his admittedly short-lived attempt to return to Judaism was not based upon a West European model but upon Buber's spiritual and mystic Hasidim. *Geist* was to be found, if at all, with the East European and not the Berlin Jews.[55]

Rathenau was by no means exceptional in this regard. The novelist Conrad Alberti (1862–1918)—born Konrad Sittenfeld—internalized the Volkish critique of the modern Jew even more precisely. Judaism, he argued, had lost all right to exist in the modern world: it was no longer a religion or a race or a nation but merely a "clique." The modern Jew was the natural enemy of progressive organic development. He incarnated the principle of modern capitalism, accumulation for its own sake. Jewish capitalists mistreated their workers far more than did their Christian equivalents. Jews liked material things, but their production was never based on honest work or basic values. They were responsible for the corruption of German culture, in the exchanges, the press, the theater. Alberti clearly had little use for the "ghetto Jew," but his portrait of the Jew as unethical parvenu was borrowed directly from the Volkish critique of the assimilated Jew.[56] Similarly, Otto Weininger (1880–1903) depicted Jews as essentially amoral, cynical, sceptical, lacking in warmth and emotion, in his classic self-hating work *Sex and Character* (1903). These were the properties that anti-Semites attributed to "deracinated" Jews. "Committed" post–World War I Jewish analysts like Hans Kohn argued that Weininger had been led astray because he was acquainted with only the superficial, inauthentic, and assimilated "coffee-house" Jews of Vienna.[57] They were the very antithesis of genuine *Judentum*, and as another critic argued, Weininger's whole understanding of an overrationalistic Judaism would have been abandoned had he known something about the Ostjuden and the fervor of the Hasidim.[58]

While German Jewish self-haters borrowed their self-images from anti-Semitic portraits of the German Jew, anti-Semites, of course, found it more politic to concentrate their fire on the dangers of foreign Jewish immigration. But this attack was often only a pretext for the attack on the local Jew. Thus Hermann Ahlwardt's 1895 proposal to the Reichstag that Germany close its borders to "Israelites who are not citizens of the Reich" was in reality a vicious attack on German Jewry and a diatribe on the impossibility of assimilation: "The Jews have lived here for seven hundred to eight hundred years,

but have they become Germans? Have they ever placed themselves
on the soil of labor? They have never dreamed of doing such a thing;
as soon as they arrived they started to cheat and they have been doing
that ever since they have been in Germany. . . . The Jew is no
German. If you say he was born in Germany, he was nursed by a
German wet nurse, he abides by German laws, he has to serve as a
soldier . . . then I say that all this is not the crucial factor with regard
to his nationality; the crucial factor is the race from which he stems.
Permit me to make a rather trite comparison which I have used
elsewhere in my speeches: a horse that is born in a cowshed is far
from being a cow."[59]

Ahlwardt's remarks must be seen in the paradoxical context of
successful Jewish acculturation: "race" became an effective explanation of "Semitic-Aryan" differences in part because the external
differences were so few. It was no longer a matter of religion or
nationality or dress or language; because so many Jews had followed
the assimilationist path, the difference now had to be found in
genetic agents that could not be affected by human will and social
amelioration. "Race" became the center of the Jewish question
because among German Jews cultural distance had all but been
overcome. It was the threat and perception of radical closeness that
made "racial theory" extremely useful. This sheds a somewhat
different light on the notion that anti-Semitism flowed from an
objectively based "clash of cultures." For Western Jews, at least, it
was the identity of culture which created the need for a new
principle of differentiation.

While it is true that ultimately the Volkish representation of "the
Jew" was used to describe both the emancipated and the ghetto
Jew—they were linked in this description by a common grasping
materialism, lack of ethics, and lack of creativity—there were
important differences in the stereotypes. While the caftan Jew
embodied a mysterious past, the cravat Jew symbolized a frightening
present. The Ostjude was too primitive, the Western Jew too modern. It was the function of racism to resolve this apparent dichotomy
by uniting the two Jewries in an indivisible fashion.

But of course, for most anti-Semites this was only an apparent
dilemma. In the first place, as we have seen, at least part of the
Eastern Jewish stereotype concerned its particularly "modern"
rather than "medieval" aspect: the perception of Russian students as
nihilists and radical agitators. More important, the "international"
image of the Jew had never been eradicated, despite determined
German Jewish efforts at Jewish denationalization. Popular historical memory retained the picture of a kind of primeval Jewish unity

which made all Jewish behavior, individual or collective, assimilationist or traditionalist, appear as somehow "essentially" Jewish. For those who clung to such an image—one that obviously predated the division of Jewry into its emancipated and unemancipated components—Jewish volition was quite beside the point. Whatever the Jew did (or did not do), his actions could be absorbed into the overall picture. This does not mean that modern German anti-Semitism took root entirely outside the realm of social reality and that it was purely the product of the demented fantasies of a rigid lunatic fringe. The myth of the Ostjude (who *was* in many ways radically different from West Europeans in appearance and outlook) and that of the assimilated Jew (who *was* disproportionately involved with those modern institutions most closely associated with liberalism and capitalism) do have some foundation in reality. But both racism and the notion of "international" Jewry (which preceded and was then tied into the racist scheme) were impervious to either empirical refutation or the possibility of Jewish reformation.

It is this undifferentiated impulse against "the Jew" which ultimately made the distinction between the German Jew and the Ostjude irrelevant. If the political venom in the pre–World War I phase was more obviously against the ghetto Jew, it was most probably for reasons of political prudence, not principle. Disenfranchised immigrants were both visible and vulnerable, and discriminatory actions against them were less likely to arouse storms of protest. But from the outset, individual thinkers and the organized political anti-Semitic movement regarded actions against the Ostjuden as *one first* step in solving the Jewish question ("*einen Schritt zur Lösung der Judenfrage*");[60] few claimed that it would be the last.

Well before the war, German Zionists were warning their fellow Jews that the classic attempt to shake off the Ostjude and see him as the source of anti-Semitism was not only morally contemptible but also a critical misunderstanding of the whole basis of the modern German hostility to the Jew. They claimed that such a dissociation, in fact, served to reinforce accusations of Jewish lack of character and spinelessness.[61] But theirs were minority views which became more plausible only in the violent years immediately following World War I. Still, they described equally well the post-1870 period. The treatment accorded the Ostjude was always a sensitive barometer of the more general attitude toward the Jews, and if the attack upon him was easier, it could, nevertheless, seldom be distinguished from a potential attack on the German Jews.

It should be clear by now that this is not merely an issue of post-facto historical judgment. German Jews themselves passionately debated these questions at the time. The majority of German Jews were inclined toward a liberal, assimilationist interpretation of the Jewish question. The modern "Jewish Question" existed only insofar as the Ostjuden had penetrated into Western Europe, impeded local Jewish assimilation, kept alive the memory of "the Jew," and made accusations of ineradicable differences between the Jews and their host nations credible. The recognition that anti-Semitism was also a new phenomenon corresponding to the rise of a new kind of Jew remained hidden from most German Jews, because such a realization would have demolished the liberal and individualistic assumptions upon which post-Enlightenment German Jewry rested. Only on rare occasions did the *Allgemeine Zeitung des Judentums* debunk its own premises, but when it did do so it was with penetrating insight. As early as 1855 one article stated, "The more the old Jew with his sometimes ridiculous aspects fades away, the more Jew-hatred increases. One disdained the Jew who made one laugh, but one tolerated and often even liked him; but one hates the Jew in equal position and with equal rights."[62] At the height of the anti-Semitic movement, little of this kind of pronouncement was heard from official liberal sources.

The Zionists, on the other hand, argued that in large degree modern anti-Semitism was attributable to a Jewish loss of national nerve and self-respect. This was an already established point of view before World War I, and Albert Einstein's 1920 letter to the Centralverein eloquently fitted into that tradition: "More dignity and independence in our ranks! Not until we dare to regard ourselves as a nation, not until we respect ourselves, can we gain the esteem of others, or rather only then will it come of its own accord!"[63]

Ironically, both positions echoed anti-Semitic sources. By emphasizing one strain over the other, each party thought that it had found an explanatory key and practical guide to action. Yet as we have seen, Volkish thought and anti-Semitic ideology, from their beginnings, attacked Jewry in all its manifestations. For most, Jewish behavior could make little difference. Apparently conflicting tendencies existed side by side, and it was this welter of ambiguous signals that made both interpretations seem plausible. But behind it all lay the fact that the historical image of the Jew had never died in Germany[64] and was available for exploitation in appropriate structural crises. Onto the traditional fear and distrust of the Talmud and ghetto Jew was grafted the notion of the modern Jew, characterless and destructive in intent.

This placed the Jew in an inescapable double bind. If he maintained his traditional characteristics he could be labeled a "ghetto" Jew; if on the other hand he tried to assimilate, this could be construed as a duplicitous exercise in camouflage and proof of a flawed character. In practice, however, the distinction was never that tight but operated on a continuum in which the one merged with the other. Racism only formalized and modernized the age-old picture of an ineradicable Jewish unity. In this sense the fear of the caftan and the cravat Jew could be fused. The Ostjude was regarded as a potential German Jew. Franz Rosenzweig saw this quite clearly: ". . . the whole German fear of the East European Jew does not refer to him as such, but to him as a potential Western Jew. . . ."[65] The satirical magazine *Simplicissimus* pointedly illustrated this feared transformation in a 1903 caricature. It portrayed the metamorphosis of "Moische Pisch" to "Moritz Wasserstrall" to "Maurice Lafontaine."[66]

On the other hand, the Enlightened Jew was regarded as dangerous because, appearances notwithstanding, he had never transcended his "internal ghetto."[67] Some feared the Eastern Jews because, as Treitschke put it, they were the "inexhaustible cradle," the demographic reservoir and lifeline of Western Jewry. Others saw the real danger as emanating from the "leaders" of the Jews, the great Western Jewish capitalists. Whatever the particular emphasis, however, Jewish interdependence was never in doubt, in the minds of anti-Semites if not in the minds of Jews themselves.

Yet we cannot leave it at that. The burden of this chapter has been to demonstrate that from its beginnings the anti-Semitic attack was focused equally on the Western and the Eastern Jew. But it has also attempted to demonstrate that the Eastern Jew performed a specific function in the cultural mythology and political practice of German anti-Semitism. The distinctiveness of the Ostjude lent him a special salience as a clearly differentiated cultural symbol. It gave him a critical role in the evolving disposition of German anti-Semitism as it emerged during World War I and its violent aftermath. We shall return to this theme after examining the other great movement that fundamentally interceded in Germany's relationship with the Ostjuden: German Zionism.

4

ZIONISM AND THE OSTJUDEN
The Ambiguity of Nationalization

THE liberal Western Jewish relationship to the Ostjude was contained within the strictly delineated limits of the prevailing ideology of Jewish "denationalization." Ideas of an equal East-West Jewish partnership could have no place within this scheme, and the notion that the East European Jew could serve as a cultural model for Western Jews was regarded as palpably absurd. We cannot look to the prevailing Jewish definitions if we are to understand the more positive role the Ostjuden were to play in the evolution and disposition of twentieth-century German Jewish identity. For this we need to examine the Zionist movement; it was from this movement that the impetus towards a radically revised Jewish self-understanding developed.

German Zionism, of course, remained a minority movement throughout its pre-Hitler history.[1] This is not surprising, given its insistence on the centrality of Jewish nationalism. Most German Jews regarded the attempt to renationalize Jewry as a dangerous doctrine upsetting the liberal foundations of a hard-won Emancipation. Yet regardless of its small membership, we need to pay attention to the world of German Zionism and to some of the even smaller minority movements it spawned, for they represented an important alternative framework for relating to Jewishness in general and to the Ostjuden in particular. German Zionism became the ideological gadfly of German Jewish life; it consistently challenged liberal assumptions and presented its own ideological options and interpretations in a manner that could not be ignored. By the questions it raised and the answers it elicited, German Zionism sharpened the temper of Jewish life and consciousness.

We should not, at least initially, construe German Zionism in its narrow institutional sense. Until World War I, Western Zionism was articulated essentially within the German-speaking cultural world. Theodor Herzl was born in Budapest and Nathan Birnbaum in Vienna, and Max Nordau lived in Paris, but their common language was German.[2] They wrote in German and appealed to a public whose sensibilities were shaped in its cultural image. This identification was reinforced by the fact that from 1905 until 1920, Germany housed the offices of the World Zionist Organization, and it was there that all the important Zionist publications such as *Die Welt* were produced.[3] Certainly the early Zionist ideologists, both East and West European, tended to use the German model as a metaphor for the larger Western Jewish experience.

Zionism threatened the Jewish liberal consensus because it asserted that the Jews, contrary to the premises of Enlightenment and Emancipation and notwithstanding all their cultural differences, were indeed one nation. It was upon this simple proposition that the Zionists based their promise of a radically reformed relationship between the Eastern and Western Jew. The national movement, so went the theory, would transform the Ostjude from a powerless object of patronizing philanthropy into the natural and equal historical partner of his Western brother. Herzl expressed this in his address to the First Zionist Congress in August 1897: "Zionism has already brought about something remarkable and heretofore regarded as impossible: a close alliance between the ultra-modern and the ultra-conservative elements of Jewry. The fact that this has come to pass without undignified concessions on the part of either side and without intellectual sacrifices is additional proof, if such proof be needed, for the peoplehood of the Jews. A union of this kind is possible only on a national basis."[4]

This does not mean that the founding fathers of Zionism denied the reality of East-West Jewish differences. The contrary is true. The Russian Jew Leo Pinsker (1821–91) wrote his famous Zionist tract *Auto-Emancipation* (1882) with this distinction critically in mind. The pogroms of 1881 had turned Pinsker away from his assimilationist position, and he now attempted to demonstrate that "Judeophobia" was inherent even in the modern world: "As a psychic aberration, it is hereditary; as a disease transmitted for two thousand years, it is incurable."[5] The only solution was for the Jews to emancipate themselves politically as a nation. But Pinsker recognized that Eastern Jewry was not capable of taking the lead in such an endeavor; they had no organizational experience, nor did they possess men of the required political stature. *Auto-Emancipation* is an explicit appeal to Western Jewry. It reinforces the East-West Jewish distinction. Only in the West, Pinsker believed, was there political experience and organizational capacity equal to the task. The work was written in German because it was addressed to Emancipated Jewry, of which he regarded Germany as the cultural and political center.

In many ways Pinsker outlined the basis of what was later to become the "philanthropic" Zionism of the West. Although he generalized the problem of Judeophobia, he stressed that the real Jewish problem existed in places, like Eastern Europe, where there was a surplus Jewish population. Perhaps as a tactical move, he assured potential Western converts to political Zionism that his idea would not involve the emigration of the entire Jewish people. In effect, he defined auto-emancipation as the rescue of the East by the Western part of the nation. Pinsker allowed Western Zionism an exceptional role even before it was born: "The comparatively small number of Jews in the Occident, who constitute an insignificant percentage of the population, and for this reason, perhaps, are better situated and even to an extent naturalized, may in the future remain where they are. The wealthy may also remain even where the Jews are not readily tolerated."[6]

All this clearly anticipated the thrust of pre–World War I Western Zionism (and certainly the first generation of German Zionists). Pinsker envisaged Zionism as a rescue movement on behalf of oppressed Eastern Jews by their more fortunate and wealthy counterparts. The only difference between liberal assimilationist efforts and this plan was its "national-political" orientation. But because Western Jews would merely organize and lead the mass rather than be a part of it, their commitment to nationalization would at best be an ambiguous one.

Pinsker's Zionist undertaking revealed the Ostjude's admiration for and confidence in Western Jewry; it took a Western Jew, the "Communist Rabbi" Moses Hess (1812–75), to be severely critical. All Zionist thinkers, of course, sought to repair the East-West Jewish disjunction and establish ties on a "national" basis, but as an East European Jew in the very early days of the Zionist movement, Pinsker attempted to coax Western Jews into leadership positions through flattery. Hess, on the other hand, tried mercilessly to expose the duplicities of Western Jewish pretensions. His *Rome and Jerusalem* (1862) was of course far ahead of its time and remained an isolated intellectual curiosity for his contemporaries, but it represented the beginning of an intellectual tradition. Western Zionism presupposed a period of secularization and was born with the critique of its own assimilationist assumptions and the recovery of Jewish commitment after a period of estrangement.[7] The modern Jew who denied his own nationality, argued Hess, was not going to gain the respect of other nations:

> It is the modern Jew who is the contemptible one; it is he who denies his nationality, just when the hand of fate lies heavily upon his nation. The petty phrases about humanity and enlightenment which he so liberally casts about himself in order to cloak his aversion for solidarity with his own people will not shield him against the strict verdict of public opinion. Put on a thousand masks, change your names, religion and manners, sneak about incognito through the world, so that the Jew in you may not be recognized; every insult of the Jewish name strikes you even harder than the honest man who admits his solidarity with his family and defends its honor.[8]

Hess combined his criticism of the Western Jew with a search for more authentic Jewish models. This again anticipated later Zionist developments. Judaism in the Occident he regarded as shallow. It was in the East that millions of Orthodox Jews had preserved the kernel of Judaism; there the Jewish grain had been maintained intact. All that was required was the secularization of these forms into the living idea of Jewish nationalism.[9] Hess discerned the dialectic of Zionism long before Zionism became an organized movement. He understood that in the West it would be a form of return, a post-Emancipationist recovery of a rejected national identity, while in the East it would lead the masses toward modernization and rebirth "in the cultivated earth of the present."

From the beginning it was clear that Eastern and Western Jewry would come to Zionism out of radically different situations and needs. Yet in Herzl's insistence that "we are a people, one people,"[10] Zionism laid the basis for a new meeting and a radically revised understanding of the relationship between emancipated and unemancipated Jewry. In many ways the responses to Herzl himself seemed to vindicate this promise. Pinsker had written to a friend in 1883 expressing the hope that while perhaps Western Jewry possessed no second Moses it could produce someone capable of leading a second Exodus.[11] Fourteen years later many East European Jews explicitly compared Herzl to Moses. Ben-Gurion, who was ten years old at the time, recalled that when Herzl visited his home of Plonsk a rumor spread "that the Messiah had arrived—a tall, handsome man, a learned man of Vienna, a doctor no less—Theodor Herzl."[12] The fact that Herzl was a *Western* Jew was central to his attractiveness for the Eastern Jews. The euphoric accord that greeted him at the First Zionist Congress in Basel in August 1897 symbolized to participants that East-West Jewish reunification had already been realized.[13] In a Congress overwhelmingly dominated by East European Jews[14] the feeling of unity, as described by an early German Zionist, was extraordinary: ". . . the whole assembly rose as one man. They sang national songs, they embraced and kissed one another, and many could not suppress tears of emotion. A historic event, one of epoch-making importance for the Jewish people, had taken place. . . ."[15]

The reassertion of nationalism clearly involved Western Zionists in a repudiation, at least in theory, of the nineteenth-century liberal Jewish attitude towards the Ostjuden. The West European Jew, wrote Herzl, regarded his East European counterpart as a kind of Caliban. This was a grave mistake built upon ignorance—one always labeled barbaric that which one did not understand. The meeting with Russian Jews at the Congress had convinced Herzl that they were not Caliban but Prospero: their cultural level was equal to that of the West Europeans, and they possessed an inner unity that Western Jews had lost. Russian Jews were nationalist but not arrogant, they were not torn by the temptations of assimilation, their nature's were "simple and unbroken." They were able to maintain their own nationalism while becoming a part of modern culture. While assimilating to no one, they still learned from others. Russian Jews were upright and genuine. "And yet they are ghetto Jews, the only ghetto Jews that still exist."[16] This glorification of the Ostjude, as we shall see, assumed many guises and became a central theme in Western Zionism, a conscious counter-myth to prevailing liberal Jewish attitudes. The image of the East European Jew as the embodiment of Jewish authenticity, exemplar of the unfragmented self, was diametrically opposed to the Franzosian perception of the ghetto Jew.

Clearly this counter-myth was related to the desire of Western Zionists to hold up an uncelebratory mirror to the assimilationist Jew. Max Nordau, for one, in his famed address to the First Zionist Congress, relied upon the East-West comparison. Jewish misery, he argued, had two forms. For the masses of Jewry—in Eastern Europe, North Africa, and Western Asia—it was a literal, material misery, one that concerned the struggle for bread and survival. In Western Europe, however, the misery was "moral." It assumed the form of perpetual injury to one's self-respect and sense of honor. "The emancipated Jew is insecure in his relations with his fellow beings, timid with strangers, even suspicious of the secret feelings of his friends. His best powers are exhausted in the suppression, or at least the difficult concealment, of his own real character. For he fears that this character might be recognized as Jewish, and he never has the satisfaction of showing himself as he is in all his thoughts and sentiments. He becomes an inner cripple." The ghetto Jew, despite material poverty and persecution, had maintained an inner integrity and "in the moral sense . . . lived a full life." Modern Jews had become a "race of new Marannos, which is sustained morally by no tradition, whose soul is poisoned by hostility to both its own and to strange blood, and whose self-respect is destroyed through the ever-present consciousness of a fundamental lie."[17]

It is not surprising that Western Zionism attempted to view the Eastern Jewish masses in a new, more positive light. This seemed to be necessary to any national self-understanding. Moreover, these masses were to be the committed ranks, the "true" Jews ready for mobilization and action. Yet the rhetoric of Herzl and Nordau, men with thoroughly assimilated backgrounds and deeply European views of the world, obscured a more ambiguous relationship to the Easterners. Much of their rhetoric, in fact, was aimed at enlisting the vital political support of the Eastern Zionists. This is not to imply that the early Western Zionists did not feel a genuine sense of solidarity with their East European counterparts, but it does oblige us to examine more carefully the specifically Western assumptions of their Zionism. Although they departed from liberal Jews on the question of defining Jewry in national terms and on finding an explicitly political solution to the Jewish question, Western Zionists shared the liberal ambivalence to the ghetto masses and mirrored the cultural biases of the very assimilationist Jews whose position they were criticizing.

In the first place, the early phase of the organized Zionist movement corresponded to Pinsker's vision. The model was based explicitly upon a relationship between an elite and the masses in which the distinction between leader and follower was never in doubt. Nordau was quite clear on this: Western Zionism had to be understood in terms radically removed from the impulses animating

East European Zionism. For Ostjuden, Zionism encompassed all of life. It affected the individual and the nation, it referred to the material and the moral dimensions of existence. In the East European context, Zionism signified the liberation from slavery and the reclamation of human dignity, it was a key to *Bildung*, a bridge to the great avenues of European progress. It was the way out of the dirt, degeneration, and poverty of the Eastern ghettoes. This was not the case for Western Zionists. They had grown up in freedom and had already acquired a progressive culture. The officers of the Zionist movement were to come mainly from their ranks to command the natural recruits of the Zionist army who were to be found in Eastern Europe.[18] This approach reproduced almost exactly the patronizing attitude of liberal Jews towards the Ostjuden. Only the solution to the problem was different. Herzl in the beginning looked upon the role of the Eastern masses in the Zionist movement as clearly subservient: in January 1896 he wrote, "We have masses of 'unskilled labourers' in Russia, Rumania, Hungary, Galicia and scattered all over the world. Those emigrant organizations and Zionist societies will have to subordinate themselves to us. . . ."[19]

Herzl, of course, was sensitive to the charge that he was guilty of the same patronizing attitude that he criticized amongst assimilated Jews. In front of an audience of over a thousand people at the Königsstädtisches Casino in Berlin in February 1898, he argued that philanthropy was antithetical to the Zionist approach. Philanthropy could apply to individuals but not to a people: "If philanthropy is practiced on an entire people, it is called politics, and the philanthropy which a people attempts to practice for its own prosperity is the politics of that people."[20] The problem of the Jewish people could be solved only by a fundamental, national approach.

This was indeed a radical departure, a solution anathema to the majority of liberal Western Jews. Yet Herzl's perception of "the people"—a synonym for ghetto Jewry—was remarkably like that of assimilated Jewry. The ghetto, oppressed, miserable, and poverty-stricken, should be eradicated. It had created a community of schnorrers. For Zionists, East European Jewish life became the very paradigm of pathological society. Herzl was speaking explicitly as a West European when he argued that "Zionism is a kind of new Jewish care for the sick. We have stepped in as volunteer nurses, and we want to cure the patients—the poor, sick Jewish people—by means of a healthful way of life in our own ancestral soil."[21] The return to Zion, he wrote elsewhere, would be an act of "physical therapy." The East European masses would leave behind their "abnormal life-style" and turn to physical labor which would make them healthy. This in turn would produce positive "moral consequences."[22]

But it was Max Nordau, not Herzl, who set out most systematically the early Western Zionist perception of the East European ghetto. His view was based essentially upon European positivism, and Nordau himself was a renowned exponent of positivism. His immensely popular works *Conventional Lies of Our Civilization* (1883) and *Degeneration* (1892), written before his Zionist conversion, defined that position clearly. It was a liberal viewpoint informed by a belief in science and progress. Clarity, order, discipline, and an emphasis on hard work were central in a basically middle-class sense of priorities. The enemies of this outlook—who in Nordau's view were gaining ground everywhere in fin-de-siècle Europe—were the romantics, the "irrationalists," the metaphysicians, and the artists of "decadence." Nordau's medical background made him particularly sensitive to the physical aspects of what he considered degeneration.[23]

All of this shaped his Zionism. He distinguished the Western Zionism of "the educated and free Jewish elite" from the East European version. There the attachment to Zion of the uneducated, tradition-bound masses was a matter of instinct rather than of reasoned reflection; they were still partly influenced by "mystical tendencies." The challenge of Zionism was to save these people from their unbearable suffering and to make them productive and cultured.[24]

Given his emphasis on work, it is hardly surprising that it was Nordau who in 1901 popularized that peculiarly Jewish notion of the *luftmensch*. Today it has come to mean a kind of spiritual, rootless intellectual figure, but this is not the meaning that Nordau originally gave to it. The luftmensch was a specifically East European Jewish phenomenon. *Luftmenschen* were an entire class of grown, tolerably healthy men who were unemployed and wandered around in the hope of obtaining a piece of bread by the end of the day. Nordau was careful to distinguish the luftmensch from other marginal and itinerant social types such as the English loafer and the Neopolitan *lazzerone*. Unlike them, the luftmensch was honest and able to work but simply lacked the opportunity. The Jews of the ghetto had become a *Luftvolk*—they had no capital for the present and no reserves for the morrow.[25]

A normal economy would create normal, healthy bodies. Nordau's original (1898) call for a *Muskeljudentum* ("muscle-Judaism") was reflected in the organization of turnverein, athletic clubs, in the West, but it was the need for physical regeneration in the Eastern ghetto that seemed especially urgent to him. And what was better suited than Zionism, Nordau asked, to organize the "helpless and chaotic" masses of the East? Emigration to the New World was no solution, for freedom there was only apparent—old conditions were merely recreated in new ghettoes. Zionism would provide bread for the hungry and discipline the "neglected and brutalized" masses. It would create reliable and strong citizens out of the feeble and powerless. Nordau defined degeneration as the loss of vital energy. The constructive reharnessing of such lost Jewish energy was what Zionism was about.[26]

Despite his criticism of assimilationism, Nordau's Zionism perpetuated many of its cultural values and perceptions. He was not beyond presenting Zionism as a kind of safety valve protecting the vital interests of German bourgeois Jewry. This was the basis of his appeal for liberal Jewish support. He argued that the belief that one could shake off the caftan Jew was a serious error and merely made one contemptible in the eyes of the anti-Semites (who attacked the Ostjuden but really had the more protected, wealthier Jews in mind). Jewry, he argued, was as strong as its weakest point, and the radical interdependence of its members made it vital for Jews always to pay attention to "the most lowly Jew." "The contempt created by the impudent, crawling beggar in dirty caftan . . . falls back on all of us." If only on the basis of self-interest, Western Jews had to raise these miserable creatures to a higher economic and spiritual level. Zionism did not require that German Jews leave Germany. It sought only to come to the rescue of those who were suffering and in need of help. Zionism would transform the Ostjuden. They would become a source of pride, not shame, for the Jewish state would demonstrate Jewish proficiency (*Tüchtigkeit*).[27]

Of course this rejection of the ghetto and disdain for its cultural and human products was shared, perhaps even more virulently, by the East European Zionists. After all, the escape from the physical and spiritual confines of ghetto life was for them an intensely personal matter. Zionism was based upon the rejection of the Galut (exile), and the Eastern ghetto seemed to epitomize all the critical abnormalities of Galut. Rejection of the ghetto was common to assimilationists and Eastern and Western Zionists, all of whom longed for Jewish "normalization," although the paths they chose and the interpretations they attached to the term differed radically.

Like the Western Zionists, East European Zionist intellectuals were post-Haskalah in sensibility, but their critique of the ghetto was grounded in personal experience. Their "modern" consciousness was housed in and constricted by an antiquated social structure, and the resulting dissonance often produced vitriolic criticism. This was reflected in the works of men like Joseph Hayyim Brenner (1881–1921) and Micah Joseph Berdichevsky (1865–1921). Vladimir Jabotinsky (1880–1940), who was not raised in its confining atmosphere, expressed a general Eastern Zionist concern when he wrote that the ghetto "was scornfully oblivious of all sensuous enjoyment . . . a microcosm of truncated, mutilated, semi-life. . . . [It] despised physical manhood, the principle of male power as understood and worshipped by all free peoples in history. Physical courage and physical force were of no use, prowess of the body . . . an object of ridicule."[28] Jewish national normalization was equivalent to the revolt against the ghetto and the reassertion of the physical, the sensual, even the martial faculties.

For sophisticated Eastern Zionists this was not merely a theoretical frustration. In 1895 Chaim Weizmann wrote a letter to his friend Leo Motzkin about the return to his hometown: "The trouble is that after Berlin, Pinsk has made such a vile, repulsive impression on me that I find it unpleasant, even distasteful, to share it, dear friend, with you. There is nothing here and no-one: instead of a town—just an enormous rubbish-heap; instead of people, one comes across creatures devoid of all personality, with no interests, no desires, no demands. . . . Hundreds of Jews push on and hurry about the streets of our town, with anxious faces marked by great suffering, but they seem to do it unconsciously, as if they were in a daze. . . . I am incredibly bored here."[29]

Weizmann was not alone. Many East European Zionists had internalized the standards of West European culture and disdained their shtetl background. Yet for all that, they were deeply aware that their Zionism was rooted in a unique East European Jewish culture. The ghetto was rejected but not the "Jewish spirit" behind it, and from the beginning the Easterners resented the Western desire to dominate and direct the Zionist movement. They regarded it as particularly unhealthy because the elite, unlike themselves, had lost all touch with Jewish national and cultural roots. Western Zionists, they believed, were leading the movement in assimilationist directions and lacked all positive Jewish cultural content.

Leading Western Zionists denied the existence of a basic East-West antagonism. Max Nordau, among them, argued that the divisions were not geographical but temperamental—that Zionism was split between the hopelessly romantic, impractical elements and the positive realists, types that could be found in both East and West. It was typical of Nordau that he should characterize the clash as one between Hegelians and positivists.[30]

Yet his 1910 remarks ignored an ideological debate that was integral to the intellectual development of the second and more radical generation of German Zionists. Immediately after the First Zionist Congress, Achad Ha'am (1856–1927) (pseudonym of Asher Zvi Ginsberg, the most prominent ideological opponent of political Zionism) wrote a withering polemic against Western Zionism. The hungry Eastern masses looked upon the Western Jews as Messianic saviors, he said, but they were mistaken. People like Nordau simply did not understand that the problems facing Eastern Jewry were fundamentally different from those confronting Western Jews: "In the West it is the problem of the Jews; in the East, *the problem of Judaism*. The first weighs on the individual; the second, on the nation. The one is felt by Jews who have had an European education; the other, by Jews whose education has been Jewish. The one is a product of anti-Semitism, and is dependent on anti-Semitism for its existence; the other is a natural product of a real link with a millennial culture, and it will remain unsolved and unaffected even if the troubled of the Jews all over the world attain comfortable economic positions, are on the best possible terms with their neighbors, and are admitted to the fullest social and political equality."[31]

For Achad Ha'am, the lines of differentiation were drawn sharply and explicitly. Western Zionist leaders, however committed they were to the Zionist cause, were so far removed from Judaism that the future would be determined "by the standards of the foreign culture which they themselves have imbibed; and they will endeavour, by moral persuasion or even by force, to implant that culture in the Jewish State, so that in the end the Jewish State will be a State of Germans or Frenchmen of the Jewish race."[32] In 1902, he published his critique of Herzl's *Altneuland*, condemning Herzl's vision of the future state. Here was a derivative society, an "apish copying," devoid of all original national characteristics. It exemplified the spirit of "slavishness amidst freedom" which according to Achad Ha'am was the hallmark of Western Jewish life. Such a spirit would permeate the new Jewish state.[33]

Achad Ha'am had raised a vital question concerning the relation of a modernizing nationalism to its traditional cultural roots. Zionism clearly combined a desire for continuity with a rebellion against the Jewish past. This was indeed a serious problem, unresolved to this day. Yet the ensuing debate did less to deal with the underlying issues than it did to expose latent Zionist antagonisms.

Nordau's response, for instance, was cast in insulting personal terms. He castigated the Russian's views as foolish and malicious; they reflected a "slavish being." Zionism had no desire to give up European culture, which was not alien to Jews who had contributed so much to it. Perhaps it was alien to Achad Ha'am, but this should make him all the more appreciative of Western Zionism for making it accessible to him. The future of the Jewish People lay within the cultural framework of Western Europe and not in an "anti-cultural, wild *Asientum* as Achad Ha'am seems to desire." Zionism was not the reversion to barbarism and would not reintroduce traditional modes of intolerance that had driven outsiders away, as in Sodom and Gomorrah. The future Jewish state was to be a liberal one based upon universal freedom. It would not be another ghetto.[34]

Nordau's *"wildes Asientum"* pointed clearly to the culture of the Eastern ghettoes, and most East European Zionists interpreted the conflict in geographical terms. The young Chaim Weizmann wrote to Nahum Sokolow that the "Achad Ha'am–Nordau business" had assumed the character of a political witch-hunt and that all who disagreed with the "Viennese" version of Zionism "must be cast root and branch out of the Party. . . . woe unto him who bears the mark of Cain in opposition to Nordau!"[35] Weizmann was himself opposed to Achad Ha'am because he was "not a political Zionist,"[36] but he and many of his colleagues regarded the issue as a clear East-West struggle for power: "I trust," he wrote to his future wife Vera Khatzman, "that we shall finally succeed in letting the world know where hegemony in Jewry rightfully belongs—in the hands of the author of *Degeneration* or in those of the young, spiritually free Eastern Jews."[37] Weizmann put the matter more diplomatically and with admirable insight to Herzl. He suggested that only his "faction"—a group of young radical "oppositionalists"—could bridge East-West differences, for they would extract the Jewish essence from the masses and pour it into a European mould: "What we regard as Jewish culture has till lately been confused with Jewish religious worship, and when culture in the literal sense was discussed, the Zionists of Western Europe thought that it referred to the improvement of educational facilities in East Europe. Perhaps it is now understood . . . that the totality of Jewish national achievement is intended—particularly that literature, art, scientific research, should all by synthesized with Europeanism, translated into modern creativity, and expressed in institutions bearing their own individual character."[38]

In Germany itself the Zionist leader Adolf Friedemann confided in his diary that although Achad Ha'am was no great thinker, he was correct in his debate with Nordau. There was little in *Altneuland* that could be said to contain Jewish content or feeling.[39] The public attack on Nordau, however, was headed, not surprisingly, by transplanted Ostjuden. Leo Wintz, who had come from the Ukraine to Berlin in the 1890s and was editor of *Ost und West*, led the attack. In an anonymous article "The Jews of Yesterday," Wintz depicted the conflict as one between "rooted" and "uprooted" Judaism. Nordau clearly belonged to the latter camp—a "Jew of yesterday" who had suddenly "come back" to Judaism at the First Congress in 1897. Nordau himself was less important than what he typified. He represented "a childish arrogance," a patronizing West European perspective. Such Jews duplicitously sought to pose as aristocrats rescuing the poor sunken Eastern masses from the lower depths. But the West Europeans were the "new" Jews, it was they who were the "guests" within Zionism. A man like Nordau, who in his *Conventional Lies of Our Civilization* had dismissed the Bible as a "childish" document replete with shocking morals, had no legitimacy as a teacher of the Jews, much less as their task-master.[40]

It is significant in terms of the evolution of German Zionism that while Herzl was outraged by defenders of Achad Ha'am,[41] younger Zionists like Martin Buber and Berthold Feiwel formulated a collective letter, circulated to various Jewish newspapers, which declared: "There is no need to defend the man who helped to create spiritual Zionism; this fearless man of truth in thought and deed; this man of ethical excellence who is regarded by the best East European Jews with honour, respect and trust. This genuine and perfect Jew who, long before the advent of political Zionism, appeared as the most radical combatant on behalf of the national movement and who issued the call for redemption of the people, the language and the land. It is superfluous to defend Achad Ha'am against the defamations and degradations contained in Nordau's article. But we consider ourselves honour-bound to protest more vigorously, in the name of many West European Jewish authors. . . ."[42]

But spiritual or cultural Zionism was not significant within German Zionism until a number of years later. At the critical August 1903 Congress when Herzl proposed Uganda as a *Nachtasyl*, a temporary source of refuge for a desperately threatened Jewry, it had virtually no influence. The East European Zionists were horrified by Herzl's proposal. They attributed "abortions" such as "philanthropic Zionism, *Nachtasyl* Zionism" directly to Western "assimilation within Zionism."[43] The German vote on the Uganda matter reinforced Russian Zionist fears. Of the fifty-four delegates in the

German camp, only seven opposed Herzl's proposal and of those at least four had East European backgrounds.[44]

The first generation of German Zionism did indeed proceed along mainly philanthropic lines. This was not limited to ideological matters. Leadership was concentrated in German hands, while the followers were often East European.[45] Ahron Sandler reminisced that "even in Berlin our meetings would have made a sorry impression if numerous *Ostjuden* . . . had not filled the room."[46] The presence of Ostjuden in the German Zionist Organization strengthened the conviction of both liberal Jews and anti-Semites that Zionism was a foreign ideology, an alien import. But it was not merely sensitivity to such accusations that kept the Ostjuden in subservient positions within the local movement. Franz Oppenheimer (1864–1943), who typified the attitudes of the first generation of German Zionists, told Kurt Blumenfeld that Zionism necessarily involved German Jews as "directors" and the Ostjuden "as actors."[47] Adolf Friedemann was convinced that the democratic statutes of the Zionist Organization were a formality and that the "real" leadership had to be Western.[48]

Statistics of Eastern Jewish membership in the German Zionist movement are incomplete, but the attraction of Zionism for Eastern Jews living in Germany was quite natural. As newcomers to Germany, most of them possessed a "traditional" national Jewish consciousness, and their status as double outsiders, marginal figures within German society and estranged from the mainstream of German Jewish life, made them obvious recruits. But they remained followers, and the student and intellectual circles with whom a creative dialogue might have developed by and large lived separate lives. These groups formed their own small sub-cultures, not really wanting integration but excitedly absorbing Germany's great cultural offerings and adapting them to their own esoteric national concerns.

The list of Zionist intellectuals and students who made their homes in Germany during the pre-war era is impressive. It includes luminaries like Chaim Weizmann, Leo Motzkin, Jacob Klatzkin, Shmaryahu Levin, and Nachmann Syrkin. Somewhat incongruously, Berlin became a center of the East European Hebraist cultural revival.[49] David Frischmann, Saul Tschernichowsky, and Micah Berdichevsky wrote and experimented at various times in Germany, and in 1909 a World Congress of Hebraists was held there. One year before World War I Schmuel Agnon took up residence in Germany.

Yet there was little cultural communication between these circles and the early German Zionists, for they seemed to inhabit different worlds. German Zionists would occasionally visit their East European counterparts at their favorite haunt, the Café Monopol. The café was frequented by Menahem Ussishkin, Shalom Aleichem, Shalom Asch, and others like them. Only Hebrew was spoken, and the waiters would greet their East European customers with *Shalom*. These intellectuals even staged Purim plays in Hebrew at the Monopol.[50] Little connected the highly acculturated middle-class early German Zionists with these somewhat Bohemian figures trafficking through Berlin society in a foreign language. The attempt to conduct a genuine dialogue would have to await the arrival of a radicalized second generation of German Zionists.

The ideology of German Zionism, then, had very little to do with a meeting of equals. The specifically *German* Zionism was grounded in the sufferings of East European Jewry and the philanthropic belief that German Jews could come to their political aid. It was characteristic that the assimilated lawyer Max Bodenheimer (1865–1940) conceived of forming a separate Zionist organization only after Karl Emil Franzos and others close to the Alliance Israelite rejected the notion of Jewish colonization in Palestine as in principle unacceptable. This prompted him to meet with men like Adolf Friedemann and Heinrich Loewe who were part of the nationalist student organization Jung Israel. Out of this nucleus the German Zionist Organization, Zionistische Vereinigung für Deutschland (ZVfD), was officially formed in 1897.[51]

But the outlines of German Zionist ideology were already implicit in Bodenheimer's *Wohin mit den russischen Juden?* of 1891, a pre-Herzl document that was a Zionism of compassion, one that referred to the colonization and rehabilitation only of the persecuted Ostjuden and contained no threat to emancipated Jewry. This set a trend. German Zionism did not advocate emigration but rather offered German Jews a renewed sense of pride in their heritage, a positive sense of Jewish identity. It countered the negative self-image that assimilation and anti-Semitism had fostered.[52]

Zionists clearly did oppose liberal Jewish psychological self-abnegation and national self-denial. The attempt to reestablish ties with the Ostjuden and to assert a Jewsh national commonality was one manifestation of this opposition. "The Russian Jews, how do they concern us?" asked one German Zionist pamphlet shortly after the Zionist Congress of 1897. "Like all other German Jews they too are our brothers. The Zionists view all Jews as brothers who have a common history and a common future."[53]

This was indeed positive, yet the newly recovered membership within the Jewish people involved radically different rights and obligations for Eastern and Western Jews. German Zionists defined their Zionist responsibilities in purely philanthropic terms. Their definition differed from even normative Herzlian Zionism in that it refused to universalize the Zionist analysis and apply its insights to the political situation of Jews in Germany. It applied only to "unfree" Jews. As Adolf Friedemann wrote in a 1903 brochure, "West Europeans will mainly provide the organizers for colonization. . . . naturally we are not about to initiate a mass emigration of German, French and English Jews."[54]

These early Zionists did not regard the tenets of their Zionism as antithetical to *Deutschtum*. There was no sweeping indictment of liberal Enlightenment presuppositions, nor was there a call for Jewish cultural reformation; they shared Nordau's impulse to bring to the oppressed Jews of Eastern Europe the cultural fruits of Enlightenment. One of the earliest German Zionists to settle in Palestine (in 1909), Elias Auerbach, wrote six years before his departure that there was no point in glorifying the "total" Judaism of the East European Zionists, because cultural assimilation was implicit in modernity. Zionism and German culture were not mutually exclusive.[55] Even when a number of years later German cultural Zionists radically questioned these assumptions, the early generation retained its position. As one of its members put it in 1912, "We German Zionists came to Zionism out of different motives from those of the *Ostjuden*. Zionism, as we understand it, is the solution from the moral and economic *Judennot*. We did not arrive at Zionism out of love for Palestine; we did not want to solve the problem of the Jewish nation in order to be able to create a Jewish culture. . . ."[56]

The differences between early and later German Zionism were in part generational. Early German Zionists remembered the Ostjuden whom they had known as children. Max Bodenheimer's father, to the amusement of his children, often invited Polish schnorrers for Sabbath meals and would send them on their way with a gift of money.[57] Franz Oppenheimer, too, associated Ostjuden with a similar childhood experience. He recalled one such "poor devil" appealing to his father for money.[58] In a sense, these youthful encounters were consistent with their later benevolent conceptions of Zionism.

The radicalized second generation, on the other hand, were so assimilated that they lacked even this paternalist contact with Ostjuden. Richard Lichtheim (1885–1963) was totally unaware that masses of Jews lived in the East until he joined the Zionist movement. He knew from sources like the *Berliner Tageblatt* only that the tzarist government was anti-Semitic and had not given Jews equal rights. Beyond that, the Eastern Jewish world remained a mystery.[59] Perhaps this *tabula rasa* made equal East-West Jewish relationships more likely. The experience of Kurt Blumenfeld is an example. Unlike the earlier Zionists, he defined his Zionism in either/or terms. Upon his "conversion" to Zionism, he deliberately switched his allegiance from *Deutschtum* "to the Polish Jews." East European Zionists now became his standard for Jewish attainment, not objects of philanthrophy. Even his choice of bride was partly ideological, for it was conditioned by his rejection of the shallowness of German Jewish middle-class life and his decision "not to marry a German Jewess." His Russian wife Jenny was the first East-European Jewish woman ever to enter his home.[60] Blumenfeld's post-assimilationist Zionism differed from the earlier Zionism in its emphasis on personal commitment. Whereas Friedemann and others had made *Aliyah* (emigration to Palestine) an East European, not a German, act, Blumenfeld argued that precisely because German Jews were so deracinated, *Aliyah* had to become a personal imperative for the German Zionist.[61]

This approach was far from characteristic of the first generation of German Zionists, however. The Zionism of the distinguished sociologist-economist Franz Oppenheimer was more typical. A specialist in land settlement, he made it quite clear at the 1903 Zionist Congress that Palestinian settlement applied to those who had been deprived of contact with Mother Earth and who needed to wipe away the terrible stamp of oppression that "half-Asia" had imprinted on its Jews. Zionism would humanize the physically degenerate masses of the ghetto.[62] The notion that Jews of the ghetto were physically (and spiritually) less than fully human conformed to the overall Zionist idea that Jewish man had to be remade. The emphasis on *Muskeljudentum* was seen as a way of reviving dignity and ensuring survival. German Zionists who had created their own turnverein, were convinced that a similar emphasis would combat the physical degeneration of the Ostjuden, and they correspondingly established a number of turnverein in various parts of Eastern Europe. Pamphlets appeared regularly with titles like *"How Do We Create a Strong Jewish Race in Russia?"*[63] Analyses of physical degeneration in the ghetto stressed that it had not only contributed to Jewish defenselessness but was also responsible for much of the Russian contempt for the Jews—how could one respect such miserable looking creatures?[64] In an address bemoaning the indecencies of "half-Asian" anti-Semitic atrocities, Franz Oppenheimer proudly pointed to the "new Maccabees" of Odessa and Kiev who had responded to the pogroms with brave self-defense. This had provided Jews all over the world with a sense of renewed dignity.[65]

There is no doubt that Oppenheimer was deeply moved by the plight of the Ostjuden. He regarded the creation of a national home as the only way to restore them to a dignified and healthy life. But he always distinguished between Russian and German Jewry. His famous essay of 1910 *Stammesbewusstsein und Volksbewusstsein* only systematized sentiments which he and other early German Zionists had expressed for many years. The relation of the Western Jew to Zionism, Oppenheimer argued, was entirely different from that of the Ostjuden. Ostjuden were characterized by *Volksbewusstsein* (national consciousness), Western Jews by *Stammesbewusstsein* (ethnic or "clan" consciousness). The latter referred to the sense of belonging to a great historical nation, a pride in a common ancestry, an identification with the past, and an acceptance of Jewish identity (which, he pointed out, differentiated Western Zionists from the self-denying assimilationists). But this national consciousness had to be distinguished from that of the Ostjuden, which referred not to past but to present consciousness, culture, and circumstance. For Oppenheimer, the two modes of consciousness were differentiated according to their opposed cultural implications:

> We are collectively [either] Germans by culture [*Kulturdeutsche*] or French by culture and so on . . . because we have the fortune to belong to cultural communities [*Kulturgemeinschaften*] that stand in the forefront of nations. . . . We cannot be Jewish by culture [*Kulturjuden*] because the Jewish culture, as it has been preserved from the Middle Ages in the ghettoes of the East, stands infinitely lower than modern culture which our [Western] nations bear. We can neither regress nor do want to. But it would be impossible for the Eastern Jews to be Russian or Rumanian. . . . They must be Jews by culture . . . for the mediaeval Jewish culture stands exactly as far above East European barbarism as it is beneath the culture of Western Europe.[66]

For Zionists like Oppenheimer as much as for liberal assimilationists, Ostjuden were a measuring rod against which to gauge the *German* Jewish sense of identity. Oppenheimer's formulation was incorporated in official C.V. proclamations regarding the relationship of German Jews to the Ostjuden on the one hand and *Deutschtum* on the other.[67] Liberal Jews and early Zionists could easily coexist, for not until the challenge of the radical second generation of cultural Zionists did Zionism threaten the basic liberal assumptions of German Jewry. Zionists and assimilationists agreed that Jewish culture was ghetto culture.

Oppenheimer based his Zionism explicitly upon the notion that Eastern and Western Jewry were radically distinct. He argued that unlike the Ostjude, the *Westjude* came to Zionism out of purely idealistic and altruistic motivations. For Ostjuden, Zionism was a matter of survival. East European Jews should remember this. They could not afford to abuse their Western colleagues, whose intelligence and capital they needed. Palestine was basically a haven for the oppressed Eastern Jews, while Western Zionists were good patriots of their home countries. They had the national consciousness of the nation into which they were born. Oppenheimer's article aroused a storm of protest from the radical minority.[68] Yet he echoed the sentiments of the great majority of German Zionists.

Most Zionists, like Oppenheimer, were sensitive to East European Jewish needs, a sensitivity often lacking in liberal Jewish consciousness. They constantly deplored German Jewish dissociation from the Ostjuden living within the Reich. Russian Jewry, a typical statement asserted, did not shame German Jewry—"on the contrary, they honor us"—for they were a proud and productive people.[69] Zionists consistently challenged the argument that Ostjuden were the source of anti-Semitism in Germany, and, for not entirely disinterested political reasons, they were in the forefront of the struggle to protect the voting rights of Ostjuden in community elections. East European Zionist mediators like Fabius Schach regularly published articles describing the difficulties of Eastern Jews in Germany, criticized disdainful German Jewish attitudes towards them, and suggested various ways of overcoming such barriers.[70]

For all that, early German Zionism separated the ideological from the personal. It presupposed a new mode of identification but not a shift in cultural identity or personal commitment. "The return to Jewishness" meant a new self-acceptance, not a change in content, a position that Adolph Friedemann formulated quite succinctly: "Zionism reconciles us with ourselves."[71] The notion of Zionism as personal and cultural Jewish totality emerged only with the second generation of German Zionists. Responding to new circumstances in new ways, these post-assimilationist Jews were deeply influenced by the spiritual Zionism of Achad Ha'am, the pervading Volkish atmosphere within German society, and Martin Buber's appeal to assimilated Jews to seek roots in *Judentum* rather than *Deutschtum*.

The radicals deeply offended their Zionist elders with the belief that Germanness and Jewishness were incompatible and that a Zionist commitment involved an uprooting (*Entwurzelung*) from Diaspora life. They were a minority that took seriously the previously abstract slogan of national renaissance. Although their ideas were those of a minority within a minority, they had an impact far beyond their numbers, and we should examine their formulations with some care, for they provided alternative directions in the search for German Jewish identity. In this process the counter-myth of the Ostjude played a cardinal and defining role. Their transvaluated perception of the East European Jew was designed to give the German Jew a new and quite different picture of himself.

5 IDENTITY AND CULTURE
The Ostjude as Counter-Myth

THE shift in German Zionism from a philanthropic approach to one of personal commitment challenged older, more conservative attitudes towards the Ostjuden significantly. Tension between the political and cultural modes had characterized the movement from its beginnings: early German Zionists had minimized, when they did not totally reject, the cultural implications of their Zionism. But German Zionism produced its own dialectic. With its radicalization by a number of post-assimilationist intellectuals, it seemed that Achad Ha'am had gained the last word over Max Nordau. Zionism was increasingly construed as an internal and spiritual matter, a cry for personal and cultural revolution. German Jews were now admonished to commit themselves to "Jewishness" and personal settlement in Palestine.

This was a transformation that early German Zionists found virtually incomprehensible. As Adolf Friedemann commented, Zionism had always propagated feelings of Jewish national solidarity, but the new notion of *Jüdischkeit* (Jewishness) was impossibly vague. What was its content? Where were its concrete manifestations? No one could seriously demand of German Jews that they cultivate East European Jewish forms of life and culture. After all, Zionism opposed assimilation only insofar as it referred to a self-abnegating denial of Jewish origins. It had never advocated disaffection from Western culture. Certainly for German Jews this was unthinkable.

100

They were totally integrated into German culture—"Goethe, Schiller, and Kant were our educators"—and this was both a positive and an irreversible process. The radicals, argued Friedemann, were deceiving themselves. Despite all their rhetoric, they themselves had no notion of Hebrew and virtually no knowledge of Jewish culture. Like their elders, they were fundamentally *kulturdeutsch*.[1] The leader of the radicals, Kurt Blumenfeld, could hardly dispute these assertions. Yet he argued that what distinguished the new from the old approach was the recognition that cultural deracination was a morally and culturally blameworthy condition.[2] Radical Zionists regarded it as a deficiency to be overcome; Jewishness must be a total commitment. Calls for renaissance were transposed from the external and the political to the existential and cultural plane, a focus that placed a strikingly different light on the Ostjude.

What were the sources of this new German Zionist perspective? Clearly the example of Achad Ha'am's cultural Zionism and the practical Zionism exemplified by Chaim Weizmann were important and mirrored a more general shift within the World Zionist movement, but more than this was involved. The radical view of Jewish renaissance was part of a wider neoromantic German mood. It consciously entailed a romantic vision of existence and an explicit break with positivist approaches to social reality. Intellectuals associated with this trend gave renewed importance to elements which a rationalist bias had repressed.[3] The new emphasis on myth and a revised understanding of the role of the irrational nurtured a new appreciation of previously castigated elements of Jewish life; perhaps the most stark example of this change was Martin Buber's radical transvaluation of the nineteenth-century German Jewish image of the Hasid. But the way was also opened for a more receptive attitude to Eastern Jewish culture as such. Whatever their other differences, Franzos and Nordau had regarded the ghetto in terms of a common positivist rationalism. Many of the younger Zionists were to attack precisely those assumptions.

There is no doubt that much of the thinking about Jewish national regeneration was influenced by German Volkish ideas. Volkish ideology was not a purely right-wing affair. The stress on "community" and "organicism" was shared by many on the Left who were disenchanted with liberalism and the impersonal, fragmented experience of living in the *Kaiserreich*.[4] The common denominator of the Volkish approach was its disaffection from bourgeois conventions and capitalist impersonality. All sought ways of creating "rooted" communities capable of engendering profound personal ties which they felt were conspicuously absent in an increasingly atomized modern Germany. Emphasis shifted from the formal institution of the state to the primal, enduring *Volksgeist* and its capacity for regeneration.

Early German Zionists had felt at home, were part of the Wilhelmine cultural consensus. The post-assimilationists, however, claimed that genuine incorporation into German society was neither possible nor desirable. On the basis of their Volkish assumptions they had to find their own people, establish their own national framework.[5] Volkish ideology without a Volk was, of course, an impossible contradiction. Zionists discovered their people in the Eastern ghettoes. It was there that the real Volk existed, not as a pale imitation, an imitative adjunct of a foreign culture, but as a living, pulsating organism with its own forms. "Genuine" Jews were to be found in the East, and for these Zionists, the Eastern Jews became the surrogate for the German nation, an alternative framework of identification. In a sense, Buber's Hasid—vibrant and rooted in human community and religious values—was the Jewish Volkish answer to the ideal figure of the German Volkish movement, the peasant.

The discovery of a primal national tie between Eastern and Western Jew required new definitions of the bonds between them and negations of older conceptions. "Return" meant viewing the ghetto in a new light. *Vom Judentum* (1913), a collection of articles by German and Czech Jewish "radical" intellectuals, illustrates the Volkish and neoromantic nature of this outlook. As Gustav Landauer put it, the Western Jew was a *Halbheit*, he would have to bow in humility before the real Jew, the Eastern Jew. At least one aspect of Jewish national return, argued Robert Weltsch, was an understanding of the basic ingredients of East European Jewish culture. Unlike Jewish life in the West it was whole and organic, not torn and fragmented. It was this fact that prompted Max Brod to invert Jewish liberal disdain and to accord to East European modern Jewish literature an authenticity that seemed impossible for German Jews to achieve. Moses Calvary inveighed against modern rationality and argued that the new Judaism would have to stress the spirit of fantasy and playfulness, vital unconscious attributes of the Volk which liberalism had repressed. This Volk spirit was embodied in the Yiddish folk song—the only folk song that Jews had. Its increasing popularity was a sign that the new spirit was gaining ground.[6] These analyses, of course, illuminated ghetto culture less than they revealed a particular Western Jewish mood of dissent. As with other

Volkish movements, there was much concern with the aesthetic and with the primal, even unconscious, creative powers, and these young Jews projected those elemental qualities onto the East European Jewish world. Yet the demand for (translated) Hebrew and Yiddish literature, newly conceived as the embodiment of the real Jewish *Volksgeist,* was less a matter of true appreciation than of dissatisfaction with bourgeois Jewish life. Western Jewish art and literature were regarded as artificial mirrors of a deracinated and contradictory existence.[7]

The call for radical Jewish renaissance threatened Western Jewish assumptions in another, more profound way. As even the moderate *Ost und West* argued in its opening statement, Jews everywhere, despite apparent differences, "shared the same inherited characteristics."[8] This was a remarkably "illiberal" conviction. If Jews were linked by inherited qualities, genetics doomed the politics of cultural assimilation. In their search to establish the deeper nature of Western Jewish ties to the Jewish Volk, the new radicals had to go beyond older, more conventional definitions. The nineteenth-century liberal slogan of "common faith" was clearly insufficient, for it purposely excluded precisely what they wanted to emphasize: the notion of an interdependent and vital national organism. The antiseptic use that early German Zionists like Franz Oppenheimer had given to the idea of *Abstammung* was equally unacceptable. *Abstammung,* after all, referred only to the fact of common origin and a shared past. It said nothing of a common present and thus effectively devitalized contemporary cultural and existential commitments. But these were the very bases of the radical position. The enunciation of Volkish rebirth required new categories capable of challenging liberal conceptions of the East-West Jewish relationship. They were found in two apparently contradictory notions, "blood" and "will."

In his famous 1909 lectures to the Prague Bar Kochba organization, Martin Buber developed the idea of "the community of blood" (*"die Gemeinschaft des Blutes"*).[9] What, he asked, were the real bases of Jewishness? Previous answers such as religion or nation were merely formal. The deeper answer was to be found in the process by which the Jew "senses in this immortality of the generations a community of blood, which he feels to be the antecedents of his I, its perseverance in the infinite past. . . . the deepest layers of our being are determined by blood; . . . our innermost thinking and our will are colored by it."[10] This blood relationship led to critical cultural consequences that drastically challenged the assumptions of liberal assimilationism. The Jew "senses that he belongs no longer to the community of those whose constant elements of experience he shares, but to the deeper-reaching community of those whose substance he shares."[11] The Western Jew was rent apart by the contradiction between "blood" and "experience," and it was this dichotomy that stood at the heart of modern Jewish loneliness. Yet there was always hope: "That his substance can, nevertheless, become a reality for the Jew is due to the fact that his origin means more than a mere connection with things past; it has planted something within us that does not leave us any hour of our life, that determines every tone and every hue in our life, all that we do and all that befalls us: blood, the deepest, most potent stratum of our being."[12]

The problem was to establish the ground and provide the means for a newly constituted "total" sense of Jewishness. Buber's solution to assimilation and the East-West Jewish disjunction, the "community of blood," was of course a spiritual metaphor couched in physical language. Its intent was not racist. Still, a more trivial notion of the Jews as a community of blood, a sense of the overarching, intangible, and yet physical basis of Jewishness, was shared by many circles, although each attached a different significance to it. For racial anti-Semites, of course, it was precisely this that rendered assimilation impossible and that linked the "modern" to the ghetto Jew. Anti-Semites repeatedly argued that despite the discarding of externals like the caftan and side-locks, the posture and mannerisms of German Jews retained their native imprint. They were radically different from "real" Germans.[13] To liberal Jews, Zionist arguments were offensive precisely because they seemed to parallel such anti-Semitic assertions.

Yet even the most assimilationist of Jews found it difficult to discard this physical dimension entirely. Some who were uncomfortable with their Jewishness regarded Judaism partly as a psychological trait and at times even as a physiological defect. Fritz Mauthner, for example, experienced it as a kind of "duct in the brain," a disease he was afraid to contract.[14] Yet one need not resort to the extremes for illustration. Ludwig Geiger, who stood at the very center of the liberal German Jewish experience, neither self-hating nor Volkish in his Jewish predispositions, was aware of this physical aspect. Geiger admitted that Jews were easily identifiable by the way they moved, by the shape of their noses, and by other bodily cues, but he drew no cultural conclusions from this. If there was a physical component, it was an unfortunate fact, not a political desideratum. Almost nothing, he wrote, connected the English

Jewish lord with the world of the Russian schnorrer.[15] Others agreed
that there were indeed physical landmarks of Jewishness but asserted that they were hangovers from the ghetto and would disappear
with the successful completion of cultural assimilation.[16] Yet for all
that, liberal Jews were often shocked by what appeared to be an
"instinctive" recognition of kinship. When Richard Beer-Hoffman
was in Berlin for rehearsals of one of his plays, he came up the stairs
of the subway on a cold, windy night, his face wrapped in a woollen
scarf so that only his eyes were visible. An Ostjude in caftan stopped
him and said, "My good sir is one of us. . . . He will tell me how I can
get to the Nollendorfplatz?"[17] Was there indeed such a thing as
"Jewish eyes"?

Many of those identified with a radical Jewish renaissance thought
so. For the socialist Gustav Landauer (1870–1919)—who envisaged
the renaissance in terms of a non-Zionist Diaspora awakening of the
Jewish Volk—Jewishness was palpably physical. All Jews were
infused with deep "racial" qualities; Landauer was convinced that
he could recognize other Jews merely by looking at them.[18] This
affinity also expressed itself in mental terms. In his review of
Buber's *The Legend of the Baal-Shem*, Landauer argued that
Judaism was not a sociological product or historical accident but an
inherent attribute (*unverlierbare innere Eigenschaft*) that united
apparently separate individuals in a deeper unity. An organic Jewish
Seelensituation overcame external differences, for it both predated
and transcended simple cultural categories.[19] There is no doubt that
Landauer's conceptions were deeply influenced by his meeting with
East European immigrants in 1906: "When I was a student, I
underwent the profound experience that within the lack of roots
which is usually called radicalism . . . I suddenly found a new
peoplehood . . . as I took refuge from the heartless world of the
bourgeoisie in the workers' movement, adopting them as my own
Volk. I never thought that in my mature years I should still find
something like a second home in an ancient people."[20]

The question of the existence of an inherent Jewish commonality
became central in the debate between the cultural and the philanthropic Zionists. Oppenheimer's controversial essay *Stammesbewusstsein und Volksbewusstsein* made the issue concrete.[21]
Dissenting and defending opinions were published in the journals,
and various local Zionist branches held special meetings to discuss
the problem.[22] One polemicist, Richard Huldschiner, applied the
well-known German distinction between culture and civilization to
the problem of East-West Jewish relations. Oppenheimer, he ar-

gued, had employed the superficial notion of *Kultur*. Culture was not learned, it was inborn, and it was only on the basis of his incorrect understanding of culture that Oppenheimer could make the East-West Jewish distinction. Jews had acquired only the externalities of *Deutschtum*, its "civilization"—the truly determinative culture, however, remained ineradicably Jewish. Because of this, German Jews were ultimately more bound to the Ostjuden than they were to the Germans.[23] An anonymous Easterner put it even more bluntly: There was a basic Jewish *Grundcharakter*, a psychological state of being that required its own milieu for its free and undistorted expression. The Jewish *Grundcharakter* belonged to both Eastern and Western Jew, it could not be washed away.[24] The need to internalize, to physiopsychologize Jewishness was of course related to the perception that Jews had shed their "objective" cultural characteristics: new criteria of identification were required. Anti-Semites found it in race. Those committed to a Jewish renaissance (and not necessarily a Zionist one) also sought interior manifestations of that identity. The notion of the blood-community was central to Franz Rosenzweig's evocation of Jewish existence in *The Star of Redemption* (1921).[25] In another, less formal context Rosenzweig explicitly enunciated what many Jews left publicly unspoken. Jewishness, he wrote, is "no entity, no subject among other subjects, no one sphere of life among other spheres of life; it is not what the century of emancipation with its cultural mania wanted to reduce it to. It is something inside the individual that makes him a Jew, something infinitesimally small yet immeasurably large, his most impenetrable secret, yet evident in every gesture and every word— especially in the most spontaneous of them."[26]

The Oppenheimer debate brought out yet another vital ingredient that proponents of an East-West Jewish national meeting regarded as critical: the notion of national will. Few paused to examine the contradiction in opposing categories like blood and will. For those who emphasized will, nationalism was surely a highly volitional, not determinist, matter. It sprang from Renan's idea that nationalism was a kind of daily plebiscite—those who wanted to become a nation did so on the basis of consensus. This was the conception that animated Jacob Klatzkin's reply to Oppenheimer. As East European editor of *Die Welt*, he argued that the Zionist was characterized not by his contemporary situation but rather by his wishes for the future. Volition was the foundation of the Jewish national idea. Only on that basis could assimilated German citizens of the "Mosaic" persuasion be transformed into nationally conscious Jews. Oppenheimer's "freezing" of East-West Jewish distinctions as the cultural norm was completely alien to the Zionist idea.[27]

It was Buber who combined the determinist (blood) with the subjectivist (will) element and most forcefully pressed for "total" Jewish transformation. The Volk could become a Volk only when commitment was total, when the person was involved with his whole being. The "new" Jew was confronted with a decision: he could never overcome his internal schism "so long as the insight that our blood is the creative force in our life has not become a living, integral part of us." This doctrine amalgamating blood with will applied not to past history but to the present moment. The test of its success would be measured in the meeting with the East European masses: an entirely new, existential openness was required.

> Those people out there—the miserable, stooped people dragging their feet, peddling their wares from village to village, not knowing where tomorrow's livelihood will come from nor why they should go on living, and those dull nearly stupefied masses, being loaded aboard ship, not knowing where to or why—we shall perceive them, all of them, not merely as our brothers and sisters; rather, made secure within himself, every one of us will feel: these people are part of myself. It is not together with them that I am suffering; *I* am suffering these tribulations. My soul is not by the side of my people; my people *is* my soul.[28]

In his reply to Oppenheimer, Buber asserted that assimilation was not merely a national question. It had deeper moral and human implications: assimilation signified the acceptance of instrumentality as the ruling force in one's life. Zionism, on the other hand, was antithetical to this, for the *decision* to live life autonomously, according to one's own ideals, was already a transcendence of the purely instrumental.[29]

To the young Zionist radicals, these ideals seemed to be embodied in the life of the Eastern Jews. The radicals turned increasingly to translations of ghetto literature, for it was only there that Jewish culture, unsullied by the influence of a foreign society, could be found. The very notion of the ghetto as fount of literary inspiration and source of rejuvenating power radically subverted the conventional wisdom. For liberal Jews and conservative Zionists alike, the ghetto, by definition, was devoid of creative power, cultureless.[30]

Yet Zionist romanticizing of ghetto literature must be seen in perspective. Not all elements of ghetto culture were idealized;

perceptions were channeled according to Zionist ideological predisposition. While the maintenance of traditional ways was praised, it was the *modern* East European Jew—Achad Ha'am, Bialik, Berdichevsky—who was the ideal figure for the renaissance. In such figures modernity and Judaism seemed to blend: they, more than the traditional ghetto Jew, were thought of as the foils to the pale, imitative assimilated Jew of the West.

We are left, therefore, with an old ambivalence in new disguise. German cultural Zionists did want a meeting with *Ostjudentum*, but the meeting would not be a Western Jewish return to the ghetto; it would involve mutual transformation in the future which was Palestine. The cultural revolution would take place in the Zionist future. Perhaps the traditional Jewish spirit of Eastern Jewry would be maintained, but certainly not its content. German cultural Zionists viewed Ostjuden as the embodiment of Jewish authenticity lost to the world of Western Jews, but they also demanded a significant modernization of that authenticity. As Hans Kohn in his introduction to *Vom Judentum* put it, "We want to revolutionize Jewry, not just Western Jewry, but *above all* Eastern Jewry."[31] Men like Bialik and Berdichevsky were admired because they had overcome their ghetto horizons, and unlike the fragmented Western Jew, had healed the dichotomy between humanness and Jewishness. The very notion of the Zionist cultural renaissance assumed flaws in both the modern Western and traditional Eastern European versions of Judaism. This was the limit of the Zionist counter-myth of the Ostjude, for Zionism was a negation, in principle, of Galut, exile. Its entire thrust was the transformation of the Jewish people in its own homeland, the attempt to recover the moral and physical health which, Zionist analysts asserted, had been conspicuously absent in the historical condition of Galut.

Most radical Zionists clung to a conception of the new Jew which they juxtaposed to the defects of the Galut Jew. Yehezkel Kaufmann has demonstrated that Zionism often portrayed the Diaspora Jew in somewhat anti-Semitic terms.[32] Certainly many radical German Zionists regarded the Galut Jew—both the traditional ghetto and modern bourgeois variety,—in a way quite consistent with the German Volkish conception of the shifty, rootless Jew: Jews were materialistic, uncreative, aridly intellectual, alienated from nature and productive labor. The Galut, with its radical dependence of Jew upon non-Jew, was regarded as the source of Jewish "deformity." Abnormal conditions had created misshapen, abnormal people. The Jew, both East and West, required fundamental reshaping, normal-

izing. At times the Zionist attack on Jewish life in the Diaspora
approached almost violent dimensions. The line between constructive self-criticism and Jewish self-hatred was often thin and occasionally invisible.

Theodor Lessing (1872–1933) personified this tension. The famous
diagnostician of the structure of Jewish self-hatred (*Der jüdische
Selbsthass*, 1930) was himself a prime example of the phenomenon
he so acutely analyzed. By the age of fifteen, he reports in his
autobiography, he had fully internalized the negative conception of
the Jew and was writing grotesque, self-destructive, anti-Semitic
verse.[33] His series of 1909 articles "Impressions from Galicia" was
filled with gross stereotypical descriptions of the Ostjuden and their
way of life.[34] The Jews were portrayed as dirty, decadent, dishonest;
prostitution was rife, and fathers offered their daughters for sale.
The articles caused an uproar and prompted numerous protests.[35]
The Galician publicist Binjamin Segel wrote an impassioned, book-
length rebuttal.[36] Lessing did not spare emancipated Jewry either.
His caricature of modern Jewish intellectuality as embodied in the
critic Samuel Lublinski[37] was almost identical to the anti-Semitic
stereotype and occasioned a reprimand from Thomas Mann,[38]
amongst others.

For all that, we cannot dismiss Lessing's case as simple self-hatred.
This would be an accurate description of his early youth and his
conversion to Protestantism in 1893, but he renounced the Protestant
connection and there is evidence that he had Zionist sympathies as
early as 1901.[39] In that year he wrote a searching review of Ludwig
Jakobowski's *Werther der Jude* in which the outlines of his analysis
and criticism of Jewish self-hatred are already apparent. He argued
that Jakobowski's work mirrored the German Jewish tragedy. German Jews wanted passionately to be a part of *Deutschtum*, but in the
process of being rejected, they had accepted the low German
evaluation of themselves. This had made them nothing better than
slaves. Anti-Semitism, he wrote, had profound and depressing psychological consequences for the Jews, but there was a way out:
"pride, consciousness of the dignity and greatness of our Judaism
and its history."[40]

These early remarks give some credence to Lessing's assertion that
his critics were wrong, that he was not attacking Jewry. He was,
rather, diagnosing the Jewish situation and was prompted by a sense
of identification and concern more than by disdain. It was necessary
to dwell on Jewish deficiencies precisely because of that concern. If,
for instance, East European Jews often seemed odious to him, his

sense of unbreakable ties to them was an even stronger feeling.[41] While Lessing's tone, as his critics charged,[42] often made it difficult to detect that concern, he consistently maintained that radical self-criticism was the only effective way to solve the Jewish dilemma. He viewed the Jewish fear of publicly admitting their own shortcomings as a key symptom of precisely the disease he sought to cure, and castigated this self-defensiveness and prickly sensitivity as a form of "social neurasthenia, a pathology of the national soul."[43] Only self-examination could lead to enlightened reform. This, Lessing insisted, pointed to Jewish commitment and identification, not to its opposite.

German Zionism had a real function for those Jews who were plagued with self-doubt and yet perceived that there was little hope for real integration within the German Volk. Lessing's return to Jewishness through Zionism manifested a change in the object of national commitment, from *Deutschtum* to *Judentum*, but no alteration in his basic ideas.[44] His Volkish premises remained intact. Zionism's search for the "new man," after all, was similar in spirit to the general fin-de-siècle expressionist search for virile activism and the reassertion of the instinctual. In his writings Lessing looked toward the metamorphosis of the Galut Jew into the "new Jew" of Palestine, forged in the spirit of "Old Testament pagan *Natur-mythos*." For Lessing, at least, the distinction between Jewish self-rejection and Zionist commitment was possible only because Zionism held out the hope for a radically new Jew of the future.[45]

Lessing was extreme in his views, but even those Zionists who genuinely admired the "authenticity" of the ghetto based their hopes for partnership with the Ostjuden upon the assumption of mutual transformation. Major Zionist ideologists argued that a new and vital synthesis would emerge as a result of the national meeting of East and West. Chaim Weizmann described this as a process of "bringing the ghetto to Europe and Europe to the ghetto."[46] Both Achad Ha'am[47] and Martin Buber[48] envisaged the meeting as one which would heal the tragic split between *Judentum* (as represented by the East) and *Menschentum* (as represented by the West). The meeting would finally bring about a fruitful synthesis, the real Jewish renaissance.[49]

Yet the very juxtaposition of Western humanity and Eastern Jewishness pointed to the limits of the Ostjude as a Zionist counter-myth. If the assimilated Jew of the West was lacking in Jewish substance, his Eastern counterpart was deficient in terms of more universal, modern requirements. In the last analysis, even for the radicalized pre–World War I German Zionists, though they recognized that the real Volk was in the East and that it was there that Jewish authenticity and potential creative power lay, the specifically Jewish culture of the ghetto could not become the model for national rebirth. In Buberian terms, the Ostjuden provided the great force but not the forms for the renaissance. The Volkish Zionists were sensitized to the Ostjuden in a way that the first generation of German Zionists were not. Yet they always viewed Eastern Jewry through Zionist spectacles. Like other ideologies, Zionism entailed a system of selective perception. Because it negated Galut life and advocated the creation of the "new Jew," it could not, by definition, adopt or endorse an empirical acceptance of Eastern Jewish life as it was.

One Zionist, Ernst Müller, put the matter quite succinctly: It would be fatal if Palestine were to be exclusively a land of Eastern Jews. National renaissance was not "Eastern Jewish" but an all-Jewish matter, an ideal that cut far deeper than the temporary division between East and West. The "new" Jewish culture would not be based on the *Golus* culture of the Eastern ghetto. There was a better, more universal model upon which Zionists like Müller could draw, and this was the primal Judaism "that still lives in our blood. Not the Talmud, but the Bible, not the *Jargon*, but the Hebrew." The Biblical past would be the standard, the mold in which the new Jew would be cast.[50] Some Zionists even denied the conventional proposition that East European Jews were indeed full *Kulturjuden*, for "total" Judaism did not yet exist. To create it was the task for the Zionist future; the distinction between the "whole" Ostjude and the "fragmented" Western Jew was mythical. Galut was, by definition, a state of incompleteness. Hasidic legends, ghetto writers who wrote in the *Jargon*—they too reflected the alienated experience which was Galut. Real Jewish culture was possible only in an independent Jewish society.[51]

At times the oppression, not the Jewishness, of East European Jewry became a metaphor for all of Diaspora Jewry. The 1912 New Year editorial of the *Jüdische Rundschau* argued that the "whole *Golus* is the ghetto." Jews everywhere were like ghetto Jews, pale, bent, and fearful. Ancient Palestinian soil would transform them all. They would become farmers and soldiers. "The ghetto Jew will become a muscle man . . . a new spirit in a new body." The Eastern Jew was still regarded as the real Jew, his culture still admired as authentically Jewish, but the meeting of Eastern and Western Jew would transcend all Diasporic forms. The new Jew would be forged in Palestine.[52]

There were, to be sure, a number of young Zionists who even in the prewar period found this attitude too disdainful, too unaccepting of the everyday reality of East European Jewish life. They were looking for a more complete integration into that way of life which they regarded as a model of a living Judaism. Some, like Max Meyer, attempted this while remaining within the Zionist movement. Along with many German Zionists, Meyer discovered his sense of Jewish identity as a result of his meeting with Ostjuden in Germany, but unlike the others, he identified with them completely. In his case, the encounter produced an experience that was akin to conversion. He married an East European woman, went to Lithuania in 1912, mastered Hebrew, and to the shame and horror of his family, made Yiddish his home language.[53] Here was an instance of conscious reverse assimilation, an attempt to recover modes and mannerisms that German Jewry had resisted for over a century. Meyer's German was filled with dreaded reminders of Mauscheln, peppered with obviously Yiddish forms of pronunciation and syntax. Fellow Zionists, as well as his family, began to feel distinctly uncomfortable in his presence.

Of course, Meyer did not entirely abandon his background; to do so would have involved even more radical steps in conscious cultural demodernization and would not have been consistent with any view of Zionism. There were, however, one or two radically unrepresentative and eccentric individual attempts at self-ghettoization that involved changes in language, religious belief, values, dress, aesthetics, and manners. Ahron Marcus (1843–1916) and Jiri Langer (1894–1943)—German and Czech respectively—undertook remarkably similar journeys.[54] Both left their familiar bourgeois environment, travelled to the ghetto, and immersed themselves in the Hasidic world. Both, in the full anthropological sense of the word, went "native" and upon their return to "society" experienced a kind of culture shock in reverse. The shock was shared by their liberal Jewish counterparts. The sight of these Western Jews dressed in archetypal ghetto garb and behaving exactly like the uncultured Ostjuden was a source of shame and bewilderment. Jiri Langer's return to Prague in 1913 is described by his brother thus:

> Father told me with a note of horror in his voice that Jiri had returned. I understood what had filled him with dread as soon as I saw my brother. He stood behind me in a frayed, black overcoat,

clipped like a caftan, reaching from his chin to the ground. On his head he wore a broad round hat of black velvet, thrust back towards his neck. He stood there in a stooping posture; his whole face and chin were covered with a red beard, and side whiskers in front of his ears hung in ringlets down to his shoulders. All that remained to be seen of his face was some white, unhealthy skin and eyes which at moments appeared tired and at others feverish. My brother had not come back from Belz, to home and civilization; he had brought Belz with him.[55]

That was true in a deeper sense as well. Both Marcus and Langer attempted to mediate and elevate the ghetto world to an Enlightened readership. Thus Marcus tried to demonstrate the profundity of Hasidic life and thought and its affinity with the most advanced theories of modern philosophy. He fitted Hasidism into the fashionable fin-de-siècle contention that the irrational was autonomous and could not be reduced to positivist rationalism.[56] His *Hartmanns inductive Philosophie im Chassidismus* (1888) asserted that Eduard von Hartmann's notion of the unconscious as expressed in his *Philosophie des Unbewussten* (1868–69) had been anticipated by Hasidic ideas of the prerational.[57] Langer, too, was fascinated by the irrational and the unconscious. His *Die Erotik der Kabbala* (1923) was a Freudian analysis of Jewish mysticism, an attempt to explain the derivation of Jewish ritual and cult in sexual terms. His *Nine Gates to the Chassidic Mysteries* (1937), published originally in Czech, was an exotic and imaginative exposition that drew upon the years he had spent as a member of that sect.

But Marcus and Langer were ostentatious exceptions to the rule. For Zionists, men like Max Meyer were already at the edge, the ultimate permissible limit of identification with the ghetto. That limit was based upon consistent Zionist rejection of ghetto and Galut. It was precisely this rejection, the dismissal of ghetto life, that prompted a small minority of Zionists to disaffect from Zionism *in the name of East European Jewry*. Zionism had spawned its own dialectic. Influenced by the Zionist opposition to assimilation and its romantic affirmation of a living and indigenous national Jewish culture, these few intellectuals came to the conclusion that only in the Eastern ghettoes did a real, vibrant, and empirical Jewish culture exist. Zionism, they believed, was a potent enemy of the very cause it pretended to champion.

A small movement, even smaller than the minority from which it broke, its ideas nevertheless require examination, for they offered yet another option for East-West Jewish relations. Even if those making up this movement remained isolated from the mainstream, they were vocal and they influenced the Jewish discourse of the time. Their outlook illustrated some of the possibilities that a pre-World War I post-Zionist national sensibility had to offer. Their thinking was extreme, and according to their contemporary critics, unrealistic, for they sought to reconcile modernity with the ghetto and to affirm what both assimilationist and Zionist had ultimately denied—that the only authentic Judaism was the Judaism of Eastern Europe. With these thinkers, the inversion of the stereotype, the Ostjude as counter-myth, reached its zenith.

The person most closely associated with this viewpoint was Nathan Birnbaum (1864–1937). Franz Rosenzweig characterized Birnbaum as a "living exponent of Jewish intellectual history."[58] His career did indeed illustrate the range and fluidity of positions that the search for an acceptable modern Jewish self-definition entailed once assimilation had been rejected. In all Birnbaum's transformations, however, the Ostjuden remained central. Birnbaum was brought up in Vienna in a moderately Orthodox atmosphere and given a German cultural education.[59] He became a prolific writer and Jewish culture critic. He was never an easy man to deal with, but through the strength of his commitment and convictions he nevertheless retained the respect even of his political opponents.[60] One of the first Western Zionists (he coined the term *Zionism*), after a break with Herzl and political Zionism he gave increasing attention to the world of the Ostjuden, its language, culture, and history. He mastered Yiddish and proceeded to formulate his own version of Golus nationalism, with the retention of East European Jewish culture as its central aim, and he explicitly opposed Zionism's attempt to "transcend" it. Having this goal in mind, he organized the first Yiddish language conference in Czernowitz in 1908. Over the years, his identification with Eastern Jewish culture drew him increasingly toward the Orthodox religious position.

Birnbaum was a prime mediator, interpreter, and champion of *Ostjudentum* to West European Jewish intellectuals. He lacked Buber's appeal, for Buber was concerned less with portraying a present reality than with describing the wisdom of a religious sect of the past, a past wrapped in myth and legend and suitably packaged for a neoromantic German audience. As Birnbaum phrased it in his review of *The Tales of Rabbi Nachmann*,[61] Buber had "over-told" his tales, their beauty was too polished. Birnbaum, on the other hand, was concerned with the here-and-now, with an understanding and appreciation of contemporary East European Jewry. In his work, the Enlightenment myth of the Ostjude was radically challenged: Yiddish and ghetto life became the standards for a new, inverted Jewish culture criticism.

Nineteenth-century German Jews had consistently regarded Yiddish as a tasteless, mongrel jargon, a bastardized vulgarization of German, the embodiment of a narrow, obscurantist ghetto spirit. Birnbaum turned this prejudice on its head. Yiddish was not the reflection of a pinched, mean existence but the mirror of a proud, creative tradition. Indeed, "it was nothing but the classical product of the hardest struggle for individuality, the wonderful, living resistance of the Jewish People against their Germanization."[62] This approach became especially ironic during World War I. Many German Jews did an about-face when the German army occupied Poland and was confronted with millions of Yiddish-speaking Jews: suddenly that language was extolled as integrally related to German and proof of Eastern Jewish loyalty to *Deutschtum*. Birnbaum, however, could accept neither German Jewish contempt for the *Jargon* nor its sudden espousal of that language as a central bastion of Germanism. Yiddish was an autonomous, valuable linguistic vehicle for the expression of unique Jewish cultural values.

Birnbaum opposed all manifestations of assimilation, particularly the assimilating intelligentsia. For him, the designation Ostjude was valid not as a geographical description but as a cultural measure of Jewish integrity. Thus he no longer looked upon the modernizing East European Jewish intellectuals as Ostjuden: spiritually sundered from their roots, they were merely fragments of *Westjudentum* in the midst of *Ostjudentum*.[63] Intellectuals who had lost touch with their national roots were like a sea without water, they were walking self-contradictions.[64] The most vital task was the formation of a new kind of committed, rooted Jewish intellectual, for the real challenge of the Jewish culture critic was to defend autochthonous East European Jewish life from the many threatening incursions of assimilation. All Western Jews confused culture with civilization. They mistakenly believed that over the years they had brought culture to the Ostjuden. But paradoxically a creative, self-generated culture was precisely what Western Jews lacked. Unlike the Ostjuden, they had lost inner depth, and the layers of accumulated traditional experience had been erased.[65] Zionists did not differ from the liberal Jews in this respect. In fact, Birnbaum's criticism applied especially to the so-called cultural Zionists, who were always talking about the future "creation of a Jewish culture," mistakenly assuming that there was no functioning, creative Jewish culture of the present.

Despite the external oppression and poverty of the ghetto, this was not so. What the Ostjuden lacked was civilization, not culture.[66]

By 1909 Birnbaum had totally inverted the liberal order of priorities, calling for the emancipation of Eastern Jewry from Western Jewry.[67] He regarded the objection that this would shatter the national unity of the Jewish people as cant, for such unity was a chimera, in any case. In the East there was a real national life, in the West none—how could one shatter that which did not exist? Perhaps the decisive emancipation of Eastern Jewry from the dominion of Western Jews would finally bring about a relationship of genuine equality. His call for separation was not based upon hatred for the West but rather was spurred by the conviction that there was an imminent danger of Jewish cultural extinction. Only separation would insulate *Ostjudentum* from the pressing danger of decomposition and growing dissension.

By World War I Birnbaum had come full circle, from an early rebellious secular political Zionism to an Orthodox religious position. Unlike most Western Orthodox Jews, however, he predicated his Orthodoxy upon the affirmation of the peculiarly East European *Golus.*[68] Only there could Jews remain free of the dangers of secular paganism and remain true to their original holy, monotheistic mission. He agreed with the liberal Jewish proposition that *Kulturjuden* were to be found exclusively in the ghettoes of Eastern Europe, but he saw this as a virtue, not a defect to be rapidly overcome. And he took issue with the Zionists who sought to create a mythical culture of the future on the basis of destroying a vibrant national life of the present.

It would be incorrect to dismiss Birnbaum as an utterly isolated, eccentric case. Certainly his position never became representative, but still, his polemical pen constantly forced Zionists to refine, defend, or change their positions. Even his opponents acknowledged that it was he who "discovered" the Ostjuden for Western Jewry[69] and who sensitized large numbers of people to a new understanding of their significance in Jewish life. Birnbaum was a central influence on Fritz Mordecai Kaufmann and the small circle of followers he attracted in Germany just before World War I.

Like Birnbaum, Kaufmann was a disenchanted Zionist who adopted the cause of *Ostjudentum* whole-heartedly. There was a remarkable similarity of outlook between these two men who were separated by twenty-four years in age. They diverged only in Kaufmann's increasingly socialist outlook and Birnbaum's growing Orthodoxy.

Kaufmann's background hardly explains his later attitudes. He was born in Eschweiler in 1888 to an established, highly acculturated German Jewish family, and at least until 1910 was passionately interested in German folk music. While still at school he formed, in rapid succession, commitments to school reform, vegetarianism, and anti-alcoholism.

Kaufmann's years in Leipzig, from 1910 until 1912, were a decisive turning point. It was then that he discovered his Judaism and came to Zionism. This brought him into contact with the East European Zionists living in Leipzig. The impact was shattering. Kaufmann threw himself into all aspects—but especially the musical—of East European Jewish culture. He mastered the nuances and intricacies of Yiddish and married a Russian Jewish woman. As one collaborator put it, he *became* an Ostjude. In 1913, together with his brother Julius, he founded the radical journal *Freistaat*. Despite his disaffection from Zionism he remained in touch with its more radical exponents. During the war he was associated with a number of projects designed to aid East European Jews. In 1920 he became general secretary of the Workers Welfare Organization, an institution established in 1919 for the purpose of regulating the affairs and protecting the rights of Eastern Jewish immigrants. He died, very young, in March 1921. Upon his death, *Der Ostjude*, the only Eastern Jewish journal in Germany, eulogized him as the "finest mediator of our being to German Jewry."[70]

Die Freistaat, with its *Alljudentum* outlook, simultaneously attacked the two groups that it considered to be the real enemies of East European Jewish culture and society, the assimilationists and the Zionists. The approach was radical and frontal, unlike that of *Ost und West*, the other, more moderate German Jewish magazine specifically designed to mediate the world of Eastern Jews. Thus Ludwig Strauss, a close collaborator of Kaufmann's, based his opposition to assimilation on grounds that were strikingly different from the more familiar Zionist position. This became clear in his controversy with the well-known theater critic Julius Bab. Bab had argued that German Jews were rooted exclusively in German culture and expressed their Jewishness only insofar as they tended to become mediators rather than creators of *Deutschtum*. Strauss interpreted this as evidence for the proposition that "the creative" Jewish instincts were repressed when under the dictates of a "foreign culture." Inner freedom of expression was possible only in a Jewish milieu suited to the structure of the Jewish soul. Cultural Zionists would not have differed with Strauss's analysis, only with his solution. *Anschluss*, he claimed—making oneself "a part of Jewish, which means Eastern Jewish, Culture"—solved the problem. For the small *Freistaat* circle, Jewish and Eastern Jewish culture were entirely synonymous.[71]

Bab's reply went to the heart of the problem of the relation between modern culture and Jewish identity. German Jews could not solve their problem by simply "attaching" themselves to Eastern Jewry. Their relation to German culture was too deep, too natural. They were advised to recognize this and be proud of the specific contributions they had made to that culture. While the Ostjuden valiantly struggled to transcend their stagnation and Europeanize themselves, he wrote, *Die Freistaat* was exhorting German Jews to deliberately indulge in an act of cultural retrogression. This might succeed in making German Jews more Jewish, but it would also cut off the sources of their humanity (*Menschentum*), their roots in the more universal European community. Ostjuden could by all means be integrated into the European community, but to propose the opposite for German Jews was absurd.[72]

Bab's position was based on an analysis of the nature and conditions of Jewish creativity. The specific Jewish contribution to culture, he claimed, consisted in interpretation, criticism, and mediation. This was not a "national" ingredient but a matter of the individual's relation to the whole. Strauss retorted that Bab accepted the false post-Emancipation dichotomy between humanness and Jewishness. The distinction between individual and national survival was fallacious: "We are human in the higher sense only when we are fully Jewish." That was why the Ostjuden were so important, for amongst them no such dichotomy existed. They did not "Europeanize" themselves, but incorporated the achievements of Europe within their own Jewish culture. There was as little conflict between national existence and human culture for them as there was for the German nation.[73]

One is struck by the fact that both Bab and Strauss automatically accepted the Volkish contention that German Jews were incapable of "creative" contributions to culture. They were mediators, not producers. In his contribution to the debate, Gustav Landauer also accepted this idea. Instead of disputing it, he argued that German Jews were not representative of the whole Jewish experience. The Bible, after all, contained great poetry, and there was much to be said for the creative originality of East European Jewish literature. It was true that the German Jewish cultural present was not creative, but it was only an ephemeral moment in Jewish history and could not be made the measure of Jewish creativity.[74]

Strauss's demand for German Jewish *Anschluss*, union, with ghetto culture was of course a sentiment few liberal Jews were even prepared to debate. Perhaps for this reason the real targets of Kaufmann and *Die Freistaat* were the Western Zionists. Kaufmann regarded their attitude to Ostjuden as duplicitous. They flirted with the nation as an abstraction but remained estranged from the flesh and blood reality of their own people. This was so because Zionism was shaped by a bourgeois intelligentsia that was radically alienated from the masses. Despite their proclamations, Jewish culture remained an alien ingredient in their psychological make-up: post-Emancipation deracination had been left untouched. Zionism was really a panacea for the pains and problems of perplexed Western middle-class Jews; it had little to do with the lives of the masses. It had, therefore, never undertaken serious, empirical investigation of the complexities of life in the East. Zionism had created the phantom of a disintegrating world, but the real phantom was Palestine. This deferment of Jewish hopes had removed Western Zionists even further from Jewish reality. Zionism did not overcome but reinforced national estrangement.[75]

Zionists, said Kaufmann, were only partially Jewish (*teiljüdisch*), while his approach was total (*alljüdisch*).[76] *Alljudentum* was a "positive" philosophy, for it took into account and identified with all aspects of the national body, no matter how peripheral. Real understanding of East European Jewry required liberation from the perspectives of Western class ideologies, of which Zionism was a part. Zionism was a product of assimilation and anti-Semitism; *Alljudentum*, on the other hand, arose from the immediate experience and consciousness of the nature and dignity of the East European Jewish masses. One could attain such totality only by freeing oneself from the nervous inadequacy of antinational Haskalah presuppositions and ridding oneself of "bourgeois instincts and decadent fragmentation." Only through a total, even sensual identification with the goals, rhythms, and pulsating reality of the people was a genuine meeting possible.[77]

Kaufmann viewed the so-called Zionist cultural renaissance as an empty literary event devoid of Jewish substance. Ideas borrowed from alien sources were applied superficially to Jewish life. The "renaissance" was merely a deflection of German Romanticism to a new object. It was not serious, but the coquettish *Kulturkritik* of dejudaized Westerners. Its literary quality had relieved these intellectuals of the dreary responsibility of actually confronting the oppressive realities burdening their people. The search for community had resulted only in pseudo-community.[78]

We do not know how many people were active in Kaufmann's circle. Certainly there were never many, and the majority of German Jews were probably unaware of its existence or singularly indifferent to it. *Die Freistaat*, after all, was an esoteric journal on the prewar fringe of German Jewish radical thought. Still, it raised new possibilities, sharpened the debate, and made Zionists sensitive to questions they had previously dismissed. Cultural Zionists had to defend themselves against charges of national elitism and were forced to define and defend their positions with more care.[79] They began to take note when radical East European Zionists socialists like Ber Borochov and Berl Locker contributed pieces to the *Freistaat* attesting to the alienation of both Eastern and Western bourgeois intellectuals from the masses.[80]

We know that most radical cultural Zionists did not translate their theories into action, nor did all the adherents of *Alljudentum*. For both groups the gulf between precept and practice persisted: their bonds with German culture were not, in fact, terribly frayed.[81] Yet these small minorities did embody a new, important form of German Jewish self-understanding. Both groups were tied to the fin-de-siècle neoromantic mood. The search for a rooted living Volk, the predisposition to think in "organismic" terms, to stress the prerational, even unconscious elements of culture, the openness to and longing for newer, more personal forms of *Gemeinschaft* made the Eastern Jew the natural focus of attention. In this process the liberal-rationalist notion of the Ostjude was turned on its head. We have seen that regardless of the direction of discourse the Eastern Jewish masses were usually portrayed in stereotypical and undifferentiated terms. This was still largely true, but now disdain was transformed into idealization. The Ostjude had become an important counter-myth for dissenting prewar Jewish minorities.

But these perceptions were contained within small minorities. It was only with Buber's presentation of Hasidism that the sectarian quality was overcome and a wider pre–World War I German audience was exposed to a specific version of the neoromantic metamorphosis of the East European Jew.

FROM RATIONALISM
TO MYTH
Martin Buber and the
Reception of Hasidism

IN the minds of most nineteenth-century German Jewish intellectuals, progressive historical development had swept away remnants of unreason—the path toward a philosophically pure monotheism had been cleared. Jewish "irrationalism" was largely purged or was increasingly relegated to a superseded past. Kabbalah—Jewish mysticism—was usually dismissed as the confused mumblings of older, more superstitious times. Lacking both philosophical and historical integrity, it was not worthy of separate consideration as an autonomous, coherent, and valid Jewish tradition.[1]

Hasidism was regarded in a similar light. Yet it was even more threatening, for it was a contemporary movement, a live reminder from Eastern Europe of the demonic powers of mysticism and unreason. Ironically, eighteenth-century Jewish Enlightenment in Western Europe coincided with the rise of this "obscurantist mass movement" in Poland. Heinrich Grätz put it thus: ". . . at the time when Mendelssohn declared rational thought to be the essence of Judaism, and founded, as it were, a widely-extended order of enlightened men, another banner was unfurled, the adherents of which announced the grossest superstition to be the fundamental principle of Judaism, and formed an order of wonder-seeking confederates."[2] This popular uprising had no immanent logic. Hasidism was merely the response to Talmudic scholasticism, the triumph of the uncivilized faculties: "It was just this excess, this

121

over-activity of the spiritual digestive apparatus, that produced such lamentable phenomena. The intellect of the Polish Jews had been so over-excited, that the coarsest things were more pleasing to them than what was refined."[3]

By the beginning of the twentieth century the rise of political anti-Semitism, an emergent Jewish nationalism, and the general antipositivist fin-de-siècle mood had begun to undermine the plausibility of a purely rationalist Jewish self-understanding. Jewish intellectuals, mostly East European and nationalist, began to focus on previously "outlawed" irrationalist phenomena of Jewish history and in the process radically transformed their meaning. Concern with the history of ideas gave way to a new emphasis on the folk aspects of a living people, nationalism encouraged the shift from abstract theology to an emphasis on social movements.[4] For these individuals, political and national considerations prevailed over the religious and intellectual predilections of the Science of Judaism. Yet the stress on popular movements was not entirely deterministic and sociological. The quest for the roots of Jewish spirituality proceeded, but now the object of the search was democratized. Only amongst the folk masses would the "historical models for the rejuvenation of the Jewish people" be found.[5]

This search for the sources of national cultural vitality entailed a new openness, even romantic receptivity, towards materials that the earlier rationalist bias had either discredited or neglected. It involved a heightened sensitivity to myth, legend, and folklore and assumed the presence of hidden but potentially regenerating Jewish counter-traditions. Hasidism, the popular pietistic movement which spread throughout Eastern Europe during the eighteenth century, was an obvious model for the irrationalists. In this mystical movement the bases of a counter-tradition were readily accessible in the form of popular tales, legends, and stories. Unlike Grätz, the new thinkers were prepared to grant those sources a coherence and logic of their own, and in their transvaluation of rationalist assumptions, attempted to lend Hasidism intellectual respectability. Well before Martin Buber, men like S. Dubnow, S. A. Horodezky, Y. L. Peretz, and Micha Yosef Berdichevsky had begun the work of collecting Hasidic tales and reevaluating the nature of the Hasidic movement.

Clearly, the Hasidic revival preceded Buber, yet to this day that movement is almost exclusively indentified with Buber's treatment of it. Gershom Scholem has pointed out that "most of us, when we speak about Hasidism, probably think primarily in terms of the concepts that have become familiar through Buber's philosophical interpretation." Buber's presentation has been endowed with a somewhat reified quality: even as early as 1906, when his Hasidic works began to appear, few of his admiring Western readers were aware that they were confronting an *interpretation*, a highly stylized and idiosyncratic mediation of that movement. When the subject became fashionable, a topic for university seminars, many German students were unaware that other sources existed.[6]

What explains this phenomenal influence? Why were Buber's Hasidim particularly attractive? Perhaps a comparison with another contemporary radical irrationalist, Micha Yosef Berdichevsky (1865–1921; pseud. Bin Gorion), will help throw some light on this question. Berdichevsky, an Ostjude from Podolien, spent the major part of his creative intellectual life in Germany, where he absorbed much of the neoromantic mood of the time. Like the early Buber, he was particularly influenced by Nietzsche and sought to apply the latter's *Lebensphilosophie* to a radical transvaluation of Jewish life.[7] Berdichevsky believed that the normative rabbinical tradition had repressed creative, life-affirming impulses. He argued that within Jewish history itself, if one paid more attention to folklore, legends, and the preachings of heretics, fragments of a subterranean Jewish counter-tradition could be found.[8] Pristine Judaism, he believed, was based on vitalistic and naturalistic elements. In his final work he attempted to demonstrate that the Torah of Moses was a late, "antinatural" imposition on the Hebrews, whose real religion was founded on a prior, unrepressed experience of the sword and nature.[9] Rabbinism had usurped life and in its stead had substituted stifling conceptions of morality and law. Berdichevsky hoped that the counter-traditions would provide the substance for new life-enhancing myths. They, in turn, would destroy the suffocating institutions of traditional Judaism and make possible a radical national "naturalization" on the soil of the ancient Hebrews. The search for a suitable myth made Hasidism particularly attractive to Berdichevsky. He praised it as a popular movement galvanized by an oral folk wisdom in apparent revolt against the rabbinical thinking and institutions of the day. These were the kind of antinomian qualities necessary for a transvalued cultural renaissance.[10]

Much of this was like Buber's early thinking (indeed, Berdichevsky clearly influenced Buber's Jewish historiography). Yet Berdichevsky never received the same wide acclaim as Buber, and the reasons are not difficult to discern. For all his immersion in German culture, Berdichevsky remained an Ostjude, grappling with the problematics of the Eastern rather than the Western Jewish situation.[11] He wrote mainly in Hebrew to an Eastern Jewish audience which had not yet made the break from the traditional world of Judaism. Berdichevsky's Nietzschean irrationalism was designed to liberate ghetto Jewry from its debilitating lethargy. Buber addressed a post-assimilationist audience, while Berdichevsky wrote for a "premodern" public. His radicalism was designed first of all to facilitate the break with traditional Judaism. Only after that was accomplished could the modern "national" reconstitution take place. In fact, his opposition to the constrictions of the Galut and ghetto eventually led him to renounce even Hasidism as yet another quietistic expression of the alienated Diaspora experience.[12] Despite their admiration for him, German Zionists grew wary of advocating Berdichevsky as a model. Eastern Jews could deal with his ideas of total revolt, but for assimilated German Jewish youth his ideas were considered dangerous. Berdichevsky's ideas of radical liberation from the tradition made sense to readers who were still being shaped by that tradition.[13]

Buber, unlike Berdichevsky, began his work by taking for granted the break from the Jewish past. He addressed himself to a West European audience which he regarded as deeply assimilated, and his radical reinterpretation of Jewish history was designed to find a new rationale for the affirmation, not the overcoming, of a rediscovered Jewishness. While Berdichevsky borrowed from German culture to shape his concept of East European Jewish reality, Buber took as his model East European Hasidism because he wanted to reshape Western Jewish cultural sensibility. Despite the fact that he often described himself as a Polish Jew (much of his youth was spent with his grandparents in Galicia), the issues which Buber confronted and the manner in which he dealt with them are comprehensible only within his specifically German-speaking context. Buber clearly regarded himself as a West European, and particularly a German, intellectual. "I could not become a Hasid," he reflected over fifty years after his first Hasidic works appeared. "It would have been an unpermissible masquerading had I taken on the Hasidic manner of life—I who had a wholly other relation to Jewish tradition. . . ."[14]

Some observers trace the genesis of Buber's concerns and achievements directly to the cultural plight of the Austro-Hungarian Empire. In that polyglot society tolerance and harmonious coexistence were of vital importance. Buber, these authors remind us, was born in Vienna, and his discovery and representation of the despised East European Jewish masses was not only a response to the need to integrate them in the Empire but was also in itself an example of the symbiosis of Jewish genius with Austrian *Humanitas*.[15] Be that as it may, there is no doubt that it was only with Buber that the world of East European Jewry as it manifested itself in Hasidism became a respectable, even admired, part of "higher" German culture.

This was so partly because of the sheer elegance and flow of Buber's writing, its imagery and polished style—writing that was strongly influenced by his wife Paula, a distinguished novelist who wrote under the pseudonym Georg Munk. But of course Buber's Hasidim exerted a fascination that went beyond matters of style. Buber deliberately addressed German cultural needs and appealed to an intelligentsia seeking new alternative forms of expression. His early works were a reflection of the renewed concern with the mythical and emphasis on the creative fruits of mystical experience. Buber's doctoral dissertation at the University of Vienna in 1904 dealt with the great German mystic Jakob Boehme. His approach to the Hasidim was suffused with elements that were paralleled in German mysticism. While Berdichevsky emphasized the nihilistic and atheistic strains in Nietzsche, Buber fused the cult of Nietzsche with the new interest in mysticism (and in the process tamed it). By emphasizing *Erlebnis* (inner experience) and sanctity, Buber answered both general and Jewish needs. His analysis of Hasidism provided a model of Jewish spirituality that was at the same time radically antiestablishmentarian in character. It applied many of the dissenting ideas of the time to an analysis of the Jewish historical experience, and provided an acceptable Jewish alternative to the more general Volkish search for rooted, creative human community.

What to Franzos was nothing but a species of medieval barbarism appeared now in Buber's hands like the very vanguard of modernism, and it was this that constituted its great appeal for many members of an intelligentsia disaffected from the liberal-positivist consensus. Key words like *myth* were radically inverted, and applied to Hasidism possessed a magic of their own: "My narration stands on the earth of Jewish myth and the heaven of Jewish myth is over it. The Jews are a people that has never ceased to produce myth. All myth is the expression of the fullness of existence, its image, its sign; it drinks incessantly from the gushing fountains of life."[16] This notion of myth as a property of the soul, a faculty that pointed to the intuitive apprehension of the Absolute, Buber explicitly contrasted with religion. Religion was synonymous with official Judaism and had always sought to repress and counter the fructifying effects of myth. Hasidism was an instance of the triumph of myth and genuine religiosity over official rabbinical religion, a natural and spontane-

ous outpouring of these subterranean, "underground" impulses:
"And suddenly, among the villages of Poland and little Russia, there
arose a movement in which myth purified and elevated itself—
Hasidism. In it mysticism and saga flowed together into a single
stream. Mysticism became the possession of the people and at the
same time assimilated into itself the whole narrative ardour of the
saga. And in the dark, despised East, among simple, unlearned
villages, the throne was prepared for the child of a thousand
years."[17]

This, of course, turned the entire German Jewish Enlightenment
rationalist tradition on its head. Here Hasidism becomes the paradigm of Jewish well-being, the proclamation of rebirth; no renaissance of Judaism was possible that did not contain its elements.[18]
Hasidism was nothing less than the sanctification of the everyday
world. This was to be Zionism's goal too. Buber did not deny that
many elements of contemporary Hasidism had degenerated, yet even
where he discussed this degeneration he was concerned with expos-
ing the wrong-headedness of liberal perceptions:

> The "cultured" speak of "wonder rabbis" and believe they know
> about them. But, as is usual with the "cultured" in such matters,
> they possess only the most superficial information. The legendary
> greatness of the grandfathers has certainly disappeared and many
> are at pains to preserve their power through all kinds of petty
> magic; but all their carryings on cannot darken the inborn shining
> of their foreheads, cannot destroy the inborn sublimity of their
> figure. . . . Certainly, the zaddik is now essentially approached for
> help in quite earthly needs. But is he not still what he once was
> imagined and appointed to be: the helper in spirit, the teacher of
> world-meaning, the conveyor to the divine sparks? Certainly, the
> power entrusted to him has been misinterpreted by the faithful, has
> been misused by himself. But is it not at base a legitimate, *the*
> legitimate power, this power of the helping soul over the needy?
> Does there not lie in it the seed of future social orders?[19]

For both Buber and his admirers the argument of historical
degeneration missed the point. Buber never hid his lack of interest
in history. What was important in the Legends was not the reconstruction of historical atmosphere but the evocation of an ecstatic
Erlebnis. Its very freedom from historical constraints made this
vision attractive. Was not a recurring, existential need the basis of
myth and its creative reworking?: "I have told it anew as one who was

born later. I bear in me the blood and the spirit of those who created it, and out of my blood and spirit it has become new."[20] Buber's poetic tales were attractive partly because they made the spirit, not the content, of Hasidic life important. The way to rebirth was open and constantly changing, dependent upon individual creativity and spontaneous activity.

It was precisely because he was not interested in history that Buber, more than any of the other mediators of Hasidism, was to be so influential. In 1943, after listening carefully and tensely to Gershom Scholem's penetrating historical critique of his Hasidism, Buber slowly replied: "If what you were now saying were right, my dear Scholem, then I would have worked on Hasidism for forty years in vain, because in that case, Hasidism does not *interest* me at all."[21] Hasidism fitted admirably into the *Erlebnismystik* of the time. More than anything else it was a spiritual phenomenon, and it functioned for Buber and his readers with an elasticity that the concrete historical phenomenon lacked. For our purposes, it is not the validity of Buber's Hasidic philosophical position that is pertinent, but rather the uses to which it was put and the role it played in reshaping the perceptions of many Jewish and non-Jewish circles.

Buber's Hasidism came suitably "packaged"—it reflected and reinforced many of the neoromantic sentiments disaffected intellectuals were expressing in their search for more meaningful forms of human community. Whereas the old rationalism saw only external form, the new mood sought concealed layers of interiority and spirituality. The Hasid embodied all these qualities and longings. Of course the enthusiasm was possible largely because of the space and time separating these intellectuals from the real world of Hasidism. In this sense, Buber's counter-myth bore little resemblance to the contemporary reality in Eastern Europe. Rather, its effectiveness was the product of Buber's sensitivity to the neoromantic orientation of German culture. The emphasis on the legendary made it possible to dissociate the living Ostjude from the Hasid of the legends; they inhabited quite separable worlds. Buber was effective because the creatures of his ghetto, unlike the characters in Franzos or Nordau's *Luftmenschen*, were received as metaphorical, not literal, phenomena.

This bifurcation—the split between the spiritual and the empirical—made Buber's Hasidim attractive for many assimilated Jewish intellectuals. It provided an alternative channel of Volkish identification, a new focus for a positive sense of Jewishness, yet it avoided any need to identify with the contemporary Hasidim. The relationship was obviously far more symbolic. As Arnold Zweig proclaimed, there was no longer any need for Jews to feel a sense of shame or inadequacy, for in Buber's legends they could find their own version of the brothers Grimm and the Greek myths. Only legends like these possessed the power to bring back an alienated youth to the wellsprings of their Jewishness.[22]

The range of appeal to assimilated Jews was indeed wide. Buber's teacher, the famous sociologist Georg Simmel (1858–1918), who was of Jewish origin, read *The Tales of Rabbi Nachmann* in 1906 and for the first time included himself within the Jewish frame: "We are surely a remarkable People," he told Buber.[23] Even for some Jews bordering on radical self-rejection, Buber exerted a kind of ambiguous fascination. Fritz Mauthner's diary notes of 31 May 1906 are revealing. Buber, he wrote, was a "strange, worthy person . . . Polish Jew . . . atheist Zionist." Of *The Tales of Rabbi Nachmann* Mauthner commented that they were "fatiguing but very interesting. And shaming, moreover. A poor Polish Jew without education [*Bildung*] and what a splendid image-maker."[24]

For these men, Buberian Hasidism recovered the qualities— aesthetic sensibility, heightened sense of the sacred in the everyday world, simplicity, rootedness in a community of values and fellowship—that they found most stunted in modern Jewish life. Of course their perceptions were aided by the real physical distance that separated Hasidic centers from German cities. Even the most hardened of self-rejecting Jews, Maximilian Harden, could characterize Buber's Baal-Shem as "strange but charming."[25] What in Berlin would have been extremely threatening here became simply exotic.

We have already seen the effect of Buber's first two Hasidic books on Walther Rathenau.[26] Here, he felt, was Jewish *Geist*. This in contradistinction to the restless philistinism and rootless materialism that he found so tasteless in his fellow German Jews. So impressed was Rathenau that he determined to go back to the sources themselves. The author of *Höre Israel*, of all people, threw himself energetically, albeit for a limited period, into the study of Hebrew.[27] But the case of Rathenau is instructive also because it demonstrates the limits as well as the strengths of Buber's appeal. Precisely because of the literary and mystical elements in Buber's writing no specific commitment seemed to be demanded, and it was therefore easy to integrate this exotic movement into almost any "spiritual" ideological framework. Rathenau was attracted to Buber's Hasidim because they were a community that exemplified his search for the *Reich der Seele*, the kingdom of the spirit, and the antithesis of the "Asiatic horde" who were crowding the theaters of Berlin. As James Joll puts it, however, this was merely a species of "salon mysticism"; it did not seriously affect Rathenau's relation to his Jewishness.[28] His opinions on Jewish matters varied according to whom he spoke. In 1902, for instance, he wrote to Herzl that while he was no Zionist, he was certainly no enemy of that movement.[29] Yet in a letter to Maximilian Harden he ruthlessly ridiculed Herzl's attempts to interest him in Zionism. "He offered me a position as guardian of Zion with the rank of lieutenant and senior cantor under the condition that I curse the Savior every Sabbath [*Schabbes*] in the *Neue Freie Presse* and arrange a small, intimate Passover dinner with Christian children a la Bearnaise. I believe, indeed, that this is not his last word and think that we should simply acquaint ourselves with side-locks [*Peijes*] and caftan."[30]

This duplicity came from Rathenau's ambivalence about his Jewishness. Certainly his ardor for the Hasidim dampened rather quickly. In 1919 he described Buber's work as "very pretty, but contrived and over-sweetened."[31] Yet the other side of his Jewishness continued to be expressed. Attraction to Jewish things coexisted with repulsion. He belonged to a literary society composed of an unlikely, even exotic combination of Westjuden, Ostjuden, and non-Jews, for example. Little is known of this somewhat anomalous but exciting "Thursday Society" that met at the Restaurant Steinert in Berlin (probably between the years 1908 and 1915), but its membership was certainly ethnically and ideologically heterogeneous.[32] It included Buber, Berdichevsky, Gerhard Hauptmann, Otto Loerke—the club published his *Gedichte*—Ephraim Frisch, Otto Müller, and others. There is even reason to believe that, through the offices of Moritz Heimann, Rathenau helped to subsidize Berdichevsky's grand project, *Legends of the Jews*.[33]

The fact that Buber's Hasidism appeared in the form of stories and legends made it amenable to people who inhabited radically different ideological worlds. Its aesthetic character cut across political and religious lines. On the Left, Gustav Landauer's admiration for Buber's Hasidic works prompted him to declare that Jewishness was a special spiritual sensibility which only Buber and his Jewish readers could fully share. George Lukacs dreamed that he might have been a descendant of the Baal Shem and asserted in 1911 that he desired nothing more than to read a complete edition of Hasidic tales. Buber's influence was clearly discernible in the 1913 essay on the Jewish revival by the young neo-Hegelian philosopher Ernst

Bloch. Bloch pictured a faceless assimilated bourgeois Western Jewry and contrasted the legalistic elements of Judaism with, among other things, the beauty and authenticity of Hasidism.[34]

On the other side of the political and religious spectrum there were even greater surprises. In the second volume of his *The Decline of the West* (1922), Oswald Spengler wove Hasidism into the texture of his morphology of civilization. Hasidism was an instance of the "Magian-mystical" mode that contrasted so sharply with Western "Faustian" consciousness. Buber's 1907 work *The Legend of the Baal Shem* was a major source in his predominantly sympathetic though philosophically idiosyncratic account: "In Baal Shem . . . a true Messiah arose. His wanderings through the world of the Polish ghettos teaching and performing miracles are comparable only with the story of primitive Christianity; here was a movement that had its sources in ancient currents of Magian, Kabbalistic mysticism, that gripped a large part of Eastern Jewry and was undoubtedly a potent fact in the religious history of the Arabian Culture; and yet, running its course as it did in the midst of an alien mankind, it passed practically unnoticed by it. The peaceful battle that Baal Shem waged for God-immanent against the Talmudic pharisees of his time, his Christlike figure, the wealth of legends that were rapidly woven about his person and the persons of his disciples—all this is of the pure Magian spirit, and at bottom as alien to us of the West as primitive Christianity itself."[35]

The Viennese aesthete Hugo von Hofmannsthal (1874–1929), whose patrician sensibility seemed radically removed from the world of *Ostjudentum*, was deeply impressed by Buber's *Rabbi Nachmann* and even inquired into other works by Dubnow and Berdichevsky.[36] What linked Hofmannsthal to Buber, who deeply admired him, was the shared emphasis on myth and mysticism in the search for the unity of life.[37] Like Buber, Hofmannsthal attempted to harness constructively and contain the irrationalism of the fin-de-siècle by fusing action with aesthetics. Hasidism was a clear instance of a social form that seemed to shape irrationalism in a positive rather than destructive manner. Somewhat ironically, Hofmannsthal's shift from the narcissistic to an engagement with political reality, his abandonment of lyric poetry for drama, had been prompted ten years earlier in 1896 by his own stark encounter with the ghetto, not by the magic of romantic Hasidic tales. His nascent social consciousness was aroused in the Jewish village of Tlumacz in Galicia, where he was billeted for military service. There he wrote, "I am correcting my concept . . . of what life is for most people: it is more joyless,

more depressed than one likes to think: much more . . . [the]
spectacle of so many miserable human beings . . . their stench and
their voices."[38]

But most German intellectuals had never been near these Galician
ghettoes. It was not Hasidism per se but its presentation as an
energizing myth, an aestheticized mysticism, that was the source of
Buber's magnetism for the great poets of his time. The most striking
illustration of this was perhaps Rainer Maria Rilke. Rilke was, of
course, not interested in Buber's theoretical pronouncements. What
attracted him were the poetic possibilities inherent in Buber's
formulation of the mystical unity of things. Rilke, like Buber,
believed romantically in self-discovery through the realization of the
unity of man and tried to transform the unity of ecstasy into one of
day-to-day existence. Like that of Buber, Rilke's work has been
criticized as a kind of tamed *Wandervogelmystik* (youth movement
mysticism).[39] Clearly there was an affinity. Rilke wrote about Buber
with great enthusiasm. Buber's poetic philosophical work *Daniel*
(1913), with its "concern for unity, realization, creativity, action and
form," directly influenced Rilke's Ninth Duino Elegy.[40] As the
admiring Buber later wrote, "We had to take similar paths. Any
other leads into nihilism."[41]

Buber's work was written in terms easily universalized. Its spiritual quality was attractive to searching Christians as well as to post-
assimilationist Jews. Of his *Baalschem* volume, the Swedish peda-
gogue Ellen Key wrote to Buber that it "was a revelation of
unsuspected depths—well, perhaps suspected, but a confirmation of
my suspicions. How wonderful this all is—how beautifully you have
poeticized all this! . . . I have only poor words for the wealth
[*Reichtum*] that partly becomes mine as a result of reading this book.
How deep, how *soul-stirringly authentic*."[42] One Christian reviewer
of *The Tales of Nachmann* in 1908 even suggested that Christians
would receive this more favorably than Jews, for it concerned itself
with "great Holy wisdom" and contemporary Jews were not yet ready
to face such a challenge.[43] The emphasis on Erlebnis had, after all, a
universal application, and as another Christian reviewer, Karl
Wilker, expressed it after reading *Der grosse Maggid*, Buber really
understood the meaning of *Er-leben* and anyone who read his
account would enter the realm of the holy. The Hasidic way, where
religious Erlebnis and everyday life were one, had to become "the
way of all of us."[44]

Buber appealed to contemporary Christians largely because of
what to them was his religiosity. For younger Jewish intellectuals,

Buber was attractive precisely because he offered a Jewish spiritual vision that was purged of Orthodox religious ritual and obligation. At times his more enthusiastic readers, like Margaret Susman, confused Buber the man with the message that he brought. The young Buber, she wrote, we regarded "not as a person but as pure spirit."[45] It was this sense of spirituality that brought Salman Schocken, who later formed an important Jewish publishing house, back to "living Judaism" after he had read *The Tales of Rabbi Nachmann*.[46]

Buber was able to "bring back" many such young Jews because he was regarded, paradoxically, as being in the mainstream of German intellectual life while at the same time forging a genuinely spiritual Jewish alternative to the established forms. Arnold Zweig (1887–1968), later to become one of the leading proponents of the cult of the Ostjuden, wrote to Buber in 1912 that he was as alienated from "establishment" Zionism as he was from other forms of institutional German Judaism and that it was only through Buber's works that he could return with renewed spiritual intensity to the problems of Jewish life.[47] In this context, Buber's Hasidic works were more important than his theoretical writings, for as Moses Beilenson wrote, here were concrete models that united Jews with their past and showed that the ghetto possessed great living powers.[48] Ernst Simon's 1922 review of *Der grosse Maggid* neatly reveals the function of Buber's Hasidim for those young Zionists. The Hasidic Legends, he wrote, were attractive because they referred to real people, "made them like us," and gave the legends vitality.[49] But the renaissance Zionist of the twentieth century did not want to imitate Jews of past centuries. Simon stressed that Buber did not want to renew Hasidism as such. The Jewish future would replicate its spirit, not its form.

This, of course, left matters very open and undefined and encouraged a sometimes absurd latitude in denoting Hasidic spirit and influence. Berthold Viertel, for example, quoting from Buber's works, imputed to the highly assimilated critic Karl Kraus a philosophy of language that was Hasidic in its "antitheoretical" quality and its religious, even mystical, intensity. In an essay memorializing Gustav Landauer, Ernst Simon called Landauer an "unwitting" Hasid: "The methodological foundation of his philosophy is language criticism, that of Hasidic thought is the practice of taking the word seriously, of deep responsibility toward the word. It is easy to see that language criticism and letterist mysticism are opposites only at first glance. In point of fact, they are different forms of the same instinct: the urge to build the world-ego out of the word-ego."[50]

Buber appealed to many dissenting circles disenchanted with the conventions of liberal positivism, but from the beginning, there were also many who took exception to his work. One non-Jewish reviewer argued that Buber had done nothing to reverse the opinion that Jews were singularly devoid of creative cultural capacity. Buber's attempt to demonstrate the poetic values of Rabbi Nachmann was a total failure. He had indeed succeeded in portraying the world of "real Judaism," but instead of closing the cultural gap he had presented a religious world which, to the West European, was as far away as the "Japanese interior."[51] Another observer regarded the Hasidic writings not as aesthetic or spiritual documents but as disguised political tracts, romantic propaganda designed to facilitate the mass migration of Ostjuden into the Reich. Anyone who was aware of the malicious reality of the contemporary "wonder-rabbis" and what problems they created for established German Jewry would read Buber's *Baal-Shem* "with different eyes." The attempt to recreate national solidarity between these obscurantist, superstitious creatures and the modern enlightened Jew could only be dangerous for the latter.[52]

The major criticism of Buber's work concentrated less on its political ramifications than on its literary and philosophical aspects, however. The source of this criticism was sometimes surprising. For instance, the brilliant Friedrich Gundolf (1880–1931), a Jewish member of the intensely neoromantic Stefan George circle—an orientation one would have expected to incline him favorably towards Buber's purpose—dismissed the *Baal-Shem* as "merely literary." Buber had attempted to write poetry and history simultaneously and had ended up with neither. The reader got no feeling for the historical ghetto, and to all intents and purposes, the Baal-Shem could have easily been an Indian mystic.[53]

The attack by liberal Jews was less surprising. Buber's style, one critic argued, was impenetrable to the ordinary reader and sank into a "sea of abstractions." The content of his work might differ from theirs, but his style was indistinguishable from that of people like Houston Stewart Chamberlain and Otto Weininger. This sort of "profundity" was synonymous with lack of clarity and yet another manifestation of antiliberal romantic *Schwärmerei*.[54]

Given Buber's denigration of official religion and his view of Hasidism as an instance of the creative outpourings of an anti-institutional Judaism, it is small wonder that from the beginning, German Jewish Orthodoxy opposed his reworking of Hasidism. Buber's influence on German Jewish youth, they charged, was deplorable, for the young viewed the Hasidim entirely through his distorted spectacles. Rather than describing Hasidism historically, Buber had transposed it into a disembodied poetic construction. In this manner he had created a variety of "romantic Christian mysticism." One reviewer charged that by 1919 Buber's elevation of Hasidism had taken on the status of a latter-day Jewish idolatory, an ideological fetish. Hasidism, the reviewer conceded, was indeed partly a response to an over-intellectualized Talmudic scholasticism, but for the rest, Buber had "Protestantized" its nature. His emphasis on universal love and Erlebnis, his one-sided interpretation, entirely ignored Hasidism's loyalty to Jewish law and the structure of traditional belief. His vacuous literary sensibility had deprived Judaism of concrete form: in the name of spirituality and aesthetics all Jewish content had been lost. The Legends were tendentious, for they fostered the mistaken notion that Judaism was a function of pure spirit and had nothing to do with religious observance of the Law.[55]

But of course, such criticism missed the main point. It was precisely Buber's antilegalism, his insistence on the openness of content, his stress on the continuous re-creation of meaning through personal Erlebnis that made him attractive to secular Jews. What in the eyes of the Orthodox was a weakness was really the source of his magnetism: for Buber historical-legal authority stifled "higher experiences" which were in principle untransmittable.

The young Gershom Scholem, who also opposed the rationalist bias of the Science of Judaism and who was deeply impressed, at first, by Buber's call for creative Jewish renaissance, made what was perhaps the most penetrating contemporary critique of Buber's assumptions.[56] Unlike the other members of the Buber Hasidic cult, Scholem proceeded to study the sources themselves. He castigated Buber's *Erlebnismystik* as a means of avoiding serious confrontation with precisely those sources that he was trying to elevate. Erlebnis itself became a species of obscurantism: ". . . because the youth cannot remain silent and cannot speak, cannot see and cannot act, they 'experience' [*erlebt*]. In these pages, the Torah has been turned into an *Erlebnis*. The vague mysticism to which Judaism is sacrificed on the altar of *Erlebnis* is the true crown of the youth movement. . . . in truth, *Erlebnis* is nothing but a chimera, the Absolute turned into idle chatter [*Geschwätz*]."[57] There was force to this argument, but again it was Buber's ahistoricity, his "existential" relation to the sources, that attracted his followers. Clearly they were more interested in Erlebnis than in an accurate historical reconstruction of Hasidic life, for Scholem's highly intellectual return to

Judaism, his remarkably penetrating study of the sources, and his reconstruction of modern Jewish historiography were, as Franz Rosenzweig saw as early as 1921, quite without parallel.[58] While Rosenzweig, too, could not approve of Buber's criterion of ecstatic feeling as a measure of authentic Jewish action, he encouraged the encounter with Hasidism as at least a positive beginning to a deepened Judaism. Buber may have been misguided in his predilections for Erlebnis, yet unlike Scholem, he did provide a positive alternative model and activity.[59]

Buber's reception amongst certain Eastern Jewish intellectuals was similarly ambiguous. Some of them—closer to the reality of that Eastern movement—formulated their critique of neo-Hasidism even as Buber popularized it in Germany. There was irony in the fact that much of this criticism should be written under the influence of Max Nordau's non-Zionist works.[60] Men like Shai Ish Hurwitz enlisted the positivism of Nordau's *Degeneration* to inveigh against the tendency to romanticize what they regarded as a fundamentally mythologized Hasidism. Hasidism should be seen for what it was—a form of decadence.[61] The East European Zionist theoretician Jacob Klatzkin analyzed the neo-Hasidic cult as analogous to nineteenth-century efforts to "spiritualize" Judaism *(Geist des Judentums)* and make it socially acceptable in a liberal Enlightenment culture. Neo-Hasidism was nothing but a "tasteful coiffured, stylized Judaism" tailored to the needs of a neoromantic generation. Like its Enlightenment predecessor, neo-Hasidism functioned as a surrogate, an ideological *ersatz* for a basically de-Judaised life. Neo-Hasidism, concluded Klatzkin, was not a precondition for Jewish renaissance but its antithesis.[62]

The fact that Buber's presentation of the Hasid seemed to fly directly in the face of the empirical reality of Hasidism was the source of both the attraction and the criticism. Of course the Legends were more appealing than the actualities of the ghetto; indeed, they obviated the need to really confront the ghetto. But as Fritz Mordechai Kaufmann warned, an uncritical appropriation of Buber's one-sided presentation was prone to the dangers of any intellectual fad. Like Burckhardt's characterization of Greece, it was destined for a popular but short life.[63]

The tension between the ideal and the real was always present in Buber's mediation of the Hasidic experience. Until World War I, this tension was fairly easily contained. After all, Buber's readers were physically remote from the real centers of Hasidic life. With Germany's occupation of Poland, however, many Germans were thrown into direct contact with the Hasidic masses. Although Buber alluded to the contemporary decline of that movement, this was never the central element of his analysis nor was it pertinent for his readers. Now they were faced with the unenviable task of reconciling Buberian aesthetics with what increasingly appeared as Franzosian reality. When confronted with the actual ghetto, few could look through the prism of the Legends—many reverted to their Enlightenment spectacles.

Thus the liberal assimilationist Adolf Grabowsky asserted that his prewar readings of Buber had persuaded him that the Hasidim were indeed a devout, mystical community practicing ideas strikingly like those of the great German mystic Meister Eckhart, but real contact demonstrated that there was no genuine mysticism amongst the Hasidim. Mysticism was merely the excuse of the Polish Jew who had grown too lazy for Talmud study. The *Zaddik* was not a *Zaddik* but indeed a *Wunderrabbi* who exploited the superstitions of his ignorant followers and who had no relationship with a genuine mystical transcendence.[64] In the middle of the war, German rabbis stressed again that the liberation of the Hasidim from ignorance was the precondition for the general cultural emancipation of all of East European Jewry.[65]

Of course those nurtured in the Enlightenment tradition of nineteenth-century German Jewish life were almost certain to view Hasidic life in this manner. But even those who were part of the cult of the Ostjuden found it difficult to view the Hasidim through Buber's stylization. Young, enthusiastic Zionists reported about such contacts with a sense of disillusionment. As Felix Rosenblüth observed, the Hasidic synagogue service was a wild, noisy, disorderly affair in which very little of Buber's Hasidic *Geist* was manifested.[66] The war, moreover, made very evident a point which Shai Hurwitz had made in 1909: Hasidism, far from incorporating the elements of a future rebirth of Judaism, was essentially a quietistic movement which, in addition, fundamentally opposed Jewish nationalism.

For all that, within Zionist circles, Buber's Hasidic myth persisted. So great was its influence that in 1919 Heinrich Löwe, the veteran German Zionist, complained that German Jewish "pseudo-Hasidism" was making the meeting with Russian Zionists, who knew the reality, impossible: "Martin Buber is not the danger but, rather, those who do not understand him. We do not desire a Christological Judaism."[67] Similarly, by 1922 incisive young Zionists such as Erich Fromm, Ernst Simon, and Leo Löwenthal grew aware that the lack of clear goals for inner Jewish development stemmed at least in part from the spiritual anarchy that (the misunderstanding of) Buber had encouraged. The shocking relativism of young German Zionists, they argued, was the product of an abysmal ignorance of Jewish sources and history. The will to transcend one's assimilated cultural state was a precondition to success but was not itself the goal.[68]

In the end, the great influence of Buber's Hasid on various groups of German intellectuals could be explained on the basis of the psychological and intellectual needs that his mediation seemed to satisfy. His Hasid could be variously interpreted as a metaphor of spiritual community, a paradigm for "unconditional" relationship, a representation of the creativity of myth as against the sterility of religion, and in general, the exemplification of a counter-community that suited the searchings of a neoromantic sensibility. Here, seemingly, was a *Gemeinschaft* that cut across conventional religious and political lines.

The Hasid for both Buber and his readers was not a real figure but an ideal type: the empirical Hasid and the Hasid of the Legends could be dissociated from one another. It is a tribute to the tenacity of Buber's presentation of the subject that this form of dissociation persists to this day. Many Jews still view the real Hasid of *Mea She'arim* or Williamsburg with disdainful Enlightenment eyes, yet read the Hasidic tales with great relish. Buber's Hasid acted as an ideal figure against which dissatisfied intellectuals could judge their own unacceptable contemporary Jewish reality. This function of Hasid as measure and idealistic escape retains its powers even in our times, as the recent memoirs of Saul Friedländer attest.[69]

We must now, however, take care to distinguish the Buber of the Hasidic legends from the Buber who championed the more general cause of the Eastern Jews. The former was a literary, even religious task, the latter a cultural and sociopolitical one. Buber himself differentiated between the two, and when, with the outbreak of World War I, the question of the Eastern Jew became a central one in German politics, a matter in need of urgent and immediate attention, he devoted his time increasingly to these more practical problems. He established *Der Jude* in 1916, and that journal, unique in the annals of German Jewish publications and of a consistently high intellectual standard, committed itself with a passion to the many dimensions of the problem.

World War I highlighted and made real as never before the problem of Germany's relation to the Ostjude. The unprecedented meeting of thousands of modern German and Austrian Jews with the ghetto Jews was fascinating in itself. Under the circumstances of a

German armed occupation and the pressures of a swelling anti-Semitism, this strange encounter was destined to reveal many of the ironies and illuminate the dialectic of the modern Jewish experience.

7 STRANGE ENCOUNTER
Germany, World War I
and the Ostjuden

THE *Ostjudenfrage* underwent a metamorphosis during
World War I, acquiring a significance and political urgency that
were new and ominous. The war raged in the most heavily populated
Eastern Jewish areas—Congress Poland, Galicia, and much of the
Pale of Settlement. Germany's occupation of Poland in 1915 provided a radically new context for an old problem. Instead of the ghetto
coming to Germany, Germany came to the ghetto. Prussian soldiers,
impoverished inhabitants of countless shtetls, and middle-class
German Jews were flung together—an unprecedented situation.
Physical contact now personalized what for many had been an
academic matter. The war became the testing ground for the validity
of the various prewar German images of the Ostjude. At the same
time, opposing forces vied with one another to influence the way in
which the Ostjude would be treated and perceived.

Eastern Jews figured prominently in a political problem of national importance, as an integral part of the question of Germany's
Ostpolitik. For the war reopened the Polish question, which since
1864 had lain dormant. Russia, Austria, and Germany alike attempted to woo the Poles by promising them fulfillment of their national
aspirations. The large Jewish population of Poland made Jews an
essential ingredient in any solution. Moreover, with the occupation
of the Baltic States and large parts of Belorussia and the Ukraine in
addition to Congress Poland, Germany was now in control of the

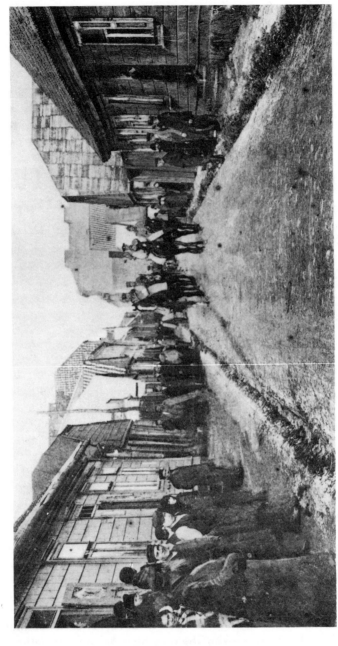

German officers entering the Jewish quarter of Mława, 129 kilometers northwest of Warsaw, 1914. Hofphotograph Kühlewindt, Königsberg, Prussia / postcard: Kunstanstalt J. Themal, Posen. From the Archives of the YIVO Institute for Jewish Research.

German soldiers looking for lodging in a Jewish home. Unidentified newspaper clipping / Gustav Eisner Collection, Archives of the YIVO Institute for Jewish Research.

bulk of European Jewry. The Germans were quite aware that the Jews could not be left out of their plans for the postwar European order under German hegemony and accordingly set up a special department of Jewish affairs in the Foreign Office.[1]

German Jews were forced to confront the problem. Their responses to the challenge not only mirrored their changing feelings and attitudes towards the Ostjuden but also provided a sensitive measure of their own self-conceptions, their understanding of the relation between *Deutschtum* and *Judentum*, between being German and being Jewish. By the war's end German Jewry had undergone transformation—defeat and radical anti-Semitism made this almost inevitable.[2]

Few German Jews were troubled when war was declared in 1914, however. Most shared in the collective euphoria.[3] Even radical Zionists like Kurt Blumenfeld, Martin Buber, and Moses Calvary breathlessly participated in the nationalist enthusiasm.[4] Of course, Jews could endorse the war with an easy conscience because the enemy was Russian absolutism; at last the despotic anti-Semitic heritage would be brought to account. Barbaric "half-Asia" would be defeated and with that defeat, finally, would come Jewish emancipation. This conviction was shared by liberal,[5] Orthodox,[6] and Zionist[7] alike. At least at the outset, it seemed to be a war in which German and Jewish interests were identical. Hermann Cohen's 1915 rendering of the harmonious relationship between *Deutschtum* and *Judentum* was merely the philosophical systematization of a popular Jewish perception.[8]

These hopes, the assumptions of an identity of interests, were quickly put to the test. German soldiers advancing to the East suddenly faced the reality of the Jewish masses in the Eastern ghettoes. An occupying German power now administered the lives and hopes of the Ostjuden. What only a minority of German Jews were prepared to admit before the war was now thrust upon their consciousness: for both Jews and non-Jews the connection between Eastern European and German Jewry seemed undeniable. The recognition of this interdependence, the realization of its possibilities as well as an acute sense of its dangers, politicized German Jewry as no question had done before. Liberals, Zionists, and Orthodox Jews all attempted to influence public opinion and shape German policy vis-à-vis the Ostjuden. Their actions were not prompted by benevolence alone, for as the war unfolded it became evident that the Eastern Jew increasingly symbolized the greater, more general Jewish question.

German Jewish responses to this problem varied according to political and ideological predilections, but all were formulated within a common context. The war placed German Jews directly in the middle: they were poised between the Jews of the Eastern ghettoes and the German authorities (ranging from the soldier at the Front to the civil administration and the political policy makers in Berlin). As patriots they had to confront the Ostjuden within a German political perspective; as Jews they had to act as champions and mediators of the Ostjuden in their encounters with the German authorities. Reactions differed. Contact with the Jews of the ghetto variously challenged or transformed or reinforced previous notions of Jewishness. Regardless of the reaction, however, it was a confrontation that the war had made almost unavoidable.

GERMAN SOLDIERS AND EASTERN JEWS

How did the German soldier respond to the sight of the Ostjude in his home surroundings? What was the nature and result of this strange encounter? How did the perceptions of the German soldier affect German Jews?

We must, at the outset, distinguish political and military policy from popular perception. In August 1914 the combined general command of the German and Austro-Hungarian armies issued a proclamation to the Jews of Poland that portrayed the Germans as the liberators of the Jews from Russian slavery and called upon the Jews to support the German troops. Many Jews did indeed regard the armies of the Central Powers as their champions, and hoped for a radical change in their fortunes, which from the outset of the war had considerably worsened. The Russian high command blamed their initial defeat on the Jews and executed over one hundred suspected Jewish spies; Jewish hostages were taken in those parts of Galicia occupied by the Russians, and the anti-Jewish campaign climaxed with the expulsion of several hundred thousand Jews from the frontline areas. Hebrew and Yiddish newspapers were banned.[9] The Central Powers were indeed welcome. The question here, however, is how the "liberators" in reality viewed the liberated.

The evidence is mixed. Many soldiers felt a sense of compassion for the Jews when they saw the ghettoes, which had become even more impoverished by the ravages of war. Yet this feeling was almost inevitably accompanied by a sensation of distaste and shock: the world of *Ostjudentum* was a strange, alien phenomenon. For many, the ghetto stereotype was confirmed: the Ostjude was no figment of the overheated anti-Semitic imagination but a stark reality. Cultural differences seemed enormous. The Vilna ghetto, one army paper reported, was inhabited by people radically different from Europeans. In the middle of a great Lithuanian city one suddenly "entered a totally different world, the world of the Orient."[10] Leading his men through the Galician battle-front, General Otto von Moser later reflected (with accompanying photographic confirmation) upon the

The ravages of war: living conditions in Poland during World War I. Gustav Eisner Collection, archives of the YIVO Institute for Jewish Research.

encounter: "What a horrible dirty Jewish nest . . . and at the same time the position of an Austro-Hungarian Cavalry regiment! Where does something like this exist in Germany—and the Austro-Hungarian officers tell us that this is by no means the worst of them. . . . The inhabitants stand lazily around with their great round eyes, the men and the boys with their dark little hats, the long black locks draped round the ears . . . so they stand, despite the summer heat, in their dirty caftans. . . ."[11]

Not all these perceptions were grounded in anti-Semitic sentiment, but of course the fright at seeing such poor and seemingly degenerate figures made it easy to transfer incipient compassion into a more manageable stereotypical judgement. It is never easy to identify with people living in dehumanized conditions. In the case of the Polish Jews, the predigested notion of the "ghetto Jew" obviated the necessity to go beyond surfaces.

Even where a degree of sympathy did exist, the nature of German–
East European Jewish contact seemed almost designed to quash the
bond. The meeting customarily took place in the marketplace, for it
was the Jews, middlemen in underdeveloped economies, who were
the main peddlers of wares to the German soldiers. One typical letter
from a soldier said of the Jews that their "one idea is to get money
out of our soldiers, who have come to protect them, as long as there is
any to be got."[12] The reality of Jewish hawkers fused easily with the
Shylock myth. German Jews voiced their concern. Report after
report, they claimed, showed that the German soldier regarded the
Ostjuden as dirty, profiteering, crooked, immoral.[13] The notion of
Jew as ruthless usurer became so ubiquitous that some German
officers gave their men permission to simply take the goods if they
thought the Jews were overcharging.[14]

This assessment was perpetuated by letters from the Front even in
journals directed to an intellectual audience. The caftan Jews,
reported *Der Kunstwart*, did nothing but business ("tun den lieben
langen Tag nichts als handeln"). Of course there were many exceptions and Ostjuden were oppressed, but this should not obscure the
fact that many were a purely parasitic presence practicing usury on a
defenseless Polish peasantry.[15] The avant-garde *Die Weissen Blätter*
published an article by the literary critic Franz Blei which stated
that even the most radical of civilizing and modernizing methods
would not expunge the basic business nature from Polish Jewish
being.[16] The "unaesthetic" nature of the Ostjuden clearly jarred the
sensibility of the young soldier readers of this journal. The editor,
René Schickele, was swamped by submissions from the Eastern
Front dealing with the perplexing and distasteful encounter.[17]

Official army publications were of course constrained to deal with
the question in more sober terms. Yet in the popular trench
newspapers, where Ostjuden were portrayed rather sympathetically
and Jewish "cleverness" praised, examples of this wit were significantly put in an economic frame and were often combined with
humor. One story told of a Jewish dealer who refused to lend
Hindenburg money. Hindenburg objected: "You lent to the Tsar,
why not to me?" The Jew replied: "The Tsar took Przemsyl—and
gave it back . . . took Lemberg, gave it back . . . but you took
Warsaw, Pinsk . . . has anyone yet heard of Herr Hindenburg giving
anything back?"[18]

The situation of the Ostjuden, however, was anything but funny.
The tremendous uprooting, poverty, and suffering caused by the war
resulted in further demoralization and breakdown in an already

German soldiers and Jewish woman in a tearoom in Galicia. Drawing by
L. Gedö, from Hirschfeld and Gaspar, eds., *Sittengeschichte des Ersten
Weltkrieges.*

pinched East European Jewry. Germans came into contact with the
Ostjuden either in the marketplace or as objects of occupation
policy. And there was yet another area of contact—with East European Jewish prostitutes.

Jewish prostitution was, as we have seen, not a new problem, but
the war made it more obvious, and the poverty and brutalization
wiped away more inhibited, less blatant trafficking. Hitler's later
exploitation of the fear of sexual impurity related specifically to
Jewish prostitution, "which remained concealed from the majority
of the German People until the War gave the soldiers on the Eastern
Front accession to see similar things, or better expressed, forced
them to see them."[19]

Defenders and detractors of Eastern Jews debated the extent and
causes of this phenomenon, but regardless of its objective dimen-

"*Herr Offizier*, please come to my sister—only half a piece of bread!"
Drawing by L. Gedö, from Hirschfeld and Gaspar, eds., *Sittengeschichte des Ersten Weltkrieges*.

sions there can be little doubt that the image of the Ostjuden as mediated by the war experience was tied in with the theme of prostitution. Jewish "criminality"—already a familiar accusation—became an increasingly important slogan. In the East this was perceived as a combination of economic dishonesty and sexual vice. The German police chief in Lodz told Adolf Friedemann that, while there were many exceptions, Polish Jewry was in a state of "shocking degeneration." Jews were heavily represented in the world of crime and their sexual mores were "indescribable." Sixty percent of all prostitutes in the area, he claimed, were Eastern Jewish women.[20]

Another, more conservative estimate claimed that in Warsaw in the years 1915 and 1916, 457 of a total of 1,778 prostitutes were Jews.[21]

No exact figures exist. There can be no doubt that the war encouraged prostitution in general. Indeed, the German army organized and controlled its activities, and amongst the brothels they established, some were on the Eastern Front.[22] Jewish prostitution in particular was facilitated by the fact that Yiddish and German were enough alike to make communication possible, which was not true of German and Polish. This afforded a veneer of sociability, and Jewish women openly sought clients in tearooms. More sordid scenes were also enacted. There were reports of small ghetto boys attempting to lure soldiers and offer their sisters for the sum of five marks.[23] Some observers understood that the brutalization of war explained this behavior, but for others, scenes like these only reinforced notions of Jewish immorality.

The conditions of war made it easy to fuse myth with reality. Ostjuden had always been stereotyped as dirty, and what the soldiers found as they entered the ghettoes of Poland, Galicia, and Lithuania vindicated that idea. They very often did find unsanitary conditions, a situation that the German occupation did excellent work in improving. Stringent medical and sanitary regulations were promulgated, houses were sprayed to prevent epidemics, streets were cleaned of years of ingrained dirt, and schoolchildren were disinfected.[24] All this was no doubt both necessary and beneficial, but still, its symbolic significance should not be overlooked. Many Germans regarded the cleansing as an explicit act of political hygiene, an effort at massive cultural purification. One German major commented that the Jewish masses could not be dealt with politically until they were raised from their state of dirt and *Unkultur.* He advocated "Soap. Only when the population has learned to wash themselves can we think of political measures."[25] Well after the war, the image of the Ostjude as unclean and carrier of infectious sexual disease was perpetuated. Seated amongst German army officers at a dinner table in 1920, Franz Kafka was told war stories about a sick East European Jew who, the evening before his unit was due to march to the Front, sprayed germs of the "clap" into the eyes of twelve other Jews. Cowards could find use even for sexual diseases.[26]

German soldiers, by and large, found the meeting with Ostjuden distasteful, yet we should not ignore another dimension of the encounter. A small minority of non-Jews "discovered" the Eastern Jews in ways remarkably like those of some (also a minority) of their

Germans spraying disinfectant in a house in Poland during World War I in an effort to combat typhus and other infectious diseases. Gustav Eisner Collection, archives of the YIVO Institute for Jewish Research.

German Jewish colleagues. Their enthusiasm had similar roots. What attracted them to the Jews of the ghetto was the observation that in the East, unlike in Berlin or Vienna, Jews were not creatures of a shallow bourgeois way of life, nor did they in any way attempt to disguise their Jewish being. This was a living, authentic Judaism, not a pale, deracinated, imitative society.

We have already seen that Volkish anti-Semites like Julius Langbehn praised the "traditional" Jew for similar reasons, but his was an ideological position not derived from any direct experience with the ghetto. The small wartime non-Jewish cult of the Ostjuden sprang from real contact. The Yiddish theater was the main instrument through which the discovery took place. German officers could not attend the Polish theater, but with some effort, they could follow proceedings in Yiddish. With little other entertainment available, they streamed into the theaters. For many, the performances demonstrated that Ostjuden were not, after all, without culture. In some cases German officers would rise at the end of a play, helmet in hand in respectful silence, as the Jewish national hymn "Hatikvah" was sung.[27] One such observer later admitted that before he met these "authentic" Jews he had been an anti-Semite; the encounter with the Ostjuden had given him a new respect and love.[28]

It was, above all, this perception of authenticity that captivated. The poet Richard Dehmel was overwhelmed. Vilna impressed him more than Rome, and he was deeply moved by the religiosity of the synagogue services. Sammy Gronemann, who was with Dehmel during the war, argued that intellectuals like Dehmel could penetrate to the core precisely because of their poetic sensibilities. Unlike most Western observers, they were able to go beyond superficial externalities.[29] For the few German soldiers who crossed the conventional barriers, the effect was profound. One even reported a total transformation. The Ostjuden, he found, represented something "eternal," their biblical being embodied a secret of which the contemporary period was badly in need.[30] For such men the Ostjuden were a standard by which, through contrast, the values of the modern world could be judged.

But these were the reactions of a small minority. For the average German soldier, the confrontation with the Jews of the ghettoes only confirmed and deepened an existing stereotype. His perceptions were not necessarily grounded in anti-Semitism, but they doubtless lent credibility and resonance to the malicious anti-Semitic propaganda against the Ostjuden that appeared in the immediate postwar years. The images and impressions did not exist in a vacuum. During the course of the war they were transmitted to German society in the form of letters, articles, conversations. They were to affect the development of the Jewish question in Germany in a fundamental way.

GERMAN JEWS AND GHETTO JEWS

Almost from the beginning of the war, German Jews realized that the popular perception of the Ostjude would not leave them unaffected. Different strategies for coping with this interdependence developed, but few could be indifferent to it. The dialectic was seen early. As one observer put it, for the soldiers all Jews were becoming "one type," and it was certain that the very notion *Jew* would find a new echo not only at the Front but also in Germany itself.[31]

It is difficult to measure with any exactitude the responses of individual German Jewish soldiers to the Eastern Jews. Certainly for many, the meeting did not lead to a reawakened pride in their Jewishness, but instead, reinforced the classic dilemma of Jewish conspicuousness. The ghetto Jews highlighted in blatant fashion what many acculturated German Jews chose to forget. Close contact shamed such Jews, who sought, above all, to establish their psychological and cultural distance from the Ostjuden. Some Jewish soldiers, when dealing with the ghetto Jews, made clear their contempt by checking and double-checking every penny in even the smallest commercial transaction and in this way demonstrated their anxiety about identification.[32] Anti-Semitic publicists boasted that Jewish officers were disgusted and shamed by the appearance and habits of their fellow religionists.[33] Even amongst Zionist students— at the forefront of the discovery and cult of the Ostjuden—these feelings manifested themselves. Their journals were full of complaints about fellow Zionists who persisted in regarding the ghetto Jews in much the same way as did their non-Jewish comrades.[34]

But by and large, the encounter left most Jews with a deepened Jewish consciousness. The experience was often moving. Nevertheless this could not dispel the familiar ambivalence. Report after report stressed the sincerity, fervor, and intensity of Polish Jewish observance and prayer, but also its strangeness and its "unaesthetic" nature, with its babbling, screaming, and gesticulating.[35] Even positive impressions served to underline East-West Jewish distinctions. Julius Marx experienced the discovery of Eastern Jewry as a kind of sentimental historical journey into his own forgotten Jewish past. Sitting in an airless synagogue in Tykocin in August 1915, Marx was reminded of his father—"my old, pious father."[36] Still others, when they saw the desperate plight of the Ostjuden, felt not only great compassion but also an intensified sense of gratitude to Germany. Next to his description of the shocking conditions prevailing in the shtetl of Olkusz, one soldier appended an appreciation of the fact of his German nationality: "Deutschland, Deutschland über alles."[37]

The point should be clear that even though many German Jews had their prejudices confirmed, even more revised them and regarded Eastern Jews in a new, more positive light. Their hospitality, their genuinely "Jewish" way of life affected many powerfully.[38] But even when the impressions were favorable, they usually also had the affect of emphasizing the historic distance. One report from the Front stated that for German Jewish soldiers celebrating the High Holidays in Vilna, services were very impressive but at the same time "an inexhaustible riddle, as mysterious as the Golem of Prague."[39]

And whatever sense of kinship may have developed, consciousness of differences were as marked as feelings of commonality. Ostjuden often refused to believe that the German soldiers who presented themselves as Jewish were indeed what they claimed. (In Eastern Europe the term *daitsch*—"German"—was synonymous with the modern, beardless, heretical Jew.) Certainly their external appearance did not betray their origins. Nor were relations improved much in areas of life like religion in which one would have expected the contact to be most fruitful. To be sure, German Jewish observers were often tremendously impressed by what they regarded as a kind of primal Jewish religiosity. Yet cultural differences frequently obtruded. For East European Jews, the synagogue functioned in a manner consistent with its Hebrew name: *Bet Knesset*, a meeting house where study and conversation as well as formal prayer took place. Levels of formality were certainly very different. A popular joke related the story of a Jew from Kowno who was told to make an appointment with the German rabbi during his consultation hours: "I can speak with God by day and night and with the field rabbi I must make an appointment?" East European Jews were aghast when German rabbis, familiar with Western models of religious decorum, insisted that children be prevented from entering the synagogue "in order not to disturb the service."[40]

Even those liberal Jews whose contact with the ghetto increased their commitment to Eastern Jewry regarded Ostjuden as in need of basic reformation under German Jewish tutelage. The confrontation served to underline the faith that Ludwig Geiger expressed in 1914. Germany stood for the great middle-class virtues: "justice and morality, order, efficiency, discipline and organization." Perhaps, Geiger suggested, the war was destiny's instrument of returning Russian Jews "to German Culture and Civilization."[41] This nagging paternalism was always present. For most, the ghetto Jews would be redeemed only by internalizing the quintessentially "German" values. Discipline and organization were fundamental prerequisites to progress. One field rabbi summed up this attitude in his complaint that every Ostjude thought he knew all the answers. No one would ever admit that others knew better or were more efficient, and as a result there existed a radical inability to organize. German Jewry, on the other hand, had learned the value of obedience and unity. What *Ostjudentum* needed above all was the inculcation of obedience, which would lead to some semblance of organized life.[42]

IMAGES, MEDIATIONS, AND APOLOGETICS

Responses to the encounter on the Eastern Front varied. Yet one point remained constant. The war had made the Ostjude an inescapable presence for the German Jew, and while many individual Jewish soldiers tried to deny the connection, organized German Jewry, sometimes acrobatically, sought ways of negotiating their way honorably between the poles of *Deutschtum* and *Ostjudentum*. This was a task that fell naturally upon them, for the war had thrown together the radically different worlds of the caftan Jews and the German army and administration. German Jews tried to function as political, linguistic, and cultural mediators, bridges spanning these mutually incomprehensible social worlds.

The war did prompt some highly unusual if not bizarre encounters. One was the meeting between Governor General von Beseler and the Gerer rabbi, arranged at the request of the former.[43] A meeting of this kind between the aristocratic Prussian and the Hasidic *rebbe* would have been unimaginable at any place but on the Eastern Front. Perhaps even more incongruous was von Beseler's meeting with the anti-Hasidic Rabbi Soleveitzchik. The General was told that this was the Jewish equivalent of a meeting with a cardinal. When the General respectfully asked if he could be of service, the Rabbi astounded him with his almost comically out-of-context reply: "Yes, I want a grocery store."[44] There were other apparent absurdities. In Lithuania, Sammy Gronemann became a translator-interpreter of Yiddish for the German administration without really knowing the language.[45] Conversations which would have been highly improbable in Germany now became commonplace. Some of these, involving unlikely participants on unlikely subjects, even appeared to bring German Jew and non-Jew closer together. Thus the Orthodox Cologne rabbi Emanuel Carlebach presided over heated and lengthy exchanges with top officials of the German administration about the history and meaning of Hasidism. After one such session, which concluded with a warm toast of mutual friendship and respect, an elated Carlebach noted in his diary, "Would this have been possible before the War"[46] Yet just as regularly, the war tended to aggravate German-Jewish differences. When a German Jewish soldier died in Kowno, Lithuania, the military wanted to bury the soldier together with his comrade-in-arms. But the German Orthodox Rabbi Rosenak intervened, and after much debate it was agreed that the Jewish religious tradition would prevail and that the soldier would be laid to rest in the local Jewish cemetery. When the soldier's family heard about this, they were outraged and immediately ordered the exhumation and transfer of the body to the German military cemetery.[47]

These were all extreme instances of the encounter. German Jews, for the most part, were concerned with less dramatic forms of mediation. Most common was the attempt to soften the negative impression that Polish Jews made on the German soldier. Apologetics were distributed as widely as possible both at the Front and at home, analyses of the Eastern ghettoes that were usually grounded in nineteenth-century liberal assumptions applied to the war situation. Ismar Freund, for example, writing in the Vilna-stationed Tenth Army's newspaper, did not deny the reality of the soldiers impressions. Ostjuden, he agreed, were indeed strange in their ways, there *was* much uncleanliness, dishonesty in economic dealings *did* occur. But such phenomena should be placed in proper perspective. Most soldiers had made the mistake of confusing these characteristics with Jewish qualities per se, which was completely incorrect—Jewish religious sources all enjoined honesty and cleanliness. The problem related not to "inherent Jewish defects" but was historical in nature. Ostjuden resembled Prussian Jewry of a century before; only their condition of oppressed disenfranchisement made them what they were. German Jews had had the good fortune to be emancipated and live in a decent, moral society. Perhaps the war had provided Germany with the opportunity of bestowing new light and freedom upon the unhappy millions of the East.[48]

Tracts like these effectively articulated Jewish liberal aims. Eastern Jewish rights were championed—on the basis of a clearly demarcated sense of distance. In this way the obligation to both *Deutschtum* and *Judentum* was satisfied. Here was a kind of vicarious identification designed as much for self-protection as to further the interests of the Ostjuden. Mediation was predicated upon the

explicit contrast that German Jews drew between Eastern and
Western Jewry.

If German Jews did not deny the negative non-Jewish impressions
of the ghettoes, how—apart from the assertion that this condition was
historical and therefore changeable—did they defend the Ostjuden?
An official Centralverein publication by Felix Goldmann, *Polnische
Juden*, was typical of its genre. Goldmann invoked a distinction that
was to become common in all these discussions. The Ostjude, he
concurred, was not a pleasing sight, but one had to distinguish
between appearance and reality. One could not generalize from the
external to the internal. What the German soldier saw in the ghetto
was not false, yet it also was not the truth, because history had
constrained the Ostjuden to lead a kind of double life. Material
conditions had created ugly, miserable-looking creatures, but the
inner being of these people remained uncrushed and their souls
were still consumed by an unquenchable faith and nobility. Jewish
backs might be bent, but deeper observation would reveal upright
spirits.

Liberal Jews were not the only ones to make this argument. The
young Zionist Nahum Goldmann, himself a transplanted Eastern
Jew, argued that only through the construction of a special ghetto
psychology would the modern observer, Jewish and non-Jewish,
begin to comprehend the Ostjuden, for they operated according to a
quite different set of mental laws. The cringing, servile exterior that
so many German soldiers had noticed was a defense, a response to
and internalization of years of Christian oppression. Once one
penetrated this exterior, one would discover a deeply rooted idealism and sense of values.[49]

The distinction between the external (hence "superficial") and the
internal (hence "authentic") was an effective means of countering
the increasingly virulent attacks on the ghetto Jew. In this battle,
people became acutely aware of the importance and political uses of
images. Replying to Franz Blei's assertion that Polish Jews were by
nature *Schacherjuden* ("petty Jew dealers"), Martin Buber made
aggressive use of the "internal-external" distinction. Although he
also produced statistics demonstrating that the Ostjuden had more
workers than "businessmen" in their ranks, this was not the basis of
his argument. Rather, he concentrated his analysis upon the implied
spiritual effects of such business dealings. Blei's accusations were the
product of superficial, misguided perception: "Yes, you soldiers of
the German and Austro-Hungarian armies in the East, you have the
Jews at your fingertips but you have not looked them in the eyes.

. . ." Ostjuden in the marketplace and at home were two quite separable figures. Yes, the Jew haggled over material things "but not with the sacredness of his soul, his home and his community. He does not haggle with his God."[50]

Polemics like these regularly spilled over into questions that went beyond the issue of the Ostjude. At such times *Ostjude* functioned as a kind of code word, a synonym for the Jew in general. The Buber-Blei debate in fact evolved into a controversy over the nature of the relative merits of Judaism and Christianity. Quoting from Blei's previous writings, in which he had bemoaned the commercialization of Christianity, Buber pointed out that no Eastern Jew had marketed Judaism. Blei's reply revealed the degree to which the ghetto Jew acted as a metaphor for the Jew as such. In a private correspondence with Buber, the Jewish God becomes simply "the Polish God." This "Polish God," Blei asserted, was a God based upon fear. Only with the advent of Christianity did the loving God enter the world.[51] Buber's reply was instructive. Blei had dogmatically confused synagogue with Judaism, but it was with such antisynagogue movements as Hasidism that true fervent Judaism was to be found: "I lived for fifteen years with the Polish Jews, in the Jewish communities of Czortkow and Sadagoria, and found at that time more vital love of God than in Christianity since then."[52] Only ideological blinders, Buber added, prevented outside observers from recognizing this.

This battle over the image of the Ostjuden did not proceed in a vacuum. Underlying it was a new and complex political reality. War, in the guise of the *Ostjudenfrage*, politicized all of German Jewry in an unprecedented manner. The pressing realization that East-West Jewish interdependence would be thrust upon them, and would work in radically undesirable directions if they did not actively try to control and channel it, made this question critical for German Jews. The varying attempts to influence the nature of the occupation and the direction and content of Germany's Polish policy reflected the social and ideological differences prevailing within German Jewry itself.[53] More than ever, the *Ostjudenfrage* acted as a sensitive barometer of German Jewish self-definition. Old conceptions were tested in the light of new reality, some were invalidated, others were reinforced. But as usual, analyses of the Ostjuden revealed as much about the authors as they did about the subjects. What might have been hidden before now became perfectly obvious: that the problem of the Eastern Jew had been transformed into an urgent problem of the Western Jew.

WAR, GERMAN JEWS, AND THE POLITICS OF THE GHETTO

The Committee for the East

Very soon after the declaration of war, the veteran Zionist Max Bodenheimer formed the Deutsches Komitee zur Befreiung der russischen Juden (German Committee for the Liberation of Russian Jews).[54] The name of the committee was changed in November 1914 to the Komitee für den Osten (KfdO, Committee for the East) to give it a more neutral connotation, but the ideology was the same: it regarded German imperial interests as identical with those of East European Jewry. Bodenheimer had already attempted to forge this German–East European Jewish alliance in 1898 when he sent the foreign office a memorandum alluding to the ties between Yiddish and German and pointing to the political uses the German Empire could make of these linguistic links.[55] Bodenheimer was convinced that his plan could simultaneously serve both German imperial and Jewish national interests. In the event of a German victory, the alliance between Germany and the Ostjuden would maintain the balance of power over the other nationalities. Jewish and German nationalism meshed, for it was in Germany's interests to maintain the Eastern Jews as a separate, autonomous (though pro-German) nationality. Throughout its career, the KfdO advocated the principle of Jewish national and cultural autonomy in Eastern Europe.

The range of membership of the KfdO was impressively broad. Not surprisingly, Bodenheimer's veteran Zionist colleagues Adolf Friedemann and Franz Oppenheimer were enthusiastic participants. But the committee's members also included figures who were far more representative of German Jewry as a whole: Eugen Fuchs, chairman of the Centralverein, Maximilian Horwitz, chairman of the Verband der Deutschen Juden, Berthold Timendorfer, president of the B'nai Brith Lodges, and Moritz Sobernheim, chairman of the Deutsch Israelitischer Gemeindebund. What made this apparently incompatible liberal-Zionist partnership possible? To begin with, only moderate Zionists remained as members of the KfdO, and as we shall see, younger and more radical German Zionists later bitterly opposed its work. The KfdO, moreover, explicitly distinguished Ostjuden from Westjuden—only in Eastern Europe were Jews a nationality, for conditions in the East had made assimilation impossible. Both liberal Jew and moderate Zionist could agree with the Jewish nationalism of the KfdO, as long as it was confined to the geographical limits of Eastern Europe. In effect, the committee based itself upon the distinction that Franz Oppenheimer had drawn in 1910 between the ethnic in the West and the national in the East. This differentiation was acceptable to Eugen Fuchs, whose wartime formulation of the relation between *Judentum* and *Deutschtum*, *Glaube und Heimat* (*Faith and Homeland*), was even patterned upon Oppenheimer's analysis.[56]

The KfdO held a broad appeal for German Jewry because it was perceived as combining a commitment to German culture with a sense of responsibility for the Eastern Jew. Sympathy was based upon the fact of cultural and political distance which had always been the position of the middle level of German Jewry as distinguished from extreme Zionists, radical assimilationists, and the Orthodox. The happy circumstance of mutual interests and the fact that the Ostjuden could be presented as pivotal to German political success in the East made this outlook broadly appealing.

In publication after publication, Eastern Jews were portrayed as pioneers of German culture and commerce in the East, natural partners and allies in Germany's Polish policy.[57] Propaganda arguing for the symbiosis of *Ostjudentum* and *Deutschtum* was so common that it became clichéd. Countless articles hammered home the need for such a partnership. Yiddish suddenly became evidence of Jewish loyalty to German language and culture rather than an example of linguistic "mongrelization." Special analyses now tried to link the *Jargon* with rather than dissociate it from German, and to demolish the notion that it was nothing but a degenerate form of *Mauscheln*.[58] The committee inundated German military authorities with its publications, which they claimed were indispensable if the occupation was to grasp the nature of its ghetto charges successfully.[59] On the home front special Yiddish cultural evenings were organized.[60]

Members of the KfdO sincerely wanted autonomous national status for East European Jewry. They genuinely regarded this as in the best interests of the Ostjuden. Yet it was the conviction that these policies were fundamentally serving Germany's *Kriegspolitik* that gave force to much of the committee's work. The appeal to German political interests was never merely tactical. An examination of the minutes of the proceedings of the KfdO reveals this quite clearly. The consensus of one meeting explicitly held that Jewish autonomy was "the best way to Germanize the East."[61] Ostjuden remained what they had been in the nineteenth century, the objects of patronizing policy. Now, however, German Jews were given much greater

leverage in determining their fate. Neither the tone nor the content
of prescriptions for the Eastern Jews was changed by the new
circumstances. As one member of the committee stated, "Only
through Prussian discipline (in the framework of a community
under a Prussian protectorate) will the Jews develop normally and
eventually attain the level to which German Jews have progressed
over the last 100 years. . . . If we want to develop the capacities and
all the good qualities of the Eastern Jews, then we must strive to
bring them under Prussian discipline."[62]

Franz Oppenheimer's 1915 letter to General Ludendorff demonstrates to what degree KfdO policy resembled liberal nineteenth-
century Jewish attitudes. Applied to the war, the emphasis on more
authoritarian Prussian values was a natural addition. Ghetto Jews,
wrote Oppenheimer, were indeed unsympathetic, but changes in
conditions would radically transform them. "Prussian discipline
and justice" would doubtless have a salutary effect. Germany's great
humanistic challenge was to bring about such a change.[63]

Yet contemporary observers were less apt to note the continuities
and more likely to see the departures of the KfdO from traditional
German Jewish liberal positions, departures that illuminated some
of the ironies of the new politics of the *Ostjudenfrage*. Perhaps the
most obvious example of the about-face was the transformed attitude
to Yiddish. But the changes in the committee's position were really
superficial. An examination of the KfdO's long-term prescriptions
regarding Yiddish demonstrate this: the liberals of the committee
made it quite clear that, regardless of the official propaganda, "the
Jargon must disappear as quickly as possible and be replaced by
High German."[64] The moderate Zionists of the KfdO did not entirely
share this view. Bodenheimer, Friedemann, and Oppenheimer were
more inclined to let Yiddish remain the language of the home and
make the transition to German gradual and a matter of free choice.
They were at one with the other committee members, however, that
Yiddish would not and could not endure. Despite the political
rhetoric, an older and deeply rooted antipathy to the language
remained. It was necessary to accede to the demands of practical
politics, but like the overwhelming majority of German Jews,
members of the KfdO never developed an affection for Yiddish on
its own merits.

There was one area of significant change, however. In its demand for national autonomy for the Eastern Jews, the KfdO departed from classical nineteenth-century Emancipation ideology. This
was an important shift, especially for those liberals identified

with the KfdO. The generalized meaning of Emancipation was now qualified. Recognition of circumstantial differences meant that for Eastern Europe, Emancipation would have to follow the nationalist pattern rather than the individualistic Western model. The war provided the circumstances for propagating and implementing this conviction, and most of the work of the committee was dedicated to that end, but it was precisely this goal that occasioned opposition from all other sectors of German Jewry. Such opposition politicized the community even further, and as voices rose to counteract the influence of the KfdO on German policy, it became clear that the Eastern Jewish question had developed into a battle about the nature of German Jewry itself.

The Liberal Reaction

Criticism of the KfdO's position was voiced by Zionists, liberals, and Orthodox Jews. There were ironies in this, also, for despite the fact that the committee was bitterly opposed by radical German Zionists, it was also attacked by leading members of the liberal Hilfsverein and the upper crust of German Jewry (such as Max Warburg, Albert Ballin, Theodor Wolff, and Ludwig Stein)[65] precisely because of its "Zionist" coloring. In September 1914 Paul Nathan formed the Interconfessional Committee for the Alleviation of Suffering in the Occupied Eastern Areas (Interkonfessionelles Komitee zur Linderung der Not in den besetzten Ostgebieten) as a conscious counterweight to the KfdO.

Nathan adhered to the traditional liberal approach. Jewry could be understood only in terms of common faith, and any attempt to view the problem as national or to seek specific Jewish political rights was misguided.[66] Consistent with this understanding, the committee continued the philanthropic tradition that claimed a purely humanitarian, nonpolitical approach. The war had reduced Polish Jewry to a terrible state of hunger and homelessness, and the philanthropic effort, under the guidance of the Hilfsverein, did do much to ameliorate the horrible suffering. By war's end approximately fifteen and a half million Reichmarks had been collected. But the war and the efforts of other Jewish organizations also politicized the Hilfsverein and its circles.

In September 1915 the Deutsche Vereinigung für die Interessen der osteuropäischen Juden (German Association for the Interests of East European Jewry) was founded. The KfdO, the organization argued, was led by Zionists who had no right to represent German Jewry. The new Vereinigung, on the other hand, was genuinely representative.[67] Any approach to the Eastern Jews had to begin with the recognition that they were *not* a nation. The path of Western Jewry was still a valid model. Enlightenment and Emancipation remained the keys to solving the Jewish question. Transformation of political conditions and internal metamorphosis (*Umbildung*) would make it possible for Jews to leave their physical and spiritual ghettoes and become equal, productive citizens in the postwar order. Given the fluidity of the situation in 1915, the question was left open whether assimilation would take place within a Polish or a German framework.

Most liberal Jews tended to support the position that in any reconstruction, Polish Jews would follow the German model and become "individual citizens of the Mosaic persuasion"—that the national model was ideologically misfounded and politically danger-ous.[68] But clearly the debate about the Ostjuden touched on very sensitive issues concerning German Jews themselves, and often the arguments came close to personal slander. The scorching criticism of KfdO policies by the publicist Benjamin Segel illustrates the emo-tions that the subject aroused.

His 1916 essay *The Polish Jewish Question* was filled with personal invective and shrewd ideological insight, and it effectively exposed many of the double standards hidden by the committee's rhetoric. Bodenheimer, he charged, was championing Hebrew and Yiddish, but how was it possible to love languages about which one was completely ignorant? Ostjuden had always been despised. Now, overnight, they were to be granted rights not enjoyed by Jewish communities anywhere else in the world! The argument that the nineteenth century was the age of individual emancipation but the twentieth was one of Volkish emancipation had no logic, for if each individual attained emancipation, so too did the whole nation, as a result. The idea of a Volk was a pure abstraction; only individuals could be emancipated.[69]

The objections were not, however, purely theoretical. In practical terms, Segel argued, would not the preservation of separate Jewish cultural and linguistic institutions merely intensify an already pol-luted anti-Jewish atmosphere? National autonomy would isolate the powerless Polish Jews even more. Far from solving the Jewish question, it would perpetuate it. Why did the German Jewish liberators not try this system of national autonomy first upon themselves? Surely the backward Ostjuden were not yet ready for such an audaciously progressive social development! Bodenheimer should organize the Jews of the Rhine and declare that henceforth Yiddish—which had suddenly become a German language—be the official language of Cologne Jewry. The KfdO, Segel asserted, was led by people who were utterly ignorant about Judaism and who regarded Polish Jewry as a mere object of policy, a pawn in their political game.

Segel's critique was especially effective because he himself was a transplanted Eastern Jew. The KfdO were so incensed and threatened by this work that they attempted to block its publication, and managed to with at least with one publisher, Stilke.[70] When it finally did appear, one reviewer commented that Segel's personal insults were "the lowest possible things a Jew could write against his fellow Jews."[71]

Segel's emphasis on the East-West double standard hit a sensitive point, one that remained problematic for many German Zionists. Although his analysis did not take sufficient account of the historical and sociological difficulties of applying the Western model of individual emancipation to a radically different East European situation, he was correct about the propensity for treating the Ostjuden as mere objects of German war policy. Segel, of course, did not mention that the same criticism could be applied with equal validity to the Nathan-Simon position. While they were more consistent than the KfdO in their advocacy of individual emancipation for both Eastern and Western Jewry, they too were not primarily interested in the real desires of Polish Jews. Their position derived from nineteenth-century German Jewish liberal assumptions, and the relationship of Western with Eastern Jew continued to be defined in paternalistic and philanthropic terms. The truth was that neither the Hilfsverein nor the KfdO related to the Eastern Jews as partners. Older modes remained intact. Their main concern was to influence the course of German policy and public opinion.

It was precisely this concern that prompted liberal Jews like Ludwig Geiger to voice their apprehension about the apparent success of KfdO propaganda, on the grounds that it fostered the dangerous impression that a few Zionists represented the real feelings of the majority of Jews.[72] Others encouraged the "legitimate leaders" of German Jewry—Nathan and Simon—to make their stand against these Zionists more evident and adamant.[73] This was ironic, because the "radical" Zionists on their side were also busily attempting to dissociate themselves politically and ideologically from the KfdO.

Zionist Radicalization

Radical Zionist disaffection from the KfdO was not purely the result of the formal World Zionist Organization's policy of political neutrality. The break was more the product of the perception that the KfdO was almost entirely motivated by German nationalism and did not have the interests of Eastern Jewry at heart. The war sharpened even further the ideological differences dividing radical from moderate Zionists.

The disagreement was made explicit with the publication of a special issue on Ostjuden by the *Süddeutsche Monatshefte* in February 1916. The issue was a major KfdO propaganda success and was filled with articles by leading Zionists (Bodenheimer, Oppenheimer, Friedemann, and others) portraying the Ostjuden as ideal allies of, and perfect pioneers for, *Deutschtum* in the East. At a special meeting convened by the German Zionist central committee on April 9, 1916, this approach was unanimously condemned.[74] The young Zionist theoretician Moses Calvary found the articles especially "shameful" because they came from the pens of identified Zionists. Kurt Blumenfeld accused the conservative Zionists of using the war to become leaders of German Jewry by adopting essentially anti-Zionist positions.

The most fervent and articulate Zionist spokesman on all aspects of the *Ostjudenfrage* was Julius Berger (1883–1948). Berger was an obvious product of the radicalization of German Zionism. At the age of twenty-two he was appointed secretary of the General Zionist Office, a position which he occupied from 1905 until 1910. He assumed the position again in the critical period from 1913 until 1920. Berger's evolution as a German Zionist, his political activities and personal metamorphosis, were integral to his commitment to the Ostjuden. He set a new standard, in his actions, for the Zionist ideal of East-West Jewish relationships. His war sojourn in Poland was personally shattering, and from that time through the early phase of the Weimar Republic he single-mindedly devoted himself to matters concerning the relation between Germany, German Jews, and the Ostjuden. He settled in Palestine in 1924.

Berger argued that the war had fundamentally altered the conditions of Jewish political existence. The Polish Jewish problem had come too close to home to be avoided. It was no longer possible to deny Jewish national unity. Terrible consequences would ensue for German Jewry if it did not adopt a new approach, for it was becoming increasingly clear that non-Jewish Germans did not distinguish between German Jews and Eastern Jews: "If the Eastern Jewish problem is not solved with the German Jews," Berger warned, "it will be solved against them."[75]

German Jewry's traditional humanitarian-philanthropic approach, he argued, was itself an ideological position, for it looked upon Polish Jews as mere objects, never as autonomous subjects. It perpetuated what German Jews despised; philanthropy reinforced *Schnorrertum.* The answer was to let the Polish Jews run their own welfare system and distribute funds according to local needs.

Even more damaging were the actions of those German Jews (Berger was clearly referring to the efforts of the KfdO) who were attempting to mediate Polish Jewry to the German authorities. On the one hand, they insisted upon the unity of the Jewish people in Poland and called upon the German authorities to recognize a separate Jewish nationality; yet on the other hand, they brazenly advocated the *Deutschtum-Judentum* connection. Demonstrating the uniqueness of a people by asserting its inextricable relation to another nation was surely a strange exercise. Moreover, the claim was duplicitous—German Jews were making statements on behalf of a Jewry that had never been consulted. This was a dangerous political game, for the Poles themselves would naturally look upon the Jews as the new propaganda presented them: the incarnation of German culture in the East. Such a policy would make Polish-Jewish relations intolerable and have unthinkable consequences in the future. In his private communications and confidential memoranda, Berger called the machinations of the KfdO the work of "criminally light-headed, irresponsible political dilettantes."[76] In a letter to Richard Lichtheim, he argued that the glorification of Yiddish by the KfdO intensified Polish distrust of the Jew.[77] To advocate Germanization through Yiddish before knowing who would rule postwar Poland was profoundly irresponsible. Clearly, assimilation along Western liberal lines was also not the answer to the Polish question. But national coexistence was. Jews would learn Polish and speak Hebrew, not Yiddish, as their national tongue. His hope was that mutual respect would develop. Hebrew did not have the Germanic associations of Yiddish and was also not tied to the unpleasant memories of the ghetto and Jewish misery.[78]

Berger's championship of the Ostjuden was not based upon blind idealization; firsthand exposure had made him acutely aware of the many shortcomings of the Polish Jews. While deploring traditional German Jewish patronizing attitudes, he maintained what he considered a realistic perspective, and it was precisely this realism that turned the problem into a personal obsession. As he wrote to Buber about the worsening situation in 1916, "the *Ostjudenfrage* gives me few quiet hours. . . . I see again the terrible danger, the horrible misery, and the absolute necessity of doing something, but also the forceful realization that almost nothing can be done."[79]

Zionists like Julius Berger were not the only ones who threw themselves vigorously into the question of Germany's *Polenpolitik*. Orthodox German Jews as well as liberals and Zionists also attempted to shape the politics of the ghetto in their own ways. In the process, they made unlikely alliances and demonstrated once again some of the ironies involved in Germany's occupation of the East.

Piety Made Political

Even before the war, Orthodox German Jews exhibited the characteristic German Jewish ambivalence toward Eastern Jews. Modern German Orthodoxy reflected, in its own way, these East-West tensions.[80] Perhaps because it took seriously what most other German Jews merely regarded as a legitimizing slogan—that Jews everywhere constituted a *Glaubensgemeinschaft*, a community of faith—such tensions were often intensified. Cultural and ritualistic differences abounded. In 1888 in one German synagogue, a fight broke out because a Polish Jew prayed with a prayer shawl over his head. In Cologne, a Galician Jew was ejected from a synagogue because he fell asleep and thus did not rise during the prayer for the welfare of the Kaiser. Only a few months before the outbreak of war, German Orthodox congregants had been complaining about the Ostjuden in their midst, some even describing them as a danger to German Orthodoxy's particular tradition.[81] Yet like the Zionists, often for similar political and theoretical reasons, Orthodox Jews defended the rights of Eastern Jews in Germany and were in the forefront of the battle for their voting rights in community elections *(Wahlrecht)*.[82]

The war magnified these contradictions. Letters from the field spoke in glowing terms of the *Ur*-Jews of the East. One writer found himself in "an ideal land of Judaism" but at the same time lamented the lack of general and secular culture.[83] This was the common perception. German Orthodoxy projected its own image onto *Ostjudentum*—the war provided the opportunity for remolding the Ostjude along German Orthodox lines. Adherence to Halakah (Jewish law) would be accompanied by the modernization of consciousness and culture. As one of the spokesmen for Orthodox Jewry, J. Wohlgemuth, put it, the key to the East European Jewish question was *Bildung*. The simultaneous maintenance of religious practice and acquisition of modern modes was the challenge. The "assimilation" of East European Jewry had to be avoided at all costs. German Orthodox Jews had to ensure that the Ostjuden synthesized modernity and the Talmud along the lines of S. R. Hirsch, although it was necessary for them to maintain indigenous institutions, like the heder, that suited the needs of their historical and class situation. Wohlgemuth, like other German Jews, tried to fuse this picture of Eastern Orthodoxy with German national interests. It was in Germany's interests, he wrote, to assure that the Ostjuden remain traditional, believing Jews, for in this way they would remain rooted in their homelands. There they would not threaten Germany with a mass invasion but could act as supporters of Germany's interests in the East.[84]

Jewish compassion vied with cultural disdain. Appeals to help refugees and alleviate the desperate plight of the Eastern Jews filled the religious journals.[85] Orthodox Jews, it was regularly pointed out, had nothing in common with those Jews who were the enemies of the Ostjuden.[86] But of course appeals not to treat the Ostjuden as mere objects of policy and philanthropy were not always successful.[87] Orthodox Jews maintained an obvious sense of cultural and national superiority. In at least one case, a rabbi instructed his pupils exclusively in German, although nobody understood the language. The grounds for this were simply stated: Yiddish was not a language *("ist keine Sprache")*, and Jews henceforth had to "serve as mediators and carriers of German culture."[88] Moreover, the Orthodox shared the general German Jewish sensitivity to Jewish conspicuousness. In the wake of refugees streaming into places like Prague and Vienna, local Jewish communities nervously attempted to persuade Ostjuden to discard their caftans and sidelocks. While Orthodox journals tried to temper this resentment,[89] some amongst their own ranks were advocating the exact course with equal fervor. One rabbi, in a militant anti-Zionist polemic, appealed to Eastern Jewry to abolish Yiddish and the caftan entirely. Not only was neither related to Judaism, but Judaism would be immeasurably strengthened "when the last caftan has disappeared from the face of the earth." Yiddish was not only ugly, it was an integral part of the etiology of anti-Semitism. It awoke mistrust amongst non-Jews, who in their lack of understanding of the language read into it "secret, dangerous, suspect" intentions.[90]

In their insistence on the disappearance of externally identifying
Jewish characteristics, German Orthodox Jews were at one with
other German Jews. "Jewishness" was a matter of religion and not
culture, much less nationality. These assumptions were shared by
liberal and religious Jews alike and formed the basis for the (on the
surface surprising) wartime political alliance between assimilationists and Orthodox German Jews, on the question of Eastern Jews.
Both upheld the principle of Jewish denationalization and opposed
Zionism. For the Orthodox, Zionism was essentially an antireligious
secular nationalism more dangerous in its way than liberal religious
laxity. The politics of piety demanded that German Orthodox policy
achieve equal rights for the Ostjuden so that they might become
Polish citizens, while retaining their traditional religious outlook. As
Orthodox Jewry grew more political, all of German Jewry's major
branches committed themselves to their own particular solutions of
the *Ostjudenfrage.*

Political success came soon and surprisingly easily. The German
authorities increasingly feared the domination of Jewish political
life by "radical elements." They regarded both the KfdO and the
Zionists as such influences and believed that religious orthodoxy
would act as a conserving, stabilizing force. Hence the Freie Vereinigung für die Interessen des orthodoxen Judentums (Free Association
for the Interests of Orthodox Judaism), under the leadership of
Rabbis Emanuel Carlebach and Pinchas Kohn, received permission
to keep a delegation in Warsaw to advise the military and civil
authorities. This action stimulated conflict between the Orthodox
and both the KfdO and the Zionists, who despite great effort were
never granted such status.[91] Zionists were incensed by Orthodoxy's
partnership with the Nathan-Simon forces. The affinity between the
two positions became evident when both liberal and Orthodox
German Jew hailed the November 1916 German decree that Polish
Jewry was to be regarded not as a national but as a religious
community.

The historian of German Orthodoxy's position has recently acknowledged that the purely religious definition did not fit the "folk"
reality or temperament of the Ostjuden. The attempt to fit Eastern
Jews into the Western model of *Torah im Derekh Eretz* reflected a
persistent sense of cultural superiority.[92] This does not mean that the
educational and philanthropic work at the Front by the Orthodox
was not outstanding, but there is little doubt that like the KfdO
whom they opposed, the Orthodox at times regarded the Ostjuden as
pawns in a German political game. This was revealed when a private
memorandum of Pinchas Kohn was publicly exposed. In the docu-

ment, Kohn discussed the political "manageability" of various groups of Eastern Jewry in the occupied territory. The Orthodox masses, he reported, were "unpolitical. . . . For the German administration they were the easiest section to control. . . ." The Yiddishists, on the other hand, were "intransigent," and the Zionists would give the authorities the most difficulty. Lithuanian Jews were "a destructive element."[93]

Perhaps the most important legacy of German Orthodoxy's wartime effort was their successful politicizing of the traditional masses through the formation of the political party *Agudat Israel.* More than any other section of German Jewry, the Orthodox managed to harness the political will of the Polish Jews who were religious. Yet mutual suspicion remained. Perhaps because there was agreement on so fundamental a matter as belief in Torah, issues that divided the two Jewries became especially salient. Traditional Eastern Jews feared the imposition of a modern Science of Judaism and regarded the notions of pulpit and pastoral work as alien and non-Jewish.[94] In effect, relations between religious Jews replicated the general East-West Jewish distinctions. One transplanted East European rabbi argued in 1916 that there were large differences in "temperament and psychology," and by war's end charged that contact had exacerbated, not lessened, the differences.[95] German Jews, instead of being inspired by the warm, pulsating Jewish life of their Eastern counterparts, had retained their coldness and formality and were estranged and distant. Nothing less than a thorough democratization of German Orthodox life, he insisted, was necessary.[96]

THE *OSTJUDENFRAGE* AND GERMAN JEWISH IDENTITY

Contact with the Jews of the ghetto did not function on the political level only; it also touched on basic issues of Jewish self-understanding. Even for people who did not go to the Front, the question of the Eastern Jew became a central topic of conversation and written analysis. Unlikely figures became involved in the problem. Thus the quintessentially European Stefan Zweig wrote to Buber about his talks with the dramatist Berthold Viertel that the few things that Viertel had told him about his own experience with Eastern Jews had made more of an impression upon him than all the things he had read.[97] The question of the Ostjuden was changing the concerns of the Westjuden.

The conscious need to articulate new conceptions and images of both East European and German Jewish life as well as the nature of their interrelationship was behind the creation of two major wartime German Jewish journals—Buber's *Der Jude* and the KfdO's *Neue Jüdische Monatshefte (NJM)*. Their differences mirrored the ways in which the question of the Ostjuden had already affected German Jewish self-definition. The founders of the *Monatshefte* originally intended to call it *Ostjüdische Revue*. They believed that common concern with the question of the East European Jews had finally made German Jewish unity possible. The paper was conceived as a nonparty paper; its advocates considered it a significant breakthrough that Zionist and liberal names such as "Oppenheimer and Cohen, Fuchs and Friedemann could appear together on the same title page."[98] Franz Oppenheimer, who was outraged by Berger's attack on the KfdO in *Der Jude*, envisaged the *Monatshefte* as a paper for all of German Jewry. Unlike *Der Jude*, it would not be partisan, and its tone would be dignified.[99]

Oppenheimer was, of course, correct in his evaluation. The war had provided an opportunity for the creation of a new, moderate liberal–Zionist unity. Precisely because of their more radical leanings sympathizers of *Der Jude* were perturbed by this noncommitting, cosy *(gemütlich)* mode of nationalism.[100] Both papers had been brought into existence by the *Ostjudenfrage*. This was further evidence that the battle over the Eastern Jews was a question that centrally affected German Jewish identity.

Der Jude's mediation and defense of Eastern Jewry was the most aggressive of the two. The stark realities of the war did much to ensure that its treatment of the question would transcend the level of prewar Zionist literary romanticism. This did not always happen, but in principle the paper attempted to combine passionate defense with a critical, unapologetic mode. Robert Weltsch's letter from the Eastern Front succeeded admirably in this respect. The war, Weltsch reported, had not only uprooted the Jewish people but had also destroyed its inner structure. It had unleashed inhibitions and loosened personal restraints, created dangerous new susceptibilities. Jewish prostitution was rife in the East, the effect of war on the women disastrous: "What the war has made of them I consider to be the greatest national misfortune that has confronted us."[101] Jewish women had become a major attraction, and Lublin was positively overflowing with German officers coupled with Jewish women. To

make the problem even worse, lamented Weltsch, many of the
women were prostituting themselves not for money alone but out of a
sense of bravado. They were not even aware of their own degrada-
tion. This was the source of the deepest shame, but the problem had
to be faced—apologetics would be counterproductive in such a
situation. Female education, Weltsch maintained, had to be made
the central task of the Jewish national movement. Without healthy
women, no healthy Jewish national society was possible.

This analysis of Jewish life in the East was hardly romantic. At the
same time, however, Weltsch retained his faith in the Eastern Jews as
the source for Jewish national regeneration. There was still hope, he
wrote, for in the East there were a number of women who were
admirable and who remained the pride of the Zionist movement.
They were deeply ashamed of the degeneration and were utterly
dedicated to the cause of national rebirth. These women were unlike
their Western Jewish counterparts, who by and large were hopelessly
superficial creatures.

Weltsch's article typified *Der Jude*'s image of itself. So, too, did
Buber's political contributions. The plethora of advice, stories, and
solutions concerning the Ostjuden elicited his scorn. Arguments had
been made, he wrote, "firstly that the Polish Jews were worthless,
hence had to disappear; secondly, that they did actually have some
worth, hence did not have to disappear, but by dint of natural and
historical necessity would disappear. . . . Everyone knows exactly.
We do not know exactly. We only see. We see only a *res sui generis*
that defies all analogies. We see the dirt and the purity, the
corruption and the uprightness, the commerce and the spiritual
fervor. We see the striving souls and the terrible suffering. We see in
the hearts of the young the old, unbroken Judaism that cannot be
bent and weakened. We see the great possibilities on all the faces.
We stretch out our hands—Brothers, let us help each other. . . ."[102]

More than ever, the German Jewish attitude to the Ostjude was a
measure of broader questions of identity. For estranged Jews the
debate aroused old insecurities. Paul Nikolaus Cossmann, the editor
of the *Süddeutsche Monatshefte*, which published the special number on the Ostjuden, typified their response. Cossmann, himself the
son of an East European cellist and music teacher, was a convert to
Catholicism, an extreme German nationalist, adherent of the Vater-
landspartei, and a tragic victim of the breakdown of the German-
Jewish symbiosis (he died in Theresienstadt).[103] Cossmann was
interested in the Ostjuden, for he thought they could serve Germany's imperial war interests. This accounted for the preponderance of
KfdO contributions to the paper's symposium. While radical Zion-

ists criticized the articles for their detachment, Cossmann castigated
them as instances of mindless Jewish solidarity. In a private letter,
he expressed his concern that almost all the contributions he had
received were entirely uncritical, portraying the Ostjuden, without
exception, as "upright and talented" people. No one even mentioned
the unpleasing effects that their emigration into Germany would
have on German life and culture, he complained. All one heard was
the platitude that if the yoke of Russian oppression were lifted, these
Jews would engage in "honest work on the soil of their homeland"
and develop in an ideal manner. This was not good enough. What
was needed above all was Jewish self-criticism (*Selbstkritik*).[104]

The extreme assimilationist position explicitly laid the blame on
the Ostjuden for the perpetuation of "the Jewish question" in the
Western world. Only the continued influx of Eastern Jews into
Germany accounted for the survival of German Jewry. In the East,
the Jewish question had an objective economic foundation, but the
problem was artificially recreated in the West by the constant
westward infiltration of Ostjuden.[105] In his *Die polnische Frage*
(1916), Adolf Grabowsky argued that while Ostjuden were ready for
European "civilization" they were unsuited for integration into
German cultural and economic life. They should remain in Poland,
where under German supervision and with suitable reforms, Poles
and Jews would live in harmony.[106]

The war was clearly a watershed in liberal Jewish self-understanding. As one observer phrased it, the encounter demonstrated the
extent of the historic East-West Jewish disjunction. A massive class
distinction divided bourgeois Western Jews from proletarian Eastern Jews. At the same time, the reality of the Easterners painfully
threatened the dream of "German citizens of the Mosaic persuasion"
that Judaism was "merely a religious confession." Certainly, for
liberal Jews associated with the Centralverein, the war highlighted
an unresolved conflict in German Jewish consciousness. The desire
to help the Ostjuden had to be balanced once again with German
Jewish self-interest.[107]

Even "committed" liberal Jews like Rabbi Felix Goldmann opposed Eastern Jewish migration into Germany—on the purported
basis that once these Jews left their traditional surroundings they
would lose all "inner restraints" and rapidly assimilate or, worse
still, become political radicals.[108] Goldmann did not deny what some
rabbis were asserting: that the future of Judaism's strength lay with
the Eastern Jews. Some had even suggested a way of combining the
solution to the *Ostjudenfrage* with a plan to help ailing German
Jewish communities. Now that so many German Jews were leaving

the small towns and villages and going to the cities, leaving behind them empty synagogues, one rabbi asked, was there not an important role for the Ostjuden? In communities where there were fewer than fifty families, Jewish workers from the East should be settled. They would not cause problems for Germany, for they would be obliged to remain in these villages for fifteen years, and since they were familiar with the coercive methods of the Pale they would not find this measure distasteful. Under such conditions the Ostjuden would be rapidly Germanized, and at the same time they would critically strengthen the waning religious life of German Jewry.[109] Goldmann opposed this scheme on the putative grounds that only a "rooted" Eastern Jewry could have a beneficial effect on German Jewry. The only solution to the *Ostjudenfrage*, he insisted, was the creation of satisfactory conditions in Poland itself.

Goldmann made his argument on "Jewish" grounds. Other spokesmen for the Centralverein were not concerned that the Ostjuden would radically assimilate and become "too German," but rather that they were not yet ready for German culture. As Kurt Alexander argued, the experience of Emancipation was the precondition for cultural preparedness amongst the Ostjuden. The logical task of German Jewry was to free the Ostjuden and emancipate them where they lived. Human groups, like trees, could not be transplanted from one soil to another without undergoing damage. Moreover, the influx of Ostjuden would have a deeply unsettling effect on German Jewry's own integration.[110]

Liberal concern for the shocking plight of the Eastern Jews was one matter, the question of their coming to Germany itself quite another. Grabowsky and Alexander typified those elements who based their sense of Jewish identity upon a particularly sharp distinction between *Ostjudentum* and *Westjudentum*. At times, the liberal expression of fear over the consequences of an Eastern influx was not very different from Volkish portrayals of the Jew. Writing in the *Allgemeine Zeitung des Judentums*, Willy Cohn voiced his concern about the phenomenon of the *nouveau riche* Ostjude. Unlike money, he said, the acquisition of culture took time, even generations. For the Ostjude in Germany the disparity between economics and culture would be too great. The war had increased contact between German Jews and Eastern Jews, and while everything should be done to help the Ostjuden, "we must draw a dividing line between them and us if we want to prevent German Jewry from being hurt at its most sensitive point. To adopt them into the community of German Jewry is to make that Jewry un-German, with the emphasis on 'German.' . . . The Jewish question in the East carries with it difficult problems; if we try to solve them we must, in the first instance, keep our German *Judentum* in the foreground, for we do not want to commit suicide. . . ."[111]

These concerns reflected the nagging sense of Jewish insecurity in Germany. Zionists claimed that Alexander's position exemplified Western Jewish anti-Semitism and mocked the depth of German Jewry's own emancipation. What kind of an emancipation was it that aroused so great an anxiety over a few Ostjuden? This was not emancipation in the real sense of the word. Because of assimilationist insecurity, ancient blood bonds were being anxiously cast off.[112] Yet regardless of Zionist scorn, liberal dissociation and the sense of insecurity was a response to a real situation. As the war continued, previously muted anti-Semitic sentiments aimed at German Jews were increasingly evident. The attack on the Eastern Jews, however, had been heard from the beginning of the war, and the negative impressions of Jews on the Eastern Front meshed with efforts by anti-Semitic elements at home.

THE WAR, OSTJUDEN, AND ANTI-SEMITISM

As we have seen, Ostjuden had always been easy targets for German anti-Semitic attacks. The attack on the alien, as opposed to the native, Jew was more likely to be tolerated, even condoned, by the authorities. At least at the beginning of the war, this tendency was intensified by the *Burgfrieden*, Germany's internal political truce and pledge of national unity. Both on the Front and at home, the Ostjude, unlike his German counterpart, was fair game for the expression of increasing anti-Jewish sentiment; he was an acceptable target. But as German Jewry only gradually and fitfully began to grasp, the animus against the Eastern Jew was often an implicit, and at times explicit, attack on German Jewry itself.

Almost as soon as war was declared, the renewed call for *Grenzschluss*, closing German borders to the Ostjuden, was issued. In the context of Germany's *Ostpolitik* the old specter of a mass Jewish invasion from the East was raised. These fears were first voiced by the pan-Germans, the Alldeutscher Verband. Their program, as articulated by Heinrich Class, linked Germany's eastward annexation and expansion to an immediate closing of Germany's borders to Ostjuden. Directly following the conquest of Warsaw in August 1915, the Wirtschaftliche Vereinigung, an extreme anti-Semitic splinter party, and the Deutschvölkische Partei presented Beth-mann-Hollweg with the same demand.[113]

The issue became a matter of widespread public attention when a large number of appeals demanding the border closing appeared in 1915.[114] All the old myths were invoked. The war had created the danger of a mass invasion of "judaised mongols";[115] the threatened flood would open the floodgates of degeneration upon the physical and moral hygiene of Germany. Ostjuden were an amalgam of cripples, mental cases, idiots, and sexually diseased people.[116] The author of the most influential of these essays, government councillor Georg Fritz, warned German Jewry to support his call, for the Ostjuden invasion would once again open up the Jewish question and gravely threaten German Jewry, whose own emancipation would no longer be guaranteed.[117] The integration of "East-West" anti-Semitism was not in doubt.

Many proponents of Grenzschluss supported Zionism. Herzl's notion that the anti-Semite had a common interest with the Zionist in furthering Jewish settlement in Palestine was here vindicated: Zionism became a safety valve, a means of keeping Eastern Jews out of Germany. This logic was not limited to the extreme right. The Center party's sympathy for Zionism was motivated, at least in part, by the same consideration. As its organ *Kölnische Volkszeitung* bluntly put it, "We do not want Germany to be flooded with Jews, as happened in the case of Austria"[118]

At the same time, anti-Semites cynically attempted to exploit East-West Jewish divisions. They often invoked the names of men like Max Marcuse and Friedrich Blach who had advocated Grenzschluss even before the war. If German Jews were interested in protecting themselves, one polemic advised, they should work toward making the Ostjuden in the East productive and prevent their entering Germany.[119] There were, to be sure, anti-Semitic circles which even early in the war made it clear that, while Fritz was correct in pointing out the dangers of an invasion by Ostjuden, emphasis on closing the borders distracted attention from the real inner danger, German Jewry itself. These sentiments were voiced in journals like the *Politisch-Anthropologische Monatsschrift*.[120] Nevertheless, until the infamous 1916 *Judenzählung*, the census of Jewish soldiers serving in the German army, the main thrust of the anti-Semitic attacks was against East European Jews.

How did these renewed attacks on the Ostjuden and the demand for Grenzschluss affect German Jewish attitudes? How did German Jewry respond to these demands? We have already seen that many liberal Jews sought to prevent the mass infiltration of Ostjuden into Germany. Men like Adolf Grabowsky, Kurt Alexander, and Willy Cohn regarded it as a significant threat to German Jewry's own security, perhaps even the reason for anti-Semitism. Even before the Grenzschluss agitation, Ludwig Geiger had warned of the dangers of postwar East European Jewish immigration into Germany.[121] Yet most liberal Jews energetically opposed attempts to create a special law *(Ausnahmegesetz)* that would apply exclusively to Jews, realizing that it would damage German Jewish interests and violate equal rights. Any law promulgated against Jews was dangerous to German Jewry. Even Kurt Alexander recognized the nature of radical Jewish interdependence here and castigated Fritz's remarks as being in effect also an attack on Western Jewry.[122]

Both a border closing and a mass Eastern Jewish presence in Germany were unacceptable to these circles. Ostjuden were to be discouraged from coming to Germany, but legislation to that effect would have to exclude the word *Jew* from the formulation. Thus the famous *Denkschrift*, prepared by Paul Nathan and Max Warburg on behalf of their Vereinigung and submitted to the German Foreign Office in October 1915, attempted to have the liberal cake and eat it too. Liberal accomplishments were to be protected by illiberal actions. Until Ostjuden raised their economic and cultural standards, they argued, there could be no freedom of movement into Germany. At the same time, however, legislation to this effect had to apply not only to Jews but to all Poles regardless of religion.[123]

The Grenzschluss question illuminated once again the ambiguities of the German Jewish liberal position. On the one hand, German Jews were extremely anxious about the effects of an "invasion," which they thought would inevitably occur after the war. Confidential memoranda advocating special institutions to regulate that traffic were circulated. "If we do not control the flow," read one warning, "we will be controlled by it."[124] At the same time, men like Ludwig Geiger and Felix Goldmann also bitterly attacked the calls for Grenzschluss. German Jews, they declared, did not need advice about "their own best interests" from anti-Semites, and in any case, legislation against particular religious groups was anathema to German notions of justice and the rule of law.[125] This was an ongoing tension. Most liberal Jews distinctly opposed the mass presence of Ostjuden in Germany, but few were prepared to prevent it by promulgating laws that explicitly singled out Jews. The conflict could be resolved by substituting the word *Pole* for *Jew*.

Members of the KfdO held similar convictions. They too were alarmed by the possibility of a postwar invasion of ghetto refugees and adamantly opposed the creation of a special "Jewish" law. Franz Oppenheimer typified their attitude in a private conversation in October 1915: it was "not in Jewish interests to see 200,000 schnorrers from the East coming into Germany," he said. The government should allow freedom of movement for the educated classes, "but the road to Germany must remain blocked for the caftan Jews."[126] The fear of Jewish conspicuousness remained. Yet Oppenheimer was a fearless critic of anti-Semitism, and when the Grenzschluss was indeed promulgated in April 1918, he was shocked and strongly condemned it, like many other German Jews. At the same time, he qualified his opposition in a private KfdO memorandum. It would be different, he wrote, if the law had been based upon "general cultural grounds" or upon protecting the German work force from foreign competition. Grenzschluss would be acceptable if it applied to all races and confessions.[127]

There was growing awareness, then, that legislation to exclude Eastern Jews could set a precedent and that the object of the anti-Semitic animus could be extended: the *Ostjudenfrage* could indeed easily be transformed into the *Westjudenfrage*.[128] The war amplified German Jewish recognition of Jewish interdependence.

Zionists, too, opposed closing the borders to Ostjuden. They bemoaned the embarrassing fact that their cause was enthusiastically championed by the anti-Semitic advocates of the Grenzschluss.[129] This was clearly an undesired alliance, one that was publicly disavowed. Privately, some Zionists recognized that such sentiments amongst ruling circles could indeed serve Zionist political aims.[130]

The most principled and aggressive opposition to the Grenzschluss, however, was contained in the pages of *Der Jude*. Significantly, the most impassioned pieces were penned by non-Zionists. Fritz Mordecai Kaufmann's scornful reply to the anti-Semites appeared in the journal of his Zionist political opponents. Another non-Zionist, Gustav Landauer, coupled his romantic defense of the Ostjuden with a critique of German Jews, arguing that the only dignified response to the anti-Semites was a contemptuous silence. Revolution, not apologetics, was the answer.[131] Perhaps the most unexpected contribution on this subject came from the intellectual leader of liberal Jewry, the neo-Kantian philosopher Hermann Cohen. Elsewhere Cohen publicly opposed the Grenzschluss, not only because the singling out of particular groups violated ethical norms, but also because Ostjuden exemplified many admirable spiritual qualities. Cohen's essay in *Der Jude* was important, for it came from the most prestigious liberal Jewish intellectual in Germany and was an endorsement of the argument that the presence of Ostjuden was compatible with the interests of German Jews.[132]

Yet Cohen raised questions about comparative East-West Jewish modes of being. He could not resist reiterating his conviction that German Judaism remained the historical ideal—an ideal worth emulating by Eastern Jews: "We free Jews, with the earnestness and the rapture of our monotheism, evince a sufficient vitality for modern religiosity. . . . We have managed to harmonize our history, as the continuance of our cult, with the innermost powers of both our religious tradition and our culture in general. . . . This unity, which the German Jew generally manifests in himself, has been lost—or, rather, was never attained—by the East European Jew."[133] The establishment of seminaries for the Science of Judaism was essential if Eastern Jews were to attain such unity, Cohen wrote. Only these German ingredients would purge *Ostjudentum* of its pre-Enlightenment characteristics and preserve Jewish religiosity in the proper manner. Once again it became apparent that Eastern Jews had to be remade in German Jewry's spiritual image.

Jewish groups and individuals opposed the Grenzschluss for a variety of reasons. All were shocked, however, when on April 23, 1918, at the urging of the Reich Chancellory and apparently without the participation or knowledge of the Foreign Office, the Prussian borders were closed specifically to Jewish workers.[134] This was justified on medical, not political, grounds. Jews were held to be the main carriers of typhus, which in Poland had reached epidemic proportions.[135] It is true that during the war, conditions amongst the Jews had so deteriorated that much of their resistance had disappeared. In a private correspondence, Julius Berger acknowledged as much.[136] Yet disinfecting and delousing measures at the German border were extremely effective. By early 1918 not a single case (amongst 150,000 handled) had been reported by the responsible German Jewish authorities.[137]

Jewish opponents of the measure argued that lice made no distinction between members of different religious confessions, but this missed the point. Underlying the decree were the swelling anti-Semitic sentiments accompanying the last few months of the war.[138] Hygiene was obviously the rationale, not the reason, for the order. The director of the Ministry of Interior, Otto Lewald, who was himself half-Jewish, expressed the real feelings behind the measure. They were classically consistent with the familiar stereotype. Jewish workers were "unwilling, unclean, morally unreliable." They used work as an excuse to insinuate themselves into Germany. Shortly thereafter they would leave their jobs, assemble in the great cities, and turn to crime.[139] The Grenzschluss was a tangible outcome of the encounter in the East and a foreshadowing of things to come.

Yet we cannot leave it at that, for the Grenzschluss refers only to the question of keeping Ostjuden out of Germany. It tells us little about the disposition of the war authorities in the East itself. Only by examining the direct encounter can a fair historical judgment of the meeting between ghetto Jewry and German authority be made. To what extent were Germany's military occupiers implicated in explicitly anti-Jewish actions?

GERMAN OCCUPATION AND *POLENPOLITIK*

A recent judgment argues that throughout the war "the German authorities treated the Jews in the Eastern Occupied Territories correctly. They abrogated the restrictions enforced under the Russian regime; elementary education was made compulsory without distinction of race or creed; secondary schools and universities were thrown open to Jewish students, whose admittance had been previously restricted by the notorious *numerus clausus*."[140] Sammy Gronemann's description of Ludendorff's attitudes during the war is vastly different from the anti-Semitic Ludendorff of the 1920s: "Ludendorff never revealed himself to be anything resembling an anti-Semite. On the contrary, he often proved that he knew how to appreciate Jewish help and cooperation and frequently and gladly made use of Jewish assistance. He fostered Jewish artists, conversed with them enthusiastically for hours and let them dedicate their works to him. He also stepped in more than once against anti-Semitic excesses. . . ."[141]

These judgments are important reminders not to impose simplistic post-facto explanations for German actions. The German army's proclamation promising liberation from tzarist oppression was not mere political opportunism. At times special efforts were even made on behalf of the East European Jews. A special department, for instance, was established allowing the distribution of Yiddish and Hebrew literature to Russian Jewish prisoners of war.[142] Certainly, in terms of political policy, what happened to the Jews was not primarily a matter of anti-Jewish sentiment; it was a function of Germany's Polish policy.

From the beginning of the war, the various sectors of German Jewry had attempted to influence the course of postwar Polish political development. The very intensity of this competition may ultimately have been responsible for their ineffectiveness. So many conflicting Jewish voices were heard that the authorities were provided with a built-in excuse for doing precisely as they wanted. One member of the Imperial Cabinet remarked contemptuously to Bodenheimer, "Every day some other representatives of the German Jews present themselves to me. One day it is James Simon and Dr. Nathan, then it is Herr Rosenheim of Frankfort and Rabbi Munk; and they maintain unanimously that the Zionists are without an influence in Eastern Europe. Whom shall I believe?" Similarly, the military governor of Lodz, General Sauberzweig, asked, "With whom are we to negotiate about the future of the Jews in Poland? They have no authorized representation. Is it the Hilfsverein or is it the Zionists?"[143]

It is true that with the outbreak of hostilities, the authorities found the KfdO's advocacy of Jewish national autonomy in the German national interest.[144] Ostjuden would be the vanguard for *Deutschtum* in the East. Hindenburg himself expressed his willingness to further the aims of the KfdO.[145] Support for a solution to the East European Jewish problem, moreover, in line with Karl Renner's philosophy of autonomy for national minorities, came from a wide variety of political interests in Germany itself.[146] With the government decree of November 1916, however, all hope for national autonomy was lost, for while political recognition was given to Polish Jewry, it was defined as a religious group. The Jewish question had always been subservient to Germany's *Polenpolitik*, and it was on this level that political policy was made.

But political policy was only one dimension of the meeting. It was on the level of daily contact, of relationships in the field, that perceptions were shaped and that the strange encounter assumed reality. This was the forum that forged attitudes critical to the postwar *Judenfrage*, and it was here that the nature of relations could most easily be gauged.

By early 1916 it was evident that a gulf of fear and hostility separated Eastern Jews from their German occupiers. What caused this gulf? It is clear that it was not all a product of anti-Jewish sentiment. Part can be traced to feelings of mutual incomprehensibility. As critics of the KfdO had predicted, the propaganda emphasizing the relation between Yiddish and German only exacerbated the problems of the Ostjuden. (In early 1915 similar propaganda distributed by the German and Austrian High Command had provided the Russians with an excuse for mass deportations of Jews from the war zone.)[147] Not only were Polish-Jewish relations worsened, but also the so-called alliance between German and Yiddish highlighted German–Eastern Jewish differences. Misunderstandings abounded: words that had meant one thing in medieval German, and thus retained their meaning in Yiddish, assumed radically altered meanings in modern German.[148] The traditional German Jewish embarrassment seemed to be vindicated: exposure to the *Jargon* reinforced the notion that Yiddish was indeed a lowly bastardized German. The experience overwhelmed the propaganda. Moreover, as Julius Berger noted, these perceptions were generalized to describe the Jewish people itself.[149] Carriers of a degenerate language were themselves degenerate. Even Max Bodenheimer saw on his 1915 tour of the occupied Eastern territories that officers regarded Yiddish in exactly the opposite way from that which he had desired.[150]

Bodenheimer's report indicates the level of estrangement and hostility that developed early on. The high prices that Jews were asking for their goods, he reported, led to the impression that all Jews were dishonest. As a result, the authorities were developing a generalized antipathy to the population as a whole.[151] In an attempt to counteract this trend, the KfdO pressed for the appointment of German Jewish officials able to mediate between the two groups. As one report stated, such people could make the strange ways of the Ostjuden comprehensible to the authorities and at the same time could win the Ostjuden over to loyalty to Germany.[152] Eventually Ludwig Haas, a member of the Reichstag, was appointed head of the Jewish department in the German civil administration of Poland. More often than not, however, this compounded rather than resolved the problem. A man of great personal integrity and political acumen, Haas was nevertheless quite unsuited to the task. He was an assimilated Jew and had no sympathy or understanding for the folk dimension of Jewish life.[153] As his daughter reports, the Ostjuden were as alien to him as those to whom he had to mediate their world.[154] Franz Rosenzweig was alarmed: "The idea of this man's being allowed to play the part of destiny for the Polish Jews," he wrote, "is a ghastly one. . . ."[155] Precisely because he acted as a *German* Jew, Haas was acutely sensitive about matters that were potentially unsettling to the German Jewish image. At official Interior Ministry meetings about the border closing he maintained a stolid silence. Participants in these meetings expressed surprise that the only Jewish participant and official representative of Polish Jewish interests did not even express an opinion on the subject.[156] It is not inconceivable that Haas's later support for East European Zionist settlement in Palestine was related to his fear of a large migration of Ostjuden into Germany.[157]

The German administration simply had not been prepared to deal with a Jewish national entity as they had been with the Poles. Moreover, the constant presentation of Ostjuden as embryonic Germans made it easier to take them for granted. The supposed symbiosis, however, made cultural differences even more obvious. The German penchant for order consistently clashed with the chaotic spontaneity of East European Jewish life. Ostjuden themselves joked that "the Germans had indeed brought order to Poland. Whereas before there was corn . . . now there is order; whereas before there were oxen . . . now there is order."[158] Even more archetypal was the confrontation over cleanliness. The much-praised sanitary relief was done in extremely harsh ways. In the early hours of bitter winter mornings, children and the aged and sick were driven to the baths. One Vilna resident caustically noted in his diary, "To become sick—but to be clean."[159] It became increasingly evident, however, that these were not merely cultural misunderstandings. Jews were regularly treated with greater harshness than the local Polish population,[160] and by the end of the war most Jewish observers agreed that the rift was, to a great extent, the product of plain anti-Semitic bias running through the ranks of both the army and occupation officials. No proper evaluation of the record can omit this factor; if it does not tell all of the story it nevertheless reveals a very important part of it.

Well before others saw this reality, Julius Berger was privately voicing his great despair. Events in Lithuania, he wrote in September 1916, were "unheard of, atrocious, . . . so shocking." Printed official reports of the administration were being circulated to the effect that the Jews should be forced to leave the country "because they were morally degenerate and an injurious element for the state. And this is said about Lithuanian Jews . . . who stand on a far higher level than the Polish Jews." The Germans, he wrote, were even more cynical and vehement about the Jews than the Russian government had ever been. Berger's letter concluded on a disturbingly prescient note: ". . . anti-Semitism is growing, growing against the Eastern Jews and growing against the Western Jews, growing enormously and preparing for a real orgy that will be celebrated after the war."[161]

Berger's perceptions were no doubt influenced by his Zionist and Social Democratic predispositions, but they were later shared by leaders of all sectors of German Jewry. There were different theories about the sources of this policy, however. Rabbi Carlebach, for instance, after conversations with Paul Nathan and members of the KfdO, concluded that anti-Semitic incidents could be attributed to specific individuals and not to any systematic policy.[162] When confronted by Jewish leaders, Gerhard von Mutius, representative of the German Foreign Office in Warsaw, did not deny that many officials came from Germany with anti-Semitic sentiments. Contact with the peculiar ways of the Ostjuden had provided the occasion to express these sentiments. But did one expect, he asked, that each German official would be provided with a special course of lectures explaining the strange world of the Ostjuden before being sent to the East?[163]

The bitter postwar reality of East European Jews—economic devastation and heightened anti-Semitic outbursts—led to the mass migrations into Germany that had been so feared during the war. Yet the feared migration was in no small degree begun by the Germans themselves during the war, by means of the policy of forced labor. Even when Jews signed up voluntarily for work in Germany they were often sent to forced labor units instead.[164] Thousands of Jews were transferred to Germany through this system. Although the decision to revoke forced labor was made soon after its official authorization in October 1916, the practice continued unofficially. As late as the end of 1917 Vilna Jews were still being removed at night and taken for forced labor.[165]

This policy significantly affected the disposition of postwar German anti-Semitism and the position of German Jewry itself. Over the course of the war tens of thousands of unemployed Eastern Jewish workers were brought to Germany, more or less forcefully, to work in war production. Thus through official German actions, the feared Eastern Jewish invasion had become a reality.

OSTJUDEN, ANTI-SEMITISM, AND THE NEW GERMAN JEWISH CONSCIOUSNESS

As the war drew to a close, many German Jews realized that the links with their fellow Germans had become increasingly fragile and tenuous. The infamous Jewish census of 1916 and the undisguised animus frequently directed at German Jews thereafter had much to do with the renewed wariness. These also increased their sensitivity to German treatment of the Ostjuden. A disillusioned Franz Oppenheimer wrote in October 1917 that, even taking into consideration the mitigating factors of the difficulties of war and the confusions that stemmed from cultural differences, Germany's treatment of the Ostjude was "totally lacking in goodwill, justice, and humanity." The country would be burdened for years with the account of its actions.[166]

By war's end, organized German Jewry had arrived at a new consensus; at the heart of this agreement was the question of the Eastern Jews. Paradoxically, the same problem that had politicized German Jewry at the outset of the war and been the occasion for division now became focus and symbol of a newly forged unity. The creation of the United Jewish Organizations of Germany (Vereinigung jüdischer Organisationen Deutschlands; VJOD) in 1918 was a direct consequence of German Jewry's concern with the Eastern Jewish question. The full name of the organization was VJOD zur Wahrung der Rechte der Juden des Ostens (VJOD for the Protection of the Rights of the Jews of the East). The leaders of Jewry—Eugen Fuchs, Paul Nathan, and Franz Oppenheimer—all regarded the unity that had been achieved over the Ostjuden as a symbol of a new era for German Jewry itself.[167]

What was the basis of this newfound agreement? In effect, it was a compromise between the liberal and moderate Zionist positions. Eastern Jews, like other citizens, were to be granted the right to free immigration, including to Palestine. In Eastern Europe they were to receive full emancipation (*Gleichberechtigung*), combined with the right to maintain their independent Jewish culture. To be sure, this did not accord with the more radical Zionist demands for political as well as cultural autonomy. But the committee was formed too late in the war to have any real effect on German policy in any case. Moreover, by then it had already become clear that the VJOD would be less concerned with the *Ostjudenfrage* in the East than it was with the same question—as well as the *Westjudenfrage*—in Germany itself. The central focus had shifted back to Germany once again. Both *Der Jude* and the *Jüdische Rundschau* endorsed the VJOD because of its opposition to the Grenzschluss, not because they supported its solution to the Eastern Jewish problem.[168] The *Rundschau* articulated a mute impulse behind the founding of the VJOD: the Grenzschluss was merely a pretext; the German Jews were the real targets of the anti-Semitic attack. "We Jews, not the Ostjuden, are the ones—we are dangerous for the country or its hygiene or its morals."[169]

Rising anti-Semitism produced a feeling of greater Jewish solidarity. The war crystallized and institutionalized a common approach to the Eastern Jewish question. For all that, the identification with the Ostjude remained encased in a basically negative frame. It was not so much contact with the Ostjude as the renewed attack upon him that aroused the concern of organized German Jewry. While interdependence was recognized, the essential division between modern Western and Eastern ghetto Jews remained. German Jewish efforts on behalf of the Easterners were still justified on the basis of this differentiation. As Franz Oppenheimer argued, German Jews had a right to be interested in Eastern Jews as "Jews, as Germans, as German Jews, as Jewish Germans, and simply as human beings."[170] The war had hardly simplified the German Jewish relationship to the Ostjude!

But for a small though significant minority, the encounter with Eastern Jews at the Front resulted in far less qualified definitions of the relationship than Oppenheimer would allow. The war dramatically enlarged the scope and magnitude of the cult of the Ostjuden. An examination of the modes, moods, nuances, strengths, weaknesses, and assumptions of that cult reveals an interesting side chapter in Jewish cultural history. It also provides a glimpse into a changing German Jewish disposition as it developed through the critical juncture of World War I and its immediate Weimar aftermath.

8

THE CULT OF
THE OSTJUDEN
The War and Beyond

ALL Western attempts to recapture Jewish roots had to come to grips with Eastern Jewish being. However one regarded the Ostjude, all agreed that he was the embodiment of archetypal Jewish characteristics, the living link in an uninterrupted historical chain of tradition. In this sense, the glorification of the Eastern Jew was always a potential, if slight, element in Western Jewish self-understanding, the positive side of a built-in ambivalence. As early as 1822, Heinrich Heine voiced, along with his negative perceptions, the essence of what many years later was to become the cult of the Ostjuden. The appearance of Polish Jews, he wrote after a visit to a typical Jewish village, was "frightful . . . the nausea I felt at the sight of these ragged, filthy creatures." They lived in "pig-sties . . . jabbered, prayed and haggled." Their language was repellent, and their intellectual outlook had degenerated into "revolting superstition. . . . Yet in spite of the barbarous fur cap which covers his head, and the still more barbarous notions which fill it, I esteem the Polish Jew more highly than his German counterpart, even though the latter wear a beaver on his head and carry Jean Paul in it. As a result of rigorous isolation, the character of the Polish Jew acquired a oneness. . . . The inner man did not degenerate into a haphazard conglomeration of feelings. . . . The Polish Jew, with his dirty fur cap, vermin-infested beard, smell of garlic, and his jabber is certainly preferable to many other Jews I know who shine with the magnificence of gilt-edged government bonds."[1]

Polish rabbi. Original etching by Hermann Struck, from *Ost und West*, 1901, no. 9.

Heine's remarks captured the basic ingredients of all future German celebrations of East European Jewry (although these often lacked his qualifying realism). The charm of the Eastern Jew consisted in his "authenticity." As early as Heine's time, Ostjuden could symbolize premodern, unfragmented "wholeness." Heine, moreover, foreshadowed the tendency to base the elevation of the Eastern Jew upon criticism of the Western Jew; the cult of the Ostjude always proceeded from a comparative East-West Jewish analysis. The Ostjude was a foil for the presentation of the Western Jew as shallow, imitative, and assimilating. Beginning with Heine, the East-West evaluation was almost always derived from predominantly antibourgeois sentiments.

Of course Heine's attitudes did not become the norm for German Jewry. How could they? Nineteenth-century German Jewish emancipation was achieved very largely through embourgeoisement. The positive perception of the Ostjude, wherever it existed, was siphoned off into unthreatening philanthropic activity. We have already seen that the counter-myth of the Ostjude was possible only under different, later conditions: the rise of political anti-Semitism and the Zionist movement, fin-de-siècle neoromanticism, and post-assimilationist Jewish consciousness. Even for participants, however, the pre-1914 Ostjuden cult was more a mood, a literary feeling, than an attempt to establish real contact with the ghetto masses and put into practice theoretical notions of East-West Jewish symbiosis. As Hugo Bergmann noted in 1915, in fact, the few circles that had venerated the Ostjude ceased to do so before the war began.[2]

World War 1 radically changed all this. For committed German Jews it put the East-West Jewish relationship to a practical test. The ghetto could no longer be admired from a safe geographical distance. The war provided a new context; personal contact could not be avoided. The question of the Ostjuden now became an existential touchstone of national commitment. For many, the exposure to Eastern Jews converted a political question into a private turning point, a watershed in their personal and ideological histories.

Physical confrontation with Eastern Jewish life was not the only aspect of the cult that distinguished it from earlier versions. There was also the matter of scale. The encounter at the front involved thousands of German Jews. It is not surprising that a great many of the fighting Zionist youth were swept up in the euphoria, and there can be little doubt that it was they who were at the forefront of this discovery and glorification of the Ostjuden. But the experience was not limited to Zionists. A number of young Orthodox German Jews were equally influenced and formulated their own version of glorification. Certain Jewish intellectuals who were neither Zionist nor Orthodox but increasingly dissatisfied with the prevailing liberal conventional wisdom also discovered the world of Eastern Jewry anew.

Jews with a nationalist predisposition were naturally the most enthusiastic. Young Zionists at the Front confronted for the first time Ostjuden in their own villages and not as uprooted refugees or transplanted intellectuals. Journals and letters home were filled with reports about this novel experience. Salli Hirsch's remarks were typical:

> We always knew of course that there in Lithuania, Poland, Galicia lived the Jewish masses and that they were essential for the construction of our new national community; we were always clear, in theory, that we were one with them, but in fact we were worlds apart. . . . It took the war to bring us to them, and amazed, we stand in their midst and cry: "So, something like this really exists!" Of course we negate the Golus and the conditions under which the Ostjuden live, but we cannot ignore them. . . . We cannot be leaders of the Volk and remain distant from the Volk. An inner contact with the Ostjuden is vital, an inner contact with the Jewish people will also serve to make us more Jewish. Only the Jewish masses in the East strike me as Jewish. The few members of the Jewish people in Western Europe possess no living Jewish actuality.[3]

This reciprocal moment—when Western leadership and material aid would be given to the Ostjuden in exchange for spiritual rejuvenation and reappropriation of Jewish content—became the leitmotif of the movement. Yet even pretensions to leadership were made increasingly insecure by the growing recognition of German Jewish inadequacy. Personal contact raised serious questions of self-definition. For one participant, the encounter was a process of "unlearning." The longer the war's duration, he maintained, the closer did German Jews get to their Eastern brothers. In this process, cognitive spectacles and national emotions were exchanged: "The touchstone of this was our attitude to political events. . . . in German uniforms we saw the *Judenpolitik* of the administration through the eyes of the Jews. At that moment we became clear about ourselves."[4]

Until the war, most Zionists knew the world of the Eastern Jew only through German translations of Hebrew and Yiddish works. Many now perceived it through such literary eyes, a confirmation

that life in the East was a kind of Jewish cultural wonderland.
"There I was suddenly in that yonder world related by Peretz and
Asch, Shalom Aleichem and Mendele Mocher S'farim. . . . How
much I would have loved to remain in these small shtetls . . . and
live with these simple, unadulterated Jews."[5] While literature did
indeed channel perceptions, the impact of the confrontation was
great precisely because of its immediacy. As another put it, only now
was it revealed "with what heated passion I love my people and my
Judaism, and here it became for the first time clear how unshakea-
bly my destiny was linked with that of my people."[6] For those open
to its influence, direct participation in Eastern Jewish culture was an
overwhelming experience. Common celebrations of the Jewish sabbath and festivals and fervent singing and dancing of Hasidic
melodies produced moments of ecstatic identification. The artist
Hermann Struck argued that this *Erlebnis* was worth more than a
thousand printed works.[7]

Paradoxically, it was the "normalcy" of Jewish life in the ghetto
that impressed many German Jews. Observers were stunned to see
Jews unselfconsciously living Jewish lives in the same way that other
"normal" cultures did.[8] Despite oppression and persecution in the
East, the psychological fragmentation besetting the Western Jew was
absent. Here there was no antithesis between being a member of the
human race and being a Jew—one flowed into the other.

Of course, these "discoveries" were facilitated and channeled by
an already existing Zionist predisposition. Right at the beginning of
the war, Zionist editorials proclaimed that this was the historic
opportunity for reversing German Jewry's self-imposed assimilationist isolation from Eastern Jewry. By October 1914 the *Jüdische
Rundschau* pronounced that the change was already taking place:
"The barriers that for centuries have divided East from West have
already fallen. . . . What a century has destroyed will take only a few
decades to repair."[9]

The mood was euphoric. In the early stages of the war only a few
young Zionists tried to examine these assumptions realistically.
Ironically, it took a Czech Zionist, Hugo Bergmann, to put the
confrontation of German Jews with Eastern Jews in a different
perspective. The war, he wrote to Buber, revealed not so much the
affinity between Jew and Jew as it did German Jewry's real attachment to *Deutschtum*. "And now, since we have fought for German
culture, we feel more than ever what that culture is to us and how
our entire being is steeped in it. . . . Only because we have Fichte
could we discover the corresponding streams of Jewish culture and

understand Judaism. . . . But then we can only enter Jewish cultural
life as Germans, and I painfully ask, Where is the community that
has a place for us?"[10]

Bergmann had identified the central problem of the growing
Ostjuden cult. The paradox of the German Zionist revolt against
German culture was that the revolt itself was couched in deeply
German terms. In many ways the cult reflected this. The difficulties
of establishing an East-West Jewish community along new Jewish
cultural lines remained unresolved. The glorification of Eastern
Jews was simultaneously a challenge to and a demonstration of the
tenacity of German cultural assumptions among even the most
radically committed German Jews.

Adherents of the cult argued that German Zionists could achieve a
living relationship with the Volk only through exposure to the
Eastern Jews. They proposed organized tours and periods of residence in ghetto areas, which would have the effect of creating "whole
Jews."[11] Some enthusiasts expressed themselves in maudlin rhetoric
dripping with Freudian allusions. One commentator, G. Wollstein,
criticized traditional paternalist attitudes to the Ostjuden and proposed that "we go to them as pupils, as supplicants, as people who
realize that their life is purposeless and after decades of wandering
astray seek peace at the mother's breast, who want to find their way
back to life after realizing that until now they have led a life that was
not a life and which led directly to Jewish death."[12] For this task of
cultural transplantation, a tremendous will was necessary, but it was
clear that salvation of the Jewish people would not come from the
West.

Although not all devotees of the cult shared this degree of German
Jewish self-rejection, the enthusiasm for the Ostjude served as a
means and measure for a radical critique of German Jewish life.
Wollstein's remarks did capture this mood. Dissatisfaction with the
modes of middle-class Jewish life was marked. So distrustful was
Wollstein that he proposed, in order to prevent the "Berlinization"
of the future Jewish state, that German Jews should marry only
Eastern Jews and that they should refrain from writing in Hebrew
journals, for such contributions would consist of Jewish words but
German spirit. Wollstein was not an isolated case. Other Zionists
called for the creation of "voluntary ghettoes." Children of German
Jews had to be isolated until they felt "totally Jewish." Only then
should the doors of European civilization be opened to them. The
writer admitted that this would be ethnocentric but argued that given
the distortions of post-Emancipation Western Jewish life, it was a

necessary precondition for the recovery of a normal relation to the self.[13]

Even amongst Zionists whose opinions were less extreme, the cult of the Ostjuden was one important expression of the rebellion of German Jewish youth against German Jewish bourgeois life. Middle-class smugness and shallowness were rejected. Eastern Jews were seen as a genuine national proletariat, authentic embodiments of a proud tradition, foil to everything that these young Jews disliked in their own homes. The antibourgeois rhetoric was coupled with generational conflict. At times it became identical with the rejection of the father, the home in which one was raised. In such instances the Ostjuden functioned as a kind of symbolic surrogate family. In some cases, as we shall see, the function became real and not merely symbolic. There was a delicious irony in this: whereas before, German Jews had been shamed by the presence of their cousins from the East, their own children were now profoundly embarrassed by the affluence and philistinism of their parents and looked East for a source of renewed pride. The great problem of Jewish life, bemoaned one Zionist, was the fact that all Jews were judged by the behavior of a small bourgeoisie.[14] The cult of the Ostjuden was one way of attempting to escape this damning judgment by association. According to this theory, identification with the Ostjude—of all figures—was an avenue of *escape* from the Jewish stereotype! Socialist Zionists argued that the presence in postwar Germany of a laboring Jewish proletariat could transform traditional prejudices and demonstrate that not all Jews were unproductive capitalists.[15]

Like so many other dissident movements of the time, the cult was overwhelmingly a movement of the young.[16] The respect for the Eastern Jew, the disaffection from middle-class conventions, and the revolt against the father were all interlinked. Franz Kafka's *Letter to His Father* (1919) is only the most famous articulation of a mood that went well beyond the author's idiosyncracies and the confines of Prague.[17] For Zionists like Max Meyer, the glorification of the Ostjude was both cause and effect of the revolt against the assimilated bourgeois standards of his home.[18] Parental antipathy to East European Jewish ways merely made the Ostjuden more attractive to rebelling Zionist youth.

When in early 1917 Gershom Scholem was thrown out of his home as a result of his antiwar activities (his father regarded Zionism, like Social Democracy, as an antipatriotic force) he found refuge in a boarding house—the Pension Struck—inhabited almost entirely by modern, intellectual Eastern Jews. This was a case in which the

Ostjuden literally became new family. One of the lodgers, Zalman Rubaschoff—later Shazar, president of the state of Israel—playfully called Scholem "a martyr of Zionism." Scholem was the only German Jew in the house, and this was a critical period in his intellectual development. Surrounded by men like Rubaschoff and Samuel Agnon, he came to know Jewish culture from the inside. For young assimilated Jews, Scholem reminisces, these men were akin to "a reincarnation of the Baal Shem Tov," embodiments of deepest Jewish being.[19]

At least in theory, such rebellions entailed a process of socialization in Jewish cultural sources. At the same time there was an implied reevaluation of one's relationship with German culture. Thus those who related seriously to Jewish languages had little sympathy with the war fashion that linked German and Yiddish in an indissoluble cultural and historical relationship. On the contrary, the value and significance of Yiddish was precisely that it was different from German. Scholem's scathing review attacking Alexander Eliasberg's German translations of Yiddish works illustrates this attitude.[20] Judaism's spiritual order, wrote Scholem, was inextricably tied to Hebrew. This double layer made Yiddish particularly difficult to translate. The religious substructure of Yiddish remained rooted in Hebrew. Words like *Tora* could be approximated only very roughly in German. Jewish worship was, by definition, a collective act, and to translate *minyan* as *Privatgottesdienst* was absurd. So, too, was the translation of the ritual *mikwe* to mean "bath." To render the Hasidic *Zaddik* as *Wunderrabbi* was perhaps suitable for works by Franzos but totally misrepresented the world of Peretz. The "cold, objective" Western outlook had been imposed upon a world saturated with fundamentally different meanings and experience. Translations like these only increased the incommensurability.[21]

Of course, the reevaluation of European and German standards grew more prevalent as the brutalizing effects of the war became more and more evident. Disenchantment with Europe's civilizing and humanizing character was widespread. This mood, of course, made the cult of the Ostjuden more attractive and also more plausible. Assertions about Western progress and Eastern primitivism no longer carried their former force. Nathan Birnbaum's *Gottes Volk* (1918) held that after the horrors of the war, secular values were deeply undermined. The West was no longer in a position to cast aspersions on traditional Eastern Jewry, whose chosen task it was to demonstrate the eternity of Israel as God's holy nation. These critiques were not the monopoly of an antisecular crusade. *Der Jude* also joined the attack. In an article entitled "Modernity and Primitiveness," the theme was made aggressively clear. Why did one equate modernity with spiritual progress? Modern Europe was obsessed with causality, but this preoccupation with the technical was dehumanizing: "The hegemony of causality is the most elemental primitiveness, is bestiality." In effect it was Western technical man who was primitive. This was the way in which the Ostjude, whose soul was still linked to God, looked upon his West European brother.[22]

Such was the mood of many increasingly disaffected Jewish youth. But for a small though interesting and influential minority, the cult of the Ostjuden went beyond the realm of sentiment and opinion. For them, the war presented a chance to rejuvenate the idea of East-West Jewish community in a tangible way. With the influx of war refugees, notably children, there was an immense practical need for educational, occupational, and social welfare work. This provided an opportunity to transform theory into practice. Such practical work was, indeed, a new element of the cult, and in many ways forced its adherents to view their theories more realistically. The experience of the new institutions through which they worked gives us the means to judge not only the noble intentions but also the weaknesses of the movement. Between 1915 and 1923 in Czechoslovakia and Austria as well as in Germany, a number of such institutions were created under radical Zionist auspices. The old philanthropy gave way to a strange amalgam of practical social work and, at times, naïve cultural experimentation.[23]

These activities were most evident in Berlin's Jüdische Volksheim. There all the main ideological currents of the cult converged. Within its walls, the moods, strengths and illusions of the movement were most clearly revealed. The product of a small, dissenting Zionist minority, it represented an attempt in microcosm to reshape the nature of Jewish life. Although it was clearly limited to a small circle, its intellectual significance was increased by the fact that people of the caliber of Martin Buber, Franz Kafka, S. Y. Agnon, and Chaim Arlosoroff were involved, at varying levels of intensity, in its educational programming and activities.

The Volksheim was opened in the ghetto section of Berlin (Dragonerstrasse 22) on May 18, 1916. In that year it had a daily enrollment of about 250 pupils, divided into subgroups ranging in age from preschool years through sixteen. It attempted to combine education with welfare, play with productive work. Music, art, and manual workshops were part of the daily diet. All activities were guided by the notion of voluntary community cooperation. The leaders were young, idealistic, middle-class German Zionists and the students mostly Eastern Jewish children.[24]

Siegfried Lehmann (1892–1958) was the moving force behind the Volksheim, its major practitioner and principal ideologue. Without his initiative, it would never have come about. Although he also considered himself a theoretician, his main talents lay in the practical educational field. Apart from founding the Volksheim, he established a home based on similar principles in Kowno in 1921, and he founded the deservedly renowned educational village of Ben Shemen in Palestine in 1927.[25]

Lehmann derived his conception of the Volksheim from various sources. His notions of Jewish renaissance were based on Buber, to whom he wrote, "Without your work, the Home was unthinkable."[26] Much of the pedagogic theory was borrowed from Ernst Joël's ideas of "settlements."[27] These were the frameworks Joël advocated for the realization of his libertarian, socialist ideals of youth culture. Such "Jewish" and pedagogic ideas were integrated into a general philosophy of community, which as Lehmann proudly acknowledged, was clearly inspired by Gustav Landauer.[28] The relation between Buber, Joël, and Landauer was not one of mere accidental ideological affinity. Buber and Landauer were close friends. Both Landauer and Joël were active members of the small, radical Aufbruch circle which met in Berlin in 1915–16. This group advocated ideas that later characterized the Volksheim: literary expressionism and German romanticism, combined with notions of socialist community and humanist nationalism.[29]

Although he was not a Zionist, it was appropriate that Landauer open the Volksheim in 1916 with his talk "Judaism and Socialism."[30] His idea of *Gemeinschaft*, community as a cooperative project based not upon party socialism but upon ethical and spiritual foundations, became the cornerstone of the Volksheim's attempts to create an antiauthoritarian, voluntaristic community. But his affinity to the Home's aims went even further. Landauer, unlike many other socialists, "did not invoke humanity so much as a humanitarian concept of the Volk."[31] He did not juxtapose Volk against humanity in the tradition of the orthodox Left, nor did he propose a nationalism that shared the chauvinism of the Right. Rather, each people, including the Jewish people, should contribute to humanity through its particular cultural and historical genius. Not only were Judaism and socialism compatible, they were necessary partners.

Lehmann incorporated all of these ideas into the theory and practice of the Volksheim. The Volksheim, he proposed, would be the vanguard of socialism amongst the Jewish people, nucleus of the process that would transform both Eastern and Western Jewish youth.[32] Ostjuden, on the one hand, would receive urgently needed practical training and "unlearn" their ghetto past so that they could participate in the growth of a healthy Volkish way of life: "The Eastern Jewish children will learn from us . . . the joy of the sun and the flowers, love for beauty and uprightness."[33] The stress on productive manual and agricultural occupations would ensure that these children would "not end up as dejudaised bourgeois in Berlin West."[34]

Such convictions may have sounded a familiar patronizing note, but this was compensated for by the fact that Lehmann always stressed the need of mutual transformation. German Jews were to be the receivers as much as they were to be the givers. If anything, the new community was more important for the assimilated German Jewish youth. The experience it offered was a precondition for the return to their own people, a basis for gaining even an elementary understanding of the Jewish masses.[35] Only through unmediated exposure to the Ostjuden would alienated Jews learn the meaning of noninstrumental values, religious subjectivity, lost Jewish modes of being. The *Volksheimidee* proposed nothing less than mutual East-West Jewish transformation. Lehmann differed with Landauer, however, on the question of Zionism. While Landauer remained "a consistent cosmopolitan nationalist,"[36] Lehmann believed that only in Palestine could this transformation be achieved and true anti-bourgeois community realized.[37]

Lehmann's romantic, even mystical nationalism and his passionate search for renewed East-West Jewish community were merely an extreme theoretical expression of the general quest for community and experience (*Erlebnis*) that characterized this generation of German Jewish youth. The Volksheim provided a focus for their energies, and many of its adherents shared in the ideological and spiritual ferment of the time. The example of Erich Gutkind (1877–1965) is instructive. Gutkind's family belonged to the wealthiest section of German Jewry and were neighbors of the Rathenau's. Like many of his contemporaries Gutkind was deeply attracted to mysticism, although not of the Jewish kind, and came very close to converting to Catholicism. Yet in 1916 he experienced a Jewish "reawakening" and (what would have been unthinkable only a few years before) became leader of the Volksheim in 1919.[38] People like

Gutkind believed that they were engaged in a noble, radical experiment at whose center lay real *Erlebnis*. The sensation of "true community" was pervasive.[39]

The feeling of dynamism and excitement was enhanced by the addresses and debates scheduled regularly at the Volksheim. Fritz Mordecai Kaufmann first presented his talk "The Western Jewish Conflict" to its leaders, and on other occasions, Ludwig Strauss, Buber, and Agnon were among the guest speakers. The attempt at community with "the Volk" satisfied real emotional and intellectual needs.

Yet the Volksheim also highlighted the problems attendant upon the creation of East-West Jewish cultural community. From the outset the relationship was based upon different needs.[40] The most urgent task for the Eastern children was to acquire cultural and occupational skills that they would need to begin their new lives. Their German leaders, on the other hand, were often lost in misty, neoromantic preoccupation. In the eyes of some outside observers, the modish intellectualism of the Volksheim appeared somewhat ridiculous. For Gershom Scholem, it represented an easy escape from Jewish content and serious study in the name of a vapid *Erlebnis*. The atmosphere, as Scholem recalls it, was one of contrived aesthetic ecstasy. In highly manneristic poses, the volunteers and visitors would listen to Lehmann recite passages from such works as Franz Werfel's poem "Conversation at the Paradise Wall."[41]

The return to Jewish sources took a peculiarly German cultural route. Scholem was not the only one to notice this ideological inconsistency. A sobered participant later reminisced how, in the middle of Berlin, East European Jewish youth who spoke hardly a word of German were fed large doses of the poetry and ideas of that arch-German cultural patrician Stefan George.[42] The debates about whether or not to hang up a reproduction of a famous portrait of the Virgin Mary must have sounded exceedingly strange to Eastern Jews raised in traditional and Orthodox homes. These questions were discussed in the framework of Buberian notions of Jewish renaissance where all things were held to be "open." Still, leaders of the Volksheim were aware of the problem, and debated whether or not their ideas were too threatening to the outlook of pupils whose background and inclinations were so different.[43]

The Volksheim's cultural bias bore out the fact that the Ostjuden received rather than provided "the sparks." This tended to contradict Lehmann's symbiotic conception in which Eastern Jewish modernization would be accompanied by increasing Jewishness for Western Jews. The reason was not merely that the German Jewish revolt took place in extremely German cultural ways and that German Jews were, quite simply, German cultural products. In a letter to Lehmann written in 1915, Landauer put his finger on some of the cultural limitations of the cult. The idea that Ostjuden would be the "giving" partner in the relationship, he wrote even before the Volksheim was opened, was based on an aesthetic and lazy form of folkloristic nationalism. The German-Jewish contribution to the Ostjuden lay in European culture. Doctrinaire denial of this proposition would result only in the repression of German Jewry's best qualities.[44]

The Volksheim did not contribute in great measure to the nascent Jewish cultural revival; its importance lay in the heightened sense of East-West community that its members believed they had achieved. Since it was clearly a product of the radical spirit of the age, it is not surprising that in the calmer post-1923 Weimar atmosphere the Volksheim was split into various components and its functions taken over by different welfare agencies. As one participant later remarked, "The real Volksheim is as unrepeatable as our own youths."[45]

Whatever the cultural results of these East-West meetings, there can be little doubt that the radical mood was vital in the attempt to create basically equal relationships between Eastern and Western Zionist intellectuals in Germany. These Jews were linked by a peculiarly spiritual conception of socialism, often mined from Jewish sources, that served to make East-West differences somehow obsolete. Nothing illustrates the nature of this radical mood better than the Safed (Zwat) society formed in 1918, as Buber formulated it, to resist the *Ungeist* in Zionism.[46] Its membership consisted of elite young German and East European Zionists. Participants included Zalman Rubaschoff and Gershom Scholem, Nahum Goldmann and Ludwig Strauss, Martin Buber and Arnold Zweig, Aron Eliasberg and Julius Berger. The society's minutes provide a fascinating glimpse of the expectations of the time. The basic drive was to synthesize radical ideas and Jewish sources. Thus Rubaschoff's paper "Marx as a Jew" insisted that despite Marx's anti-Jewish sentiments, his belief in ultimate good and the realization of justice as part of the general scheme of things was a restatement of the central ideas of Judaism itself: "No caprice in history, rather eternal Law . . . based on ethical foundations. Marxism manifests these Jewish ideas: the redemption of the world. For the first time, in

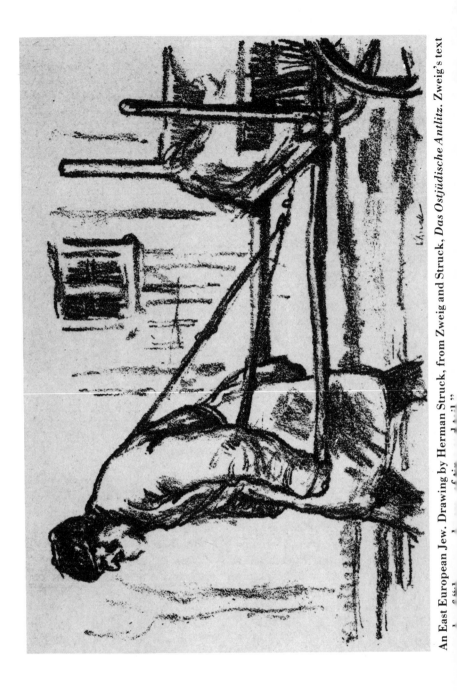

An East European Jew. Drawing by Herman Struck, from Zweig and Struck, *Das Ostjüdische Antlitz. Zweig's text*

different garb, victory of the Jewish spirit in the non-Jewish world!"[47]

This was essentially a Kantian form of socialism that from Rubaschoff's perspective had its roots in the prophetic and messianic strains of Judaism.[48] Like many other left-wing Jewish intellectuals of the time, Rubaschoff was more concerned with the ethical and humanistic dimensions of socialism than with the economic and political details of the restructuring of society.

This clearly socialist direction distinguished the postwar Zionist cult of the Ostjuden from the prewar version. Zionist rhetoric, Eastern Jews, and socialism were melded into a new whole. Arnold Zweig (1887–1968) epitomized this strain. In 1919, with the publication of his *Das ostjüdische Antlitz (The Eastern Jewish Countenance)*, the radical glorification of the Ostjude reached its height. The work was important, because it accompanied illustrations of East European types drawn by the well-known Jewish artist Hermann Struck during the war. Handsomely produced, designed for the coffee table, Struck's portraits inverted the older stereotype. The Eastern Jewish countenance was not hideous nor depraved but reflected beauty, hidden strength, and great sensitivity.

Zweig's commentary again revealed the "Rorschach" nature of the Ostjuden: villified or romanticized, they were always convenient objects upon which to project one's own values and world view. Zweig's ideas were radically antithetical to Franzos, yet both men revealed as much about themselves as they did about the world of which they wrote. The symbolic content underwent change but not the function.

Zweig's war experiences in Lithuania shaped his conception of the Eastern Jew. The encounter provided the basis for his attempt to integrate ghetto Jews into a radical philosophy of socialist Zionism and make them the touchstone for his critique of both German Jews and German anti-Semitism. He was one of the key defenders of the Eastern Jews in Germany during the critical period of 1919–23.[49]

Das ostjüdische Antlitz is filled with romantic allusions. The Ostjude becomes the great counter-symbol, emblem of spirituality in a materialistic world. The traditional Ostjude had perhaps paid a price for his religious life, for it had produced a certain helplessness and political fatalism. But at the same time there was a spirituality that was the very opposite of crass modernity. The old Jew exemplified contempt for pure materialism. This spirituality extended to the political realm. The Ostjude stood for values that had nothing to do with the Western deification of power and force: "The Ostjude is the

An East European Jewish "woman of the people." Drawing by Hermann Struck, from Zweig and Struck, *Das Ostjüdische Antlitz.* Her outer appearance is the result of eternal sorrow, unending labor, and misery, according to Zweig.

Jewish woman and child. Drawing by Hermann Struck, from *Das Ostjüdische Antlitz*. Zweig writes that a woman with a child in her arms and a wise
man holding the Torah are the two figures most representative of Eastern
Jewish life. His text describes the life of sorrow and labor led by Jewish
women. This woman "doesn't know that she is a heroine; she laughed when
we admired her."

denial of the coercive state . . . because he lives in a vital *Volksge-meinschaft*": community was realized through voluntary, coopera-tive principles rather than through the imperatives of an authoritar-ian state.[50] Close-knit community, wrote Zweig elsewhere, even solved the classical problem of modern artistic alienation. Unlike Western Jewish writers, Eastern Jewish poets like Chaim Nachman Bialik did not have to contend with an impersonal public but articulated the deepest longings of a community with whom they were intimately linked.[51]

Zweig's work illustrated the degree to which the war served to make Ostjuden the repository of values that a brutalized Europe seemed to have irretrievably lost. The perception of European decadence and the search for redeemers of innocent and authentic experience were related integrally to the cult. At the same time, the cult also tamed Jewish radicalism by channeling disaffection into alternative modes of Jewish identification. The revolt against Jewish bourgeois modes did not necessarily lead to Jewish disaffection. The Ostjude now became the keeper of spiritual integrity: "The Jew is eternal," wrote Zweig, "for spiritualized Man is eternal and Amalek is transient. . . ."[52]

For Zweig as well as for many others, the idealization of the Eastern Jew was tied to a critique of the modalities of Western life. Those who complained about the punctuality and poor workman-ship of Eastern Jewish laborers were using one-dimensional cultural judgment, for they regarded work as a disembodied, reified quality with no spiritual dimension. But the Ostjude, with his slow tempo, his different rhythms, was a reminder of the integrated whole, of the unbroken relationship between the person and the work he per-formed.[53]

Zweig's stylized romanticism, to be sure, did not preclude some criticism; it is in fact as revealing of his radicalism as are his celebratory comments. Perhaps the most pertinent aspect here is his analysis of the Eastern Jew's denial of the body, the repression of sexuality. Historical Judaism had created repressive mechanisms, the products of a religious conception in which freedom consisted in submission to God. Renunciation of the sensual and the aesthetic was the price paid for Jewish spirituality.[54] The solution to this predicament lay in radical socialist Zionism, in a process linked to what Zweig termed "re-mediterraneanization." Land and work would not only bring about the long-awaited East-West Jewish reunification but would also overcome the sensual repression of the ghetto. The joy of the body, the pleasure of nudity, the feel of one's own muscles—all this would accompany the creation of the new Jewish man in socialist Palestine.[55]

Zweig's later disillusion with Palestine, especially its East European nationalist components, is well known.[56] But at its height, his Zionism was linked crucially to the Ostjuden and his image of their role in the creative rebirth of Jewry. His particular brand of socialist, even sexual-liberationist, Zionism was clearly in tune with and a product of the radical postwar atmosphere.

In this atmosphere many romantic schemes for the reshaping of German as well as East European Jewry were drawn up. Alfred Lemm's *Der Weg der Deutschjuden* (1919) illustrated both the radicalism and the lack of realism of this mood.[57] The long-awaited Jewish renaissance, Lemm announced, had still not developed, and the war generation was too assimilated to bring it about. What was needed was the deliberate creation of a generation gap in which a sharp dividing line would be drawn between German Jewry and their offspring. This was undoubtedly harsh, but only a radical divorce from German culture could produce the necessary national vitalization. In preparation for life in Palestine, special colonies, consciously removed from German reality, would have to be set up. But to what model could these youths be directed?

Direct imitation of the Eastern Jews was out of the question. They were less developed both culturally and economically than their German counterparts. There were even more significant differences. Employing a favorite Buber dichotomy in a new context, Lemm categorized Ostjuden as orientals, German Jews as occidentals. Ostjuden still lived naïve, prescientific lives, but in the modern world one had to recognize that chemistry, not God, ruled the earth. The occidentals, for their part, had to recognize that preoccupation with science had led to an overinstrumentalized world. Ostjuden still carried with them vital values of noninstrumentality and soul. Creative Jewish rebirth would consist in an exchange of respective East-West virtues synthesized in a new whole.

The notion that Eastern Jews carried deep spiritual qualities was especially pronounced in the restless postwar era. "Time and again I had the feeling that the people in the West were searching for something that I could give them," one Eastern Jewish participant in the Volksheim recalled.[58] Ostjuden were viewed as embodying a unity lost to more sophisticated cultures.

Such perceptions, it should be clear, were not limited to declared Zionists. Other important Jewish intellectuals viewed Ostjuden in similar ways. What linked these disparate people was their opposi-

tion to established liberal attitudes. We have already seen how
Gustav Landauer played an important role in the cult of the
Ostjuden. Landauer opposed Zionism because he believed that it
negated the special calling of the Jews. They had a task for all of
humanity, and given their Diaspora history, were particularly well
suited to help in the creation of socialism outside the framework of
states and political parties. Jews generally, Landauer claimed, were
less addicted than others to the cult of the state,[59] but Ostjuden
particularly could teach their assimilated Western counterparts an
important lesson: how to once again feel like a stranger to a system of
states that was tearing Europe into pieces.[60]

Franz Kafka's discovery of Eastern Jews was a classic illustration
of the major impulses behind the movement of young intellectuals
seeking a post-liberal Jewish commitment. Like many of his German
contemporaries, Kafka's Jewish return was predicated upon conflict
with his parents. Judaism, Zionism, and the Ostjuden became of
interest to him precisely because of his father's frivolous, dismissive
approach to such matters: "Had you shown interest in them, these
things might, for that very reason, have become suspect in my
eyes."[61] Kafka's involvement with the Ostjuden, his enthusiasm for
the Yiddish theater,[62] his passionate interest in the workings of the
Volksheim—as he wrote to his fiancée, Felice Bauer, "It is positively
the only path that can lead to spiritual liberation"[63]—sprang from
and was reinforced by his "hatred" of his parents "appalling"
attitudes towards Eastern Jews.[64]

As early as 1911, Kafka's exposure to Yiddish was the stimulus for
biting criticism of German. His remarks illuminated the role of
language as an instrument in the creation of particular cultural and
human types and qualities:

> Yesterday it occurred to me that I did not always love my mother
> as she deserved and as I could only because the German language
> prevented it. The Jewish mother is no "Mutter," to call her
> "Mutter" makes her a little comic (not to herself, because we are in
> Germany), we give a Jewish woman the name of a German mother,
> but forget the contradiction that sinks into the emotions more
> heavily. "Mutter" is particularly German for the Jew, it uncon-
> sciously contains, together with the Christian splendor, Christian
> coldness also, the Jewish woman who is called "Mutter" therefore
> becomes not only comic but also strange. Mama would be a better
> name if only one didn't imagine "Mutter" behind it! I believe that
> it is only the memories of the ghetto that still preserve the Jewish

family, for the word "Vater" is too far from meaning the Jewish father.[65]

Kafka's dismissal of German coldness was linked to a self-abasing appreciation of the "hidden qualities" of the Eastern Jews: "And I should like to run to those poor Jews of the ghetto, kiss the hem of their coats, and say not a word. I should be completely happy if only they would endure my presence in silence."[66]

A similar complex of attitudes is to be found in Franz Rosenzweig's euphoric wartime encounter with Eastern Jews. Certainly no nationalist, this neo-Orthodox figure also derived much of his admiration for the simple ghetto Jews from a singular distaste for shallow, middle-class German Jewish attitudes. In a letter from Rembertow, addressed significantly to his mother, he wrote: "The Jewish boys are magnificent and I felt something I rarely feel, pride in my race, in so much freshness and vivacity. . . . I can well understand why the average German Jew no longer feels any kinship with these East European Jews; actually he has very little kinship left; he has become philistine, bourgeois; but I, and people like me, should still feel the kinship strongly."[67]

Rosenzweig's mother characterized his attitude as fanaticism.[68] This, of course, only fed the fuel of his enthusiasm. The secret of Eastern Jewish life, wrote Rosenzweig, was its integration. There was nothing "barbaric" about that. Rather, the individual who chose to relinquish such a culture had to be considered a barbarian. Like Kafka, Rosenzweig articulated a strange theory of Jewish linguistic alienation in his *The Star of Redemption:* "While every other people is one with its own language, while that language withers in its mouth the moment it ceases to be a people, the Jewish people never quite grows one with the languages it speaks. Even when it speaks the language of its host, a special vocabulary, or at least, a special selection from the general vocabulary, a special word order, its own feeling for what is beautiful or ugly in the language, betray that it is not its own."[69]

Landauer, Kafka, and Rosenzweig were not Zionists, yet they could be regarded as identifying, committed Jews. More surprising was the role of the Ostjuden in the Jewish reawakening of certain radically disaffected intellectuals. The case of the highly assimilated left-wing novelist Alfred Döblin (1878–1957)—himself of East European Jewish origins—is the most outstanding example.[70] At an early age, Döblin officially withdrew from Judaism. His discovery of the

Jewish Volk, as a part of the cult, was belated. As late as 1921 he wrote a caustic pro-assimilationist polemic in which, with no apparent humorous intent, he proclaimed: "Perhaps there are Jews in Poland. An expedition by a geographical society should be set up to establish this. . . . it must be confirmed whether in fact millions of Ostjuden live in Poland and Galicia."[71] Döblin, in a less facetious manner, undertook this expedition himself in 1924. His trip to Poland, which resulted in the book *Reise in Polen* (1925), was a revelation. This was a real Volk, here were genuine Jews living a vibrant culture, far removed from the pale ways of assimilated Jewry. To be sure, the confrontation with the ghetto served to underline the fact that as an assimilated Jew one could not "go back."[72] Yet it was precisely Döblin's compassion for the poverty and suffering of the Polish Jews, his admiration for their traditions and culture, his envy of their unbroken sense of community, which clearly placed him in that countergroup of people who radically transvalued traditional conceptions of the Ostjude. With the rise of fascism, Döblin pressed for a non-Zionist "territorialist" solution for Eastern Jewry[73] and attacked German Jewish assimilationists for denying the national component of Jewish life.[74]

Döblin's enthusiasm for the Ostjuden, however, was by and large not annexed to an institutional framework but was basically an ingredient in his personal and intellectual evolution. Even there it was diluted by his later conversion to Catholicism, a religious orientation which began on that same trip to Poland, where Jesus stood as the symbol of universal compassion.[75] We need, therefore, to return to that point where the cult was most obvious and organized, the Zionist camp. Many Zionists were indeed swept away by the enthusiasm; yet if we are to keep the movement in proper perspective, it must be noted that there were always dissenters. There was never consensus on the subject of the Ostjude. As a result of the war encounter with the ghetto, the prejudices of some Zionists against Eastern Jews were in fact reinforced.[76]

Even as the cult spread, opposing Zionist voices were heard. One sceptic, Gustav Witkowsky, declared that the notion that Ostjuden would somehow make German Zionists more Jewish was romantic cant. The shattering effects of the war on the Ostjuden demonstrated that they were a civilization in decline. The only solution was the negation of both ghetto and Galut. The argument of Eastern Jewish cultural superiority was wrong: "Even if I were in position to exchange my being for a spiritually Slavic-oriented Jewishness I could not accept the illusion that I had become a total Jew. . . . this kind of 'natural' Jewishness is tied to economic and political backwardness. . . ."[77]

Attacks like these made adherents of the cult moderate their positions. Gerhard Holdheim, for example, responded that the Ostjuden could never replace Palestine in the Zionist scheme of things. Moreover there was no question of aping the Ostjuden. There was a need, however, for German Jews to mix with them, for this would facilitate the process of internal transformation and help overcome Jewish national alienation.[78] Kurt Blumenfeld argued that the turn to *Ostjudentum* was not romanticism but a vital pragmatic necessity, if one was to take seriously the realities of contemporary Jewish life. Yet he was acutely aware of the dangers of the enthusiasm as well as of its ambiguous qualities. Shocked, instinctive distaste of the Ostjuden existed side by side with passionate, uncritical admiration. A true love of the Jewish people would carry with it the power of objectivity and make unrestrained cultism unattractive.[79]

These debates raised perennial issues of modern Jewish identity: what was Jewishness and how did one define its content? Certainly for the most radical proponents of the cult like Birnbaum and Kaufmann, Jewishness was equivalent to Yiddish-speaking East European Jewish culture (although Birnbaum increasingly stressed the traditional religious over the modern cultural dimensions). But to proceed along this path was to indulge in nothing less than an act of cultural demodernization, or as some contemporaries termed it, "backward assimilation." Despite the disenchantment with Europe, the vast majority of German Jews regarded such a step as historically retrogressive, sociologically impossible, and culturally undesirable. The more extreme versions of the cult succeeded only in highlighting the gulf between rhetoric and action and demonstrated the intractable nature of social reality. Like most romantic antimodern movements, the cult of the Ostjuden based itself on essentially modern presuppositions.

The possibility and desirability of such a "backward assimilation" were the subject of heated polemics in the Zionist movement. Fritz Mordecai Kaufmann's efforts to transform the musical sensibility of German Jews occasioned one such debate. In a number of articles, Kaufmann argued that a vital ingredient of the "return" to Jewishness consisted in the removal of German musical roots. Yiddish music would provide a critical bridge in the move from the German to the Jewish culture. Kaufmann scorned even those Zionists actively identified with the Eastern Jewish cult as being still culturally alienated from their Jewish roots. Their song books, for instance, showed that not only were the vast majority of songs they sung still in German, as opposed to Hebrew and Yiddish, but most of them were even of the German nationalist or military variety. All talk of cultural revolution was pointless until this disposition changed.[80]

Georg Strauss scathingly replied in the Zionist youth leaders' journal that there was indeed a disinclination towards the Yiddish musical mode. Western Jews might have routinely undervalued the cultural products of the ghetto, but Kaufmann had committed the opposite sin. His praise of the ghetto was totally undiscerning and one-dimensional. He proposed "nothing less than the assimilation of West European Jewry to Eastern Europe . . . trying to create an Ostjude out of a Goy." But this was a consciously backward movement, for despite fleeting moments of beauty, Eastern Jewish music reflected the misery to which it was witness, it echoed the material and spiritual confinement of the ghetto. From the European point of view, Jewish melody was "like a roof without a house," alien in "its oriental harmony and musical system."[81]

Strauss was of course correct in his diagnosis. The war had not made the connection (*Anschluss*) with the Ostjuden any more feasible than before. Ideas that it was possible were based upon sentimentality rather than realism. Even the satirical Zionist journal *Schlemiel* recognized this and caricatured the cult of Yiddish music: when workers sang Yiddish songs they became "folk songs," when the bourgeoisie sang them they were pure "kitsch."[82] Strauss's remarks demonstrated again that for many German Zionists the ghetto remained materially and spiritually incapable of producing significant cultural products.

Despite the rhetoric, the glorification of the Ostjude often did not penetrate older, more negative attitudes. Constant postwar invocations by German Zionists to build bridges with resident Eastern Jews and overcome the mutual alienation attested to the fact that for many, relationships had not undergone any fundamental change.[83] The veneration of the Ostjude once again points to the symbolic and cultural function of the East European Jew. It served less as a practical way of transforming the conduct of daily East-West relations than as a psychological measure, a means toward radical Zionist self-definition.

This problem of uniting theory with practice was never resolved in German Zionism. Buber's warning to Jewish youth in 1919 was ironic: the war, he commented, had finally removed the illusion that Western Jews had organic ties to other nations. Yet at the same time they remained cut off from their own national existence. This had deepened their longing for community. Youth, he declared, "must no longer permit itself the illusion that it can establish a decisive link to its people merely by reading Bialik's poems or by singing Yiddish folksongs nor by the addition of a few quasi-religious sentiments and lyricisms . . . something bigger is at stake . . . one must join, earnest and ready for much struggle and work, in Judaism's intense creative process . . . one must recreate this process from within."[84] But in many respects, Buber himself had fathered the literary cult of the Ostjuden, and his vague pronouncements about the "openness" of Jewish content were themselves part of the difficulty in putting these ideas into practice. As the years went on, many of Buber's disciples were increasingly irritated by Buber's own reluctance to practice the precept he encouraged in others (especially since one of his favorite words was *realization*).[85]

The cult was a product of the turbulent times in which it was formulated. By 1923 even *Der Jude* reflected the more sober, realistic mood. Paul Zucker's review of *Das ostjüdische Antlitz* was symptomatically entitled "Myths of the Present." Progressives were always satirizing those writers who invoked *German* loyalty, *German* spirituality, *German* culture, he said. Yet here were Zweig and Struck doing exactly the same thing with East European Jewry. Their intentions were no doubt honorable, but it was necessary to say a decided no to their work. The problem lay not so much in its unconsciously apologetic nature as in the total dimunition of critical distance that could have given form and perspective to their vision. The wheel had come full circle. Not dissociation but overidentification had become the problem. Precisely because Jewish instinct tended toward undiscerning, total affirmation, it was subject to suspicion. Had Struck retained even the minimum of sympathetic distance, he could have attained portraits of the quality of Käthe Kollwitz rather than celebratory pieces suited only to a Zionist party newspaper. The issue was vital, Zucker went on, for sentimentality threatened the very basis of authentic sensibility. Jewish art should never become an ideological instrument, or it would degenerate into mere Volkish dilettantism.[86]

Zucker and Scholem voiced their criticisms of the cult from within the Jewish national camp. They attacked the glorification of the Eastern Jews only insofar as it seemed a hindrance to authentic Jewish national liberation. The liberal attack on such Zionist notions, however, was based upon very different assumptions. Most retained intact the nineteenth-century conception of German *Kultur* and ghetto *Unkultur.* The attempt to impose East European culture upon German Jews, one observer wrote, was clearly absurd and was linked to the misguided notion that German and Jewish modes were irreconcilable polarities.[87] Berlin's wealthy Reform congregation made its attitude clear: German Jews had always felt for their East European counterparts, but this did not mean that the Ostjuden were closer to German Jews than were German Christians. That was simply a falsehood, "and no Zionist suggestion could make that true. . . . our development has so formed us that a national cultural community with them [the Ostjuden] is out of the question."[88] Referring to the Volksheim, the writer F. Coblenz blamed "Zionist agitation" for removing children from their homes in Berlin West to live in the northern sections of the city, where they worked with their Galician "brothers": "This goes beyond romanticism; it verges on the immoral: the Galician 'brother' is closer to these young people than their own mother and father."

Felix Goldmann, a rabbi in Leipzig (which had an overwhelmingly East European Jewish population) characterized the cult of the Ostjuden as a "modern mania," "a sickness of the mind." In a review of Sammy Gronemann's satirical 1920 novel *Tohuwabohu,* Goldmann correctly diagnosed the glorification of Eastern Jewry as deriving from a dislike of German Jewry. The uncritical admiration for *Ostjudentum,* he proclaimed, was accompanied by a blindness to the praiseworthy aspects of German Jewish life.[89]

A critique of great insight was written by Binjamin Segel. The veteran East European publicist adopted an essentially nineteenth-century *Maskil* position. The veneration of the Ostjuden, he argued, revealed something entirely new: "The ignorance, the superstition, the economic helplessness, the lack of worldliness, in one word the culturelessness in which they vegetate is increasingly revered, surrounded by a romantic aura. A veritable cult of the 'Ostjuden' prevails." Eastern Jews, with their misery and dirt, had been transformed into models. Their unkempt appearance now became "aesthetic," superstition became "mysticism," ignorance was "poetic." No work—under Buber's obvious influence—was complete without homage to Jesus, Marx, and Gustav Landauer. Great German figures like Mendelssohn and Geiger were declared obsolete, while obscurantist Hasidic rabbis and fashionable revolutionaries were transformed into Jewish heroes.[90]

Perhaps the most ironic and scorching criticism of the Zionist cult of Eastern Jews was made by an Eastern Jew in the name of Eastern Jews. In a 1920 "Open Letter" (written in Yiddish) to Martin Buber,

Max Brod, and others, the neoromantic Galician writer Moshe Zilburg mounted a "Yiddishist" attack. The war, he wrote, had turned Ostjuden into refugees, and German Zionists had tried to teach and help them. Ostjuden were "discovered" anew, and no Yiddish or Hebrew work remained untranslated. But behind this enthusiasm there lay another aim: "You applied all your powers to make the real Yiddish physiognomy disappear, to make the Jewish masses *like you*." The vision of a new *Gemeinschaft* was quite unsuited to the real needs of the masses. The Zionists who attempted this were tainted by total alienation from "the real Jews." They were "a foreign body in our organism. You have been raised in a foreign alma mater, far from the people and its daily experience." The great tragedy, Zilburg continued, was that the decline of the Jewish masses was in large measure a product of Western Zionist intrusion; the masses had to be warned about the predatory effects of these people. Not for nothing were words like *Daitsch* ("German") living synonyms for assimilation, symbols of a spirit alien to Yiddish being. The danger was compounded by the fact that these Zionists were different from the earlier modernizing *Maskilim*, who at least had their roots in Jewish culture. Now historical errors were being perpetuated by people who were entirely cut off from that tradition and yet posed as "committed" Jews. They were full of advice for their Eastern brethren, yet failed to live up to the first precondition: that a Jew live among and for his people and share actively in their trials and tribulations. Inaction was rationalized by the doctrine of the "negation of the Galut." But the "genuine Jew of the ghetto is normal, healthy"; it was the "new Jew"—indistinguishable from everyone else—who was the real Philistine. These Western Jews were rejected at home and so they sought to bring their unrealizable dreams to the Ostjuden and impose them upon the ghetto masses.[91]

Orthodox Jewry also criticized the Zionist approach. Yet they too elaborated their own version of the cult consonant with their religious world view. Once again it was the war that marked a turning point, at least for a minority of Orthodox youth. Letters from the field exhorted German Jews to go and live amongst their brothers in the East and help them in ways that transcended the old philanthropy.[92] Orthodox youth, though in fewer numbers, exhibited the same enthusiasm as the Zionists. After the war, many German Jewish students went East (especially to Lithuania), where they supped at the fount of "authentic Jewish learning" in the religious academies, the *yeschiwoth*.[93] Their elders were sensitive to these sentiments and attempted to direct the movement within acceptable channels. The editor of the important journal *Jeschurun* wrote in 1920 that the influx of Ostjuden into Germany provided the basic precondition for the revival of serious Jewish learning in Germany, but of course this was to be a reciprocal process. "Science" would rescue the Ostjuden from the premodern approach, while German Jews, under Eastern Jewish influence, would recover a lost ardor for Judaism.[94]

All this was explicitly distinguished from the Zionist version of the cult. One Orthodox rabbinical leader claimed that the two movements were "incomparable." Zionists merely borrowed some formal Eastern cultural elements and used them as aesthetic props, exotic additions to ideals that were fundamentally alien to Judaism. Orthodox Jews, on the other hand, regarded their Eastern cousins not as interesting cultural objects but as real guides towards the establishment of a vital Torah culture. Older Orthodox adherents had to value rather than bemoan these trends.[95] Another commentator endorsed the religious version of the cult on the explicit condition that the renaissance be predicated on a clearly religious and not national basis.[96]

But for all that, older Orthodox attitudes by and large prevailed. For many, "Polonization" was regarded as a danger rather than an opportunity. The older distaste persisted. Even those not unsympathetic to the new religious idealism were determined to maintain the East-West distinction. As one commentator put it, the "return to *Ostjudentum*" defied all rational conceptions of historical causality—one could never turn back the clock. Polish Jewish immigration into Germany was undesirable for the Ostjuden themselves: under the influence of Feuerbach, Haeckel, and Wellhausen, Talmud youth would be overwhelmed and a general decline in morals and religiosity would be the effect. German Jewry, no doubt, was in need of reinvigoration, but it needed to find its own way.[97]

The cult of the Ostjuden, in any of its various versions, can easily be caricatured. It is simple to point to its limitations and contradictions: the gap between precept and practice; the persistence of cultural barriers that in the realm of social relationships highlighted rather than removed East-West differences; modish ideas and radical pretensions; the obvious use of the Eastern Jew as a symbolic weapon in the revolt against the middle-class Jewish home. Yet it would be wrong to leave it at that. This cult was an important manifestation of a mood that spread to a significant minority of German Jewry's war generation. It reflected the intellectual currents and radical sentiments of youth increasingly dissatisfied with conventional middle-class German Judaism. Despite the hyperbolic rhetoric, it was a small but revealing fragment of cultural history. In the end, the cult represented an attempt by idealistic youth to personalize the long-awaited Jewish renaissance in new and concrete ways. Once again Eastern Jewry became the natural "partner" for such efforts, a vital presence through which the old dilemma of German Jewish identity could find a new resolution.

Yet it was less the physical and practical than the symbolic dimensions that endowed these representations with their effectiveness. Ostjuden retained their salience, their accessibility as metaphors for both social commentary and personal identity. The shtetl—affectionate synonym for the negatively loaded term *ghetto*—functioned as a recognizable historic entity, nostalgic antithesis to the disenchantment of European life. It symbolized totality, organic community, lost spiritual values. Increasingly and into our own times, the ghetto of memory was transformed into the embodiment of authentic and warm human community, *Gemeinschaft*, a counter-utopia to values lost in the world of impersonal society, *Gesellschaft*.[98]

At the same time, because they lived in defined areas and in recognizable "Jewish" ways, the Ostjuden never lost their paradigmatic Jewish qualities. In a recent essay attempting to revise negative perceptions of German Jewish life, Gerson D. Cohen bemoans the fact that while the post-Holocaust period has produced "affectionate memorializers" of the East European Jewish experience, no "wistful literature of nostalgia" has been generated by the memory of German Jewry.[99]

But as Cohen points out, it is precisely because German Jewry's historical importance lies in its pioneering confrontation with modernity that it was less amenable to myth-making, less accessible as an archetypical Jewish model. The romanticizing of the Ostjuden, both before and after the Holocaust, derived its force from the fact that Eastern Jews for the most part lived their lives in what appeared to be a distinctively Jewish culture. This seeming integration was able to embody the myth of the *Ur*-Jew far more easily than could the complex experience of German Jewry. The latter may in the end be more instructive in terms of the continuing search for modern alternative models, but it was this very modernity that precluded it as an inspirational source for Jewish counter-myths.

For Ostjuden the immediate post–World War I German reality was anything but nostalgic and ethereal, however. In the wake of defeat and in the presence of revolution, German Jewry entered a new, deeply disturbing era in which the Eastern Jews among them played a vital but quite different, symbolic role. In these turbulent times of rampant anti-Semitism, the glorification of the Ostjude seemed like a hopeless irrelevancy.

9 JEWISH IDENTITY, OSTJUDEN, AND ANTI-SEMITISM IN THE WEIMAR REPUBLIC

THE shock of defeat, fear of revolution, unparalleled economic collapse, and brutalization of political life were inescapable realities in the Weimar Republic between 1918 and 1923. The accompanying anti-Semitism was both an expression of the general crisis and an opportunity for previously outlawed sentiments to surface publicly. For the first time in twentieth-century Germany, anti-Semitism gained political respectability and mass support.[1] A few prescient observers had feared such a development well before the war had run its course. In 1916 one Zionist argued that Zionists all over the world should support Germany in the war, for defeat would inevitably heighten Jew-hatred in that country, while victory would mean its final overcoming.[2] Defeat certainly gave credence to the old slogan "The Jews are our misfortune." So great were popular anti-Semitic passions during 1919–23 that one eminent historian, Golo Mann, has concluded that they were even more rabid than during the years 1930–33 or 1933–45.[3]

Once again, the *Ostjudenfrage* symbolized the wider Jewish problem. Although now the anti-Semitic attack was generalized and clearly included native Jewry, the obviously vulnerable and alien nature of the Ostjuden made them particularly salient victims. Accusations that the invasion by ghetto Jews had already materialized were made plausible by the fact that during the war 70,000 Eastern Jews—workers, prisoners, civil internees—were added to the prewar population of 90,000.[4] In addition, thousands more sought refuge from the brutal pogroms that rocked Eastern Europe after the war. These refugees needed political protection and economic assistance desperately, and to a large degree the organized German Jewish community provided them.[5] At the same time, German Jews were themselves facing an unprecedented political situation.

Most historians agree that the war and its aftermath induced a transformation in German Jewish attitudes.[6] Many contemporary observers also believed that it had sharpened German-Jewish differences and greatly deferred Jewish hopes for a place in the German sun.[7] In a surprisingly frank "Confession" Georg Hermann, author of the optimistic German-Jewish novel *Jettchen Gebert* (1907), articulated what he thought amounted to a general change in sensibility.[8] Before the war, wrote Hermann, he had regarded himself as a typical *Westjude*, disdainful of the uncivilized Ostjuden and deeply identified with German culture. Jewishness had been peripheral to his essential Germanness. The war, however, had produced a massive sense of disillusionment and an increasing awareness of Jewishness. In an apparent repudiation of liberal self-understanding, Hermann argued that Jewishness was an internal quality, a quality inhering in Jewish being. No Jew, he proclaimed, regardless of the degree of assimilation, would succeed in becoming a German. Whether or not one liked it, it was necessary to become conscious of Jewishness. The war had clearly demonstrated the mutual incompatibility (*Wesensfremdheiten*) of *Deutschtum* and *Judentum*.

Hermann's remarks reflected the degree to which the Right had succeeded in forcing political discourse into its own frame of reference. Through their actions, anti-Semites had pushed liberals like Hermann into acknowledging German-Jewish incompatibility. They then used these Jewish statements as proof for their own assertions of that incompatibility.[9] But of course Hermann's estrangement from *Deutschtum* did not result in Zionism. Indeed, his solution indicated that transformed consciousness and a new commitment to Jewishness could leave older attitudes to the Ostjuden intact and bypass nationalist avenues entirely. His was a call addressed explicitly to Western Jews—"I can only speak for them"—to unite and form a common community. They would then dedicate their service to the good of humanity. Such service was to be limited to the community of Western Jews and implied no cultural or poltitical link to the Jewish masses in the East.

This "confession" demonstrated the dilemma of the disillusioned German liberal Jew. Ethnicity now became important, but Hermann was determined to avoid the obvious implication that Eastern Jews and Western Jews were substantively part of the same ethnic group. His Zionist critics reminded him that through his presentation of Eastern Jews in *Jettchen Gebert* he himself had added to the stockpile of anti-Semitic literature—the Jacobys were merely a modern rendering of the Shylock myth.[10] His "new vision" of Judaism, they argued, was mere embroidery, disembodied ideas, devoid of feeling for the real people and their sufferings, cut off from tangible Judaic forms of language, culture, and religion. Others, while agreeing that the time for fundamental change had arrived, argued that the only way to Jewish recovery was through the Ostjuden. Hermann's rejection of nationalism was wrong. Particularity was the necessary precondition of universality.[11]

Hermann's solution was not quite as idiosyncratic as might appear. It represented one way out of the dilemma by, paradoxically, placing Jewish ethnicity (of the Western variety) at the center of a new universalist mission. At a time when old liberal assumptions no longer seemed effective, this was a comforting notion, for while it emphasized a specifically Jewish component, Enlightenment rationalism was preserved intact. Even the nationalist *Der Jude* published a similar suggestion by Rudolf Kayser, the critic and editor of *Neue Rundschau*. Kayser proposed a "new Covenant" in which Jews would act as agents of a universal mission in a mechanized Europe. The Ostjuden were not suited to such a task since they were not a purely spiritual entity but constituted "a nation in the old (physical) sense." As such they required a tangible state of their own. Western Jews, on the other hand, were Jews only in a spiritual sense.[12]

Both Hermann and Kayser symptomized liberal Jewish recognition of changed circumstances. Their solutions acknowledged the failure of assimilation and gave Judaism a heightened role in their new self-definitions. Yet it was a commitment whose political content and requisite action remained purposely vague. Despite self-proclaimed metamorphosis, the old division between Eastern and Western Jewry was explicitly perpetuated.

If German Jewish liberals, by and large, tried to define their increased commitment to Jewishness in non-national and non-"cultural" terms, this did not mean that they avoided their responsibilities for their Eastern counterparts either within Germany or abroad. The organized community was aware of the need to support the refugees, and responsible leaders increasingly understood that they could not siphon off anti-Semitic hostility onto the Ostjuden. Yet while all this was positive, it was still done for reasons of political exigency and did not really point to a fundamental transformation in German Jewish attitudes.

The leading spokesman of the Centralverein, Eugen Fuchs, continued to base his conception of German Jewry upon the distinction between East and West.[13] Jews all over the world did indeed belong to a common community, but they had to be understood as different segments of that whole. Eastern Jewry had developed nationally, while Western Jews were fully assimilated both culturally and nationally. It was not the differences between the Jewries that constituted the problem, but the misguided Zionist effort to make such radically different entities identical.[14] It is true that Fuchs now placed more emphasis on the *Stamm* (ethnic) components of Jewish identity, but this entailed little movement from older positions, except perhaps to complicate even further the building blocks of an ever-more-complicated definition and justification of Jewish identity. "We are Germans of Jewish faith and ethnicity for whom *Deutschtum* is nation and people, Judaism faith and ethnicity, divided from the Germans by means of faith and ethnicity but not by Volk. We are German nationals not Jewish, only a Jewish religious community and not a Jewish Volk, at least in Germany. We are no Volk," he wrote in 1919.[15]

Zionists scorned the Centralverein's apparent change of attitude. Its opposition to assimilationist positions, they argued, was only skin-deep. In one such statement, Moritz Bileski pointed to the continuing disdain of the ghetto and its caftan products as evidence of an assimilationist outlook. The underlying psychology of assimilation—the need to make Jews inconspicuous and place them in an identical mold with others—was untouched. Even the new slogan of distinctive ethnicity (*Stammeseigentümlichkeit*) did not lead back to the Jewish people. The German nationalism of the CV Jews remained as it was before the war. In response to Zionist radicalization, in fact, they had intensified the stress on *Deutschtum* to a point where the most obvious double standards were employed: Jewish nationalism was totally outlawed, while German Jews were driven to an almost chauvinist German nationalism. The Centralverein, Bileski concluded, despite its new, committed Jewish rhetoric, was as deeply penetrated by the spirit of assimilation as when it was originally founded.[16]

But the creation of the VJOD and the Workers' Welfare Agency (Arbeiterfürsorgeamt) did represent a change. For the first time, a concerted effort by representatives of the major institutions of the Jewish community was made to protect the rights of and provide employment and housing to a minority whose presence in Germany could not have made itself felt at a worse time.[17] Throughout the economic collapse and the polarized political atmosphere, German Jews, on the whole, intensified their efforts on behalf of their East European counterparts. Of course these duties did not evoke enthusiasm. In troubled times, the Ostjuden were a potential "provocation," an irritant, a burden without which German Jewry's load would have been much lighter.

Because the radical right had converted the *Ostjudenfrage* into a German *Schicksalsfrage*, a matter of national destiny, German Jews had to define the balance between Jewish responsibility and German loyalty with added caution. Paul Nathan's formulation was typical of the leadership's approach. It was clear, he wrote, that in view of Germany's crippled situation, the presence of large foreign groups was not desirable. But expulsion would not be effective nor was it morally appropriate, especially since so many Eastern Jews had been brought to Germany by force. Deportation would be both unpatriotic and harmful to Germany's international reputation.[18] Nathan tirelessly rebutted anti-Semitic charges. His apologia on behalf of the Ostjuden was clothed in the language and limited by the premises of *Deutschtum* in its liberal, Enlightenment guise.[19] This was a vision of German culture, however, that was being rapidly and severely eroded.

All Jewish responses had to come to grips with the assertion that the problem of the Eastern Jews was not a Jewish problem but was a German one and would have to be treated as such. The Centralverein's Kurt Alexander took the middle position on this. On the one hand, he scoffed at anti-Semitic propaganda that claimed there were 400,000 Ostjuden living in Berlin alone, and he demonstrated the fallacy of generalizing a group criminality to all Eastern Jews simply because there were a few lawbreakers among them. Yet as a matter of course he wrote, "That the German Jews do not encourage this immigration must be obvious to all reasonable people." The Ostjuden would move on as soon as circumstances permitted.[20] The only solution, an editorial in *Im deutschen Reich* proclaimed, was the reconstitution of East European political life. Mass migration was impossible anywhere in the postwar world, and certainly Germany was in no position to absorb more workers. It was to be hoped that reconstitution would facilitate the return of most Ostjuden to Eastern Europe. Their plight invited compassion, but Germany itself had become a poor country and the Ostjuden were widely regarded as taking bread from the mouths of the local inhabitants. Old hatreds had been given a new economic basis, and only the cessation of this Eastern Jewish immigration would relieve the Jew-hatred directed against the German Jews also.[21] In the same vein, the Berlin Reform congregation accepted responsibility for Ostjuden already in Germany but believed, as one typical article put it, that many "dubious" elements were in their ranks and that the majority of Germans did not desire their presence. Reform Jews had far more in common with Christian Germans than with Ostjuden, whose spirit was quite alien.[22]

These positions reflected the continuing, unresolved ambivalence of liberal German Jews towards the Ostjuden. Yet we need to make a new distinction here. As the Reform rabbi Coblenz put it, the Zionists and Orthodox wanted German Jews to "become" Ostjuden. Reform Jews, on the other hand, were willing to deal with Eastern Jews if Eastern Jews were willing to become more like German Jews. Reform Jews did not oppose gradual naturalization of Ostjuden already in Germany, provided they could be divorced from the ghetto.

This was one of the main points distinguishing official Reform Jewry from Max Naumann's Deutschnationale Juden, founded in March 1921. Certain leading Reform Jews such as Alfred Peyser were also active in Naumann's circle, but the connections were personal rather than institutional. Naumann's group was clearly a product of the postwar collapse of liberal certainties. It attempted to placate the fury of the Right by appropriating its values and advocating the overtly antiliberal, proconservative position of the Deutschnationale party. Although Naumann specifically designated his group as "German National *Jews*," he argued that the German national viewpoint was supreme in all political questons. The only political criterion, he repeated tirelessly, was the welfare of the German Fatherland. Given Germany's precarious situation, "whoever comes from 'half-Asia' is a dangerous guest. . . . this does not . . . imply the disappearance of all feelings of Jewish solidarity, if one makes Germany's interests in questions like this the decisive matter. But it would mean the abandonment of *Deutschtum* if, out of sympathy for foreign Jews, we allowed the German Fatherland to come to grief."[23]

Ostjuden were simply not assimilable into German life.[24] The hope for their gradual Germanization was misplaced, their "oriental" natures were too set for that. If Eastern Jews were allowed to stay, the opposite would occur: German Jews would increasingly resemble them. Most Weimar German Jews who believed that the Ostjuden were the "real cause" of the prevailing anti-Semitism voiced these convictions privately. Naumann's group, however, made the East-West Jewish distinction the pivot of its arguments and clearly attempted to siphon anti-Jewish hostility onto the Eastern Jews. There were times when it was almost impossible to distinguish the statements of this group from those of the gutter anti-Semitic press. Under Naumann's auspices, the following appeared in the *Kölnische Zeitung* of December 18, 1922:

> That they come in swarms, who will deny this? We don't need statistics to know this. Everywhere we look into their strange eyes . . . everywhere we hear the coarse noises of their excited conversations. In all the railway carriages they crouch and draw numbers in their greasy pocket books. In all the cafés they go in gesticulating groups, they proceed shouting, wallet in hand, from table to door to the next notary to buy a house. . . . entire areas of Berlin are falling into their hands without any of the owners ever getting their worth. . . . they have contempt for everyone. . . . All they care for is the "object." . . . Whatever is worth money becomes for them only an object, for buying and selling. . . .[25]

In the same paper Naumann published an article entitled "Is Berlin in Germany?"[26] Germany was starving, wrote Naumann, and there were hordes of half-Asian Jews penetrating into Germany with their criminal business mentality and dangerous radical notions. Through all kinds of crooked speculation, they insured themselves against disaster and demoralized everyone else. These Jews were quite different from the German Jews. Their rapid departure from Germany was to be strongly encouraged. Citizenship for Ostjuden was out of the question, and all those whose activities were harmful to Germany were to be "ruthlessly expelled."[27]

Naumann's group, although numerically small,[28] symptomized Germany Jewry's increased anxiety over its postwar position. The option of dealing with that anxiety by focusing hostility on the Ostjuden was always present, yet only Naumann's small group made this a part of its official platform. As even assimilated Jews of the time pointed out, the attempt to take Volkish ideology seriously, to deal with anti-Semitism through the total Germanization of Jews, seriously misunderstood the nature and intent of the anti-Semitic animus. Naumann argued that full Jewish identification and integration with the German people on a politically conservative basis would overcome the historic tensions. He did not advocate the

Grenadierstrasse, Berlin. Caricature of a street in the Jewish quarter, by Karl Arnold, one of the series "Berliner Bilder." Originally printed in *Simplicissimus*, 1921. From Fuchs, *Die Juden in der Karikatur.*

Street in the Jewish quarter of Berlin, the 1920s. Photograph by Walter Gircke, Berlin. Courtesy Beth Hatefutsoth, the Nahum Goldmann Museum of the Jewish Diaspora, Tel Aviv.

disappearance of Jewish identity but rather its absolute denational-ization. Of course, he disputed racial definitions of national belong-ing and argued that the real test of loyalty to *Deutschtum* was not an external matter but a question of inner attitudes.[29] There was no doubt, he wrote, that Jews needed to transform themselves. There was a core of justification in Jew-hatred. Jews would have to overcome their parvenu mentality, their tactlessness, their inner servility.[30] Only then would they be ready for proper membership in the German Volk. When the Nazis came to power, Naumann adopted a similar strategy. Racism, he argued, was justified in view of Jewish liberal abuses against Germanism, but correcting feeling and attitudes was the solution to the problem, not "purifying" blood.[31]

Two groups of Jews were outlawed from Naumann's vision: Ostjuden and Zionists. For Naumann, the two were practically synonymous. Both epitomized the Jewish national sensibility, both contradicted *Deutschtum*. They represented alien, disloyal elements. They worked hand in hand with each other and had no place in the German scheme of things.[32]

Naumann's group never received popular support from the Jewish community and was bitterly attacked by the Orthodox, the Zionists, and the spokesmen of the Centralverein.[33] Liberal Jews did not deny Naumann's contention that the *Ostjudenfrage* was a German problem, but they did point out that it was also a Jewish problem, for the animus against the Ostjuden could spread to and often really included German Jews.[34] Linking Jews to political conservatism would not affect this question. Ostjuden as such were not the issue; their problem had to be seen within the general postwar context of stateless refugees.[35] Fabius Schach argued that the war had demonstrated both the political folly and the moral bankruptcy of German nationalism.[36] The Kapp putsch had shown that the only protectors of the Jews were socialist, and this would be true in the future also. The turn to conservatism was doomed before it began.

For all that, Naumann's group manifested a faith in Germany and in German nationalism that was not entirely unlike that of the CV.[37] There was at least a grain of truth in the contention of one of Naumann's supporters that although they used different words, the membership of the Centralverein shared the Deutschnationale Juden's negative opinions of the Ostjuden.[38] But the essential point was that publicly organized German Jewry tried to balance the competing pressures within some kind of traditional, liberal synthesis. Naumann's group, on the other hand, was the first institutional attempt to place Jewish fate squarely in the conservative, nationalist camp.

This reorientation was linked directly to the postwar anti-Semitic mood and attempted to harness it by appropriating key values of the potential aggressor. Clearly, anxiety was not limited to Naumann's dissenting circle. There can be no question that fear and concern were widespread. Perhaps Peter Gay exaggerated when he wrote that "Jewish cringing at Jewish conduct, the most common and most banal expression of Jewish self-hatred, grew markedly during the Weimar Republic, far beyond what it had been before World War I."[39] Modern German Jewish history generally, and in particular the Wilhelmian period, as we have seen, lacked neither the banal nor the pathological versions of self-hatred. Maximilian Harden, Conrad

Alberti, Otto Weininger, Walther Rathenau, and others all published their anti-Jewish tracts well before the First World War.
Indeed, the "banal" manifestation of self-hatred, the desire to
control and eliminate conspicuous Jewish behavior, was inherent in
the Enlightenment-Emancipation pact. As we have seen in chapter 1,
much of the first half of the nineteenth century was taken up with
Jewish efforts to expunge conspicuous "ghetto" characteristics.

Still, the postwar era did sharpen sensitivities and seemed, for
many, to polarize choices. The famous novelist Jacob Wassermann
(1873–1934), in his tortured 1921 work *Mein Weg als Deutscher und
Jude (My Life as German and Jew)*, reflected this heightened
bewilderment and anxiety. Here Wassermann explicitly expressed
his distaste for the Ostjuden: "When I saw a Polish or a Galician Jew
I would speak to him, try to peer into his soul, to learn how he
thought and lived. And I might be moved or amazed, or be filled
with pity and sadness; but I could feel no sense of brotherhood or
even of kinship. He was totally alien to me, alien in every utterance,
in every breath, and when he failed to arouse my sympathy for him
as a human being he even repelled me. . . . I do not solicit imitation
nor claim that what I did, how I conducted myself was proper; I am
simply describing my experience and struggle."[40]

Wassermann was describing a genuine feeling. It was more than
prejudice that divided this acculturated German Jew from the Jews
of the Eastern ghettoes. A real sociocultural gap stood in the way.
Wassermann did not deny his Jewishness but defined it in an
exclusively German way. He drew a fundamental distinction between a "Jewish" Jew and a German Jew: "Are those not two distinct
species, almost two distinct races, or at least two distinct modes of
life and thought?" Even though he found few admirable German
Jewish models—as a youth one blonde rabbi attracted him—he
regarded himself as "simultaneously and irrevocably" both German
and Jewish. Yet this was an insecure vision. It took Wassermann's
troubled unconscious to reveal the fragile mental moorings of the
purported synthesis. His formulation may have mirrored the mute
collective apprehensions of many German Jews: "The German and
the Jew: I once dreamed an allegorical dream. . . . I placed the
surfaces of two mirrors together; and I felt as if the human images
contained and preserved in the two mirrors would have to fight one
another tooth and nail."[41]

Many Jews were conscious of the growing polarity, although the
strategies for dealing with the problem varied enormously. On the
one extreme there were those who advocated total assimilation and

attributed the "Jewish problem" to the fact that Jews still functioned as a separate community with recognizable cultural features. This nonpluralistic conception held that there was simply no place for Jewish separatism in Germany. One advocate of this position, Otto Lubarsch, argued that the Ostjuden were responsible for both anti-Semitism and the continuation of Jewish life in Germany. The gates should have been closed to them long ago. Now they were streaming into the country and bleeding it dry.[42]

Lubarsch accepted the aggressor's stereotype of the Jew. Jewish existence simply lacked legitimacy. Yet even the most self-hating Jews of the postwar period stopped short of an all-encompassing racial determinism. Unlike Otto Weininger,[43] who in 1903 took his own life because he found no escape from his self-defined hatred of Jewishness, men like Arthur Trebitsch (1879–1927) invented at least partial solutions to the racial dilemma. Trebitsch—son of a Viennese Jewish silk-merchant and brother of Siegfried Trebitsch, the distinguished German translator of George Bernard Shaw—was, according to one Jewish commentator, the führer of Austrian National Socialism for a short period during its infancy.[44] While this is not certain, Trebitsch's theories certainly conformed to most Nazi notions.

He developed his racist ideas during the war, but they were first published in 1919 under the title *Geist und Judentum*. Jews, Trebitsch argued, were the fundamental menace to Europe's well-being. The choice was clear. German *Geist* stood poised to resist its antithesis, Jewish *Ungeist*. Europe's recovery was dependent upon the rapid development of an antitoxin to the fatal Jewish poison. Since the best antitoxins were derived from toxins, the most sensitive and effective fighters for *Deutschtum* would come from among Jews who had "overcome" their Jewishness. Trebitsch himself was the ideal leader for the fight against *Judentum*.

Of course, for Trebitsch the real center of Jewish *Ungeist* lay in the East. As a result of the Eastern Jewish invasion the whole of Europe had been infected with *"morbus judaicus."*[45] As the title of his 1921 work *German Geist—or Judaism: The Road to Liberation*[46] indicated, this was an either-or, life-and-death struggle. The Aryan race would have to exert iron pressure on the poisonous creatures from the East and expel all but a select few whose sons would be put to work in compulsory labor battalions. Three generations of physical labor would extract their Judaic poisons, after which purification they would be welcomed as honorable Aryans.[47] Even in demented Jewish minds there was some room for escape from racial determinism.

But this was Jewishness as pathology. Most Jews sought an acceptable combination of *Deutschtum* and *Judentum*, a way of defining
Jewishness in terms of Germanness. Wherever possible the identity
of the two was stressed. The "banal" preoccupation with Jewish
conspicuousness was a way of minimizing overt social distinctions. It
was not self-denial. On the contrary, it signaled recognition of
identity and was governed by the acute self-consciousness of a
minority sensitive to its vulnerability. In a potentially hostile environment German Jews were insecure and anxious. As the executive
director of the Centralverein, Ludwig Holländer, remarked, "German Jews are stepchildren and stepchildren must be doubly good."[48]
Toward this end, Adolph Asch, in 1922, founded a "self-discipline"
organization whose aim was to cut down on Jewish ostentation of
dress and the unnecessary display of luxuries.[49] But special emphasis
was placed on controlling the negative and conspicuous habits of the
obviously Jewish Ostjuden.

Because of the financial dependence and political disenfranchisement of the Eastern Jews in Germany, German Jewish organizations
possessed a significant degree of control over them. Already in 1917
one Jewish community in Saxony had set up a special internal legal
institution (*Rechtsstelle*) to deal with the problem of their local
Ostjuden. As its delegate explained to the annual assembly of the
Centralverein, the behavior and business mentality of the Eastern
immigrants had destroyed established, genial modes of commerce.
The Gentile's judgment of native German Jews had in turn been
affected. To keep the Ostjuden in check and ensure that they
conformed to German standards of morality, the *Rechtsstelle* had
been established. This institution, the delegate Dr. Goldberg from
Plauen announced, had the advantage of containing sensitive matters
within the community itself. The court's task was to arbitrate matters
which if aired publicly would have a negative effect on the way
German Jews were perceived. To much applause, Goldberg announced that the system worked well and that while it had not
eliminated local anti-Jewish sentiment entirely, it had certainly
limited it considerably.[50]

This clearly was not a matter of dissociation but a form of
aggressive confrontation with an unpleasant reality. Shame implied
reluctant acknowledgment of relationship and acceptance of responsibility. Jacob Wassermann formulated it well: "To be ashamed of
someone else is an uncommonly painful situation; most painful of
all, of course, when a blood and racial kinship is involved, and when
an unyielding inner decree as well as moral self-schooling demand

that one bring some sort of defense of every utterance and every action of that other. True responsibility is like a pact signed in one's heart blood."[51]

The drive to hide undesirable Jewish characteristics was a continuing theme. Of course, it was a matter of perceived self-interest rather than positive identification. One observer, writing in the midst of the postwar economic collapse, bewailed the unavoidable fact that all Jews were held responsible for the negative acts of some Jews. Unfortunately, he wrote, any attempt to create a "Society of Honorable Jews" that would be differentiated from the criminal elements of Jewry would not work. Outsiders always generalized Jewish actions. The only solution was to establish a Jewish Community Chamber (*Gemeindekammer*) endowed with punitive powers. This would ensure the maintenance of Jewish honor by internal means.[52]

Jewish honor was understood in very broad terms. Thus the "tactless'" *Jüdeln* (a mishmash of Jewish expressions spoken in *Mauscheln*) performed by Jewish cabaret artists in the nightclubs of avant-garde Berlin was the subject of irate comment by Jewish observers.[53] By emphasizing the comic vulgar "Jewish" element, they complained, Jews were publicly and dangerously fouling their own nest.

Tactlessness, in large part, was understood as the public presentation of what were considered to be ghetto characteristics. German Jewish liberalism, always committed to the exercise of reason, the cultivation of an Enlightenment sensibility that transcended collective prejudicial judgments, never overcame its antipathy to the ghetto and its products. Ghetto Jews, or concretely, Ostjuden, represented the outer limits of this rationalist consciousness; they often induced a selectivity in that liberalism, a double standard that went against the grain of its self-defined humanistic criteria. Ostjuden and "national" Jews seemed to betray the very basis of such liberalism, for they symbolized Jewish particularity (*Sonderleben*), which in its cultural and national forms was antithetical to the Enlightenment pact.

Ghetto Jews, Zionists, and anti-Semites, regardless of their other differences, agreed that Jews were a recognizably separate group. This insistence on Jewish differentiation went against the grain of the classical nineteenth-century Emancipation vision. German Jewish liberals like Constantin Brunner were therefore able to attack all three groups with equal vehemence and without a sense of inner contradiction.

Brunner (1862–1937), born Leo Wertheimer, the son of an Altona rabbi, expressed this faith in its most extreme form. His works on the Jewish question, published in 1919 and 1930, were tenacious reassertions of classical liberal assumptions written at a time when the lights of liberalism in Germany were rapidly being extinguished.[54] A distinguished philosopher, Brunner did not deny Judaism's contribution to civilization. On the contrary, he believed that Judaism, along with Christianity, formed the spiritual basis of the Western heritage. His attacks on anti-Semites, moreover, were uncompromising. So, too, were those on the Zionists and the Ostjuden, however. For Brunner, all fell short of the standards required by his conception of German culture as a culture of *Bildung*, one to whose tenets he remained consistently faithful. He was almost incapable of admitting that German culture had another, more brutal face than the one he championed.[55]

Still, he made a great effort to comprehend the postwar anti-Jewish reality. In Germany, he argued, there was no Jewish question, only an anti-Semitic question—this in contradistinction to Russia, where there *was* a Jewish problem. In Russia there were Jews, whereas in Germany there were only Germans of Jewish origin. But in the last analysis, he maintained, anti-Semites were as unrepresentative of Germany as Zionists were of German Jewry. For Brunner, the threat of Zionism and the threat of the Ostjuden were synonymous. Ostjuden were antithetical to German being; at a time of German suffering, they were not welcome guests, and for the most part they remained alien and unsympathetic creatures.[56]

Brunner wrote these words at the height of the anti-Semitic outbursts of 1919. It is true that he sought to refute anti-Semitic myths of monolithic Jewish unity. Yet his strategy was hardly designed to improve the image of the Ostjuden, and his language about them came perilously close to the language of the anti-Semitic enemy he was attacking. Brunner was aware that this represented a double standard, the blind spot in his liberalism. But in effect he rationalized away any cognitive dissonance by arguing that the prejudice and hatred of both Jew and non-Jew would last as long as external separatist "Jewish" characteristics persisted. Jews had to transform themselves, and their names, and prove their worth. They had to experience Germany as their "natural" home, they had to cease their servile ways and yet avoid sounding arrogant.[57]

Naumann, Wassermann, and Brunner, in effect, regarded Ostjuden as a major cause of the postwar anti-Semitic animus and attempted to deflect that animus upon them and away from German

Jewry. They did not represent the response of organized, main-stream German Jewry. Regardless of the nature of any particular response, however, it is only within the context of effective, radical-ized anti-Semitism that German Jewish life in the Weimar Republic is comprehensible. The war had transformed "the Jew" into Germany's most critical cultural symbol. The historical image of the Jew, always present but less germane in periods of social stability, was now successfully galvanized as an explanation for the German disaster.

The period 1918–23 made clear what many German Jews attempt-ed to deny in the pre-Weimar period. It became painfully obvious that the *Judenfrage* was not merely an *Ostjudenfrage* but went directly to the heart of German Jewry. The attack was regularly aimed at Jews who were most assimilated into German life and culture. Rathenau and the rich Jews, the liberal establishment and the Jewish press, these were presented as the real villains, authors of "the stab in the back." Precisely because distinctions between German and foreign Jewry were increasingly blurred in the lexicon of radical right anti-Semites, accusations about the diabolical nature of "international" Jewry acquired greater plausibility.

But for all that, the Ostjuden still played a specific role in the mythology and practice of the anti-Semitic camp; the traditional stereotype of the ghetto Jew was especially salient in this time of political chaos and economic collapse. An obviously alien presence dramatized the Jewish danger. Indeed, in both the rhetoric and action directed against the Ostjuden, the postwar brutalization of the Jew was most acute and achieved its first real success. In the perspective of hindsight, the representation and treatment of the East European Jew during the early years of the Weimar Republic seems like a foreshadowing, an unconscious rehearsal, of what was to happen to German Jewry itself a decade later.

Against the postwar background of defeat and economic disinte-gration, it was easy to present the "mass invasion" of Ostjuden as a fundamental threat to German morality, economy, sexuality, poli-tics, and culture. Old accusations took on renewed significance. Most prominently, Eastern Jews were presented in terms of the Shylock myth. Statistics were quoted demonstrating how they had used the war as a means of immense self-enrichment at the expense of poor and honest folk who were performing their patriotic duties. Prewar Vienna, declared one anti-Semitic writer, had only 100 millionaires. By 1919 that figure jumped to 8,000, 7,200 of whom were Jews. Of these Jews, 5,400 were Ostjuden who had made their money in the most scandalous, dishonest ways. The lack of ethics was a defining Eastern Jewish trait.[58] Lawyers debated whether or not Ostjuden obeyed an alleged Talmudic injunction that freed them from telling the truth in secular courts.[59]

Radical Right publications like Theodor Fritsch's *Hammer* regularly employed what can only be termed "parasitological" descriptions. They routinely wrote about Ostjuden in dehumanized language—a habit that later became normative for German Jewry as well: "A horrible sight, these faces of animals of prey: in them there is nary a sign of human feeling. . . . they stand before us as the embodiment of Jehova's promise: Thou shalt devour all other Nations! Yes, devour greedily, pitilessly. The myth that Jews were forced to become usurers and liars by their environment is exposed the minute these Ostjuden take their first step into our land. . . . they are the conscious products of Talmudic criminal schools. . . ."[60]

The idea of Eastern Jewish criminality, the refusal of Ostjuden to do honest labor and their determination to enrich themselves at the expense of impoverished workers, was a theme that Hitler employed masterfully in the early years of his career.[61] Ostjuden, moreover, were not only held responsible for taking bread from the mouths of German workers but were also accused of monopolizing urgently needed space in a period of desperately short housing.[62]

The myths that circulated about the Ostjuden were effective because like all myths they had some basis in reality. The war and its immediate aftermath did witness a sharp rise in the number of Ostjuden in Germany. Right-wing agitation vigorously exploited this, especially because Eastern Jews were such visible, obviously alien targets. Their concentration within specific areas, moreover, made it easy to exaggerate their numbers, and this their opponents did with regularity.[63] Still, according to a government memorandum, 45,000 of the Eastern Jews who had entered the country between 1914 and 1920 had already left Germany by 1922, leaving no more than 55,000.[64] In objective terms, this was not a mass invasion, but subjectively, Eastern Jewish visibility provided the accusation with a modicum of plausibility.

Perhaps these myths were especially effective because they merged with the fear of radical political change. After the success of the Russian Revolution, the German revolutions were viewed by millions as the ultimate threat to the traditional German way of life. Bolshevism, the alien import, became an immediate threat. The prominent role of Jews in the Russian Revolution and Bela Kun's

"Underground Russia: A Picture without Words, for Framing." Kikeriki, Vienna. From Fuchs, *Die Juden in der Karikatur.*

radical regime in Hungary made the equation of Judaism and
Bolshevism seem credible. Moreover, many of the leading radical
activists in Germany were indeed Ostjuden (even though they were
almost all totally disaffected from their Jewish origins). Rosa Luxem-
burg, Leo Jogiches, Karl Radek, Towia Axelrod, and Eugen Leviné
are only the best known among many such figures.[65] Gustav Noske,
the right-wing Social Democratic leader, characterized the ideas of
these Eastern Jewish Marxists as a "secret science" that "remained
incomprehensible to the German workers."[66] Even radicals who
were clearly not Ostjuden were branded as such. Kurt Eisner, the
leader of the Bavarian Socialist Republic, who was born in Berlin,
became widely known as a "Galician Jew,"[67] symbol of the Jewish
revolutionary, "a Shylock . . . with a dirty little hat covering his
head." The revolution was described as the "Stern Judas" by the
radical right.[68] International Jewry had carefully paved the way to
German disintegration. The seeds of the postwar disasters had been
sewn during the war with the infiltration into Germany of Russian
and Polish Jewish workers. Only a concerted effort by Germans
would save the country from these conspirators. Alfred Roth of the
Deutscher Schutz- und Trutz-Bund expressed the paranoiac mood of
the radical right in his 1920 pamphlet *Judaism and Bolshevism—
Disclosures of Jewish Secret Documents: An Exhortation and Warning in the Last Hour.* The revolution revealed once again the old
battle lines. The war between Siegfried and Ahasver was one of life
and death. The Russian Revolution was evidence of the triumph of
Talmudic Jewry. Now these same Talmudic Jews were spreading
their tentacles in order to fulfill the ancient prophecy that Jews
would rule the world. An integral part of that plan was the extermination of the Aryan peoples. To that end, Russian and German Jews
were working in conspiratorial harmony.[69]

Beneath the slogan of "the international Jewish revolution" all
distinctions between ghetto Jews and modern Jews evaporated. For
Roth, quintessential Talmud Jews were locked in partnership with,
of all people, Walther Rathenau, "King of the Jews in Germany."
This was not a contradiction in the conspiratorial scheme of things.
It simply meant that the Talmud-Bolshevists of the East had become
the storm troopers of the great Western Jewish capitalists. Even
amongst less extreme anti-Semites, little remained of the older
distinctions between assimilated and unemancipated Jewry.[70]

There were a few exceptions to this rule, however. Friedrich von
Oppeln Bronikowski, for example, a Conservative, attempted to
deal with the Jewish problem by distinguishing Eastern from Ger-

Anti-Semitic election poster, Austria, 1920, by Von Bernd Steiner. From Fuchs, *Die Juden in der Karikatur.*

man Jewry and establishing the former as a legitimate target of animosity, the latter as an illegitimate one.[71] Notions of an international Jewry, he wrote, were palpably absurd. The real distinctions between cultured, assimilated German Jewry and backward Ostjuden were quite obvious. German Jewish support for the Eastern Grenzschluss should have quashed forever the legend of universal Jewish solidarity. If anything, German Jews—Zionists apart—were characterized by their fervent sense of *Deutschtum*. They should not pay for the Bolshevist misdeeds of the Ostjuden. Bronikowski's attempt to deflect anti-Semitism onto the Ostjuden and away from German Jews was quite explicit. Indeed, on the eve of Nazi accession to power he sharpened his attack on Ostjuden and Zionists and insisted even more strongly on the absolute necessity for distinguishing between ghetto Jews and assimilated Jews.[72]

But this distinction had never been clear in the minds of anti-Jewish forces, and the conservative Deutschnationale Volkspartei was split on the question. Certainly in the postwar turmoil Bronikowski's ideas found few supporters amongst committed anti-Semites. In his reply to Bronikowski, the literary critic Adolf Bartels asserted that external differences merely camouflaged inner unity. Jews retained their invisible bonds. In any case, the extent of German Jewish assimilation had been drastically exaggerated. Jews remained ineradicably Jewish regardless of the culture to which they purportedly belonged. The great danger was that Eastern Jews would come to Germany and in the superficial sense be rapidly assimilated by their Western brothers.[73] This perception, that *Ostjudentum* functioned as a massive reservoir for the continual revitalization and strengthening of Western Jewry, was voiced repeatedly.[74]

Yet the success of anti-Semitic propaganda against the Ostjuden cannot be explained purely on the basis of their alleged identity with Western Jews; its effectiveness derived from the resonance that was still evoked by the traditional stereotype of the ghetto Jew. Eastern Jews—alien, visible, and vulnerable—could be attacked with greater impunity than could native Jewry. Election propaganda in both Austria and Germany constantly exploited ghetto Jews through caricature. The Austrian Christian Socials, for example, pictured a snake with the head of a repulsive, side-locked Ostjude strangling its victim to death. The 1920 caption read, "Vote Christian Social, Save Austria!" Similarly, a 1919 German National Democratic Party election poster tapped ancient fears of the dark, mysterious powers of the ghetto. It pictured a priest, candle in hand, walking in front of a simple German worker who is pulling a coffin through the streets.

Anti-Semitic election poster, Germany, 1919, by Max Lieberwein. From Fuchs, *Die Juden in der Karikatur.*

Behind the coffin walks a gloating Ostjude. The only escape from this fate was to vote National Democratic.[75]

It is clear that the attack on the Eastern Jew was particularly vehement in the anti-Semitic camp, but what was the response of other sectors of German society? In a time of mass upheaval, how deeply had the stereotype of the ghetto Jew penetrated? With conservatives like Bronikowski, as we have seen, the answer is clear. Amongst Volkish activists like Hermann Popert, founder of the *Vortrupp* Youth Movement and a person obsessed with the need to reinvigorate a degenerating Germany through alcohol abstinence, there was a similar response. Popert, himself half-Jewish, was deeply concerned with German racial hygiene, but his notion of race was territorial, not genetic. All Germans who lived in Germany could be members of the Volk if they lived up to the requisite national demands. His movement explicitly disavowed racial anti-Semitism and insisted that it not touch any *German* citizens. Ostjuden were a different matter; these Popert portrayed in radically stereotypical terms, basing himself, in the main, on the works of Jakob Fromer, Solomon Maimon, and Karl Emil Franzos. Ghetto Jews, with their filth and unclean sexual habits, were fundamentally undesirable and the cause of German anti-Semitism.[76] Journals such as the Jesuit *Hochland*, which actively opposed racial anti-Semitism, also distinguished "ghetto" Jews from German Jews.[77]

The strength of the anti-Jewish onslaught during this period enabled it to influence the nature of political discourse decisively and to exert pressure on, and successfully penetrate, previously unaffected groups. Even the bastions of opposition to anti-Semitism, the Liberal and Social Democratic parties, were affected. The German Democratic Party maintained its public position against all manifestations of anti-Semitism. Its decision to nominate fewer Jewish candidates, however, was a concession not only to the mood of the times but to the opinions of individual party members as well. Many conveniently attributed anti-Semitism to the presence and behavior of the Ostjuden.[78] (In so doing they were able to avoid confronting the full range of intentions of Volkish anti-Semitism.) Certainly many of the top leaders advocated an aggressive policy against the Eastern Jews. Otto Fischbeck, the party's Prussian minister of trade and commerce, publicly opposed the unsavory presence of the Ostjuden, while insisting that this in no way made the Democrats, who deeply respected the law-abiding German Jews, anti-Semitic.[79] In this manner some of the more democratically inclined political forces concentrated the animus on the Ostjuden and away from German Jewry. This had always been a more respectable position and, under the new circumstances, obviated the need for examining the deeper sources of the widespread racist agitation.

The response of the Social Democratic Party to the *Ostjudenfrage* illustrates the nature of the competing forces at work. Both during the war and after, there were certain people within the party who expressed general anti-Semitic sentiments, but they never became dominant. Indeed, right through the Weimar period the Social Democrats provided German Jews with their most significant organized German support.[80] With regard to the Eastern Jewish question, however, the picture is a little murkier, the evidence more ambiguous. In the prewar period, the party had defended the rights of Jewish aliens in Germany and urged Jews in Eastern Europe to participate actively in the class struggles that would bring about an age of universal socialist emancipation. There can be no doubt about this humanist orientation. Yet like so many other groups in Germany, the Left accepted the negative conception of the ghetto and its products. Karl Kautsky's analysis of the East European ghetto fitted perfectly into that tradition. Although utterly opposed to all racist conceptions and a proponent of Eastern Jewish emancipation, Kautsky regarded Judaism as a reactionary force. Judaism's natural habitat was the ghetto, which Kautsky saw as the symbol of reaction and obscurantism as opposed to progress and enlightenment.[81] Some members of the party invoked the stereotype as a justification for excluding Eastern Jews from Weimar Germany. Ostjuden, remarked one Socialist, had unclean habits and morals that were virtually ineradicable. Strong barriers had to be erected dividing the ghetto from Germany.[82]

The democratic parties were caught between the need to come to terms with popular opinion, on the one hand, and their desire to maintain a reasoned, compassionate policy, on the other. Thus they constantly argued that Germany's problem had objective socio-economic roots and that apart from a few profiteers and black market operators, the small minority of Ostjuden could not possibly be blamed for Germany's collapse. The demagogic notion that these Jews were the foremost danger to Germany's well-being, the source of postwar misery, was palpably absurd.[83] The November 1919 edict concerning the Ostjuden, signed by Wolfgang Heine, Prussian minister of the interior, illustrates this approach. After long discussions with interested Jewish organizations, the Prussian government undertook to deal with the problem in an orderly and understanding fashion. Working through the Jewish workers' welfare organizations, employment for Ostjuden would be procured, even where employment possibilities of local workers might be affected. Of course, this was predicated upon the assumption that Eastern Jews would move on as soon as it became feasible. Those Ostjuden who had committed a crime or were considered a threat to public law and order were to be forthrightly expelled—although this too would be done in consultation with the Jewish organizations, who would look after the interests of the persons in question. Moreover, the *Arbeiterfürsorgeamt* had priority in finding unemployed aliens work. This would then save them from the legally required expulsion.[84]

Anti-Jewish forces obviously interpreted this as evidence of a plot to prefer foreign Jewish over native German workers. The pressures on the Social Democrats in this regard were obvious. The situation was made more difficult by the fact that although the edict was remarkably free of anti-Jewish sentiments, Heine's past was not,[85] and his subsequent remarks and policies demonstrated this. Commenting on Popert's essay, Heine referred to the Ostjuden as "half-barbarian." As Robert Weltsch remarked, this was an indication of the degree to which the stereotype had penetrated even the most "progressive" circles.[86] Only one month after the publication of his edict, Heine made his ambivalence a matter of public record. Despite his attempts to temper the political agitation against the Ostjuden, he conceded that matters were getting progressively worse and asserted that he was considering expelling all "undesirable" Eastern Jews from the cities and interning them in special concentration camps.[87]

These remarks epitomized an unresolved split in Social Democratic attitudes. The traditional compassion and humanity of the Left was pitted against the equally ingrained distaste for the "anachronistic" ghetto Jews. In ideological terms Kautsky's formulation was standard. It was only with Eduard Bernstein's postwar publications that there was any inclination at all to see value in the ghetto Jew as such. Bernstein's arguments that, external appearances apart, there were no fundamental moral distinctions between Germans and Ostjuden was a radical departure from older approaches.[88]

The ambivalence was reflected in political actions as well as attitudes. The November 1919 edict itself was partly the product of German Jewish protests against previous anti-Eastern Jewish actions undertaken by the Social Democratic Government. In a memorandum to the Foreign Office in April 1919, Julius Berger, himself a Social Democrat, objected to the widespread expulsions of Ostjuden from all areas of Germany and especially Prussia.[89] These expulsions were carried out so brutally, wrote Berger, that they had no precedent in previous German regimes. The grounds for the expulsions (unemployment, black-marketeering) were flimsy excuses for a basically anti-Jewish policy that dominated all levels of Prussian bureaucracy. Blaming the Ostjuden for the German collapse was merely a way for the government to cover its own inability to formulate a rational economic policy. If one really wanted to end profiteering one "should close the stock exchange" rather than make a helpless minority the scapegoat for Germany's misery.[90]

Expulsions were not the only official actions perpetrated by the Social Democrats against the Ostjuden. Arbitrary arrests were far from unknown. In early 1920, with full ministerial sanction, security forces engaged in a full-scale raid on the Berlin ghetto. Under the pretext that it was necessary to ferret out black-marketeers, the Grenadierstrasse was cordoned off, and between seven hundred and one thousand people were arrested. Social Democratic Police Chief Eugen Ernst told Minister Heine that these Eastern Jews were a "cancerous sore" on the national body, a real danger to Germany. Unless they were placed in internment camps, he warned, he would not be able to control the growing tide of anti-Semitism. Although all those arrested were eventually released and although the Social Democratic journal *Vorwärts* condemned the incident (while simultaneously putting the blame on the army), this event was firmly imprinted on Jewish, and especially Eastern Jewish, consciousness.[91]

There were, to be sure, law-breakers amongst the Ostjuden, and it was not only the anti-Semites who praised the police raid. The *Berliner Tageblatt*, for example, approved of it, citing the unproductive, criminal nature of many of the ghetto's inhabitants. The initiative to rid the city of these "pests" was welcome.[92] The same newspaper complained only a short time later that security measures had not been sufficiently stringent and that more undesirable Eastern elements were finding their way across the border.[93] But as one sympathetic Jewish commentator argued, the general situation was responsible for economic lawlessness and was not limited to some Ostjuden. German Jews, non-Jews, and other foreigners were all doing the same thing. To make the Ostjuden singularly responsible was shameful.[94]

This was a theme that occupied social critics and dramatists on the extreme Left. Thus while they had little admiration for ghetto Jews, they did use them as a foil to uncover some of the major hypocrisies of postwar bourgeois German morality and society. Kurt Tucholsky's biting *Avrumele Schabbesdeckel und Prinz Eitel-Friedrich von Hohenzollern* (1921) caricatured the system of social and judicial double standards under which ghetto Jews and aristocratic natives were treated quite differently for the same offenses. A few years later he mocked the pathetic efforts of middle-class German Jews, as exemplified by the philistine Herr Wendriner, to justify anti-Semitism when it was aimed at Ostjuden.[95]

Walter Mehring's highly controversial play "The Merchant of Berlin" (1929) was more ambiguous about the Eastern Jew. Directed by the prestigious Erwin Piscator, with ingenious sets designed by Laszlo Moholy-Nagy of the Dessau Bauhaus, this was a tragicomic reconstruction of the 1923 inflation.[96] With Piscator and Mehring— who lived in the Grenadierstrasse for eight weeks so that he could faithfully reproduce its types—the figure of the Eastern Jew was placed at the very center of the action (and the economic crisis). In the midst of the 1923 inflation, Simon Chaim Kaftan (!) arrives in Berlin with one hundred dollars in the lining of his cap. In partnership with a crooked right-wing lawyer (Mueller) Kaftan becomes a billionaire, exploiting the inflation and speculating in war-surplus arms and scrap metal. Typically, as he succeeds, Kaftan sheds his caftan for a cravat and begins to mingle with high society. Yet with stabilization of the mark Kaftan is bankrupted, while Mueller and his nationalist backers go on with their successful speculations and manipulations.

Mehring and Piscator regarded Kaftan as a typical advocate of capitalism, an exploiter who perishes with capitalism. Piscator's claim that they did not intend to provide grist for the anti-Semitic mill, that the question of racial and religious affiliation was a matter of indifference and that the only matter of consequence was the "social or class problem," rings a little hollow. The attention to Yiddish, the acknowledged affinities with *The Merchant of Venice*, the Hebrew words boldly emblazoned on stage made the Jewish ingredient both obvious and central. In the highly inflamed political atmosphere of 1929, the expectation that Kaftan could symbolize the tragic-comic situation of the middle classes under capitalism, bereft of Jewish ethnic connotations, was naïve to say the least. For all that, Kaftan is in the end a victim, not a victor. It is the German lawyer Mueller who is painted in the most unpleasant shades; unscrupulous and demagogic, it is he who ultimately succeeds and maintains his fraudulently acquired wealth at the expense of others. While some liberals saw the play as feeding anti-Semitism, the right wing heatedly condemned it as pro-Jewish and anti-German, a scandal to German national pride.[97]

Anti-Semitic pressure could not be ignored by any Weimar government, however. The Social Democratic government was constantly torn between preventing anti-Semitic outbreaks and making concessions to anti-Semitism.[98] Unwilling to summarily expel all Eastern Jews and expose them once again to the "barbarism" of Eastern European anti-Semitism, Heine made good his promise to intern "undesirable" Ostjuden. On December 27, 1919, the Prussian government officially announced that "criminal" Ostjuden were to be placed in special camps.[99] Camps at Stagard and Cottbus were in fact employed for this purpose, although they were not activated until 1921 when the Social Democrats left the government and the Ministry of Interior was taken over by Alexander Dominicus of the Democrats.

Beginning with the March 1920 raid in Berlin, raids and physical harassments occurred throughout Germany. The attack on the Ostjuden appeared now to have official sanction. Government was working in tandem with, rather than against, forces of the radical Right. Hindsight lends to these events a portentous nature. Raids, expulsions, violence, special camps, all bear a striking resemblance to later developments. But of course, in no way can this be interpreted as a conscious rehearsal. The importance of the period lies in the fact that it demonstrated the degree to which both anti-Jewish rhetoric and action had achieved popular support. It set an ominous precedent.

Some of the actions were indeed extreme. Reports from the internment camps regularly told of verbal and physical abuse. Beatings were part of the daily routine. According to one account, the sound of screaming could be heard through the day.[100] Until August 1923 many who had not been officially tried and convicted were arbitrarily interned. With the return to government of the Social Democrats in 1923 the internments were ended.

Events were grim in Prussia, but the Bavarian situation was even worse. Munich was a hotbed of postwar anti-Semitism, and resident Ostjuden predictably bore the brunt of the fury.[101] Many of the political parties demanded the exclusion of Jews from public office and the immediate expulsion of Ostjuden. Contemporary observers believed that the Reichswehr was preparing a pogrom against the Eastern Jews.[102] In April 1922 an attempt was made to expel all Jews who had settled in Bavaria after 1914. Although this failed, the measure was passed in 1923.[103] Ostjuden, many of them established and respected residents, were expelled from Munich and other Bavarian cities.[104] An equally disturbing sign, one that betrayed underlying anti-Semitic intentions, was the fact that many non-Bavarian German Jews were also expelled.

Similar anti-Semitic outbursts occurred simultaneously in Austria. An almost identical pattern of agitation developed in Vienna. The climax of a concerted campaign against Eastern Jews occurred in June 1920. Slogans protesting their presence were shouted, Jews beaten. Zionists counter-demonstrated, and real violence was averted only by the intervention of security forces.[105]

Vienna was not the only place where local Jews attempted physically to defend the Ostjuden. In the early months of 1920, in Berlin's Grenadierstrasse, there was continual anti-Semitic agitation and violence directed against Ostjuden. Right-wing demagogues constantly attempted to incite restless crowds into violent action. Close observers of these scenes, among them Julius Berger, were convinced that in the light of police sympathy for the anti-Semitic forces a pogrom was imminent.[106] A number of Jewish groups—veterans and Zionist and non-Zionist student organizations—convened to discuss possible strategies of defense. One suggestion, that the group act as a deterrent guard, was dismissed as too provocative. In the end, a simple information service was decided upon. Regular patrols would report signs of trouble to the Volksheim headquarters, from whence the appropriate authorities would be informed. In this crisis atmosphere old Jewish fears reasserted themselves. Jewish conspicuousness was no longer merely inadvisable, it was now regarded as a dangerous provocation. Ostjuden were urged to keep off the streets, desist from all trading, and discard their caftans in public.[107] Although violent incidents continued, the expected pogrom was averted.

It came, however, in 1923, the year the attack on the Ostjuden reached its climax. Between November 5 and 8, Germany's first twentieth-century pogrom shook the Berlin ghetto.[108] On November 5, with over ten thousand people roaming the streets of the Scheunenviertel, the plundering and looting began. Although the event was also a hunger riot, there was no doubt that it was a pogrom. Anyone who was Jewish or looked it was robbed and beaten. Not until late on November 7, after massive police reinforcements had arrived, was some order restored.

This new reality naturally threatened older German Jewish perceptions of the Fatherland. The actions of the Reichsbund jüdischer Frontsoldaten (Jewish Veterans' Association) are a salutary reminder of the complexity of postwar mainstream German Jewish attitudes. Like other veterans' organizations they were intensely patriotic and enormously proud of their war contributions.[109] Yet they stood on their dignity as Jews and came to the physical aid of their imperiled Eastern brethren, for whom they felt responsible despite obvious cultural differences. During the pogrom the Bund, along with other Jewish organizations, broke up into groups of twenty-five men armed with cudgels and pistols and went into the Jewish quarter. In a clash with the looters, one person was killed and a member of the Bund (Max Goldlust) arrested. Later, Bund publications boasted that Bund members had prevented a pogrom directed not only against the Ostjuden but against all of Berlin Jewry. This pogrom, they argued, had been part of a systematic plan to create a Hitler state.[110]

The November outbreaks were merely the climax of anti-Jewish outbreaks which had taken place that year throughout Germany in Beuthen, Königsberg, Nuremberg, Saxony, and elsewhere.[111] For those Jews who were wedded to the humanist conception of German culture as a culture of *Bildung*, the events obviously imposed a strain on ideological and perceptual frameworks. All analyzed events in their own way. Thus in its commentary on the Berlin incident, the Orthodox newspaper acknowledged that there had been an increase in anti-Semitism but questioned Zionist arguments that a pogrom had occurred. Moreover, they wrote, the Zionist call for a "united front" against anti-Semitism was an empty slogan that merely fed anti-Semitic fears of a Jewish monolith. The notion that only Jews could help themselves was untrue. Before anything else it was God's help that was needed.[112] Liberals spoke of "our turbulent times," but often left unanalyzed the specifically anti-Jewish components and implications of the period.[113]

Only the Zionists were equipped with an ideological and explanatory framework that took seriously the radical nature of anti-Semitism. (This does not mean, of course, that they were able to foresee the unthinkable mass horrors of the Holocaust. They were, however, exceedingly alert to the novelty and seriousness of German anti-Semitism. The German Zionist tragedy consisted not in faulty analyses of the situation but in the failure to act upon their convictions and to leave while they still could.) Many years before the essential dynamic of Nazi bureaucratic methods became evident, the *Jüdische Rundschau* analyzed the Bavarian expulsions as a new kind of anti-Semitism, one in which the state itself became the main actor, a systematic organizer of an "administrative pogrom."[114] This, the paper went on, was the first major success of the anti-Semitic movement and a warning to all of German Jewry. Those who still believed that the Enlightenment ideals of the German people would solve the problem were deceiving themselves. Anti-Semitism was propelled by an inner dynamic that would never be satiated and would not stop with the "foreign" Jews. In the wake of the Berlin riots, the Zionists dramatically announced that the achievements of Jewish emancipation in Germany had been shattered and that the hour of fate for German Jewry had arrived.[115]

One decade before the accession to power by the Nazis, this seemed like irresponsible, overblown rhetoric. But the anti-Semitic attack on the Ostjuden was never completely distinguishable from the attack on the native Jew. The salience of the Ostjuden as a cultural symbol made them the first real victims of a brutalized German anti-Semitism, but as the appropriately named journal *Ost und West* remarked, the "Ostjuden are a convenient pretext. One strikes at them but intends the Westjuden."[116] The Ostjuden were clearly a metaphor for all Jews well before the undiscriminating devastation of the Holocaust.

10 THE INVERTED IMAGE

THE romantic cult of the Ostjuden was a mood whose relation to social reality never ceased being tenuous. There was always tension between the idealization of Eastern Jewry and its actual condition. Certainly, it became increasingly difficult to sustain this ideology in the face of postwar breakdown. In 1920 Nahum Goldmann described a situation of almost total collapse. The war, abject poverty, and growing anti-Semitism had uprooted Ostjuden from their traditional milieu, shattered internal and external structures, and resulted in massive demoralization. All that remained, he declared, was egoism, an all pervasive materialism. Eastern Jewry required spiritual as much as physical redemption.[1]

The assimilation of Ostjuden had, of course, been proceeding for many years. But now the assimilated Eastern Jew became almost as prominent a figure in German Zionist mythology as the "real" Jew whom the Ostjude had symbolized. The postwar Galician Jew, one concerned observer wrote, was of a new type, interested only in money and contemptuous of spiritual matters. At least the assimilated Western Jew was sensitive and cultured. The new Galician Jew, on the other hand, was dejudaized and yet used European culture merely as an instrument towards self-enrichment. He was a truly rootless, transitional character.[2]

The most trenchant presentation of the problem of the uprooted Ostjude was made by the Austrian writer Joseph Roth (1894–1939) in

his *Juden auf Wanderschaft* (1927). Here Roth, himself a transplanted Eastern Jew, chronicled the decline of Eastern Jewry and its
dissolution in the West. The work is a sustained cry of despair, a
warning about the moral illusions of assimilation. Ostjuden were
eagerly adapting themselves to a duplicitous civilization, and in the
process they were losing themselves and all the beauty associated
with their warm, meaningful lives. They were leaving *Gemeinschaft*
for a deeply fragmented, impersonal world. Their enthusiasm was
misplaced.[3]

The same criticism was aimed at Ostjuden living in Germany.
Socialist Zionists lashed out at those who rapidly acquired wealth,
fled the ghetto, and raced towards total assimilation.[4] This new
bourgeoisie, intent on establishing its Germanness and denying its
origins, was as ridiculous as it was distasteful. The Germanizing of
names was the least offensive manifestation of the process.[5] The
groping, self-serving *noveau riche* Ostjude, they proclaimed, symbolized *Ostjudentum* at its worst.[6]

But radical assimilation was not limited to the new middle class. It
also seriously affected the working masses, the Eastern Jewish
proletariat in Germany. Socialist Zionists again perceived that a
process of atomization was powerfully at work and that only great
effort could stem the tide.[7] The working-class Eastern Jews belied
older notions of the Ostjude. For many, the jump to modernity
meant not religious reform but radical secularity. The drive to
assimilation entailed an almost complete rejection of the past. A
disappointed Zionist observed that these proletarians saw no reason
for mixing with German Jews and in fact studiously avoided them.[8]

This drive to leave Judaism behind, the generational conflict and
inner disintegration, the radical lack of unity and organization
amongst the Eastern Jewish minority in Germany were the very
opposite of the monolithic picture painted by anti-Semites. To be
sure, the creation in 1920 of a representative body of Eastern Jews in
Germany (Verband der Ostjuden) was a considerable improvement
over the prewar situation. Yet it never received wide popular
support, and the few records and publications of the community
reflect a despairing sense of powerlessness and alienation. From the
moment of its inception, the Verband was plagued by problems of
disunity, apathy, and fragmentation. Its leaders constantly complained that despite the concerted attacks upon them, Ostjuden
refused to make a serious, unified response. How could German
Jewry be expected to defend Eastern Jews, they asked, when
Ostjuden did not even bother to defend themselves?[9]

As a minority in Germany, Eastern Jews felt doubly alien. In the midst of the anti-Semitic agitation an editorial in the Yiddish journal *Der Ostjude* lamented, "We are a Galut within Galut, pathetically dependent upon the goodwill of others."[10] It was vital for Ostjuden to expose the barbarism of anti-Semitism, but internal disunity and external weakness made this very difficult. One of the leading Eastern Jewish figures, Jakob Reich, attempted to define a rational minority *Politik*. In many ways it resembled German Jewish liberal strategies. On the one hand, the general public needed to be educated as to the real nature of the Ostjuden. On the other, self-education and the exertion of the strictest *self-control* were up to the Eastern Jews themselves.[11] Other Eastern leaders exhorted Ostjuden to speak German, for Yiddish only widened the divisions.[12]

Part of the problem, as Reich analyzed it, was the fact that being an Ostjude carried a stigma. This explained the lack of leadership among Ostjuden, for as soon as they could, the better elements fled the ghetto. In their conspicuous situation, Germanization, either through total assimilation or by becoming "German" Jews, must have appeared to them the safest course of action. Without the safeguards of a pluralist social structure such as that of the United States, the creation of distinctively "Eastern" Jewish forms and institutions never seemed like a real option.[13] Clearly, these tendencies weakened even further their solidarity and capacity for resistance. Almost all the Verband's work reflected and attempted to overcome this demoralization. "We Ostjuden have to learn the basic principles of political and social life," one typical analysis read. "We have to start at the beginning and learn the elementary A-B-C. We hold ourselves to be very intelligent, children of the Book, yet we are illiterate. We do not know how to deal with the most important, critical, and dangerous aspects of our existence." The only possible answer was self-reliance. Leadership and organization were the preconditions for this. One could not rely upon German Jewry to do all the work.[14]

From the beginning, *Der Ostjude* did all it could to define the East-West Jewish relationship as a mutually enriching symbiosis. Acutely aware of their dependence and yet proud of their Eastern Jewish origins, the editors of the journal pleaded for greater unity, and proposed that if German Jews would overcome their social distance from Ostjuden their isolation from World Jewry would be decreased.[15] But to a large degree these were rhetorical exercises. As Zalman Rubaschoff pointed out as early as 1918, the presence of a Jewish proletariat in Germany was itself an anomaly.[16] Germany had become yet another sanctuary in the continuing Jewish search for shelter. Now, after the immense sufferings of the war, the Ostjuden were plunged into a new double estrangement, far removed from the cultural world of the German worker and having little in common with bourgeois German Jews.

Rubaschoff viewed German Jewry in the framework of Eastern Jewish nationalist categories. Although he was an incisive commentator on German Jewish life and avoided simplistic judgments, he shared the generally negative Eastern Jewish evaluation of German Jews, who were regarded as the foremost exemplars of Western assimilation. In a series of articles on the Wissenschaft des Judentums, Rubaschoff argued that genuine revival of Jewish scholarship was possible only under conditions of a prior, inner national rebirth.[17] Without this living national ingredient, all intellectual efforts like the attempted synthesis between *Deutschtum* and *Judentum* were bound to lead to de-Judaization.[18]

It is important to recognize that the stereotyping was not limited to German Jewish conceptions of Eastern ghetto Jews. German Jews also had their particular place in the folklore and popular literature of East European Jewry. In many ways the respective East-West stereotypes were inverted images of each other. During the course of the nineteenth century, when German Jewry was representing the Ostjude as its distasteful, anachronistic antithesis, modernizing Eastern Jewish intellectuals looked upon the *Daitsch* as the ideal figure of enlightened Jewish existence. Solomon Maimon's eighteenth-century pilgrimage from his backward Polish ghetto to Berlin was only the beginning of a long tradition.[19] As late as 1896 in his work *Be'emek habahah (In the Valley of Tears)*, Mendele Mocher S'forim (Sh. Y. Abramovitsch), father of modern Hebrew literature, portrayed the German Jew as the locus for Eastern Jewish aspirations.[20] Little Hirschele from the shtetl goes to Leipzig and returns, transformed, as the cultured Heinrich Kohn, contemptuous of the backwardness of the ghetto's inhabitants.

The master folklorist Shalom Aleichem was perhaps the best at catching the half-admiring, half-mocking incredulity of the traditional Jew when confronted with the German Jew. His shtetl child says, "What value in my eyes had the German Jew who lodged with us—the contractor Herr Hertz Hertzenherz, when he spoke Yiddish, went about without a cap, had no beard or earlocks, and had his coattails cut off? I ask you, how could I have helped laughing into his face, when that Jewish-Gentile, or Gentile Jew talked to me in Yiddish, but in a curious Yiddish with a lot of A's in it." Yet for all that, "I loved him so well that I did not care if he said no prayers, and ate his food without saying the blessings. Nevertheless, I did not understand how he existed, and why the Lord allowed him to remain in this world. . . . I had heard from my teacher, Mottel, the 'Angel of Death,' from his own mouth, that this German Jew was only a spirit. That is to say a Jew was turned into a German; and later on he might turn into a wolf, a cow. . . ."[21] Fiction became fact during World War I, when many Eastern Jews refused to believe that German Jewish soldiers were indeed Jewish. Even when this was acknowledged, German Jews were widely regarded as lacking in the "essential" Jewish qualities. They were cold, lacking life and "soul."[22] The popular image of the _Yekke_, the German Jew in Israel, perpetuated this idea. German Jews were held to be assimilated, formal, cold, pompous.

But this was not merely a matter of popular stereotyping. Changes in perception were also the result of new ideological formulations. While "modern" Eastern Jews continued to admire German _culture_, the adulation of the German _Jew_ gave way, under the influence of Zionism, to withering criticism. Achad Ha'am's essays "Slavery in Freedom" (1891) and "Imitation and Assimilation" (1894) set the tone.[23] Western Jews, he argued, possessed external freedom but were characterized by their inner servitude, spineless imitativeness, and national decomposition. This perception soon dominated Eastern Jewish ideas of German Jewry. The great Hebrew poet Chaim Nachman Bialik summed up this judgment in a well-known 1921 statement. Western Jews, by abandoning Hebrew as their national language, had acted as their own gravediggers, ensuring the disappearance of Jewish culture and community. All the sophistication and privilege that had been gained were of no avail. Only the persecuted East had kept Jewish civilization alive and vibrant. Post-Enlightenment Western Jewry was like a corpse buried in foreign cultures and incapable of returning to its source of life.[24]

This developing negation of German Jewish ways was ironic, for as it was being formally articulated, a minority of German Jews were challenging Franzosian stereotypes and creating their own romantic, celebratory stereotype of the "authentic" East European Jew. Yet these inverted East-West Jewish images of one another, whether of the celebratory or dismissive kind, seldom transcended external, stereotypical judgment. In most cases they were exercises that obscured rather than illuminated the reality of their objects.

The work of the great Hebrew writer S. Y. Agnon represents a partial exception to this rule. Much of his writing is as concerned

with grasping the nature and complexity of the modern German Jew
as it is with detailing the traditional East European Jewish world.[25]
Agnon understood the great need for bridging the estranged worlds
of Ashkenazic Jewry. His catholic Jewish vision, his deep sense of
the unity of the Jewish people and its tradition, impelled him to
surmount simplistic stereotypes. In his story *Ad hena* he even breaks
the flow of the narrative to make the following angry remarks:

> All our traditional notions of German Jews are nonsensical; and if
> we praise the Jews of other countries for their knowledge of the
> Torah, their reverence, their righteousness, their piety, their inno-
> cence, we should praise German Jews for their integrity, their
> keenness of mind, their sense of responsibility, their faithfulness in
> keeping their word. Also . . . most of the knowledge we have is
> nothing but the sawdust which fell from the tools of the great
> craftsmen, that is, the German-Jewish scholars.[26]

Yet Agnon's viewpoint remained that of the outsider, the observer
of a different culture. He was sympathetic but also sceptical, critical,
at times even mocking. Like Bialik and Rubaschoff, he respected
German Jewish learning but believed that it could have meaning
only within a living Jewish culture.[27] Because the Ostjude was the
product of a vibrant Jewish reality he possessed qualities lost to
assimilated German Jews. As the narrator comments in "Behanuto
shel Mar Lublin" ("In Mr. Lublin's Store")

> How has this Galician Jew achieved something which the Leipzig
> Jewish notables could never achieve? It is that they themselves are
> too similar to the leaders of the city in their deeds, in their
> thoughts, in their minds. For years, they and their fathers and their
> forefathers strove to emulate the leaders of the city, and they
> succeeded. Thus, in spite of themselves, they became superfluous;
> the leaders of the city have no use for them. Not so with the Galician
> Jew. Even if he tries to emulate the Germans, his own flavor
> remains; his mind does not grow stale. So when one of the members
> of the City Council meets him, he finds in him something which he
> cannot find in himself, nor in anyone else.[28]

Agnon's defense of German Jewry, its contributions to scholarship
and pioneering role in the Jew's complex encounter with modernity,
sat uncomfortably side by side with his critique of its dissipation of
Jewish culture and the exhaustion of Jewish resources in a world of
assimilation. His ambivalence, indeed the conflict itself, went to the

heart of the problem of Jewish identity in the modern world. The
nature and meaning of Jewish culture, commitment, and assimilation remain as unresolved today as they were in the past. For that
reason the debate about the historical essence of German Jewry
retains its contemporary flavor.[29] As East European Jews moved
slowly out of the ghetto, there was a realization that the predicament
of the German Jew was a general predicament. Modernity brought to
all Jews the dilemmas that had confronted German Jewry. The
predicament is still with us.

The context, however, has changed. Today there is no "emancipated" as opposed to "unemancipated" Jewry: the ghetto has been
wiped out. Yet most of post-Enlightenment Jewish history was
conditioned by the dialectics of the rift between the two. The
existence of the ghetto, as myth and reality, colored profoundly the
fate and disposition of emancipated Western Jewry. The "Ostjude"
and "German Jew" were archetypal representations of the dichotomy, major actors in a new kind of confrontation marked by both
tension and creativity. Mirror opposites, they remained bound to
each other. Whether negatively or positively conceived, idealized or
despised, the Ostjude was regarded as the "real" Jew and the living
model of *Ur* Jewishness lost to German Jewry. For Germans, both
Jew and non-Jew, the inhabitants of the Eastern ghettoes kept alive
the historical memory of "the Jew." Their power as cultural symbols
made them essential ingredients of German Jewish self-definition.
Their changing image reflected the complex and contradictory face
of German Jewry itself.

REFERENCE MATTER

ABBREVIATIONS

A	*Die Arbeit*
ALBI	Archives of the Leo Baeck Institute
AZdJ	*Allgemeine Zeitung des Judenthums*
CAHJP	Central Archives for the History of the Jewish People
CVZ	*Centralvereins-Zeitung*
CZA	Central Zionist Archives
F	*Freistaat*
IDR	*Im deutschen Reich*
IF	*Israelitisches Familienblatt*
J	*Der Jude*
JR	*Jüdische Rundschau*
JS	*Jüdische Student*
JSS	*Jewish Social Studies*
JW	*Jüdische Wille*
KCB	*K. C. Blätter*
LBIYB	*Leo Baeck Institute Year Book*
MBA	Martin Buber Archives
MVNDJ	*Mitteilungsblatt des Verbandes nationaldeutscher Juden*
NJM	*Neue Jüdische Monatshefte*
O	*Der Ostjude*
OW	*Ost und West*
W	*Die Welt*

NOTES

CHAPTER 1

1 Jack L. Wertheimer, "German Policy and Jewish Politics: The Absorption of East European Jews in Germany (1868–1914)," (Ph.D diss., Columbia University, 1978), p. 15. Wertheimer argues that use of the term before the twentieth century is anachronistic. Yet as he himself points out (p. 9), equally negative epithets such as *schnorrer* and even *Polish pigs* were regularly employed. Absence of the specific term should not blind us to the reality of an emerging generalized picture which nineteenth-century German Jews were painting of their "half-Asian" counterparts. Here was a case of a stereotype awaiting its name.

The most common designation during the nineteenth century was simply *Polish Jews*, which as Raphael Patai points out was used in two senses: "in a narrow sense, it referred to those Jews who were the natives of the historical Great Poland and Lesser Poland, the core area of Poland bounded by East Prussia in the north and Galicia in the south; in the wider sense, the term 'Polish Jews' was applied to all Jews living in the territory which, under the Jagellons, constituted the Polish-Lithuanian kingdom, whether they came under Prussian, Austrian or Russian rule after the partition of Poland. This broad usage of the term included Jewish communities which differed greatly in cultural and personality traits, summed up in such Yiddish designations as *Polak* (Polish), *Litvak* (Lithuanian), or *Galizianer.*" *The Vanished Worlds of Jewry* (New York: Macmillan Publishing Co., 1980), p. 19.

2 Jacob Katz, *Tradition and Crisis* (New York, 1971).

3 Moses A. Shulvass, *From East to West* (Detroit, 1971), pp. 29–32, 47–50, 112–13. Shulvass's book tells of a relatively unknown but vital chapter in Jewish social and migratory history and has not received the attention it deserves.

4 See "Jewry and Judaism in the Nineteenth Century," in Jacob Katz, *Emancipation and Assimilation* (Farnborough, 1972), p. 3.

5 Shulvass, *East to West*, pp. 12–13.

6 See Isaac Eisenstein Barzilay, "The Jew in the Literature of the Enlightenment," *JSS* 17, no. 4 (October 1956), pp. 245–46.

7 See George L. Mosse, "Thoughts on the German-Jewish Dialogue" (Paper delivered at the 1979 Association of Jewish Studies Conference), pp. 2–3.

8 See introduction to Katz, *Emancipation and Assimilation*, p. x.

9 Quoted in Wilhelm Stoffers, *Juden und Ghetto in der deutschen Literatur bis zum Ausgang des Weltkrieges* (Graz, 1939), p. 69.

10 Ibid., pp. 68–69.

11 Barzilay, "Literature of the Enlightenment," pp. 251–60.

12 Ibid., p. 254.

13 For a good enunciation of this, see Jacob Toury, *Soziale und politische Geschichte der Juden in Deutschland 1847–1871* (Düsseldorf, 1967); also "Die Enstehung der Judenassimilation in Deutschland und deren Ideologie," in Katz, *Emancipation and Assimilation*, p. 226.

14 Mosse, "German-Jewish Dialogue," pp. 5–9.

15 W. H. Bruford has done pioneering work in this area. See his *Culture and Society in Classical Weimar, 1775–1806* (Cambridge, 1962), and *The German Tradition of Self-Cultivation* (Cambridge, 1975).

16 Mendelssohn to Klein, 29 August 1782, in Moses Mendelssohn, *Gesammelte Schriften*, vol. 5, ed. Dr. G. B. Mendelssohn (Leipzig, 1844), pp. 604–5. See, too, Michael Meyer, *The Origins of the Modern Jew* (Detroit, 1967), p. 44.

17 See Franz Kobler, *Jüdische Geschichte in Briefen aus Ost und West* (Vienna, 1938), pp. 145–46.

18 Emanuel Wohlwill, "Bemerkungen über Sprache und Sprachunterricht als Beförderungsmittel der allgemeinen Bildung," *Sulamith* 7 (1812), p. 87.

19 "Die Muttersprache in jüdischen Schulen," *Israelitische Annalen*, no. 29 (16 July 1841), p. 229.

20 "Die Juden in Volhynien, Podolien und der Ukraine," *Jeschurun* 1 (1855), p. 210.

21 See John M. Cuddihy, *The Ordeal of Civility* (New York, 1974). Much in this work lacks historical rigor, but the emphasis upon the importance of manners and etiquette in the assimilation process is correct.

22 "Einige Ideen über Erziehung und öffentlichen Unterricht," *Sulamith* 1 (1806), pp. 46–47.

23 David Friedländer, *Ueber die Verbesserung der Israeliten in Königreich Pohlen* (Berlin, 1819), p. 11.

24 See Alfred Rubens, *A History of Jewish Costume* (New York, 1973). Commentary on page 161; reproduction of portrait on page 171.

25 Anton Rée, *Die Sprachverhältnisse der heutigen Juden im Interesse der Gegenwart und mit besonderer Rücksicht auf Volkserziehung* (Hamburg, 1844). I thank Professor Jacob Katz for this reference.

26 Ibid., p. 40.

27 The work was given generally favorable reviews. See *AZdJ* 1, no. 11 (10 March 1845), p. 158.

28 See Jacob Katz, *Out of the Ghetto* (New York, 1978), p. 86.

29 See Jacob and Wilhelm Grimm, *Deutsches Wörterbuch*, vol. 6 (Leipzig, 1855), pp. 1819–20. They trace the word *Mauscheln* to 1680. Friedrich Kluge and Alfred Götze, *Etymologisches Wörterbuch* (Berlin, 1951), trace *Jüdeln* as far back as 1522.

30 For facts and statistics about the conditions of East European Jewry during this period, consult Louis Greenberg, *The Jews in Russia* (New York, 1976), and Arthur Ruppin, *The Jews in the Modern World* (London, 1934).

31 Jakob Fromer in his introduction to Solomon Maimon's *Lebensgeschichte* (Munich, 1911), pp. 7–8. This is particularly revealing because Fromer (like his subject, Maimon) was himself a transplanted, Westernized Ostjude. He believed that he had transcended the ghetto and viewed it through German Enlightenment eyes. Clearly, modern Jewish self-rejection was by no means limited to its German Jewish variant. Fromer stressed the inappropriateness of Judaism in the modern world as well as its lack of the "aesthetic" dimension. See his *Das Wesen des Judentums* (Berlin, 1905).

32 See, for instance, Leopold Zunz, *Die gottesdienstlichen Vorträge der Juden historisch entwickelt* (1832; Frankfurt, 1892), p. 458.

33 Heinrich Grätz, *History of the Jews*, vol. 5 (Philadelphia, 1895). On the disastrous "Polonization" see pp. 16–17; on the effects of language, pp. 205–6. Grätz thought these early Polish immigrants "used to lord it all over the Jews in Europe." His attitude to the East European Jewish culture of his own time was also not particularly favorable. He refused to allow publication of his *History* in Yiddish, although six years after his death (1897) a translation did appear. See Josef Meisl, "Grätz und das Ostjudentum," *Die jüdische Presse* (1917).

34 Wohlwill, "Bemerkungen," p. 87.

35 Ibid., pp. 88–89.

36 Friedländer, *Verbesserung der Israeliten*, p. 39.

37 I am following David Biale's excellent account of *Wissenschaft des Judentums*. See his *Gershom Scholem* (Cambridge, 1979), esp. pp. 1–25.

38 Zunz to Ehrenburg, 3 October 1820, in Leopold Zunz, *Leopold Zunz*, ed. Nahum N. Glatzer (Tübingen, 1964).

39 Abraham Geiger, *Abraham Geigers nachgelassene Schriften*, ed. Ludwig Geiger (Berlin, 1875), pp. 313, 319.

40 "Aus Galizien," *Der Israelit des 19. Jahrhunderts* 7, no. 6 (8 February 1846), p. 46.

41 Markus Jost, *Geschichte der Israeliten seit der Zeit der Maccabäer bis auf unsere Tage*, vol. 9 (Berlin, 1828), p. 47.

42 "Der sogenannte Chassidismus," *Der Israelit* 7, no. 22 (May 1866).

43 Friedländer, *Verbesserung der Israeliten*, pp. 22–25, is only one example among many.

44 Grätz, *History*, pp. 5–6, 206.

45 "Einige Ideen über Erziehung und öffentlichen Unterricht," pp. 46–47.

46 "Aus Galizien," p. 46.

47 Geiger, *Schriften*, p. 323.

48 "Galizische Zustände," *Der Israelit* 7, no. 12 (22 March 1846), p. 93.

49 Geiger to Joseph Naftali Dernberg, 3 August 1840, in Abraham Geiger, *Abraham Geiger and Liberal Judaism*, comp. Max Wiener (Philadelphia, 1962), pp. 87–88.

50 See "Emancipation," *Der Israelit* 2, no. 1 (January 1861).

51 "Die Judenfrage im künftigen Europa," *OW*, 1919, no. 11–12, pp. 305–6.

52 Friedländer, *Verbesserung der Israeliten*, pp. 48–49, xlvi, xlvii.

53 Ibid. On education and its importance, see pp. 1 ff.; on the comparison of Polish with other Jews, pp. 19–20.

54 For use of the term (although in a later context), see Henry Wassermann, "Jews and Judaism in the Gartenlaube," *LBIYB* 23 (1978), p. 52.

55 Geiger, *Schriften*, p. 298.

56 Mosse, "German-Jewish Dialogue," pp. 9–10.

57 See Max Lilienthal, "My Educational Mission in Russia," in Lucy S. Dawidowicz, *The Golden Tradition* (Boston, 1967). See, too, Leon Scheinhaus, *Ein deutscher Pionier* (Berlin, 1911).

58 This was a widespread attitude. See, for only one example, "Die Juden in Galizien," *AZdJ* 48, no. 46 (11 November 1884).

59 This was made clear not just by theorists but also by communal activists who worked directly with the refugees. See the *Denkschrift des Hauptgrenzkomites zu Königsberg*, 14 October 1869, CAHJP, M 1/3.

60 Kobler, *Briefe aus Ost und West*, p. 39 (12 May 1837).

61 Ibid., p. 62. He made these remarks in an address to the rabbinical assembly in Frankfurt on 24 April 1845.

62 See Helmut Neubach, *Die Ausweisungen von Polen und Juden aus Preussen 1885–1886* (Wiesbaden, 1967). Also valuable in this connection is Werner Conze, *Polnische Nation und deutsche Politik im Ersten Weltkrieg* (Cologne, 1958).

63 Zunz, *Leopold Zunz*, p. 453.

64 "Galizische Zustände," *Der Israelit des 19. Jahrhunderts*, 7, no. 12 (22 March 1846), p. 93.

65 Shulvass, *East to West*, has the most comprehensive treatment of the *Betteljuden*. See esp. pp. 12–14, 100–104.

66 Toury, *Geschichte der Juden*, p. 32.

67 See Ismar Schorsch, *Jewish Reactions to German Anti-Semitism, 1870–1914* (New York, 1972), chap. 1 and esp. pp. 23–25.

68 *Deutsch Israelitische Gemeinschaft: Bericht über den Gemeindetag zu Leipzig,* August 1869, CAHJP, M 1/3.

69 *An die Herren Vorsteher, Vertreter der Wohltätigkeitsvereine und Notabeln der Israelitischen Gemeinden in Russland und Polen,* August 1871, CAHJP, M 1/8, doc. 4.

70 *Verhandlungen der constituierenden Versammlung des Deutsch-Israelitischen Gemeindebundes,* Leipzig, 14 April 1872, CAHJP, M 1/8, file U.

71 *Armenpflege betreffend,* CAHJP, M 1/3, file U. The report claimed that success was more complete in some areas than others.

72 I. Horowitz, "Ein Blick auf die Juden in Galizien," *Monatsschrift für Geschichte und Wissenschaft des Judentums* 16 (1867). See esp. pp. 43–46, 92, 130–33.

73 On all these writers, see Stoffers, *Juden und Ghetto,* pp. 265–303.

74 The work is reproduced in Gellert's *Sämtliche Schriften,* vol. 5 (Leipzig, 1775). See Michael Meyer, *The Origins of the Modern Jew* (Detroit, 1967), p. 185, n. 27, for perceptive comments on the difference between Gellert's and Lessing's treatment of the Jew.

75 The review appeared in the *Frankfurter gelehrte Anzeigen,* September 1, 1772. See also Alexander Altmann, *Moses Mendelssohn: A Biographical Study* (Philadelphia: The Jewish Publication Society of America, 1973), p. 337. In her *The Origins of Totalitarianism,* new ed. (New York, 1966), Hannah Arendt has a fascinating analysis of Goethe's and others' expectations of Jewish exoticism (pp. 56 ff).

76 See Herbert Kupferberg, *The Mendelssohns: Three Generations of Genius* (New York: Charles Scribner's Sons, 1972), pp. 183–84.

77 For an interesting review of the way in which Jewish women were represented in the German theater between 1800 and 1850, see chap. 4 of Charlene A. Lea, *Emancipation, Assimilation and Stereotype: The Image of the Jew in German and Austrian Drama (1800–1850)* (Bonn: Bouvier Verlag Herbert Grundmann, 1978).

78 See, for instance, his *Polnische Judengeschichten* (Leipzig, 1878) and *Neue Ghettogeschichten* (Leipzig, 1881).

79 Much of what follows is borrowed from David Biale's "Masochism and Philosemitism: The Strange Case of Leopold von Sacher-Masoch" (forthcoming in *The Journal of Contemporary History*).

80 On Schiff, see Mary Lynne Martin, "Karl Emil Franzos: His Views on Jewry as Reflected in His Writings on the Ghetto" (Ph.D. diss., University of Wisconsin, 1968), pp. 24–25.

81 See *Monatsschrift für Geschichte und Wissenschaft des Judentums* 16 (1867), pp. 33–38.

82 Much of this background information has been culled from an extremely useful dissertation by Miriam Roshwald, "The Stetl in the Works of Karl Emil Franzos, Shalom Aleichem and Shmuel Yosef Agnon" (Ph.D. diss., University of Minnesota, 1972).

83 See his "Familien-Geschichten," *IDR,* 1895, no. 1 (July), p. 7.

84 See Amos Elon, *Herzl* (New York, 1975), pp. 14–15.
85 See the foreword to Franzos, *Aus Halb-Asien*, vol. 1 (Stuttgart and Berlin, 1914), pp. xvii–xviii. This had already reached its fifth edition. Franzos's other famous work on this theme is *Der Pojaz* (1905). See, too, his *The Jews of Barnow* (New York, 1883).
86 Franzos, *Halb-Asien*, 1:xiii–xiv.
87 Ibid., p. xxv.
88 Roshwald, "The Stetl." This comparative analysis owes much to her insightful work.
89 Mark Scherlag, "Karl Emil Franzos," *JR* 16, no. 50 (15 December 1911), p. 598.
90 Binjamin Wolf Segel, *Die Entdeckungsreise des Herrn Dr. Theodor Lessing zu den Ostjuden* (Lemberg, 1910), p. 65.
91 See Ludwig Geiger's enthusiastic "Zu K. E. Franzos' Gedächtnis," *AZdJ* 79, no. 22 (28 May 1915), pp. 258–59.
92 Joseph Wohlgemuth, "Deutschland und die Ostjudenfrage," *Jeschurun* 3, no. 2 (February 1916), p. 65 ff.
93 "Der 'Polnische Jude,' " *AZdJ* 70, no. 36 (7 September 1906), p. 421.
94 "Vom nationaldeutschen Juden: Eine Erwiderung," *IDR*, 1921, no. 1, p. 30.
95 See, for instance, Erich Bischoff, *Klarheit in der Ostjudenfrage* (Dresden and Leipzig, 1916), p. 56.
96 Friedrich von Oppeln Bronikowski, *Gerechtigkeit! Zur Lösung der Judenfrage* (Berlin and Wilmersdorf, 1932), p. 94.
97 See "Ostjudendebatte im Preussischen Landtag," *JR* 27, no. 95 (1 December 1922), p. 625.

CHAPTER 2

1 For an excellent summation of this period and its consequences for world Jewry, see David Vital, *The Origins of Zionism* (Oxford, 1975), chap. 3.
2 In 1880, of the world's ten million Jews, 75 percent were concentrated in Eastern Europe. By 1933 that figure had been reduced to 46 percent. In 1880 only 3.5 percent lived in the United States, on the other hand, but by 1930 the figure had reached 30 percent. See Howard Morley Sachar, *The Course of Modern Jewish History* (Cleveland, 1958), p. 315.
3 Vital, *Origins*, pp. 51–53. On Mauthner, see Wertheimer, "German Policy and Jewish Politics," pp. 135–36.
4 "Was unsere russischen Glaubensbrüder zu thun haben," *AZdJ* 45, no. 16 (19 April 1881), p. 251.
5 "Wie ist den russischen Juden zu Hilfe zu kommen?" *AZdJ* 10, no. 5 (26 January 1846), pp. 62–63.

6 Zosa Szajkowski, "The European Attitude to East European Immigration (1881–1893)," *American Jewish Historical Quarterly* 41, no. 2 (December 1951). See esp. pp. 130–31.

7 On the outbursts (at Stettin), see Fritz Stern, *Gold and Iron* (New York, 1977), p. 526. On the beginnings of the anti-Semitic movement, consult Paul Massing, *Rehearsal for Destruction* (New York, 1949); Peter G. J. Pulzer, *The Rise of Political Anti-Semitism in Germany and Austria* (New York and London, 1964); and Uriel Tal, *Christians and Jews in Germany* (Ithaca and London, 1975).

8 Szajkowski, "The European Attitude," p. 138.

9 Ibid., p. 140.

10 Stern, *Gold and Iron*, p. 526.

11 *Deutsches Central Komitee für die russischen Juden: Erster Bericht, streng vertraulich*, July 1891, CAHJP, INV-1409/318.

12 See Bernhard Kahn, "Die jüdische Auswanderung," *OW*, 1905, nos. 7–8; and Zosa Szajkowski, "Sufferings of Jewish Emigrants to America in Transit Through Germany," *JSS* 39, nos. 1–2 (Winter–Spring 1977).

13 From a report by Charles Netter of the Alliance, quoted in Vital, *Origins*, p. 60.

14 Mary Antin, *The Promised Land* (Boston and New York, 1912), p. 172. See the entire passage pp. 172–75.

15 Ibid., pp. 174–75.

16 Sammy Gronemann, "Errinnerungen," in Monika Richarz, ed., *Jüdisches Leben in Deutschland im Kaiserreich* (Stuttgart, 1979), pp. 407–10. See, too, Szajkowski, "Sufferings," esp. p. 108.

17 Karl Emil Franzos, "Die Kolonisationsfrage," *AZdJ* 55, nos. 47, 48 (20, 27 November 1891). Franzos made these comments in his capacity as chairman of a commission to investigate the possibilities of new areas for Russian Jewish colonization. In the end, Brazil was recommended, a country with relatively few Jews, little anti-Semitism, and a good climate.

18 See Ernst Feder, "Paul Nathan: The Man and His Work," *LBIYB* 3 (1958), p. 71.

19 S. Adler-Rudel, *Ostjuden in Deutschland, 1880–1940* (Tübingen, 1959), pp. 2–4.

20 See Zosa Szajkowski, "Conflicts in the Alliance Israelite Universelle and the Founding of the Anglo-Jewish Association, the Vienna Allianz and the Hilfsverein," *JSS* 19, nos. 1–2 (January–April 1957).

21 *Erster Geschäftsbericht des Hilfsvereins der deutschen Juden 1901–1902, CAHJP*, M 2/1, p. 11.

22 Szajkowski, "Conflicts," p. 47.

23 Feder, "Paul Nathan," p. 67.

24 See, for instance, "Das Galizische Werk," *AZdJ* 49 (1 September 1885).

25 Adolf Hitler, *Mein Kampf*, trans. R. Manheim (Boston, 1971), p. 59.

26 For an account of the facts of Jewish prostitution and the campaign to combat it, see Marion A. Kaplan, *The Jewish Feminist Movement in Germany* (Westport, 1979), chap. 4.

27 See Sidonie Werner, "Mädchenhandel," *Referat gehalten auf dem 2. Delegiertentage des jüdischen Frauenbundes*, October 1907; and Marion Kaplan, "German Jewish Feminism in the Twentieth Century," *JSS* 38, no. 1 (Winter 1976), p. 46.

28 Kaplan, *Jewish Feminist Movement*, pp. 125–37.

29 Fabius Schach, "Ein notwendiges soziales Hilfswerk," *OW*, 1903, no. 6, pp. 424–25.

30 Kaplan, *Jewish Feminist Movement*, pp. 129–30.

31 Franzos, "Kolonisationsfrage," esp. pp. 555, 567.

32 See "Das ostjüdische Problem," *AZdJ* 55, no. 42 (6 November 1891).

33 See "Der polnische Jude," *AZdJ* 70, no. 36 (7 September 1906).

34 Among them, *Von Cheder zur Werkstätte: Eine Erzählung aus dem Leben der Juden* (Vienna, 1885); *Der Freiwillige des Ghetto: Kulturbilder aus Vergangenheit und Gegenwart* (1903); and *Reiseerinnerungen aus Galizien* (1900).

35 Moritz Friedländer, "Politische Strömungen im heutigen Judentum," *Zeitschrift für Politik* (1911), pp. 169 ff.

36 Wertheimer, "German Policy," has a detailed analysis of the various administrative and legal measures adopted by the German authorities to ensure this. See pp. 39–90.

37 For a more detailed demographic breakdown, see Adler-Rudel, *Ostjuden*, p. 164.

38 A representative sample of these attacks and the various Jewish responses is to be found in Walter Boehlich, ed., *Der Berliner Antisemitismusstreit* (Frankfurt am Main, 1965).

39 Heinrich von Treitschke, "Unsere Aussichten," *Preussische Jahrbücher* 44 (1879), pp. 559–76. See also chap. 3 below for a more detailed treatment of the question.

40 See Boehlich, *Antisemitismusstreit*, for examples of this.

41 Salomon Neumann, *Die Fabel von der jüdischen Masseneinwanderung* (Berlin, 1881).

42 See Helmut Neubach, *Die Ausweisungen von Polen und Juden aus Preussen 1885–1886* (Wiesbaden, 1967), pp. 18–21.

43 See the *AZdJ* of 9 February 1886 and 16 February 1886. Quoted in Neubach, *Ausweisungen*, pp. 148–49.

44 Neubach, *Ausweisungen*, pp. 150–51.

45 Wertheimer, "German Policy," pp. 151–53.

46 Ibid., pp. 162–63.

47 Jehuda Reinharz, "*Deutschtum* and *Judentum* in the Ideology of the Centralverein deutscher Staatsbürger jüdischen Glaubens 1893–1914," *JSS* 36, no. 1 (January 1974). This remained the official position throughout its history.

48 For the numbers of Eastern Jews generally in Germany, see Wertheimer, "German Policy," pp. 193–207. Ostjuden concentrated in three states: Prussia, Bavaria, and Saxony (in 1910, 82.5 percent of the immigrants lived in these states). In Leipzig and Dresden they were the majority of all resident Jews.

49 For an analysis of these settlement patterns, see Klara Eschelbacher, "Die ostjüdische Einwanderungsbevölkerung der Stadt Berlin," *Zeitschrift für Demographie und Statistik der Juden* 16 (1920) and 17 (1923).

50 Adolf Grabowsky, "Ghettowanderung," *Die Schaubühne* 6, no. 5 (3 February 1910), p. 124.

51 Wertheimer, "German Policy," has a good analysis of their occupational structure, pp. 240–96. See, too, Fabius Schach, "Die russischen Juden in Deutschland," *OW*, 1905, nos. 10–11, pp. 719–30.

52 Chaim Weizmann, *Trial and Error* (Philadelphia, 1949), p. 165.

53 For details, see Wertheimer, "German Policy," chap. 7. On the eve of World War I, over three thousand students were enrolled at the various German institutions of higher education. From a more general perspective, see Robert C. Williams, *Culture in Exile* (Ithaca, 1972).

54 See, for instance, "Zur Lage der russisch-jüdischen Studenten in Deutschland," *W* 6, no. 15 (11 April 1902), p. 3.

55 Such accusations were of long standing. They were already part of the justification for the 1885–86 expulsions. See Neubach, *Ausweisungen*, p. 220.

56 Quoted in Wertheimer, "German Policy," p. 368.

57 See Gustav Krojanker, "Wille und Kampf," *JR* 17, no. 37 (11 September 1912), p. 351. In 1913, however, the Kartell-Convent der Verbindungen deutscher Studenten jüdischen Glaubens (K.C.) did protest measures which they believed were specifically anti-Jewish.

58 Peter Gay, "At Home in America," *The American Scholar* 46, no. 1 (Winter 1976–77), p. 42.

59 Eugen Ehrlich, *Die Aufgaben der Sozialpolitik im österreichischen Osten* (Czernowitz, 1909; Munich and Leipzig, 1916), p. 32. Koestler's somewhat eccentric work is entitled *The Thirteenth Tribe: The Khazar Empire and Its Heritage* (London, 1977).

60 Ernst Lissauer, "Deutschtum und Judentum," *Der Kunstwart* 25, no. 13 (April 1912), p. 7.

61 See Theodor Lessing's autobiography, *Einmal und nie wieder* (Gütersloh, 1969), p. 112.

62 Ehrlich, *Aufgaben*, p. 33.

63 Werner Sombart, ed., *Judentaufen* (Munich, 1912).

64 See Werner Sombart, *The Jews and Modern Capitalism* (New York, 1969), esp. pp. 347–51. The quotation appears on p. 349.

65 Sombart, *Judentaufen*, p. 15.

66 Ibid., p. 21.

67 Ibid., p. 38.

68 Ibid., p. 31.

69 See, for instance, the contributions by Ludwig Geiger and L. Gurlitt.

70 See Mauthner's piece, pp. 74–77.

71 "Die Wirklichkeit von morgen," *JR* 19, no. 44 (30 October 1914), p. 403.

72 Friedrich Blach, *Die Juden in Deutschland* (Berlin, 1911), p. 42.

73 Ibid., pp. 20–21.

74 "Über die christlich-jüdische Mischehe," *Sexualprobleme: Zeitschrift für Sexualwissenschaft und Sexualpolitik*, 1912. See esp. pp. 702, 713, 745–49.

75 See Sigmund Freud, *Jokes and Their Relation to the Unconscious*, trans. James Strachey (New York, 1963), p. 111.

76 Sammy Gronemann, *Zikhronot shel Yekke* [Memoirs of a Yekke] (Hebrew) (Tel Aviv, 1946), pp. 16–17. Quoted in Wertheimer, "German Policy," p. 327.

77 From Loewenberg's autobiographical novel *Aus zwei Quellen* (Berlin, 1914), quoted in Ernst L. Loewenberg, "Jakob Loewenberg: Excerpts from His Diaries and Letters," *LBIYB* 15 (1970), p. 206.

78 Loewenberg, "Excerpts," pp. 183–84.

79 We do not yet have enough comparative information on this question. The evidence is mixed in the collection of village and small-town memoirs contained in Richarz, *Jüdisches Leben* (sec. 2); and Werner J. Cahnman, "Village and Small-Town Jews in Germany: A Typological Study," *LBIYB* 19 (1974).

80 "Gebt richtige Wanderarmenfürsorge!" *AZdJ* 78, no. 31 (31 July 1914), pp. 367–69.

81 See the memoirs of Abraham A. Fraenkel, *Lebenskreise* (Stuttgart, 1967), p. 25.

82 Kurt Blumenfeld, *Erlebte Judenfrage* (Stuttgart, 1962), p. 27.

83 "Bemerkungen über mein Leben," *Bulletin des Leo Baeck Instituts*, no. 20 (1962), pp. 288–89.

84 "Aus dem Karlsbade," *AZdJ* 56, no. 28 (2 July 1892), p. 335.

85 The quotations are taken from the English translation, *Hetty Geybert* (New York, 1924), pp. 134, 146–47.

86 "Die russische Seuche," *JR* 11, no. 13 (30 March 1906), pp. 180–81.

87 Mauthner was born in Horitz near Königgrätz in Bohemia. Ehrlich heralded from Czernowitz, Bukowina.

88 Gronemann, "Erinnerungen," p. 407.

89 Ludwig Jacobowski, *Werther, der Jude* (Dresden and Leipzig, 1903), p. 151.

90 Ibid., pp. 138–39.

91 Wertheimer, "German Policy," pp. 414–74, has a full account of this development.

92 See, for instance, A. Michaelis, "Steht den ausländischen Juden in den preussischen Synagogengemeinden ein Wahlrecht zu?" *AZdJ* 76, no. 22 (31 May 1912). See, too, Ahron Sandler, "The Struggle for Unification," *LBIYB* 2 (1957).

93 See Fabius Schach, "Die Fremdenfrage (Zum Fall Duisburg)," *OW*, 1914, no. 1.

94 Michaelis, ". . . ausländischen Juden," p. 254.

95 "Ausländer," *Der Israelit* 54, no. 1 (2 January 1913), p. 2. See, too, Heimberger, "Das Wahlrecht ausländischer Juden in preussischen Synagogengemeinden," ibid., no. 33 (14 August 1913).

96 Thus Harry Epstein, "Das Stimmrecht der Ausländer—nach dem preusischen Judengesetz," *JR* 18, no. 34 (22 August 1913), pp. 353–54. The same paper also published Blöde, "Ausländer und kein Ende" (no. 5 [31 January 1913]); and Viktor, "Nochmals das Gemeindewahlrecht" (no. 7 [14 February 1913]).

97 For details, see Ismar Schorsch, *Jewish Reactions to German Anti-Semitism, 1870–1914* (New York, 1972), chap. 7; and Jehuda Reinharz, *Fatherland or Promised Land* (Ann Arbor, 1975), chap. 5.

98 "Zionismus und Deutschtum," in *Die Stimme der Wahrheit: Jahrbuch für wissenschaftlichen Zionismus* (Würzburg, 1905).

99 Moritz Goldstein, "Deutsch-jüdischer Parnass," *Der Kunstwart* 25, no. 12 (March 1912).

100 Lissauer, "Deutschtum und Judentum," p. 7.

101 Julius Goldstein, "Moritz Goldsteins 'Deutsch-jüdischer Parnass,' " *IDR*, 1912, no. 10, pp. 447 ff. Translation from Reinharz, *Fatherland*, p. 198.

102 See, for instance, Felix Goldmann's evaluation of Eastern Jewish culture in "Assimilation," *IDR*, 1914, no. 7/8 (July/August), pp. 313–14.

CHAPTER 3

1 Hitler, *Mein Kampf*, pp. 56–57.

2 See Mosse's path-breaking essays "Culture, Civilization and German Anti-Semitism" and "The Image of the Jew in German Popular Literature: Felix Dahn and Gustav Freytag," in his *Germans and Jews* (New York, 1971).

3 This was claimed in a petition by Ballnus of Czichau. Quoted in Jacob Toury, *Soziale und politische Geschichte der Juden in Deutschland 1847–1871* (Düsseldorf, 1977), p. 31. See Toury for other examples of later rhetoric against the Eastern Jew.

4 Heinrich von Treitschke, "Unsere Aussichten," *Preussische Jahrbücher* 44 (1879), pp. 559–76.

5 Heinrich von Treitschke, *Treitschke's History of Germany in the Nineteenth Century*, vol. 7, p. 450.

6 Helmut Neubach, *Die Ausweisungen von Polen und Juden aus Preussen 1885–86* (Wiesbaden, 1967), p. 10.

7 Hans Fischer [Kurt Aram], *Der Zar und seine Juden* (Berlin, 1914), p. 168.

8 There are many examples of this. See, for instance, Richard Andree, *Zur Volkskunde der Juden* (Bielefeld and Leipzig, 1881), pp. 68–69; or the discussion by Gustav Jäger in *Entdeckung der Seele* 1 (1884), pp. 246–48. The discussion went on through the Weimar period. See Hans F. Günther, *Rassenkunde des jüdischen Volkes* (Munich, 1930), p. 266.

9 "Ehren—unn Loblied oufn Knoblich . . . ," in Eduard Fuchs, *Die Juden in der Karikatur* (Munich, 1921), pp. 282–83.

10 Franz Kafka, amongst others, was struck by this. See his "Travel Diary: Trip to Weimar and Jungborn, June 28–July 29, 1912," in *The Diaries of Franz Kafka, 1914–1923* (New York, 1976), p. 301.

11 This appears in Joseph Nedava, *Trotsky and the Jews* (Philadelphia, 1972), p. 245. Quoted in Wertheimer, "German Policy and Jewish Politics," p. 127.

12 "The Anti-Christ," in Walter Kaufmann, ed., *The Portable Nietzsche* (New York, 1974), p. 625. The work was originally published in 1888. See also Nietzsche's ambivalent remarks concerning an attempt to close Germany's borders against the Eastern Jews, in *Beyond Good and Evil* (New York, 1966), sec. 251, pp. 186–89.

13 Neubach, *Ausweisungen*, pp. 219–20; Wertheimer, "German Policy," chaps. 2 and 3.

14 Fritz Stern, *Gold and Iron* (New York, 1977), p. 526.

15 See J. Herzberg, "Die Ostjudenfrage am Ausgange des achtzehnten Jahrhunderts," *IDR*, 1916, March–April. See, too, Eduard Roditi, "Wandering Jews," *Commentary* 68 (August 1979), p. 55.

16 Examples of such expulsions include those discussed in *AZdJ* 59, no. 7 (15 February 1895), p. 76; *JR* 11, no. 19 (8 May 1906), p. 289; and *JR* 19, no. 18 (1 May 1914), p. 189.

17 Not unexpectedly, there was much opposition to East European Jewish students from the German *Studentenschaft*. See Julius Heilbronner, "Die Aufnahme von Ausländern an deutschen Hochschulen," *KCB* 6, no. 10 (March–April 1916), esp. pp. 603–6.

18 It is surprising that in his scrupulously documented study of Bleichröder, Bismarck, and the Jewish question, *Gold and Iron*, Fritz Stern mentions Busch three times but never alludes to his anti-Semitism. For details on Busch, see Paul Massing, *Rehearsal for Destruction* (New York, 1949), pp. 84–85. On the background of Busch's publication and the possibility that it reflected Bismarck's ideas, see Neubach, *Ausweisungen*, p. 9. Peter G. J. Pulzer, *The Rise of Political Anti-Semitism in Germany and Austria* (New York and London, 1964), p. 98, says that Bismarck "tolerated" Busch's writings.

19 Moritz Busch, *Israel und die Gojim* (Leipzig, 1880). See esp. p. 175. Parts of the book were serialized in *Die Grenzboten* 39 (April–June 1880).

20 Chapter 2 above gives various examples of this. For organized political *opposition* to *Grenzschluss*, see Wertheimer, "German Policy," pp. 123–31.

21 See, for instance, "Im Ghetto von Berlin," excerpt from *Deutsche Zeitung*, quoted in *JR* 12, no. 9 (1 March 1907), pp. 88–89.

22 See George L. Mosse, *Nazism* (New Brunswick, 1978), p. 59.

23 See, for instance, Leon Poliakov, *Harvest of Hate* (New York, 1979), pp. 304–5.

24 This was the stated position of such Jews as Eugen Ehrlich, Max Marcuse, and Fritz Mauthner (examined in chap. 2 above). Many other German Jews shared the sentiment even if they declined to state it in print.

25 See Wilhelm Stoffers, *Juden und Ghetto* (Graz, 1939), pp. 131–32.

26 For commentary on this play and the history of its reception, see Stoffers, *Juden und Ghetto*, pp. 110–21; and Elizabeth Frenzel, *Judengestalten auf der deutschen Bühne* (Munich, 1940), pp. 86–113.

27 For the German Jewish response, see Frenzel, *Judengestalten*, esp. p. 96. Michael Meyer has also demonstrated why many opponents of Emancipation opposed reforming Jewish religious practice and belief: "Jewish political segregation could be justified if one could point to a (largely distorted) image of an alien and unchanging orthodoxy as the only 'authentic Judaism.'" See his *German Political Pressure and Jewish Religious Response in the Nineteenth Century*, Leo Baeck Memorial Lecture no. 25 (New York, 1981), p. 8.

28 C. W. F. Grattenauer, *Ueber die physische und moralische Verfassung der heutigen Juden* (Berlin, 1791). See Hannah Arendt, *The Origins of Totalitarianism* (Cleveland, 1961), pp. 61–62, for details of this and the perception of the Jew as "philistine."

29 Friedrich Bucholz, *Moses und Jesus* (Berlin, 1803), pp. 208–9, quoted in Jacob Katz, *From Prejudice to Destruction* (Cambridge, Mass., 1980), p. 57.

30 This translation, by M. Gelber, is to be found in Paul R. Mendes-Flohr and Jehuda Reinharz, eds., *The Jew in the Modern World* (New York, 1980), p. 259.

31 See Frenzel, *Judengestalten*, pp. 96 ff.; and Jacob Katz, *Out of the Ghetto* (New York, 1978), p. 86.

32 Jacob Toury, "'The Jewish Question': A Semantic Approach," *LBIYB* 11 (1966). See esp. pp. 90–94.

33 Katz, *From Prejudice*, p. 176.

34 Eduard Meyer, *Gegen L. Börne, den Wahrheit-, Recht- und Ehrvergessnen Briefsteller aus Paris* (Altona, 1831), p. 14. Quoted in Katz, *From Prejudice*, p. 178.

35 Heinrich Laube, *Struensee* (Leipzig, 1847), cited after his *Gesammelte Schriften* (Leipzig, 1909), pp. 130–31. Quoted in Katz, *From Prejudice*, p. 183.

36 "Judaism in Music," in *Richard Wagner's Prose Works*, trans. William Ashton Ellis, vol. 3, *The Theatre* (London, 1907), p. 84.

37 Ibid., p. 80.

38 Ibid., pp. 87–88.

39 Julius Langbehn, *Rembrandt als Erzieher* (1890; Leipzig, 1896), pp. 43, 193.

40 For excellent accounts of Volkish antimodernity, see George L. Mosse, *The Crisis of German Ideology* (New York, 1964); and Fritz Stern, *The Politics of Cultural Despair* (Berkeley, 1974).

41 Langbehn, *Rembrandt*, p. 292.
42 The financial background is related in most histories of anti-Semitism. See Stern, *Gold and Iron*; Pulzer, *Political Anti-Semitism*; and Katz, *From Prejudice*.
43 Quoted in Stern, *Cultural Despair*, p. 63.
44 See the English version *Debit and Credit* (London, 1858), p. 66.
45 This translation of Treitschke's "Unsere Aussichten," "A Word about Our Jewry," appears in Robert Chazan and Marc Lee Raphael, eds., *Modern Jewish History* (New York, 1974), pp. 81–82.
46 Ibid., p. 81. This was a dubious statement compounded by a semantic irony. In terms of their origins, German Jews were not "part of the Polish branch" but vice versa. The generic term for both Polish and German Jews is *Ashkenazi*—i.e., German Jews. In that semantic sense Ostjuden were German Jews.
47 Wilhelm Ender, "Zur Judenfrage," in Walter Boehlich, ed., *Der Berliner Antisemitismusstreit* (Frankfurt, 1965), pp. 106–7.
48 Busch, *Israel*, esp. pp. 228, 273, 304–12.
49 The story is reproduced in *New German Critique*, no. 21 (Fall 1980). The quotations appear on pp. 66, 69, 77, and 79 respectively. The story is translated by Jack Zipes, who also contributes an introduction, "Oscar Panizza: The Operated German as Operated Jew," in the same number. Panizza immediately brings to mind the work of Franz Kafka. In many ways he prefigures, albeit in a different manner, some of Kafka's main themes. "The Operated Jew" should be compared with both "The Metamorphosis" and "A Report to an Academy." A study of the differences as well as the similarities would be instructive.
50 *Der Giftpilz* (Nuremberg, 1938).
51 Massing, *Rehearsal*, pp. 39–40.
52 Stoecker's speech was delivered in September 1879. It is reprinted in Massing, *Rehearsal*, pp. 278–87; quotation on p. 286. Stoecker was no racist, for he sought to solve the Jewish problem ultimately through conversion to Christianity. It is instructive that Wilhelm Marr, founder of the Anti-Semitic League, also distinguished old from new Jews, despite his racism. "The Reform Jew," he wrote, "is a creature of which one never knows where the Jew begins and where he ends. . . . God save German representative institutions from Reform Jews. Better the most orthodox Polish rabbi!" Wilhelm Marr, *Der Weg zum Siege des Germanenthums ueber das* Judenthum (Berlin, 1880), pp. 12–14. Quoted in Michael A. Meyer, *German Political Pressure and Jewish Religious Response in the Nineteenth Century*, Leo Baeck Memorial Lecture no. 25 (New York, 1981), p. 20.
53 Published under the pseudonym W. Hartenau in, *Die Zukunft* 18 (6 March 1897), pp. 454 ff.
54 See the insightful review by James Joll, "The contradictory capitalist," *Times Literary Supplement*, 25 August 1978.
55 For Rathenau's interest in Hasidism, see Buber to Harry Graf Kessler, 16 January 1928, letter 261 in *Martin Buber: Briefwechsel 1918–1938*,

vol. 2, ed. Grete Schaeder (Heidelberg, 1973), p. 300. See chapter 6 below for more on Rathenau's relation to Hasidism in particular and to Judaism in general.

56 See Conrad Alberti, "Judentum und Antisemitismus," *Die Gesellschaft* 5 (1889), pp. 1719–33.

57 Hans Kohn, "Das kulturelle Problem des modernen Westjuden," *J* 5 (1920–21), pp. 287–90.

58 See Oskar Baum, "Otto Weininger," in Gustav Krojanker, ed., *Juden in der deutschen Literatur* (Berlin, 1922), pp. 130–31.

59 Reprinted in Massing, *Rehearsal*, pp. 300–305.

60 This was the response of Reichstag member Pickenbach to the 1885–86 expulsion of Ostjuden from Prussia. See Neubach, *Ausweisungen*, p. 220.

61 See, for instance, Gustav Krojanker, "Wille und Kampf," *JR* 17, no. 37 (11 September 1912), p. 351.

62 Quoted in Toury, "Jewish Question," p. 102, n. 73.

63 Letter of 3 April 1920. Quoted in Ronald W. Clark, *Einstein: The Life and Times* (New York, 1971), p. 461.

64 See Mosse, *Crisis*, p. 127.

65 Letter of 7 June 1916. See Nahum N. Glatzer, ed., *Franz Rosenzweig: His Life and Thought* (New York, 1961), p. 37.

66 *Simplicissimus*, no. 10 (1903). Quoted in Wertheimer, "German Policy," p. 105.

67 This was a constant theme. See, for instance, Busch, *Israel*; and Adolf Bartels, *Die Berechtigung des Antisemitismus* (Berlin, n.d.).

CHAPTER 4

1 In 1901, membership of the German Zionist Organization was just over 2,000. By 1904 it stood at 6,000 and had grown to close to 10,000 by 1914. It reached its pre-Nazi peak, 33,339, when the Weimar anti-Semitic *Stimmung* was at its strongest in 1922–23. For a detailed breakdown of membership in the Zionist Organization, see table 3, "Membership of Zionistische Vereinigung für Deutschland Annual Totals," in Stephen Poppel, *Zionism in Germany 1897–1933* (Philadelphia, 1977), pp. 176–77.

2 Nordau's residence in Paris did not prevent him from taking an active role in German cultural life. His books were written in German, he wrote the annual political review for Vienna's *Neue Freie Presse*, and he was foreign correspondent to Berlin's *Vossische Zeitung*. See George L. Mosse's introduction to Nordau's *Degeneration* (New York, 1968), p. xvi.

3 See Jehuda Reinharz, *Fatherland or Promised Land* (Ann Arbor, 1975), pp. 103–5.

4 "Opening Address at the First Zionist Congress," in Theodor Herzl, *Zionist Writings*, vol. 1, *1896–1898* (New York, 1973), p. 133.

5 Leo Pinsker, "Auto-Emancipation: An Appeal to His People by a Russian Jew," in Arthur Hertzberg, ed., *The Zionist Idea* (Garden City, N.Y., 1975), p. 185.

6 Ibid., p. 196.

7 For an excellent analysis of the preconditions of modern Jewish national consciousness, see "The Jewish National Movement: A Sociological Analysis," in Jacob Katz, *Emancipation and Assimilation* (Farnborough, 1972), esp. p. 137.

8 "Fifth Letter," in Moses Hess, *Rome and Jerusalem* (New York, 1958). p. 34. Hess's portrait of the assimilated Jew was clearly drawn from the German experience.

9 Ibid., p. 37.

10 See "The Solution of the Jewish Question" (1896), in Herzl, *Zionist Writings*, 1:23.

11 Pinsker to Lev Osipovich (Yehuda Leib) Levanda, 26 October 1883. Quoted in David Vital, *The Origins of Zionism* (Oxford, 1975), p. 126.

12 Quoted in Amos Elon, *Herzl* (New York, 1975), p. 182. See also p. 239.

13 See Ben Ami's description of and reaction to this scene, in Vital, *Origins*, p. 356.

14 Ibid., p. 359.

15 Max Bodenheimer, *Prelude to Israel* (New York, 1963), p. 107.

16 "The Basel Congress" (1897), in Herzl, *Zionist Writings*, 1:152–54.

17 Hertzberg, *Idea*, pp. 235–41; Vital, *Origins*, pp. 362–64.

18 "Der Zionismus der westlichen Juden" (1901), in Max Nordau, *Zionistische Schriften* (Cologne and Leipzig, 1909), pp. 311, 317.

19 "The Solution of the Jewish Question," in Herzl, *Zionist Writings*, 1:25–26.

20 "Who Fears a State?" ibid., pp. 213–14.

21 "The Family Affliction" (1899), in Herzl, *Zionist Writings* vol. 2, *1898–1904*, (New York, 1975), p. 45.

22 "The Jews as a Pioneer People," ibid., pp. 70–71. Herzl was not above viewing all Jews in stereotypical terms. For an interesting analysis of his ambivalence, see Jacques Kornberg, "Theodor Herzl: A Reevaluation," *The Journal of Modern History* 52, no. 2 (June 1980), esp. 229–32.

23 For a good elucidation of Nordau's philosophy and place in European intellectual history, see Mosse's introduction to Nordau, *Degeneration*.

24 "Der Zionismus" (1902), in Nordau, *Schriften*, pp. 24–25, 37.

25 "Kongressrede" (1901), ibid., pp. 117 ff.

26 Nordau, *Schriften*, p. 137. For his conception of *Muskeljudentum* see pp. 379–81. On Nordau's notion of degeneration and energy and an interesting if controversial treatment of the relationship between his liberalism and his nationalism, see P. M. Baldwin, "Liberalism, Nationalism, and Degeneration: The Case of Max Nordau," *Central European History* 13, no. 2 (June 1980).

27 "Der Zionismus und seine Gegner" (1898), in Nordau, *Schriften*, pp. 117 ff.

28 See Jabotinsky's introduction to *Chaim Nachman Bialik: Poems*, (ed.) L. V. Snowman (London, 1924), pp. ix–xv.

29 Weizmann to Motzkin, 2 June 1895, letter 11 in Chaim Weizmann, *The Letters and Papers of Chaim Weizmann*, vol. 1 (London, 1968), pp. 48–49.

30 Max Nordau, "Über den Gegensatz zwischen Ost und West im Zionismus," *W* 14, no. 11 (18 March 1910).

31 Asher Zvi Ginsberg [Achad Ha'am], "The Jewish State and the Jewish Problem" (1897), in Hertzberg, *Idea*, pp. 262–69.

32 Ibid., p. 268.

33 Achad Ha'am's critique first appeared in the Hebrew *Hashiloah* 10, no. 60 (December 1902). It appeared in German in *OW*, 1903, no. 4, pp. 227–43. "Slavery in Freedom" was written as early as 1891. The English translation can be found in Asher Zvi Ginsberg [Achad Ha'am], *Selected Essays of Achad Ha'am*, ed. Leon Simon (Cleveland, 1962), pp. 171–94.

34 Max Nordau, "Achad Ha'am über Altneuland," *W* 7, no. 11 (13 March 1903).

35 Weizmann to Sokolow, 7 June 1903, letter 358 in Weizmann, *Letters and Papers*, vol. 2 (London, 1971), p. 366.

36 Weizmann to Kalman Marmor, 25 July 1903, letter 413, ibid., p. 439.

37 Weizmann to Khatzman, 15 March 1903, letter 292, ibid., p. 271.

38 Weizmann to Herzl, 6 May 1903, letter 316, ibid., pp. 312–13.

39 See A. Friedemann's (early) diary in CZA A8/2/4, entry for 19 March 1903.

40 Leo Wintz, "Die Juden von gestern (Eine Erwiderung)," *OW*, 1903, no. 4, pp. 217–26. There was some confusion about the authorship of this article. Martin Buber at first thought that it was the work of the Galician publicist Binjamin Segel. We know, however, that it was written by Wintz. See his explanatory letter of 15 August 1903 to Adolf Friedemann, in M. Heymann, ed., *The Minutes of the Zionist General Council: The Uganda Controversy*, vol. 1 (Jerusalem, 1970), pp. 68–71.

41 See Herzl's letters to Martin Buber (nos. 59 of 23 May 1903 and 61 of 28 May 1903) in Martin Buber, *Martin Buber: Briefwechsel aus sieben Jahrzehnten*, ed. Grete Schaeder (Heidelberg, 1972), 1:196–97, 199–200.

42 This was first published in *Hatzefirah* (23 March–5 April 1903). The text is reproduced in Weizmann, *Letters and Papers*, 2:270–71, no. 11.

43 Weizmann to Jacob Bernstein-Kohan, 29 September 1903, letter 29 in Weizmann, *Letters and Papers*, 3:32.

44 See Elias Auerbach, *Pionier der Verwirklichung* (Stuttgart, 1969), p. 145.

45 Reinharz, *Fatherland*, pp. 134–36; Poppel, *Zionism*, pp. 38–39.

46 Quoted in Poppel, *Zionism*, p. 39.

47 Kurt Blumenfeld, *Erlebte Judenfrage* (Stuttgart, 1962), p. 52.

48 Ibid., p. 59.

49 See Elias Hurwicz, "Shay Ish Hurwitz and the Berlin He'atid: When Berlin Was a Centre of Hebrew Literature," *LBIYB* 12 (1967).

50 An account of this East European circle and its activities at the Monopol is contained in a Hebrew article by Stanley Nash, "Temunot Mi-hug Soharei Ha'Ivrit be'Berlin (1900–1914)," in *AJS* (Association of Jewish Studies) *Review* 3 (1978).

51 Bodenheimer, *Prelude*, pp. 74–75.

52 Recent historians of German Zionism like Poppel and Reinharz agree that this psychological function was critical. See, too, Ismar Schorsch, *Jewish Reactions to German Anti-Semitism 1870–1914* (New York, 1972), pp. 184–85. For a critical and opposed view see Evyatar Friesel, "Criteria and Conception in the Historiography of German and American Zionism," *Zionism* 2 (Autumn 1980).

53 Quoted in Reinharz, *Fatherland*, p. 119.

54 ZVfD, *Was will der Zionismus?* (Berlin, 1903), p. 17. Quoted in Poppel, *Zionism*, p. 27.

55 Elias Auerbach, "Deutsche Kultur im Zionismus," *JR* 8, no. 7 (13 February 1903), p. 50.

56 See Isaak Zwirn in *JR* 17, no. 22 (31 May 1912), p. 206. The translation is from Reinharz, *Fatherland*, p. 127.

57 Bodenheimer, *Prelude*, p. 35.

58 See Franz Oppenheimer, *Erlebtes, Erstrebtes, Erreichtes* (Düsseldorf, 1964), pp. 213–14.

59 See his memoirs: Richard Lichtheim, *Rückkehr* (Stuttgart, 1970), p. 72.

60 Blumenfeld, *Judenfrage*, pp. 28, 32, 46–47.

61 Kurt Blumenfeld [Maarabi], "Deutscher Zionismus," *JR* 15, no. 35 (2 September, 1910), p. 414.

62 The address "Der Aufbau einer jüdischen Genossenschaftssiedlung in Palästina" is reprinted in Oppenheimer, *Erlebtes*, pp. 281–96.

63 *Wie schaffen wir ein starkes jüdisches Geschlecht in Russland?* (Committee of Jewish Gymnasts) (Berlin, 1906).

64 "Degeneration-Regeneration," *OW*, 1901, no. 8.

65 "Alte und neue Makkabäer" was a 1906 address in memory of victims of the Russian pogroms. It is reprinted in Oppenheimer, *Erlebtes*, pp. 297–305.

66 Oppenheimer, "Stammesbewusstsein und Volksbewusstsein," trans. from Poppel, *Zionism*, p. 58. This essay appeared in *JR* 15, no. 8 (25 February 1910); and in *W* 14, no. 7 (18 February 1910).

67 See Julius Goldstein, "Moritz Goldsteins 'Deutsch-jüdischer Parnass,' " *IDR*, 1912, no. 10 (October), pp. 447–48.

68 See Reinharz, *Fatherland*, p. 133.

69 Eliaqim, "Verständige oder anständige Juden," *JR* 11, no. 19 (11 May 1906), p. 268.

70 Many of these appeared in *Ost und West*. As its name indicates, the magazine was meant to bridge Jewish East-West differences. See Schach's articles in that magazine: "Die Ausländerfrage in Deutsch-

land" (1902, no. 2); "Ein notwendiges soziales Hilfswerk" (1903, no. 6); "Die russischen Juden in Deutschland" (1903, nos. 10–11).
71 Quoted in Poppel, *Zionism*, p. 27.

CHAPTER 5

1 Adolph Friedemann, "Der IV. Delegiertentag in Leipzig am 14. und 15. Juni 1914," *JR* 19, no. 25 (19 June 1914), p. 267.
2 Ibid., pp. 268–69.
3 For a good analysis of this mood, see Mosse, *The Crisis of German Ideology*, chap. 3.
4 The best evocation of the humanitarian and left-wing possibilities of Volkish ideology is to be found in Eugene Lunn, *Prophet of Community: The Romantic Socialism of Gustav Landauer* (Berkeley, 1973). See, too, Paul Breines, "The Jew as Revolutionary: The Case of Gustav Landauer," *LBIYB* 12 (1967), pp. 81–82.
5 The pioneering analysis of this tendency is George L. Mosse's "The Influence of the Volkish Idea on German Jewry" in his *Germans and Jews.*
6 Gustav Landauer, "Sind das Ketzergedanken?" in *Vom Judentum: Ein Sammelbuch* (Leipzig, 1913), p. 255; Robert Weltsch, "Theodor Herzl und Wir," ibid., p. 162; Max Brod, "Der jüdische Dichter deutscher Zunge," ibid., p. 261; Moses Calvary, "Das neue Judentum und die schöpferische Phantasie," ibid., pp. 109–10.
7 This is well analyzed by Ruth Gladstein-Kestenberg, "Athalat Bar Kochba" (Hebrew), in Felix Weltsch, ed., *Prag v'Yerushalayim* (Jerusalem, 1954).
8 "Ost und West," *OW*, 1901, no. 1.
9 See especially his "Judaism and the Jews," In Martin Buber, *On Judaism* (New York, 1967), pp. 15–19.
10 Ibid., p. 15.
11 Ibid.
12 Ibid., p. 17.
13 Thus "Zur Judenfrage" (1880), in Walter Boehlich, ed., *Der Berliner Antisemitismusstreit* (Frankfurt, 1965), p. 107.
14 See Gershon Weiler, "Fritz Mauthner: A Study in Jewish Self-Rejection," *LBIYB* 7 (1963), p. 144.
15 Ludwig Geiger, "Zionismus und Deutschtum," in *Die Stimme der Wahrheit: Jahrbuch für wissenschaftlichen Zionismus* (Würzburg, 1905).
16 Ernst Lissauer, "Deutschtum und Judentum," *Der Kunstwart* 25, no. 13 (April 1912), p. 8.
17 This story is recounted by Eric Kahler in "What are the Jews?" in his *The Jews Among the Nations* (New York, 1967), p. 6.
18 Breines, "Jew as Revolutionary," p. 76.

19 Gustav Landauer, in *Das literarische Echo* (1 October 1910), MBA MS Var 350–5/13. See the translation by J. Hessing in Mendes-Flohr and Reinharz, eds., *The Jew in the Modern World*, p. 241.

20 "Ein paar Worte der Dankbarkeit an Martin Buber" (handwritten note, MBA Mappe 141). I thank George L. Mosse for drawing my attention to this reference. See, too, George L. Mosse, *Masses and Man* (New York, 1980), p. 260.

21 The full background of the essay is discussed in chap. 4 above.

22 For a report on the Berlin meeting, in which Buber participated, see *W* 14, no. 13 (1 April 1910), p. 287. Wiesbaden and Hamburg, amongst others, also arranged special discussions.

23 Richard Huldschiner, "Stammesbewusstsein—Volksbewusstsein," *W* 14, no. 9 (4 March 1910), p. 185.

24 "West und Ost im Zionismus" (Von einem Östler), *JR* 15, no. 20 (20 May 1910), p. 235.

25 See especially pt. 3, bk. 1 of Franz Rosenzweig's *The Star of Redemption* (1921; Boston, 1971).

26 "On Being a Jewish Person," in Rosenzweig, *Franz Rosenzweig*, ed. Nahum N. Glatzer (New York 1962), p. 216.

27 Jacob Klatzkin, "Die Grundlagen," *W* 14, no. 12 (25 March 1910), p. 260. See also no. 15 (April 15, 1910) of the same journal.

28 Martin Buber, "Judaism," p. 20. See his discussion on pp. 18–21.

29 "Zur Oppenheimer Debatte," *W* 14, no. 13 (1 April 1910), p. 287.

30 On this point see Berthold Feiwel, "Moderne Ghetto Literatur," in *Dokumente d. Fortschritts* (no. 3, 1910), MBA MS Var 350–13/5.

31 Hans Kohn, in *Vom Judentum*, p. 17.

32 Yehezkel Kaufmann, "The Ruin of the Soul" (1934), reprinted in Michael Selzer, ed., *Zionism Reconsidered* (New York, 1970).

33 Theodor Lessing, *Einmal und nie wieder* (Gütersloh, 1969), pp. 112–13.

34 Theodor Lessing, "Eindrücke aus Galizien," *AZdJ* 73 (3, 17, 24, and 31 December, 1909).

35 Amongst the various responses, see "Der Fall Lessing," *JR* 15, no. 6 (11 February 1910); and "Noch einmal 'Der Fall Lessing,' " *JR* 15, no. 9 (4 March 1910).

36 Binjamin Segal, *Die Entdeckungsreise des Herrn Dr. Theodor Lessing zu den Ostjuden* (Lemberg, 1910). Segel not only took issue with Lessing but also bitterly attacked both Ludwig Geiger and the Mosse publishing house for allowing this "defamation" to be published in a journal under their control.

37 See Theodor Lessing, "Samuel zieht die Bilanz," *Die Schaubühne* 6, no. 3 (20 January 1910).

38 In *Literarisches Echo* (1 March 1910). Lessing replied in "Wider Thomas Mann," *Die Schaubühne* 6, no. 10 (10 March 1910). See, too, Buber to Lessing, 17 May 1910, letter 153, *Martin Buber Briefwechsel*, 1:281–83.

39 See the perceptive paper by Lawrence Baron, "Theodor Lessing and the Problem of Jewish Self-Hatred" (presented to the American Historical Association, San Francisco, 28 December 1978), esp. pp. 5–6.
40 Theodor Lessing, "Ludwig Jacobowski," *OW*, 1901, no. 8, esp. p. 567.
41 See Theodor Lessing, "Jiddisches Theater in London," *Die Schaubühne* 6, no. 17 (28 April 1910), p. 486.
42 See Kalischer, "Noch einmal 'Galizien,' " *JR* 15, no. 12 (20 March 1910), p. 135. Tone was not the only issue. In an editorial "Noch einmal 'Der Fall Lessing,' " *JR* 15, no. 9 (4 March 1910), it was argued that Lessing's concern could not be genuine, for it was published in a journal (the *Allgemeine Zeitung des Judentums*) that had no interest in "positive" Judaism.
43 Theodor Lessing, "Galizien: Zur Abwehr," *AZdJ* 74, no. 7 (18 February 1910), p. 78.
44 On this point, see Baron, "Theodor Lessing," p. 6.
45 For an example of Lessing's Zionism, see "Jüdisches Schicksal," *J* 9 (1928). The quote appears on p. 17. For a description of the fin-de-siècle concept of the "new man," see George L. Mosse, "Introduction: The Genesis of Fascism," in Walter Lacqueur and George Mosse, eds., *International Fascism 1920–1945* (New York, 1966).
46 Weizmann to Abraham Idelson and Michael Kroll, 17 February 1913, letter 272 in Weizmann, *Letters and Papers*, 2:253.
47 See "Ost und West: Ein Brief Achad Ha'ams und die Monatsschrift 'Der Jude' (1903)," in *J* 1 (1916–17).
48 See especially "Renaissance und Bewegung" (1903), in Martin Buber, *Der Jude und sein Judentum* (Cologne, 1963).
49 "Renaissance und Bewegung" (1910), ibid., pp. 278–79.
50 Ernst Müller, "Nationales Bewusstsein und nationales Sein," *W* 14, no. 10 (11 May 1910), pp. 208–9.
51 See D. Pasmanik, "Nationales Schaffen und nationale Phrase," *W* 14, no. 13 (1 April 1910), pp. 282–83.
52 "Zum neuen Jahre," *JR* 17, no. 37 (11 September 1912).
53 Max Meyer, "A German Jew Goes East," *LBIYB* 3 (1958).
54 For details of Marcus's life, see Marcus Markus, *Ahron Marcus: Die Lebensgeschichte eines Chossid* (Basel, 1966); Langer's life history is retold by his brother Frantisek Langer in the foreword to Jiri Langer's *Nine Gates to the Chassidic Mysteries* (New York, 1976).
55 Langer, *Nine Gates*, p. xv.
56 Ahron Marcus [Verus] *Der Chassidismus* (Pleschen, 1901).
57 See, too, Biale, *Gershom Scholem*, pp. 115, 255 n. 5.
58 Rosenzweig to Maximilian Landau, February 1924, letter 387 in Franz Rosenzweig, *Briefe* (Berlin, 1935), p. 495.
59 For an account of Birnbaum's career see chap. 4, "Nathan Birnbaum," in Emanuel S. Goldsmith, *Architects of Yiddishism at the Beginning of the Twentieth Century* (Rutherford, 1976).

60 See the comments by Hans Kohn in "Zur Geschichte der zionistischen Ideologie," *J* 8, no. 6 (June 1923), p. 328.

61 Originally published in *Jüdische Zeitung*, no. 15 (25 October 1907). Reprinted in Nathan Birnbaum's *Ausgewählte Schriften*, vol. 2 (Czernowitz, 1910), p. 302.

62 "Die Juden und das Drama," Birnbaum, *Schriften*, 2:256 (originally in *W*, 1901).

63 This is a recurring theme in Birnbaum's work. See, for instance, "Noch einmal Ost- und Westjudentum," in *Der Freistaat* 1 (1913–14), esp. p. 571.

64 "Zur Frage des jüdischen Theaters" (1910), in Birnbaum, *Schriften*, 2:269.

65 "Ostjüdische Aufgaben" (1905), ibid., 1:261–63.

66 "Zur Kritik des politischen und kulturellen Zionismus" (1905), ibid., pp. 185–90.

67 "Die Emanzipation des Ostjudentums vom Westjudentum" (1909), ibid., 2:26–33.

68 The most developed statement of this position is contained in his *Gottes Volk* (Vienna and Berlin, 1918).

69 See the article by Adolf Böhm on the occasion of Birnbaum's fiftieth birthday, "Dr. Nathan Birnbaum," *JR* 19, no. 18 (1 May 1914), pp. 187–88. Böhm respected Birnbaum's achievements but disagreed with his contention that Eastern Jewry was synonymous with *Volljudentum*.

70 *O* 2, no. 10 (11 March 1921). For details of Kaufmann's life, see Ludwig Strauss's introduction to Kaufmann's *Gesammelte Schriften* (Berlin, 1923).

71 Ludwig Strauss, "Ein Dokument der Assimilation," *Der Freistaat* 1 (1913–14). This was a reply to Bab's "Der Anteil der Juden an der deutschen Dichtung der Gegenwart," which appeared in *Mitteilungen des Verbandes der jüdischen Jugendvereine Deutschlands* (December 1913).

72 Julius Bab, "Assimilation," *Der Freistaat* 1 (1913–14):172–76.

73 Ludwig Strauss, "Entgegnung," ibid., pp. 238–44.

74 Gustav Landauer, "Zur Poesie der Juden," ibid., pp. 322–23.

75 See "Die Erstarkung der Westlichen Judenheit," *Der Freistaat* 1 (1913–14), reprinted in Kaufmann, *Schriften*.

76 See "Alljüdische Kritik," in Kaufmann, *Schriften*.

77 "Alljudentum und Zionismus," ibid., pp. 103–4. This article originally appeared in *KCB* of January 1914.

78 "Westjüdische Erneurung," in Kaufmann, *Schriften*. Kaufmann used *Vom Judentum* as the basis for his critique of the Zionist cultural renaissance.

79 For some Zionist replies to *Der Freistaat*, see Daniel Pasmanik, "Die Legende von der 'ostjüdischen Kultur,'" *W* 17, no. 29 (18 July 1913); and A. Coralnik, "Verstiegenheiten," ibid., no. 24 (13 June 1913).

80 Ber Borochov, "Alljüdische Probleme und der Sozialismus," *Der Freistaat* 1 (1913–14); Berl Locker, "Über Zionismus und jüdische Kultur," ibid.

81 The area in which the radical reorientation of German Zionism should have been most apparent, *aliyah* (emigration) to Palestine, was not affected significantly. Zionism for the radicals, as for the generation before them, performed a psychological function related to their position in Germany more than to Palestinian reality. See Stephen Poppel, *Zionism in Germany 1897–1933* (Philadelphia, 1977), esp. chap. 5.

The career of Ludwig Strauss (1892–1953), Buber's son-in-law, was a fairly typical one for an adherent of *Alljudentum*. Under Kaufmann's influence, Strauss and Werner Senator also left the Zionist movement for a time. Strauss translated *Ostjüdische Liebeslieder* (1920) and *Chaim N. Bialiks Gedichte* (1921). Yet despite his proclamations of German Jewish *Anschluss* to East European Jewish culture, he remained deeply rooted in German cultural affairs and became an authority on classical German literature. He emigrated to Palestine in 1935.

CHAPTER 6

1 See especially the introduction and chapter 1 of Biale, *Gershom Scholem.* I rely heavily upon Biale's excellent rendering of the nineteenth-century background and his treatment of Jewish "irrationalism."

2 Grätz *History of the Jews*, 5:374–75.

3 Ibid., p. 383.

4 The most famous exemplar of this sociological approach to Jewish history was the East European historian Simon Dubnow (1860–1941). See Biale, *Gershom Scholem*, p. 33.

5 The phrase is from Biale, *Gershom Scholem*, p. 34.

6 See "Martin Buber's Interpretation of Hasidism," in Gershom Scholem's *The Messianic Idea in Judaism* (New York, 1971), pp. 229–30. See also Scholem's *From Berlin to Jerusalem* (New York, 1980), p. 74.

7 As an Eastern Jew, Berdichevsky also attempted to mediate his world to a German audience. See his *Vom östlichen Judentum* (Berlin, 1918), written under his pseudonym Bin Gorion.

8 The fruits of this interest resulted in *Die Sagen der Juden* (2 vols., published in 1913 and 1919). They have appeared in English under the title *Mimekor Israel* (Bloomington, 1976).

9 Micha Yosef Berdichevsky [Bin Gorion], *Sinai and Gerizim* (Hebrew) (Tel Aviv, 1962).

10 See his *Sefer Hasidim* (1900). See too David Jacobson, "The Recovery of Myth: M. Y. Berdyczewski and Hasidism," *Hebrew Annual Review* 2 (1978).

11 In a highly respectful eulogy, Moritz Heimann pointed out that after all his years in Germany, Berdichevsky was still regarded as strange, his appearance unreal. See "Micha Josef Gorion: Seinem Gedächtnis," *Die Neue Rundschau* 33 (1922):69.

12 See Micha Yosef Berdichevsky [Bin Gorion], "On Expansion and Contraction" (Hebrew), *He-Atid* 5 (1913). See also Biale, *Gershom Scholem*, p. 236, n. 38.

13 Gerhard Holdheim and Walter Preuss, *Die theoretischen Grundlagen des Zionismus* (Berlin, 1919), p. 41. For a contemporary evaluation of Berdichevsky as a negator of the Galut, see Baruch Krupnick, "Micha Josef Berdyczewski: Seine Wahrheiten und Dichtung," *J* 3 (1918–19).

14 "Hasidism and Modern Man," in Martin Buber, *Hasidism and Modern Man*, ed. and trans. Maurice Friedman (New York, 1958), p. 24. For an evaluation of Buber as a German intellectual, see Ernst Simon, "Martin Buber and German Jewry," *LBIYB* 3 (1958).

15 See the insightful chapter by Friedrich Heer (which touches on some of the consequences of the presence of *Ostjudentum* on Austrian cultural and intellectual development), "Judentum und österreichischer Genius," in his *Land im Strom der Zeit* (Vienna, 1958). See, too, Grete Schaeder, *The Hebrew Humanism of Martin Buber* (Detroit, 1973), p. 39.

16 Martin Buber, *The Legend of the Baal-Shem* (New York, 1955), pp. x–xi. Originally published as *Legende des Baalschem* (Frankfurt, 1907). For a good explication of Buber's concept of myth, see Schaeder, *Humanism*, pp. 91–106; and Mosse, *The Crisis of German Ideology*, p. 63. Buber used the word *myth* in different ways, and his meaning for the word was never entirely clear.

17 Buber, *Baal-Shem*, p. xii. For the notion of "underground" Judaism, see *Legende des Baalschem*, p. 6.

18 Buber was not the first to establish a connection between Hasidism and national rebirth. Already in 1862 Moses Hess had perceived this and argued that the Jewish national movement of the future should harness Hasidism to its own cause. See Moses Hess, *Rome and Jerusalem* (New York, 1958), pp. 42–43. Hess's ideas appeared too early to receive a sympathetic echo.

19 "My Way to Hasidism," in Buber, *Hasidism and Modern Man*, pp. 51–52. Written originally in 1917.

20 Buber, *Baal-Shem*, p. x.

21 See "Martin Buber's Conception of Judaism," in Gershom Scholem, *On Jews and Judaism in Crisis* (New York, 1976), pp. 166–67.

22 Arnold Zweig, Über jüdische Legenden," *Mitteilungen des Verbandes der jüdischen Jugendvereine Deutschlands* (1914), pp. 16–17.

23 See Buber's remarks in Michael Landsmann and Kurt Gersen, eds., *Buch des Dankes an Georg Simmel* (Berlin, 1958). Simmel's appoint-

ment at Heidelberg was thwarted, Buber reports in this same interview, because of the fear that he would draw "undesirable students from the East."

24 See Gershon Weiler, "Fritz Mauthner: A Study in Jewish Self-Rejection," *LBIYB* 3 (1963), p. 147.

25 Quoted in the S. Krauss review of *Baalschem*, in *Literarisches Zentralblatt für Deutschland* 61, no. 11 (12 March 1910).

26 See chapter 3 above for earlier comments on Rathenau.

27 See Buber to Harry Graf Kessler, 16 January 1928, letter 261 in Buber, *Buber Briefwechsel*, 2:300.

28 "Walter Rathenau: Prophet without a Cause," in James Joll, *Intellectuals in Politics* (London, 1960), p. 67.

29 Rathenau to Maximilian Harden, letter of 20 December 1902, in Rudolf Kallner, *Herzl und Rathenau* (Stuttgart, 1976), p. 292.

30 Kallner, *Herzl und Rathenau*, p. 292.

31 See his comments to Lore Karrenbrock as reported in Kurt Blumenfeld, *Erlebte Judenfrage* (Stuttgart, 1962), p. 141.

32 Little is known of this club. Minutes of its proceedings would undoubtedly be interesting. See *Stammtisch der Donnerstagsgesellschaft* (MBA 112/7) for the information that is available.

33 See the undated letter from Heiman appealing for financial aid for Berdichevsky, who, he said, had "transcended the narrowness of the ghetto" and yet still embodied Judaism in its primal depth. All that would be needed was the modest sum of 350 marks a month for three or four years. The letter was probably written to Rathenau. MBA, MS Var 350/89a/18.

34 See Mendes-Flohr and Reinharz, eds., *The Jew in the Modern World*, p. 241, for a translation by J. Hessing of this Landauer review. It first appeared in *Literarisches Echo*, 1 October 1910. For Lukacs, see Mosse, *Masses and Man*, p. 70. See also, for Lukacs, MBA Mappe 457 (Lukacs note to Buber of 10 December 1911); I thank George Mosse for this reference. Bloch's essay, "Symbol: Die Juden (1912–1913)," is reprinted in his *Durch die Wüste* (Frankfurt, 1964). I thank Anson Rabinbach for this reference.

35 Oswald Spengler, *The Decline of the West*, vol. 2, *Perspectives of World History*, auth. trans. Charles Francis Atkinson (New York, 1980), pp. 321–22.

36 See *Buber Briefwechsel*, 1:243, letter 102 of 20 June 1906.

37 See Schaeder, *Humanism*, pp. 67–68, 96.

38 See Carl Schorske, *Fin-de-Siècle Vienna* (New York, 1980), pp. 315–16.

39 On this point and for a general evaluation of Rilke and his influence, see Peter Gay, *Weimar Culture* (New York, 1970), pp. 52–57.

40 See Maurice Friedman's introduction to Buber's *Daniel* (New York, 1964), pp. 15, 18. See, too, Allan Janik and Stephen Toulmin, *Wittgenstein's Vienna* (New York, 1973), p. 90.

41 Friedman introduction to *Daniel*, p. 15.

42 Ellen Key to Buber, 23 September 1908, letter 134 in *Buber Briefwechsel*, 1:265. Emphasis in the original.

43 *Neue Metaphysische Rundschau*, 1908, no. 2–3. See the collection of reviews in the Martin Buber Archives: MBA MS Var350/49/13.

44 Karl Wilker, "Religiöses Erleben," in *Das Werdende Zeitalter* (July 1922), pp. 91–92, MBA Var 350/49/13.

45 Margaret Susman, *Ich habe viele Leben gelebt* (Stuttgart, 1966), p. 78.

46 Letter 234 of 4 February 1914, *Buber Briefwechsel*, 1:356.

47 See letter 199 of 16 December 1912, *Buber Briefwechsel*, 1:321–22.

48 Moses Beilenson, "Zu Martin Bubers 'Maggid,' " *JR* 27, no. 29/30 (11 April 1922), p. 187.

49 See *JR* 27, no. 36 (26 May 1922).

50 Berthold Viertel, *Karl Kraus* (Dresden, 1921), pp. 61–62. See also pp. 63–69, 89–94; and Wilma Abeles Iggers. *Karl Kraus: A Viennese Critic of the Twentieth Century* (The Hague, 1967), p. 26. Ernst Simon's essay on Landauer, "The Maturing of the Man and the Maturing of the Jew," appears in Arthur Cohen, ed., *The Jew: Essays from Martin Buber's Journal "Der Jude," 1916–1928*, trans. J. Neugroschel (Alabama: University of Alabama Press, 1980), p. 142.

51 Frieda Freiin von Bülow, *Tägliche Rundschau*, in MBA MS Var 350/49/13.

52 T. H., review of *Baalschem*, in *Hamburger Nachrichten* (14 June 1908), ibid.

53 Friedrich Gundolf, in *Preussische Jahrbücher*, 1 July 1908, pp. 149–51, ibid.

54 See the review of *Vom Geist des Judentums* by Hochschild in *KCB* 6, no. 10 (March–April 1916).

55 Armin Blau, "Gedanken zu Alfred Lemms: 'Der Weg des Deutschjuden,' " *Jeschurun* 6, nos. 9–10 (September–October 1919), esp. pp. 476 ff.

56 For an analysis of Scholem's ambivalent relationship with Buber, see Biale, *Gershom Scholem*, esp. chap. 3.

57 Quoted ibid., p. 64. Scholem wrote this in 1918–19; his criticism of Buber began with World War I, however.

58 Rosenzweig to Rudolf Hallo, 12 May 1921, letter 309 in Rosenzweig, *Briefe*, pp. 399–400.

59 Rosenzweig, *Briefe*. See, for instance, Rosenzweig to Mawrik Kahn, letter 266 of 26 February 1919, pp. 355–57.

60 Stanley (Shlomo) Nash, "Temunot Mi-hug Soharei Ha-Ivrit be-Berlin 1900–1914" (Hebrew), in *AJS Review* 3 (1978), esp. p. 11.

61 See Shai Ish Hurwitz, "Hasidism and Haskalah" (Hebrew), *He-Atid* 2 (1909).

62 Jacob Klatzkin, *Probleme des modernen Judentums* (Berlin, 1918), p. 127.

63 "Westjüdische Erneuerung," in Kaufmann, *Schriften*, p. 138.

64 Adolf Grabowsky, *Die polnische Frage* (Berlin, 1916), pp. 24–25.

65 See Felix Goldmann, *Die Stellung des deutschen Rabbiners zur Ostju-denfrage* (Frankfurt, 1916), pp. 17–20.

66 Felix Rosenblüth, "Juden des Ostens: Aus West-Galizien," *JS* 12, no. 3 (12 August 1915), pp. 66–67.

67 These comments are to be found in the proceedings of the XV. Delegiertentag der zionistischen Vereinigung für Deutschland, *JR* 24, no. 3 (4 January 1919), p. 28.

68 Erich Fromm, Fritz Goethin, Leo Löwenthal, Ernst Simon, and Erich Michaelis, "Ein prinzipielles Wort zur Erziehungsfrage," *JR* 27, no. 103–4 (29 December 1922).

69 In his *When Memory Comes* (New York, 1979), Saul Friedländer writes that after settling in Israel he spent the year 1957 in Sweden, where he discovered Buber's Hasidic works. He read them several times, "and as the result of being in a foreign country, and of a certain solitude too, I felt . . . the hidden grace of the secret world of Hasidism. . . . But, more than this, for the first time I began to feel a clear difference between my identification with Israel, which for a time at least seemed to me to be superficial and almost empty of meaning, and a feeling of my Jewishness, certain aspects of which appeared to me in this unusual setting to be suddenly endowed with a new, mysterious, powerful, magnificent dimension" (pp. 103–4). This "magnificent dimension" also maintains its appeal for non-Jewish intellectual romantics. In the highly successful film *My Dinner with André*, André speaks admiringly of Buber's works on Hasidism and Buber's conception of prayer as liberating live spirits from usually inanimate things.

CHAPTER 7

1 The best treatment of this question is to be found in Egmont Zechlin, *Die deutsche Politik und die Juden im Ersten Weltkrieg* (Göttingen, 1969), esp. section #2. See also Antony Polonsky and Michael Riff, "Poles, Czechoslovaks and the 'Jewish Question,' 1914–1921: A Comparative Study," in Volker R. Berghahn and Martin Kitchen, eds., *Germany in the Age of Total War* (London: Croom Helm, 1981), pp. 66–70. Polonsky and Riff also argue that the Jewish Question had propaganda value for the Central Powers, since in deference to their Russian ally, Britain and France did not raise the question.

2 See Eva Reichmann, "Der Bewusstseinswandel der deutschen Juden," in Werner E. Mosse, ed., *Deutsches Judentum in Krieg und Revolution, 1916–1923* (Tübingen, 1971). The entire volume is invaluable for an understanding of German Jewry in this period.

3 For an overview of reactions to the outbreak of war, see Zechlin, *Deutsche Politik*, pp. 86–100. For an interesting evaluation, see, too,

George L. Mosse, "The Jews and the German War Experience, 1914–1918," in his *Masses and Man.*

4 See Martin Buber, "Die Losung," *J* 1, no. 1 (April 1916); Moses Calvary, "Feldbriefe," *JR* 19 (26 November 1914), p. 4.

5 See the remarks by Eugen Fuchs in *IDR* 21 (1915), p. 12; also Hochfeld, "Kriegsbetrachtung," *AZdJ* 78, no. 37 (11 September 1914), p. 433.

6 See, for instance, J. Wohlgemuth, "Deutschland und die Ostjudenfrage," *Jeschurun* 3, no. 1 (January 1916).

7 Thus "Feinde ringsum," *JR* 19, no. 32 (7 August 1914); "Zwei Feldpostbriefe," ibid., no. 52 (25 December 1914), p. 470; and Max Simon, *Der Weltkrieg und die Judenfrage* (Leipzig and Berlin, 1916), esp. pp. 2–3.

8 Hermann Cohen, *Deutschtum und Judentum* (Giessen, 1915).

9 For the text of this German proclamation, see S. Adler-Rudel, *Ostjuden in Deutschland 1880–1940* (Tübingen, 1959), pp. 156–57.

10 "Das Wilnaer Ghetto," from *Kownoer Zeitung*, reprinted in *Der Israelit* 58, no. 26 (28 June 1917), pp. 9–10.

11 Otto von Moser, *Feldzugsaufzeichnungen* (Stuttgart, 1928), p. 70. I thank Steve Lampert for this reference.

12 Letter from Ernst Günter Schallert from the Galician front, 27 April 1915. See A. F. Wedd, ed., *German Students' War Letters* (New York, 1929), pp. 101–2.

13 See Kurt Alexander, "Deutschland und die Ostjudenfrage," *IDR* 12, no. 1–2 (January–February 1916), p. 21; Walter Preuss, "Die K.J.V.-er und die Ostjuden," *JS* 13, no. 4 (18 August 1916), p. 237.

14 See Feldwebel C., *The Diary of a German Soldier* (New York, 1919), pp. 168–69.

15 Hermann Ullmann, "Polen, Juden, Deutsche: Hinter der östlichen Front," *Der Kunstwart* 29, no. 4 (1915), pp. 144–45.

16 "Die polnischen Juden," reprinted in *Menschliche Betrachtungen zur Politik* (Munich, 1916), pp. 341–44.

17 See *Die Weissen Blätter* 2, no. 2 (November 1915), pp. 1408–19. I thank George L. Mosse for this reference.

18 In *Die deutschen Schützengraben- und Soldatenzeitungen*, ed. Fred B. Hardt (Munich, 1917), p. 29.

19 *Mein Kampf* (Boston, 1971), p. 59.

20 A. Friedemann's diary, p. 17, CZA A8/2/4.

21 Julius Berger, "Deutsche Juden und polnische Juden," *J* 1 (1916–17), p. 147.

22 For excellent treatment of these questions, see Magnus Hirschfeld and Andreas Gaspar, *Sittengeschichte des Ersten Weltkrieges* (Hanau am Main, 1929); and Stephen Kern, *Anatomy and Destiny* (Indianapolis, 1975), esp. the chapter "Eros in Barbed Wire." On German brothels in the East, see Zosa Szajkowski, "East European Jewish Workers in Germany during World War 1," in *Salo Wittmayer Baron: Jubilee Volume*, vol. 2 (Jerusalem, 1974), pp. 900–901.

23 Hirschfeld and Gaspar, *Sittengeschichte*, p. 277. See also H. C. Fischer

and E. X. Dubois, *Sexual Life during the World War* (London, 1937), pp. 351–53.

24 See "Körperliche Regeneration der Ostjuden" (Von einem Warschauer Arzte), *NJM* 1, no. 4 (25 November 1916), p. 92.

25 See *Protokoll der Unterredung mit Major Simon in Warschau* (13 February 1916), CZA A15/viii/9c.

26 Only Kafka could ask the question "Is that possible?" after hearing this story! See Kafka to Max Brod, May 1920, in Franz Kafka, *Letters to Friends, Family and Editors* (New York, 1977), p. 237.

27 See Sammy Gronemann, *Hawdoloh und Zapfenstreich* (Berlin, 1924), pp. 183–84. See also Wilhelm His, *A German Doctor at the Front* (Washington, 1933), p. 84.

28 Hans Reiman, "Von Kowno nach Bialystok und retour," *Die Schaubühne* 22, no. 29 (20 July 1926). Many soldiers went to the homes of the local Jews and attended festive Passover services, something they had not done in Germany.

29 Gronemann, *Hawdoloh*, pp. 61–62. For all that, Dehmel notes in his war diary that he never saw an attractive East European Jewish woman. He comments that only the ideological proclivities of the Zionist artist Hermann Struck permitted him to see beauty in these women. Dehmel, on the other hand, was married twice to German Jewish women. See his *Zwischen Volk und Menschheit: Kriegstagebuch* (Berlin, 1919), p. 451. For his marital background, see Werner Sombart, *Judentaufen* (Munich, 1912), p. 29.

30 Arnold Ulitz, "Augen des Ostens," *NJM* 7, nos. 19–20 (10–25 July 1919), esp. p. 423.

31 Edmund Hirsch (in the field), "Der russischen Juden Not und Trost," *IDR* 22, nos. 1–2 (January–February 1916), pp. 15–16.

32 Berger, "Deutsche Juden," p. 145.

33 See Erich Bischoff, *Klarheit in der Ostjudenfrage* (Dresden and Leipzig, 1916), p. 19.

34 Thus Walter Preuss, "Die K.J.V.-er und die Ostjuden," *JS* 13 (August 1916); Georg Ehrlich, "K.J.V.er und Ostjuden," ibid. (May 1917).

35 See Alfred Zweig, "Ein Feldpostbrief statt der Fortsetzung einer wissenschaftlichen Abhandlung," *Monatsschrift für Geschichte des Judentums* 59 (1915), esp. p. 56; Dr. Sali Levi, "Aus meine Erlebnissen bei den Juden in Russisch-Polen," ibid. 60 (1916), esp. p. 5.

36 Julius Marx, *Kriegstagebuch eines Juden* (Zurich, 1939), pp. 76–77.

37 "In einer jüdischen Stadt." Letter of 25 September 1914 in *Kriegsbriefe deutscher und österreichischer Juden*, ed. Eugen Tannenbaum (Berlin, 1915), p. 41.

38 Tannenbaum, *Kriegsbriefe*. See "Do is er, der Jid," 26 September 1914, pp. 48–49; "Als Feldwache an der Grenze," 4 November 1914, p. 112.

39 "Die hohen Feiertage jüdischer Soldaten in Wilna," *AZdJ* 81, no. 44 (2 November 1917).

40 The story of the Ostjude and the field rabbi can be found in the German

Zionist satirical journal *Schlemiel*, no. 1 (1919), p. 35; on sending the children out of the synagogue, see Felix Hirschmann, "Ein Gottesdienst im Osten," *AZdJ* 81, no. 30 (27 July 1917), p. 355.

41 See "Der Gemeindebote," *Beilage zur AZdJ* 78, no. 43 (23 October 1914).

42 Army rabbi S. Levy, "Disziplin und Organization," *KCB* 7, no. 9 (1916).

43 See Alexander Carlebach, *Adas Yeschurun of Cologne* (Belfast, 1964), pp. 55–56.

44 This story was related to me by Alexander Carlebach in an interview conducted in Jerusalem, 7 August 1978.

45 Gronemann, *Hawdoloh*, pp. 33–36.

46 See Alexander Carlebach, "A German Rabbi Goes East," *LBIYB* 6 (1961). Diary entry of Emanuel Carlebach for January 1917, pp. 105–6.

47 Gronemann, *Hawdoloh*, p. 102.

48 Ismar Freund, "Zwei Aufsätze über die Ostjuden," *Sonderabdruck aus der Zeitung der 10. Armee* (Wilna), nos. 23, 25 (27 January, 1 February, 1916).

49 See his "Zur Psychologie der Ostjuden," *Süddeutsche Monatshefte* (February 1916). This was one of many contributions to this journal's *Sonderheft* on Ostjuden.

50 "Die Polnischen und Franz Blei," *J* 1 (1916–17), p. 775.

51 Blei to Buber, 25 November 1915, MBA MS Var 350/1031.

52 Buber to Blei, 26 November 1915, ibid.

53 The full political history of this question has been related by Zechlin, *Deutsche Politik.* I therefore deal with the political question only insofar as it relates to the particular focus of my own study.

54 See Zechlin, *Deutsche Politik*, p. 118; Bodenheimer's own account can be found in the chapter "The First World War" of his book *Prelude to Israel* (New York, 1963).

55 Bodenheimer, *Prelude*, pp. 233–34; see also his *Auszug aus einer Denkschrift an das Auswärtige Amt vom Jahre 1901 über das Interesse des deutschen Reiches an dem zionistischen Plan, CZA* A15/VIII/6.

56 Eugene Fuchs, "Glaube und Heimat," *NJM* 1, no. 22 (25 August 1917).

57 For a typical example of this genre, see Adolf Friedemann, "Die Bedeutung der Ostjuden für Deutschland," *Süddeutsche Monatshefte* (February 1916), esp. p. 677.

58 Amongst many, see "Die russischen Juden als Pioniere des Deutschtums im Osten," *IDR* 20, no. 10–12 (October–December 1914); Heinrich Löwe, "Die Jüdisch-deutsche Sprache der Ostjuden," *Süddeutsche Monatshefte* (February 1916); Wladimir W. Kaplun-Kogan, *Die Juden in Polen* (Berlin, 1915), and by the same author, *Die jüdische Sprach- und Kulturgemeinschaft in Polen* (Berlin and Vienna, 1917); Rabbi Porges, "Jüdisch-Deutsch und Deutsch," *AZdJ* 79, no. 45 (November 1915).

59 Thus the KfdO distributed copies of the *Sonderheft* of the *Süddeutsche Monatshefte* to various authorities. See the letters from the Police Prasidium, Lodz (3 March 1916), and from von Beseler in Warsaw (18

March 1916), thanking them for copies and commenting upon their usefulness. CZA A15/VIII/9c.

60 See the circular advertising one such evening: *Schutzverband deutscher Schriftsteller* (6 April 1916), CZA Z3/1684.

61 *Protokoll der Sitzung des geschäftsführenden Ausschusses,* 23 March 1915, CZA A15/VIII/9a.

62 *Protokoll,* 23 March 1915. See the statement by the orientalist Eugen Mittwoch.

63 Oppenheimer to Ludendorff, 6 July 1915, in CZA A15/VIII/7.

64 See CZA A15/VII/2d., p. 4; see, too, Zechlin, *Deutsche Politik,* p. 191.

65 See Zechlin, *Deutsche Politik,* p. 134.

66 For a good exposition of Nathan's outlook and activities, see Ernst Feder, *Politik und Humanität: Paul Nathan* (Berlin, 1929).

67 Zechlin, *Deutsche Politik,* p. 169.

68 For liberal support of Nathan's basic position, see, for instance, A. Bruchner, "Das Ostjudentum am Scheidewege," *AZdJ* 80, no. 5 (4 February 1916); and Martin Philippson, "Die Zukunft der Juden des Ostens," *AZdJ* 79, no. 41 (8 October 1915).

69 Binjamin Segel, *Die Polnische Judenfrage* (Berlin, 1916). Segel also wrote a passionate pro-German war tract, *Der Weltkrieg und das Schicksal der Juden* (Berlin, 1916).

70 See the letter to Julius Berger, probably from Viktor Jakobson, of 25 February 1916, in CZA Z3/162.

71 Egon Zweig, *Jüdische Zeitung* 10, no. 11 (17 March 1916).

72 See Geiger's article "Ostjuden," in *AZdJ* 80, no. 10 (10 March 1916), p. 110.

73 See *Bericht des Herrn Professor Sobernheim über seine Reise nach München vom 26. bis 28. April 1916,* in CZA A15/VIII/9c.

74 Minutes of the proceedings can be found in CZA Z3/1684.

75 Berger, "Deutsche Juden."

76 See his "highly confidential" manuscript "Die polnischen Juden im Weltkrieg," in the National Library, Hebrew University, Jerusalem, p. 13.s.

77 4 May 1916 in CZA Z3/161/.

78 Berger, *Polnischen Juden,* pp. 9p, 1.

79 See his letter of 1 October 1916 in CZA Z3/716.

80 The definitive study of German Orthodoxy, its social and intellectual basis, its peculiar blending of traditional with modern elements, still awaits its author. Baruch Kurzweil argues the petit bourgeois nature of German Orthodoxy in an article in *Ha'aretz* (Hebrew), 26 September 1965. See the dissenting reply by Alexander Carlebach, "The Image of German Orthodoxy," *Niv Hamidrashia* (1966).

81 See Wertheimer, "German Policy and Jewish Politics, p. 423. See also Samuel Rathhaus, *Der Zurückgang der israelitischen Religionsgesellschaft* (Frankfurt, 1914); I thank Jack Lieberles for this reference.

82 See, for instance, "Ausländer," *Der Israelit* 54, no. 1 (2 January 1913). See, too, chapter 2 above, for a discussion of these actions.

83 Jacob Levy, "Von den Juden Ostgaliziens und ihrer Jugend," *Jeschurun* 5, no. 5–6 (May–June 1918), p. 302.

84 J. Wohlgemuth, "Deutschland und die Ostjudenfrage," ibid. 3, no. 1 (January 1916); Wohlgemuth, "Erziehungsfragen in Ost und West," ibid. 4, no. 2 (February 1917).

85 Thus G. Meisels, "Der Fremde," *Der Israelit*, no. 19 (10 May 1917); "Neologe Urteile über das Ostjudentum," ibid., no. 8 (24 February 1916), p. 2.

86 Oskar Wolfsberg, "Jüdische Kultur," ibid., no. 20 (18 May 1916).

87 See "Wie ein Bruder zum Bruder," ibid., no. 46 (4 November 1915), for such an appeal.

88 See *Abschrift! Bericht über die ökonomische und kulturelle Lage der Juden Kownos vor dem Kriege und während des Krieges*, CZA A15/VIII/9c.

89 "Kaftan und Peos," *Der Israelit*, no. 32 (29 July 1915), pp. 31–32.

90 The polemic was written partially in retaliation against Zionist attacks on Emanuel Carlebach by his father Solomon Carlebach: *Der Zionismus in seiner jetzigen Gestalt und in der heutigen Zeit: Eine Gefahr der Judenheit* (Lübeck, 1917); see esp. pp. 39–49. I thank Alexander Carlebach for this reference.

91 For accounts of this, see Alexander Carlebach, "A German Rabbi"; and by the same author, *Adas Yeschurun*, pp. 55–73. For German perceptions of the stabilizing role of Orthodox politics, see Polonsky and Riff, "Poles, Czechoslovaks and the 'Jewish Question,' " p. 68.

92 Carlebach, "A German Rabbi," pp. 65–66. See also Emanuel Carlebach's diary for 17 November 1916, p. 81, where he complains about the terrible smells of "Polack" food and where he places signs in his waiting room prohibiting spitting.

93 See "Alljüdische Politik," *Der Israelit* 59, no. 3 (17 January 1918).

94 Carlebach, *Adas Yeschurun*, pp. 60–62.

95 Rabbi J. Weinberg, "Schulfragen im Ostjudentum," *Jeschurun* 3, no. 9 (September 1916), p. 495. See also Army Rabbi Neufeld, "Warum verachten uns die Ostjuden," *Der Israelit*, no. 32 (8 August 1918).

96 Rabbi J. Weinberg, "Die Demokratisierung der Orthodoxie," *Der Israelit* no. 25 (20 June 1918). These accusations were heatedly denied in accompanying editorial comments. See also in the same paper, no. 26 (27 June 1918), an argument that only through the good offices of German Orthodoxy did Polish Orthodoxy become a significant organized political factor.

97 Zweig to Buber, 24 January 1917, letter no. 333, 1:464. Viertel also participated in the written discussion. See his articles in *Die Schaubühne*, nos. 50, 51, 52 (1916).

98 W. Kaplun-Kogan to Bodenheimer, 8 July 1916, CZA A15/VIII/2f.

99 See his letter of 16 July 1916, CZA A15/VIII/2f.

100 See Leo Hermann to Hugo Bergmann, 29 August 1916, CZA Z3/1688.

101 Robert Weltsch, "Ein Feldpostbrief aus dem Osten," *J* 1 (1916–17).

102 Buber, "Argumente," ibid., p. 64.

103 For biographical details, see Hermann Sinsheimer, "Paul Nikolaus Cossmann," in Hans Lamm, ed., *Von Juden in München* (Munich, 1959), pp. 295–97; and Wolfram Selig, *Paul Nikolaus Cossmann und die Süddeutschen Monatshefte von 1914—1918* (Osnabrück, 1967).

104 Cossmann to Kaplun-Kogan, 24 December 1915, CZA A15/VIII/2d.

105 Thus Eugen Ehrlich, *Die Aufgaben der Sozialpolitik im österreichischen Osten (Juden und Bauernfrage)* (1909; Munich and Leipzig, 1916), pp. 27–43.

106 Adolf Grabowsky, *Die polnische Frage* (Berlin, 1916), esp. pp. 14–34, 104–7.

107 Siegbert Feuchtwanger, *Die Judenfrage als wissenschaftliches und politisches Problem* (Berlin, 1916), esp. p. 47.

108 Felix Goldmann, *Die Stellung des deutschen Rabbiners zur Ostjudenfrage* (Frankfurt, 1916).

109 Rabbi Gelles, "Die Ostjudenfrage vom Standpunkt der Religion," *IF* 18, no. 9 (2 March 1916).

110 Kurt Alexander, "Deutschland und die Ostjudenfrage," *IDR* 12, no. 1–2 (1 January–February 1916).

111 Willie Cohn, "Zukunftsfragen des deutschen Judentums," *AZdJ* 79, no. 48 (26 November 1915).

112 M. M. (probably Max Meyer), "Jüdischer Antisemitismus," *JR* 21, no. 10 (10 March 1916), pp. 81–82.

113 See Zechlin, *Deutsche Politik*, pp. 266–67.

114 Amongst many, the most quoted are Georg Fritz, *Die Ostjudenfrage, Zionismus und Grenzschluss* (Munich, 1915); Wolfgang Heine, "Ostjüdische Einwanderung," *Preussische Jahrbücher* 162 (October 1915); Paphnutius, "Die Judenfrage nach dem Kriege," *Die Grenzboten* 74, no. 39 (September 1915).

115 Fritz, *Ostjudenfrage*, pp. 39, 42.

116 Heine, "Einwanderung," pp. 65–66.

117 Fritz, *Ostjudenfrage*, p. 43.

118 "Deutschland und der Zionismus," 23 June 1918. Quoted in Isaiah Friedman, *Germany, Turkey and Zionism 1897–1918* (Oxford, 1977), p. 402.

119 Bischoff, *Klarheit*, pp. 45–59.

120 See Otto Diebhart, " 'Die Ostjudenfrage (Zionismus und Grenzschluss)': Eine Erwiderung," *Politisch-Anthropologische Monatsschrift* 14 (1915–16), pp. 582–90.

121 See *JR* 20, no. 6 (1915), p. 45; ibid. no. 10 (1915), p. 80.

122 Kurt Alexander, "Gefahr," *IF* 17, no. 40 (7 October 1915), pp. 1–2.

123 See Zechlin, *Deutsche Politik*, p. 272. When the memorandum became known amongst American Jews, it created a major scandal and the Jewish Relief Committee (many of whom were themselves Ostjuden) decided to stop distributing welfare through the Hilfsverein. See *Abschrift*, letter from Strauss to Oppenheimer, 28 June 1916, CZA Z3/204.

124 See *Streng vertraulich—Jüdische Emigrations-Org. (J.E.O.): Gesell-schaft zur Regelung der Auswanderungsfrage der Ostjuden* (undated, anonymous publication).

125 Ludwig Geiger, "Kriegsliteratur," *AZdJ* 80, no. 9 (3 March 1916), p. 103; Felix Goldmann, "Deutschland und die Ostjudenfrage," *IDR* 20, no. 10–12 (October–November 1915), pp. 195–213.

126 "Besprechung zwischen Dr. Oppenheimer, Rechtsanwalt Rosenbaum und Dr. Jacobson," 14 October 1915, CZA Z3/204.

127 Memorandum addressed to Hermann Struck, 3 May 1918, CZA Z3/205. For his public opposition to Grenzschluss, see "Der Antisemitismus," *NJM* 2, no. 23 (10 September 1918), esp. p. 529.

128 See "Die Ostjudenfrage," *OW*, 1916, no. 2–3. The German Orthodox were also among those opposing Grenzschluss. See, for instance, "Der Ruf nach Grenzsperre," *Der Israelit* 56, no. 42 (7 October 1915).

129 Leo Hermann, "Die chinesische Mauer," *JR* 20, no. 42 (15 October 1915).

130 See Franz Oppenheimer's letter of 19 October 1915 to Viktor Jakobson, CZA Z3/204. For an examination of the resemblances and connections between Zionist and anti-Semitic assumptions, see Jacob Katz, "Zionism vs. Anti-Semitism," *Commentary* 67 (April 1979).

131 Fritz Mordecai Kaufmann, "Grenzsperre," *J* 1 (1916–17); Gustav Landauer, "Ostjuden und Deutsches Reich," ibid.

132 For Cohen's opposition to Grenzschluss see "Grenzsperre," *NJM* 1, no. 2 (25 October 1916). His "Der polnische Jude," *J* 1 (1916–17), has been translated and appears as "The Polish Jew" in Arthur A. Cohen, ed., *The Jew: Essays from Martin Buber's Journal, "Der Jude," 1916–1928* (Alabama, 1980).

133 Cohen, *The Jew*, p. 56.

134 Zechlin, *Deutsche Politik*. See chap. 15 for details of this whole development.

135 Abschrift II.6414, *Aufzeichnung über die Gründe für die Sperrung der Ostgrenze gegen die Einführung jüdisch-polnischer Arbeiter*, CZA Z3/203.

136 Letter of 30 May 1918 from Julius Berger to the Zionist Central Bureau, CZA Z3/203.

137 Theodor Behr, "Grenzschutz," *J* 3 (1918–19), p. 249.

138 Zechlin, *Deutsche Politik*, pp. 276–77.

139 Ibid., p. 275.

140 Isaiah Friedman, *Germany, Turkey and Zionism*, p. 234.

141 Gronemann, *Hawdoloh*, pp. 143–44. The translation is taken from Sander Gilman, "The Rediscovery of the Eastern Jews: German Jews in the East, 1890–1918," in David Bronsen, ed., *Jews and Germans from 1860–1933* (Heidelberg, 1979), p. 355.

142 See *Ausschuss zur Beschaffung jiddischer und hebräischer Literatur für russische Kriegsgefangene* (Berlin), CAHJP, Inv/149.

143 Bodenheimer, *Prelude*, pp. 263–64.

144 See, for instance, *Abschrift. Kaiserlich Deutsches Polizeipräsidium, Lodz* 15.1.1916 gez. von Oppen to KfdO, CZA A15/VIII/2e; also Governor v. Puttkamer, "Eine Kulturfrage im Osten," Sonderabdruck *Tags,* no. 300 (23 December 1915).

145 See Bodenheimer, *Prelude,* p. 251.

146 Zechlin, *Deutsche Politik,* pp. 180–81.

147 Friedman, *Germany, Turkey and Zionism,* p. 235.

148 Some of these (hilarious) misunderstandings are reported in Gronemann, *Hawdoloh,* p. 39.

149 *Die polnischen Juden im Weltkrieg,* p. 17d.

150 *Bericht über die im Auftrage des Komitees für den Osten im Mai–Juni 1915 unternommene Reise nach Russisch-Polen: Vertraulich,* CAHJP INV/1431 (10), p. 6.

151 Bodenheimer, *Bericht,* p. 14.

152 See KfdO to Excellence den Civil-Governeur von Polen: Herrn von Brandenstein, 27 January 1915, CZA A15/VIII/7.

153 Zechlin, *Deutsche Politik,* p. 160; Friedman, *Germany, Turkey and Zionism,* pp. 374–75, has a different view.

154 Judith Schrag-Haas, "Ludwig Haas: Erinnerungen an meinen Vater," *Bulletin des Leo Baeck Instituts* 4 (1961), p. 80.

155 See Nahum N. Glatzer, ed., *Franz Rosenzweig* (New York, 1961), letter of 3 June 1918, pp. 76–77.

156 See Julius Berger's letter to Zionist Central Bureau, 13 September 1918, CZA Z3/163.

157 Friedman, *Germany, Turkey and Zionism,* p. 375.

158 *Schlemiel,* no. 9 (1919), p. 127.

159 Szajkowski, "East European Jewish Workers," p. 900.

160 Szajkowski, "East European Jewish Workers," provides details of these anti-Jewish policies and a description of local Jewish reactions.

161 See Berger to Helene Hanna Cohn, 26 September 1916, CZA Z3/716.

162 "A German Rabbi," letter from Rabbi Carlebach of 10 May 1916, pp. 94ff.

163 Quoted in Zechlin, *Deutsche Politik,* pp. 200–201.

164 Szajkowski, "East European Jewish Workers," p. 902.

165 See *Protokoll der Sitzung des vorbereitenden Komitees zur Gründung einer jüdischen Arbeitsfürsorgestelle,* 9 October 1917, CZA A15/VIII/9d, p. 11.

166 "Antisemitismus," *NJM* 2, no. 1 (10 October 1917), p. 4.

167 See the statements by Fuchs, Nathan, and Oppenheimer, ibid., no. 11 (10 March 1918).

168 See Behr, "Grenzschutz," p. 267; "Verhinderung der jüdischen Rückwanderung," *JR* 23, no. 34 (23 August 1918).

169 "Grenzschluss gegen Juden in Deutschland," *JR* 23, no. 30 (26 July 1918), p. 229.

170 "Gemeinbürgschaft," *IDR* 24, no. 4 (April 1918), esp. pp. 146–47.

CHAPTER 8

1 Heine to Christian August Keller, 1 September 1822. See Hugo Bieber, ed., *Heinrich Heine: Jüdisches Manifest* (New York, 1946), pp. 11–12. Heine later published his "Memoir on Poland" in *Der Gesellschafter* (January 1823). For the present translation, see Heinrich Heine, *The Poetry and Prose of Heinrich Heine*, ed. F. Ewen (New York, 1948), pp. 690–91.

2 Bergmann to Buber, 11 May 1915, *Buber Briefwechsel*, 1:388.

3 "Unsere Arbeit nach dem Kriege," *JS* 12, no. 10 (27 November 1916), p. 325. See, too, H. G.-r. "Kriegsbeitrag," *JR* 22, no. 12 (23 March 1917), pp. 99–100.

4 L. Barth, "Juden und Judenpolitik im ehemaligen General-Governement Warschau," *JW* 1, no. 6 (February 1919), p. 321.

5 Benno Grzebinasch, "Eindrücke über Juden und Judentum während meiner russischen Kriegsgefangenschaft," *JW* 1, no. 6 (2 February 1919), p. 362. See, too, Barth, "Juden und Judenpolitik," p. 321, for similar observations of literature coming to life.

6 Hugo Hein, "Aus Russisch-Polen," in the series "Juden des Ostens," *JS* 12, no. 3 (12 August 1915), p. 75.

7 Gronemann, *Hawdoloh*, p. 200.

8 Ibid., p. 145.

9 Leo Rosenberg, "Die Wirklichkeit von morgen," *JR* 19, no. 44 (30 October 1914), pp. 403–4.

10 Bergmann to Buber, 11 May 1915, in *Buber Briefwechsel*, 1:388–89. See, too, Bergmann's "Der jüdische Nationalismus nach dem Krieg," *J* 1 (1916–17).

11 Gerhard Holdheim, "Rückblicke und Ausblicke," *JS* 15 (January 1917).

12 G. Wollstein, "Neue Kompromisse," *JS* 15 (January 1917), pp. 353–54.

13 Arnold Kutzinski, "Freiwilliges Ghetto," *JS* 15 (June 1917), pp. 506–9.

14 This mood became most pronounced in the immediate postwar period. See Hans Sachs, "Der Jude und der Bourgeois," *J* 3 (1918–19).

15 See, for instance, Israel Reichert, "Die jüdische Arbeiterfrage in Deutschland," *A* 1, no. 2 (31 January 1919); Walter Preuss, "Jüdische Arbeit in Deutschland," *JS* 18, no. 4 (June–August 1921).

16 Thus the periodical in which Zionists most frequently voiced this mood was the self-consciously youthful *Der Jüdische Student*. Most of the leaders of the cult were born in the 1880s or even later. Julius Berger was born in 1883, Arnold Zweig in 1887, S. Lehmann in 1892, and Fritz Mordecai Kaufmann in 1888.

17 Franz Kafka, *Letter to His Father* (New York, 1965), p. 85. See, too, pp. 75 ff.

18 Max Meyer, "A German Jew Goes East," *LBIYB* 3 (1958).

19 See Gershom Scholem, *From Berlin to Jerusalem* (New York, 1980), pp. 44, 83–84. For Scholem's appreciation of Shazar and Agnon, see chap. 5.

See also Scholem's *On Jews and Judaism in Crisis* (New York, 1976) for "Agnon in Germany: Recollections."

20 Eliasberg (1878–1924) was born in Minsk, Russia, but came as a young man to Germany. A prominent translator, he became a major mediator of Eastern Jewish life. He lived with his family in Munich but in the wake of postwar anti-Semitism was expelled from there and found asylum in Berlin. Amongst his translations are *Ostjüdische Theater* (1917), *Die Sagen polnischer Juden* (1916), and *Ostjüdische Novellen* (1917).

21 G. Scholem, "Zum Problem der Übersetzung aus dem Jiddischen," *JR* 2, no. 2 (12 January 1917), pp. 16–17. For a similar approach, see Fritz Mordecai Kaufmann, "Über Mendele und die Übersetzbarkeit seiner Dichtungen (Bemerkungen zu einer Übersetzung)," in his *Gesammelte Schriften*, p. 182. These men were more likely to call the language Yiddish than *Jargon*.

22 Markus Reiner, "Modernität und Primitivität," *J* 1 (1916–17), pp. 702–4.

23 For Max Brod's pedagogic efforts in Prague, see his "Erfahrungen im ostjüdischen Schulwerk," *J* 1 (1916–17), pp. 32–34. For Austria, see Siegfried Bernfeld, *Kinderheim Baumgarten (Bericht über einen ernsthaften Versuch mit neuer Erziehung)* (Berlin, 1921). Like the Jüdische Volksheim, the latter attempted to combine new educational theories with Zionism and socialism.

24 For details of the conception and workings of the Volksheim, see S. Lehmann, *Das jüdische Volksheim: Erster Bericht* (Berlin, 1916); and S. Adler-Rudel, *Ostjuden in Deutschland, 1880–1940* (Tübingen, 1959), pp. 51–56.

25 On the Kowno project, see S. Lehmann, *Von der Strassenhorde zur Gemeinschaft (Aus dem Leben des jüdischen Kinderhauses in Kowno)* (1926).

26 Lehmann to Buber, 14 November 1916, MBA MS Var 350/373.

27 Lehmann to Buber, 10 October 1915, in *Buber Briefwechsel* 1:401–2.

28 See Lehmann, "Gustav Landauer und das jüdische Volksheim," *A* 2 (June 1920). The entire issue of this Zionist Socialist journal was devoted to Landauer's work.

29 For details on this circle, see Eugen Lunn's excellent study *Prophet of Community: The Romantic Socialism of Gustav Landauer* (Berkeley, 1973), pp. 249–51.

30 "Judentum und Sozialismus" appears in *A* 2 (June 1920).

31 These are Lunn's words, in *Prophet of Community*, p. 6. I follow his account of Landauer's philosophy.

32 S. Lehmann, "Die Verwirklichung des Sozialismus und die Volksheims-idee," *A* 1, no. 4 (28 February 1919). This was the text of a speech Lehmann gave at the home.

33 Salomon Lehnart (S. Lehmann), "Jüdische Volksarbeit," *J* 1 (1916–17), p. 110.

34 *Idee der jüdischen Siedlung und des Volksheims* (n.p., n.d.).

35 See, for instance, Lehmann's "Notwendigkeit der neuen Gemein-schaft," *Jerubbaal* 1 (1918–19).

36 Lunn, *Prophet of Community*, p. 271.

37 "Über die erzieherischen Kräfte von Erde und Volk," *J* 9 (1927–28).

38 Scholem, *From Berlin*, pp. 80–82.

39 See, for instance, Georg Lubinski, "Erinnerungen an das jüdische Volksheim in Berlin," *Der junge Jude* (July–August 1930); and Gertrude Weil, "Vom jüdischen Volksheim in Berlin," *Jüdische Wohlfahrtspflege und Sozialpolitik* (1930), p. 281.

40 For a report of how a participant saw the problem, see Sophie Steinhaus, "Aus dem jüdischen Volksheim," *JW* 1, no. 4–5 (October–December 1918).

41 Scholem, *From Berlin*, p. 78. See, generally, pp. 76–80.

42 Lubinski, "Erinnerungen," p. 135.

43 Wilhelm Levy, "Gesetzestreue oder Auflehnung," *Jerubbaal* 1, no. 4 (1918–19), esp. p. 155. See also Hede Bloch's remarks in *Jerubbaal* 1 (1918–19), pp. 277, 278.

44 Landauer to Lehmann, 30 October 1915, reprinted in *Der Junge Jude* 2 (November 1929).

45 Lubinski, "Erinnerungen," p. 134.

46 See the "Nachschrift" of his letter (no. 386) to Hugo Bergmann of 4 February 1918, in *Buber Briefwechsel*, 1:527.

47 See Zwat Protocols, MBA MS Var 350/40/11. For Rubaschoff's paper, see pp. 15 ff.

48 For an analysis of the Kantian nature of this socialism, see "Left-Wing Intellectuals in the Weimar Republic," in Mosse, *Germans and Jews*.

49 See, for instance, "Nochmals zur Tragik des deutschen Juden," *Hochland* 2 (April–September 1921), pp. 748–51; "Aussenpolitik und Ostjudenfrage," *NJM* 4, nos. 11, 12 (10, 25 March 1920); "Die Summe," *JR* 28, no. 97 (20 November 1923); "Ostjuden und Abwehr," *JR* 28, no. 100–101 (30 November 1923); *Das Los der Geflüchteten* (Berlin, 1929). I thank Gad Ben-Ami for the last reference.

50 All quotes are taken from the reproduction of *Das ostjüdische Antlitz* that appeared in *Herkunft und Zukunft* (Vienna, 1929). See esp. pp. 19 and 24.

51 See Zweig, "Bekenntnis zum Neid," *JR* 27, no. 103–4 (29 December 1922). See, too, in the same issue, Robert Weltsch, "Chajim Nachman Bialik: Zum 50. Geburtstag."

52 Zweig, *Antlitz*, p. 32.

53 Ibid., pp. 64–66.

54 Ibid., pp. 67ff.

55 Ibid., esp. pp. 141–48.

56 See Zweig to Freud, 1 September 1935, in Sigmund Freud and Arnold Zweig, *The Letters of Sigmund Freud and Arnold Zweig*, ed. Ernst L. Freud (New York, 1970), pp. 108–9, where Zweig complains that at a

demonstration of left-wing workers they "tried to keep up the fiction that they did not understand me when I spoke German and so they had my speech translated into *Iwrith*—as though all 2500 of them did not speak Yiddish at home."

57 Alfred Lemm, *Der Weg der Deutschjuden: Eine Skizzierung* (Leipzig, 1919).

58 Dora Dymant, an *Ostjüdin* who attended the Volksheim. See her comments reprinted in Franz Kafka, *I Am a Memory Come Alive* (New York, 1974), p. 232.

59 Landauer, "Judentum und Sozialismus," pp. 50–51.

60 See Landauer, "Ostjuden und Deutsches Reich," *J* 1 (October 1916).

61 Kafka, *Letter to His Father*, p. 85.

62 This, of course, was a prewar discovery. His *Diaries*, 1910–1913, ed. Max Brod (New York, 1965), are filled with references to the subject. See also Evelyn Torton Beck, *Kafka and the Yiddish Theater* (Madison: University of Wisconsin Press, 1971). Beck not only documents Kafka's passionate relationship with the Yiddish theater but suggests that it was a fundamental part of his art, reflected in his narratives "by his use of cultural symbols, his choice of themes and characters, his manipulation of language, and his attitude toward his heroes" (p. 30).

63 See Franz Kafka, *Letters to Felice* (Middlesex, 1974), entry for 12 September 1916, pp. 616–17. See, too, Elias Canetti's introduction to this volume, esp. p. 84. For Kafka, the Volksheim became a vicarious obsession, a means of changing the image of Felice Bauer. After succeeding in persuading her to join the Home, Kafka constantly tried to guide her work from afar.

64 See *Diaries, 1910–1913*, entry for 31 October 1911, p. 125; and *Diaries, 1914–1923* ed. Max Brod (New York, 1965), entry for 11 March 1915, p. 117.

65 See entry for 24 October 1911, *Diaries, 1910–1923*, p. 111.

66 Kafka, *I am a Memory Come Alive*, p. 232.

67 Letter of 23 May 1918, in Rosenzweig, *Franz Rosenzweig*, ed. Glatzer, pp. 73–74.

68 *Rosenzweig*, ed. Glatzer. See the editorial comment on p. 80.

69 On the "barbaric," see *Rosenzweig*, letter of 9 July 1916, pp. 37–38. On language, see Rosenzweig, *Star of Redemption* (Boston, 1971), p. 301.

70 For biographical details, see *Nachwort* by Walter Muschg in the new reprint of Döblin's *Reise in Polen* (Olten, 1968).

71 Döblin, "Zion und Europa," *Der Neue Merkur* (August 1921); see pp. 338–42.

72 Döblin, *Reise*, p. 258.

73 See, for instance, Döblin, *Jüdische Erneuerung* (Amsterdam, 1933), and *Flucht und Sammlung des Judenvolks* (Amsterdam, 1935).

74 Döblin, "Jüdische Antijuden," *Das Neue Tagebuch* 3, no. 45 (1935).

75 Döblin, *Reise*, p. 366.

76 See Walter Preuss, "Die K.J.V.-er und die Ostjuden," *JS* (18 August 1916), p. 237; Georg Ehrlich, "K.J.V.er und Ostjuden," *JS* (March 1917), p. 410.

77 Gustav Witkowsky, "Hie Zwirn!" *JS* (May 1917), 439; see also pp. 431, 438.

78 See Holdheim's reply to Witkowsky in *JS* (August 1917), pp. 570–72.

79 Blumenfeld reply to Witkowsky, *JS* (June 1917), esp. pp. 476, 478.

80 See Kaufmann, "Das jüdische Volkslied," *Freistaat* 1 (1913); "Die Aufführung jüdischer Volksmusik vor Westjuden," *J* 2 (1917–18); "Das Volkslied der Ostjuden," *Jüdische Turn-und Sport-Zeitung* (1920), in *Gesammelte Schriften;* "Das Blauweiss Liederbuch," *Jerubbaal* (1918–19). For an excellent discussion of the theoretical components of "demodernization," see part 3 of Peter Berger, Brigitte Berger, and Hansfried Kellner, *The Homeless Mind* (New York, 1974).

81 George Strauss, "Das jüdische Lied im Blau-Weiss und das Blau-Weiss Liederbuch," *Blau-Weiss Blätter: Führerzeitung* 2, nos. 1, 2 (October, November 1920); see esp. pp. 20, 22–23, 25.

82 *Schlemiel,* no. 15 (1920), p. 204.

83 There are many examples of this. See, for instance, Fritz Strauss, "Soziale Arbeit als Aufgabe der jüdischen Jugend," *JR* 24, no. 16 (28 February 1919), pp. 119–20; "Gemeinsame Arbeit," *JR* 24, no. 25 (4 April 1919), p. 185.

84 "Herut: On Youth and Religion," in Martin Buber, *On Judaism* (New York, 1967), pp. 159–60.

85 See Gershom Scholem's telling remarks in "Martin Buber's Conception of Judaism" in his *On Jews and Judaism in Crisis,* p. 127.

86 Paul Zucker, "Mythos der Gegenwart," *J* 7, nos. 7, 8 (July 1923), pp. 464–65.

87 David Krombach, "Auf dem rechten Wege: Zur Geschichte des K. C. Gedankens," *KCB* 7, no. 13 (September–October 1916), pp. 728–36.

88 F. Coblenz, "Nationales oder religiöses Judentum," *Mitteilungen der jüdischen Reformgemeinde zu Berlin,* no. 4 (23 March 1919), p. 2.

89 See F. Goldmann, "Einheitsfront," *IDR* 26, no. 11 (November 1920), pp. 330–31. Gronemann's book was published in 1920.

90 Verax, "Jüdische Rundschau," *IDR* 27, no. 1 (January 1921), pp. 18 ff. For evidence that Segel was the author, see Eva Reichmann, "Der Bewusstseinswandel der deutschen Juden," in Werner Mosse, ed., *Deutsches Judentum in Krieg und Revolution, 1916–1923* (Tübingen, 1971), p. 562. It is interesting that as late as 1921 Segel still placed the word *Ostjuden* in quotation marks.

91 Moshe Zilburg, "Vos ich hob euch zu sagen" (Yiddish), in his own short-lived Yiddish journal *Kritik,* nos. 1, 2, 3 (February, March–April, September 1920). For details on Zilburg, see Sol Liptzin, "Galician Neoromanticism," *YIVO Annual of Jewish Social Science* 14 (1969).

92 See, for example, "Helfen," *Der Israelit,* no. 49 (7 December 1916).

93 See Alexander Carlebach, *Adas Yeschurun of Cologne* (Belfast, 1964), p. 122. By the same author, see too "The Image of German Orthodoxy," *Niv Hamidrashia* (1966).

94 J. Wohlgemuth, "Nachwort des Herausgebers," *Jeschurun* 7, nos. 11–12 (November–December 1920), pp. 508–9.

95 Jacob Rosenheim, "Abrahamitisches oder mosaisches Judentum? Eine Auseinandersetzung mit zeitgenössischen Strömungen," *Ausgewählte Aufsätze und Ansprachen* (Frankfurt, 1930), pp. 180–83.

96 See Armin Blau, "Gedanken zu Alfred Lemms: 'Der Weg der Deutsch-juden,'" *Jeschurun* 6, nos. 9–10 (September–October 1919), pp. 482–83.

97 Wiener, "Bemerkungen zu dem Kapitel: Wir und die Ostjuden," *Jeschurun* 7, nos. 3–4 (March–April 1920), pp. 189–94.

98 For an excellent account of the symbolic uses of *Ostjudentum* in general, and specifically in the works of the Austrian writer Joseph Roth, see Claudio Magris, *Weit von wo: Verlorene Welt des Ostjudentums* (Vienna, 1974). I thank Klaus Berghahn for this reference.

99 "German Jewry as Mirror of Modernity," *LBIYB* 20 (1975), p. xi.

CHAPTER 9

1 For a detailed analysis of these developments, see Werner Jochmann, "Die Ausbreitung des Antisemitismus," in Werner E. Mosse, ed., *Deutsches Judentum in Krieg und Revolution.*

2 Max Simon, *Der Weltkrieg und die Judenfrage* (Leipzig and Berlin, 1916), p. 79.

3 Golo Mann, "Deutsche und Juden: Ein unlösbares Problem." Quoted in Saul Friedländer, "Die politischen Veränderungen der Kriegszeit," in Mosse, *Deutsches Judentum*, p. 49.

4 See Adler-Rudel, *Ostjuden in Deutschland*, pp. 60–63.

5 Part 3 of Adler-Rudel, *Ostjuden*, details the history of these efforts.

6 See Eva Reichmann's excellent "Der Bewusstseinswandel der deutschen Juden," in Mosse, *Deutsches Judentum*. See also Ruth Louise Pierson, "German Jewish Identity in the Weimar Republic," (Ph.D. diss., Yale University, 1970).

7 See, for instance, Reinhold Lewin, "Der Krieg als jüdisches Erlebnis," *Monatsschrift für Geschichte des Judentums* 63, no. 1–3 (January–March 1919); Franz Oppenheimer, "Der Antisemitismus," *NJM* 2, no. 23 (10 September 1918).

8 Georg Hermann, "Zur Frage der Westjuden," *NJM* 3, nos. 19, 20 (10, 25 July 1919).

9 See the use made of Hermann's remarks by Theodor Fritsch in *Handbuch der Judenfrage* (Leipzig, 1939), p. 490

10 Felix Theilhaber, "Offener Brief an Herrn Georg Hermann," *NJM* 3, no. 22 (25 August 1919), pp. 483–84.

11 Julius Simon, "Offener Brief an Georg Hermann," *NJM* 4, no. 5 (December 1919), pp. 113–14. For yet another response, see Katzenstein, "Zur Frage der Westjuden," *NJM* 4, no. 7–8 (10–25 January 1920).

12 Rudolf Kayser, "Der neue Bund," *J* 3 (1918–19). See, too, Arnold Zweig's reply, "Entgegnung."

13 Eugen Fuchs, "Ein Nachwort," *NJM* 3, no. 22 (25 August 1919).

14 Eugen Fuchs, "Eine Auseinandersetzung," *IDR* 25, no. 6 (June 1919), p. 250.

15 Eugen Fuchs, "Was nun?" *NJM* 3, no. 7–8 (10–25 January 1919), pp. 139–40.

16 Moritz Bileski, "Der Kompromiss des Deutschen Judentums," *J* 5 (1920–21).

17 Adler-Rudel, *Ostjuden*, p. 71.

18 Paul Nathan, "Nachschrift," *IDR* 27, no. 1 (January 1921).

19 See, for example, his *Die Ostjuden in Deutschland und die antisemitische Reaktion* (Berlin, 1922).

20 Kurt Alexander, "Zeitschau," *IDR* 26, no. 7–8 (July–August 1920), esp. p. 237.

21 "Wandersturm," *IDR* 26, no. 12 (December 1920).

22 F. Coblenz, "Über die Ostjudenfrage in Deutschland," *Mitteilungen der jüdischen Reformgemeinde zu Berlin*, no. 2 (1 July 1921), pp. 22–23; and by the same author in the same journal, no. 4 (23 March 1919), "Nationales oder religiöses Judentum?"

23 Max Naumann, "Von nationaldeutschen Juden: Eine Erwiderung," *IDR* 27, no. 1 (January 1921).

24 "Von nationaldeutschen Juden, Ostjuden und Dissidenten," *Mitteilungen der jüdischen Reformgemeinde zu Berlin*, no. 3 (15 September 1921), esp. p. 8.

25 Quoted in "Angstpsychose," *JR*, no. 101–2 (22 December 1922).

26 Max Naumann, "Liegt Berlin in Deutschland?" quoted in *JR* 27, no. 26 (31 March 1922), pp. 167–68.

27 Max Naumann, "Ausländergefahr und Ostjudengefahr," *MVNDJ*, no. 1 (January–February 1923).

28 For a list of the eighty-nine founding members, see Klaus J. Hermann, *Das Dritte Reich und die deutsch-jüdischen Organisationen, 1933–1934* (Cologne, 1969), pp. 36–38.

29 See Max Naumann, *Von mosaischen und nicht-mosaischen Juden* (Berlin, 1921), p. 25.

30 See *Von nationaldeutschen Juden* (Berlin, 1920), pp. 12–13, for a catalogue of distasteful Jewish characteristics.

31 George L. Mosse, *Germans and Jews*, p. 112. In 1933, Hans Joachim Schoeps and his Vortrupp also attempted to go beyond liberalism and solve the Jewish problem within the Volkish framework. He submitted a memorandum to the Nazis defining the Jews as a *Stand*, possessed of

equal rights and responsibilities within the Volk. Ostjuden and Zionists were excluded from this scheme. See his *Bereit für Deutschland!* (Berlin, 1970), pp. 23–24.

32 For Naumann's perception of the interrelationship, see his "Liegt Berlin in Deutschland?"

33 See Ludwig Holländer, "Verband nationaldeutscher Juden und CVDSJG," *IDR* 27, no. 4 (April 1921).

34 See Holländer's confidential manuscript concerning Naumann's attempt to attach German Jewry to the Volkspartei: *Denkschrift über die Bestrebungen des Rechtsanwalts Dr. Max Naumann in Berlin auf Begründung eines Verbandes nationaldeutscher Juden* (Berlin, 1921), esp. pp. 7–8.

35 Berthold Haase, "Der gegenwärtige Stand der Ostjudenfrage," *CVZ* 2, no. 41 (25 January 1923), p. 26.

36 Fabius Schach, "Nationaldeutsche Juden," *AZdJ* 86, no. 2 (20 January 1922).

37 For the judgment of Sidney Bolkosky, among others: see *The Distorted Image* (New York, 1975), p. 163.

38 Alfred Peyser, *Nationaldeutsche Juden und ihre Lästerer* (Berlin, n.d.), p. 12.

39 Peter Gay, "Hermann Levi: A Study in Service and Self-Hatred," in his *Freud, Jews and Other Germans* (New York, 1978), p. 201.

40 Jacob Wassermann, *My Life as German and Jew*, English trans. S. N. Brainin (New York, 1933), pp. 196–97.

41 Ibid., pp. 197–98, 234, 220–21.

42 See his biography: Otto Lubarsch, *Ein bewegtes Gelehrtenleben* (Berlin, 1931), pp. 539 ff. I thank George L. Mosse for this reference.

43 For an account of this aspect of Weininger's life, see Theodor Lessing, *Der jüdische Selbsthass* (Berlin, 1930).

44 See Solomon Liptzin, *Germany's Stepchildren* (Philadelphia, 1944), pp. 189–94. On the other hand, F. L. Carsten in his book *Fascist Movements in Austria* (London, 1977) does not mention Trebitsch. For more on Trebitsch, see Lessing, *Selbsthass*, pp. 101–31.

45 Arthur Trebitsch, *Geist and Judentum* (Vienna and Leipzig, 1919), pp. 236–39.

46 Arthur Trebitsch, *Deutscher Geist—oder Judentum: Der Weg der Befreiung* (Vienna and Leipzig, 1921).

47 Trebitsch, *Geist und Judentum*, pp. 279–80.

48 Quoted in Kurt Blumenfeld, *Erlebte Judenfrage* (Stuffgart, 1962), p. 51.

49 See "The Berlin-Jewish Spirit," in Peter Gay, *Freud, Jews and other Germans*, p. 183.

50 See "Stenographischer Bericht über die Hauptversammlung der CVDSJG vom 4. February 1917," *IDR* 23 (1917), pp. 50–51.

51 Wassermann, *My Life*, p. 188.

52 See M. Grunewald, "Eine Gemeindekammer," *AZdJ* 85, no. 18 (2 September 1921), pp. 203–4.

53 Fritz Goetz, "Jiddisch und Jüdeln: Ernsthafte Schriftsteller und takt-
lose Kabarettisten," in *Vossische Zeitung*, no. 534 (1924), as quoted in
CVZ 3, no. 46 (14 November 1924), p. 708.

54 Constantin Brunner, *Der Judenhass und die Juden* (Berlin, 1919); and
Von den Pflichten der Juden und von den Pflichten des Staates
(Berlin, 1930).

55 See his semi-autobiographical *Vom Einsiedler* (Potsdam, 1924), esp. pp.
79–82.

56 Brunner, *Judenhass*, pp. 77, 162, 192.

57 Ibid., pp. 192–93, 299, and the section beginning p. 375.

58 Leo Haubenberger, "Das Judentum in Österreich," *Deutschlands Erneuerung* 4, no. 10 (1920), p. 619.

59 See "Der Eid der Ostjuden," excerpted from the *Kölnische Zeitung*
report of a court case, quoted in *CVZ* 3, no. 30 (24 July 1924).

60 This excerpt appears in "Die Hetze gegen die Ostjuden," in *Mitteilungen aus dem Verein zur Abwehr des Antisemitismus* 30, no. 1 (10
January 1920), p. 3.

61 See his speech of 12 April 1922, "Die 'Hetzer' der Wahrheit!" quoted in
Friedländer, "Politische Veränderungen," p. 55.

62 See Klara Eschelbacher, "Die Wohnungsfrage," *NJM* 10, no. 11–12 (10–
25 March 1920), p. 257.

63 See Wilhelm Treue, "Zur Frage der wirtschaftlichen Motive im deutschen Anti-semitismus," in Mosse, *Deutsches Judentum*, esp. p. 399.
Although in 1925 Ostjuden constituted only 19.1% of German Jewry,
their relative percentages increased in the larger centers. Thus in Berlin
they were 25.4%, in Munich 27%, and in Dresden 60%. In Leipzig the
figure was an overwhelming 80%.

64 "Die Denkschrift der Reichsregierung vom 30.3.1922," in Adler-Rudel,
Ostjuden, p. 120.

65 For an excellent account of this whole question, see Werner T. Angress,
"Juden im politischen Leben der Revolutionszeit," in Mosse, *Deutsches
Judentum*.

66 Robert S. Wistrich, *Revolutionary Jews from Marx to Trotsky* (London,
1976), p. 90. Quoted in Wertheimer, "German Policy and Jewish
Politics," p. 310.

67 Friedländer, "Politische Veränderungen," p. 51.

68 Reinhold Wulle, "Der Stern Judas," *Deutsche Zeitung* 24, no. 111 (13
March 1919); quoted in Jochmann, "Ausbreitung," p. 451.

69 Alfred Roth, *Judentum und Bolschewismus: Enthüllungen aus jüdischen Geheimakten. Ein Mahn- und Warnruf in letzter Stunde* (Hamburg, 1920); for similar views, see Rudolf von Sebottendorf, *Bevor
Hitler kam* (Munich, 1933).

70 See, for instance, Paul Busching, "Die Revolution in Bayern," *Süddeutsche Monatshefte*, no. 2 (June 1919).

71 *Antisemitismus?—Eine unparteiische Prüfung des Problems* (Charlottenburg, 1920), esp. pp. 8, 18, 47–49, 53–54, 64.

72 Friedrich von Oppeln-Bronikowski, *Gerechtigkeit! Zur Lösung der Judenfrage* (Berlin-Wilmersdorf, 1932). See also Arnold Paucker, " 'Gerechtigkeit': The Fate of a Pamphlet on the Jewish Question," *LBIYB* 8 (1963).

73 Adolf Bartels, *Die Berechtigung des Antisemitismus: Eine Widerlegung der Schrift von Herrn v. Oppeln-Bronikowski, "Antisemitismus"* (Berlin, n.d.), p. 11. Bartels had written similarly in "Ein deutsch-jüdisches Weltbündnis?" (1915) and "Nota iudaica" (1917), in his *Rasse und Volkstum: Gesammelte Aufsätze zur nationalen Weltanschauung* (Weimar, 1920).

74 See, for instance, Alfred Piech, "Slawentum und Judentum," *Deutschlands Erneuerung* 3, no. 2 (1919), p. 102.

75 For details on Popert, see George L. Mosse, *The Crisis of German Ideology*, pp. 104–6.

76 Hermann Popert, "Ostjuden," *Der Vortrupp* 8, no. 22 (2 November 1919). Many Zionists who identified with his Volkish youth movement aims were scandalized. See the critique in the Zionist Socialist paper, *A* 2, no. 1 (15 January 1920), entitled "Ostjuden." See also "Neuorientierung," *JR* 24, no. 1 (19 February 1919).

77 See Paul Wohlfarth, "Die Tragik des deutschen Juden," Arnold Zweig's reply, "Nochmals zur 'Tragik des deutschen Juden,' " and the comments by the editor Karl Müth, in *Hochland* 2 (April–September 1921).

78 See Werner Jochmann, "Ausbreitung," esp. pp. 491–97.

79 See Fischbeck's remarks in "Ostjudendebatte im preussischen Landtag," *JR* 27, no. 96 (5 December 1922), p. 632.

80 See Donald L. Niewyk, *Socialist, Anti-Semite, and Jew* (Baton Rouge, 1971), p. 221. Niewyk's point is well taken, but he seems to underplay the dualities and ambivalences of the Socialists concerning the Ostjuden, especially when the Socialists had official responsibility for the problem.

81 For the general attitude of the Left, see George L. Mosse, "German Socialists and the Jewish Question in the Weimar Republic," *LBIYB* 16 (1971). Kautsky's *Rasse und Judentum* appeared in 1914, and an expanded edition was published in 1921. See the English translation, *Are the Jews a Race?* 2d ed. rev. (Connecticut, 1972), esp. chap. 12, "The Last Stages of Judaism."

82 See Theodor Müller, "Die Einwanderung der Ostjuden," *Neue Zeit* 39 (24 June and 1 July 1921).

83 For an idea of the content and extent of these ideas, see "Die Hetze gegen die Ostjuden," *Mitteilungen aus dem Verein zur Abwehr des Antisemitismus* 30, no. 1 (10 January 1920), pp. 2–3. Traditional student opposition to Ostjuden also continued. See "Der Kampf gegen die Ausländer," *JR* 25, no. 2 (9 January 1920), p. 10.

84 For this history and that of Jewish social welfare efforts, see Adler-Rudel, *Ostjuden*, esp. pp. 63–66. The edict itself is reproduced on pp. 158–61.

85 Ibid., p. 66.

86 R. W., "Halb-Barbaren," *JR* 25, no. 9 (3 February 1920), p. 56.

87 See the address to the Prussian *Landesversammlung* on 16 December 1919, in "Konzentrationslager," *JR* 25, no. 1 (6 January 1920), p. 3.

88 See "Die Mizrach-Yidn in Daitschland," in the American Yiddish journal *Die Zukunft* 28, no. 11 (November 1923). See also Mosse, "German Socialists," for an account of the stereotype and Bernstein's role.

89 See Berger's private memorandum to Prof. Sobernheim of the Jewish affairs section of the Foreign Office, 2 April 1919, CZA Z3/718.

90 See his memorandum of 27 February 1920, CZA Z3/720. Also C. Z. Klötzel, "Zur Lage der ostjüdischen Arbeiter in Deutschland," *Volk und Land* 1, no. 8–9 (20–27 February 1919), p. 263.

91 On the arrests, see "Die Ostjudenverhaftungen," *JR* 25, no. 22 (31 March 1920), p. 154. On the raid, see C. Z. Klötzel, "Razzia," *NJM* 4, no. 11–12 (10–25 March 1920), and "Jagd auf Juden," *JR* 25, no. 15 (24 February 1920), p. 99; and Niewyk, *Socialist, Anti-Semite, and Jew*, p. 100. Niewyk minimizes the significance of this action.

92 *Berliner Tageblatt*, 10 February 1920, quoted in Oppeln-Bronikowski, *Gerechtigkeit!* pp. 94–95.

93 *Berliner Tageblatt*, 26 April 1920, quoted ibid.

94 Klötzel, "Razzia."

95 Reprinted in Kurt Tucholsky, *Gesammelte Werke (1907–1924)*, vol. 1 (Hamburg, 1960), pp. 805–8. On "Herr Wendriner steht unter der Diktatur" (1930), see Tucholsky, *Ausgewählte Werke* (Hamburg, 1966), p. 483.

96 The play can be found in Günther Rühle, *Zeit und Theater* 2 (Berlin, 1972). See also the commentary on the play, pp. 803–9. (I thank Reinhold Grimm for this reference.) A detailed account is provided by Piscator himself in his work *The Political Theatre: A History 1914–1929* (1929; Avon: New York, 1978). See esp. pp. vi–viii, pp. 314–17, 330–35. This was Piscator's most elaborate attempt at "machine theater" (although in execution it proved to be cumbersome and slow-moving). Still, the idea was impressive. Piscator (p. 331) describes it thus: "In accordance with the subject, I saw the play from the start in three stages: a tragic stage (proletariat), a tragicomic stage (middle class), and a grotesque stage (upper classes and the military). This sociological division produced the three-tier system of staging, which we constructed with the aid of elevators and bridges. Each of these social classes was to have a stage of its own—upper, middle, lower—and the classes were to meet from time to time wherever the focus of the dramatic action demanded it."

97 For Piscator's treatment of all these questions, see esp. pp. 332–33. Piscator argues in relation to the unsympathetic portrayal of Jews (p. 333): "I cannot concede that in a theater based on the principle that

every truth must be uttered, certain things should remain unsaid because of potential sensitivity." For samples of reviews and the controversy the play aroused, see Günther Rühle, *Theater für die Republik 1917–1933* (Frankfurt, 1967), pp. 961–68.

98 See Adler-Rudel, *Ostjuden*, p. 114.

99 See Jochmann, "Ausbreitung," pp. 505–6. It is only fair to note that this decision was taken against Interior Minister Severing's vote.

100 "Di I'nuyim Fon Di Mizrach Yid'n In Stagard," in the official newspaper of Eastern Jews in Germany, *Der Ostjude* 2, no. 22 (3 April 1921); see also the Socialist Zionist journal *Die jüdische Arbeiterstimme* 1, no. 6 (1 June 1921).

101 See Jakob Reich, "Eine Episode aus der Geschichte der Ostjuden," in Hans Lamm, ed., *Von Juden in München* (Munich, 1959).

102 These parties included the Bayerische Volkspartei, Deutschnationale Partei, Deutsche Mittelpartei, Bauernbund, and others. See the undated memorandum to the Comité des Délégations de la Nation Juive (Paris), probably written by Julius Berger, CZA Z3/721.

103 For details, see Reich, "Episode," pp. 120–21.

104 "Judenaustreibung aus Bayern," *JR* 28, no. 94 (2 November 1923), pp. 547–48.

105 This is reported in *AZdJ* 84, no. 26 (25 June 1920), p. 291. In Austria, as in Germany, the Ostjuden were a primary target for political anti-Semitism from its beginnings. See Carsten, *Fascist Movements*.

106 Julius Berger, *Bericht* (23 March 1920), CZA Z3/201. Ulrich Dunker, *Der Reichsbund jüdischer Frontsoldaten 1919–1938* (Düsseldorf, 1977), mistakenly attributes this report to Alfred Klee (p. 252).

107 Berger, *Bericht*.

108 For an account of the pogrom, see Dunker, *Reichsbund*, pp. 49–56.

109 For an English analysis of this organization, see Ruth Pierson, "Embattled Veterans; The *Reichsbund jüdischer Frontsoldaten*," *LBIYB* 19 (1974).

110 "Die November-Pogrome vor Gericht," *Der Schild*, no. 7 (1 June 1924); "Memento," ibid., no. 13 (3 July 1925).

111 See "Die Hauptversammlung des Reichsbundes jüdischer Frontsoldaten, 21, 22 Oktober 1923," ibid., no. 18 (November 1923).

112 "Die Berliner Vorgänge und ihr Echo," *Der Israelit* 64, no. 46 (15 November 1923).

113 See Fritz Neulander's comments, quoted in "Die judenfeindliche Welle in Deutschland," *JR* 28, no. 97 (20 November 1923), p. 561.

114 "Judenaustreibung aus Bayern," ibid., no. 94 (2 November 1923).

115 "Die Schicksalsstunde des deutschen Judentums," ibid., no. 95 (9 November 1923), p. 557.

116 "Die Weltgefahr der Judenhetze in Deutschland," *OW*, 1920, no. 3–4, p. 71.

CHAPTER 10

1 Nahum Goldmann, "Zionismus und nationale Bewegung," *J* 5 (1920–21), pp. 45–46.
2 Ben Nathan, "Galizien," *JW* 1, no. 4–5 (October–December 1918), pp. 299–300.
3 See Joseph Roth, *Werke*, vol. 3 (Berlin, 1956).
4 Eros, "Das Problem der Grenadierstrasse," *A* 2, no. 4 (15 March 1920), pp. 45–46.
5 See Abraham Schwadron, "Von der Schande eurer Namen," *Jerubbaal* 1 (1918–19), esp. p. 448.
6 See Otto Abeles, "Der Olreitnik," *Begegnung mit Juden* (Vienna and Jerusalem, 1936).
7 "Das Problem der Grenadierstrasse," p. 46.
8 Max Eschelbacher, "Ostjüdische Proletarier in Deutschland," *J* 3 (1918–19). See also Alfons Pacquet, "Rücklauf und Sammlung," *Freie Zionistische Blätter*, no. 1 (January 1921), where he argues that Ostjuden were attracted to Socialism rather than Zionism, yet as outsiders were unwilling and unable to join German Socialist organizations.
9 See "The Conference of Ostjuden in Germany," *O* 2, no. 26 (7 July 1921). For a view of how Ostjuden in France dealt with the question of anti-Semitism, see David H. Weinberg, *A Community on Trial* (Chicago, 1977).
10 "The Torture of Ostjuden in Stagard," *O* 2, no. 22 (3 April 1921). For an account of life in the Berlin ghetto, see Mischket Liebermann, *Aus dem Ghetto in die Welt* (Berlin, 1977). I thank Gad Ben-Ami for this reference.
11 Jakob Reich, "Deutschland (Rundschau)," *NJM* 4, no. 11–12 (10–25 March 1920), p. 266.
12 M. Gantzer, "Sprechen Ihr Daitsch," *O* 2, no. 4 (29 January 1921), pp. 14–15.
13 For a good analysis of modes of Eastern Jewish assimilation into German life, see Wertheimer, "German Policy and Jewish Politics, pp. 542–44.
14 Israel Uerbach, "Die ostjüdische Aleph-Bet," *O* 2, no. 23 (10 June 1921).
15 See Josef Lin, "Der Mizrach Yid," *O* 1, (10 September 1920); Y. Kirschbaum, "Gesamtorganisation und Mizrach Juden," *O* 1 (19 November 1920).
16 Zalman Rubaschoff, "In der Neue Achsanya," in the short-lived Yiddish journal *Oif der Schwell* [On the threshold], no. 1 (1918).
17 See Zalman Rubaschoff, "Der Lehrstuhl," *J* 2 (1917–18).
18 Rubaschoff republished Eduard Gans's address to the Verein für Kultur und Wissenschaft der Juden under the caustic title "First Fruits of Dejudaisation." See "Erstlinge der Entjudung," *JW* 1 (1918–19).

19 See Solomon Maimon, *An Autobiography* (New York, 1967).

20 See Baruch Benedikt Kurzweil, "The Image of the Western Jew in Modern Hebrew Literature," *LBIYB* 6 (1961), pp. 171–72.

21 In "The Pocket Knife," in *The Jewish Children* (New York, 1922), pp. 191–92.

22 See the analysis by Mordecai Ehrenpreis of the coldness which he as a Galician Jew experienced when a student in the Berlin school of the Science of Judaism, in *Bein Mizrach Le'Ma'arav* (Hebrew) (Tel Aviv, 1963), p. 36. See, too, the complaints of German Orthodox coldness by an East European rabbi, Ben Zion Berman, in a Hebrew article "Mizrach U'Ma'arav" [East and West], *Jeschurun* 8, no. 11–12 (November–December 1921), esp. p. 146.

23 The two essays are reprinted in Achad Ha'am, *Selected Essays by Achad Ha'am*, ed. Leon Simon (Cleveland, 1962). See, too, K. Baruch, "Die Juden des Westens im Urteil Achad Ha'ams," *J* 1 (1916–17).

24 "Brief an die Herausgeber des 'Dvir,' " in *Chaim Nachmann Bialik: Essays* (Berlin, 1925).

25 For a list of pertinent Agnon works dealing with German Jewry as well as a sensitive commentary on the issue (a commentary upon which the following is based), see Dan Miron, "German Jews in Agnon's Work," *LBIYB* 23 (1978).

26 Ibid., p. 269.

27 Ibid., p. 277.

28 Ibid., p. 275.

29 For a good summary of the issues, see Michael R. Marrus, "European Jewry and the Politics of Assimilation: Assessment and Reassessment," *Journal of Modern History* 49, no. 1 (March 1977).

SELECTED BIBLIOGRAPHY

ARCHIVES

New York. Archives of the Leo Baeck Institute.

Asch, Adolf. "Posener und Berliner Erinnerungen 1881–1931."
Gronemann, Sammy. "Erinnerungen."

Jerusalem. Jewish National Library. Martin Buber Archives.

Mappe 141. Gustav Landauer.
112/7. *Stammtisch der Donnerstagsgesellschaft.*
MS Var 350/89a/18. Moritz Heimann.
MS Var 350/1031. Buber–Franz Blei Correspondence.
MS Var 350/373. Buber–Siegfried Lehmann Correspondence.
Mappe 457. George Lukacs to Buber.
MS Var 350/49/13. Reviews of Buber's Works.
40/11. Minutes of the Safed (Zwat) Circle.

Jerusalem. The Central Archives for the History of the Jewish People.

M/1. *Deutsch-Israelitischer Gemeindebund*, Berlin.
M/2. *Hilfsverein der deutschen Juden*, Berlin.

INV/149. *Ausschuss zur Beschaffung jiddischer und hebräischer Literatur für russische Kriegsgefangene*, Berlin. 1916–18.
INV/1409/318. *Deutsches Central Komitee für die russischen Juden.*
INV/1431(10). *Komitee für den Osten*, Berlin. 1915–17.

Jerusalem. The Central Zionist Archives.

Z2. Central Zionist Office, Cologne. 1905–11.
Z3. Central Zionist Office, Berlin. 1911–20.
A8. Adolf Friedemann.
A15. Max Bodenheimer.
A22. Kurt Blumenfeld.
A124. Hermann Struck.
A135. Sammy Gronemann.
A136. Leo Winz.
A161. Franz Oppenheimer.
A206. Julius Berger.

NEWSPAPERS AND PERIODICALS

Jewish

Allgemeine Zeitung des Judenthums. Leipzig and Berlin.
American Jewish Historical Society Publications. Baltimore.
Die Arbeit: Organ der zionistischen volkssozialistischen Partei Hapöelhaza'ir Deutscher Landesverband der Allweltlichen Zionistischen Arbeitspartei Hitachdut. Berlin.
AJS Review. Association of Jewish Studies. Cambridge, Massachusetts.
Blau-Weiss Blätter: Führerzeitung. Monatsschrift für jüdisches Jugendwandern. Berlin.
Bulletin des Leo Baeck Instituts. Tel Aviv.
Centralvereins Zeitung: Blätter für Deutschtum und Judentum. Berlin.
Commentary: A Jewish Review. New York.
Freie Zionistische Blätter. Berlin.
Der Freistaat: Monatsschrift für jüdische Kultur und Politik. Berlin.
Im deutschen Reich: Zeitschrift des Centralvereins deutscher Staatsbürger jüdischen Glaubens. Berlin.
Der Israelit: Ein Centralorgan für das orthodoxe Judentum. Frankfurt and Mainz.
Der Israelit des 19. Jahrhunderts: Eine Wochenschrift für die Kenntnis und Reform des Israelitischen Lebens. Hersfeld.
Israelitische Annalen: Ein Centralblatt für Geschichte, Literatur und Kultur des Israeliten aller Zeiten und Länder. Frankfurt.

Israelitisches Familienblatt. Hamburg.
Jerubbaal: Zeitschrift der jüdischen Jugend. Vienna.
Jeschurun: Ein Monatsblatt für Förderung jüdischen Geistes und jüdischen Lebens in Haus, Gemeinde und Schule. 1855–70, Frankfurt.
Jeschurun: Monatsschrift für Lehre und Leben im Judentum. 1914–30. Berlin.
Jewish Social Studies: A Quarterly Journal Devoted to Contemporary and Historical Aspects of Jewish Life. New York.
Der Jude: Eine Monatsschrift. Berlin.
Die Jüdische Arbeiterstimme. Berlin.
Die Jüdische Presse: Organ für die Gesamtinteressen des Judenthums. Berlin.
Jüdische Rundschau. Berlin.
Der Jüdische Student: Monatsschrift des Bundes Juedischer Corporationen. Berlin.
Jüdische Welt: Rundschau. Jerusalem.
Der Jüdische Wille: Kartell jüdischer Verbindungen. Berlin.
Jüdische Wohlfahrtspflege und Sozialpolitik: Zeitschrift der Zentralwohlfahrtsstelle der deutschen Juden. Berlin.
Der Junge Jude. Berlin.
K. C. Blätter: Monatsschrift der im Kartell-Convent vereinigten Korporationen. Berlin.
Kritik (Yiddish). Vienna.
Leo Baeck Institute Yearbook. London.
Mitteilungen aus dem Verein zur Abwehr des Antisemitismus. Berlin.
Mitteilungen der jüdischen Reformgemeinde zu Berlin. Berlin.
Mitteilungen des Verbandes der jüdischen Jugendvereine Deutschlands. Berlin.
Mitteilungsblatt des Verbandes nationaldeutscher Juden. Berlin.
Monatsschrift für Geschichte und Wissenschaft des Judentums. Berlin.
Neue Jüdische Monatshefte: Zeitschrift für Politik, Wirtschaft und Literatur in Ost und West. Berlin.
Oif der Schwel. Yiddish. Berlin.
Ost und West: Illustrierte Monatsschrift für das gesamte Judentum. Berlin.
Der Ostjude: Jiddisches Wochenblatt: Zentralorgan des Verbandes der Ostjuden in Deutschland. Berlin.
Der Schild: Zeitschrift des Reichsbundes jüdischer Frontsoldaten. Berlin.
Schlemiel: Jüdische Blätter für Humor und Kunst. Berlin.
Die Stimme der Wahrheit: Jahrbuch für wissenschaftlichen Zionismus. Würzburg.
Sulamith: Eine Zeitschrift zur Beförderung der Kultur und Humanität unter den Israeliten. Dessau.
Volk und Land: Jüdische Wochenschrift für Politik, Wirtschaft und Palästinaarbeit. Berlin.
Die Welt: Zentralorgan der zionistischen Bewegung. Berlin.
YIVO Annual of Jewish Social Science. New York.
Zeitschrift für Demographie und Statistik der Juden. Berlin.

General

The American Scholar. New York.
Berliner Tageblatt. Berlin.
Central European History. Atlanta.
Deutsche Zeitung. Berlin.
Deutschlands Erneuerung: Monatsschrift für das deutsche Volk. Munich.
Die Gesellschaft: Monatsschrift für Literatur und Kunst. Leipzig.
Die Grenzboten: Zeitschrift für Politik, Literatur und Kunst. Berlin and Leipzig.
Hochland: Monatsschrift für alle Gebiete des Wissens, der Literatur und Kunst. Munich.
Journal of Modern History. Chicago.
Der Kunstwart. Dresden and Munich.
Literarisches Echo. Berlin.
Literarisches Zentralblatt für Deutschland. Leipzig.
Der Neue Merkur. Berlin.
Die Neue Rundschau. Berlin.
Das Neue Tage-Buch. Paris.
Neue Zeit: Wochenschrift der Deutschen Sozialdemokratie. Stuttgart.
New German Critique. Milwaukee.
Politisch-Anthropologische Monatsschrift. Leipzig.
Preussische Jahrbücher. Berlin.
Die Schaubühne. Berlin.
Sexualprobleme: Zeitschrift für Sexualwissenschaft und Sexualpolitik. Frankfurt.
Süddeutsche Monatshefte. Munich.
The Times Literary Supplement. London.
Der Vortrupp: Deutsche Zeitschrift für das Menschentum unsrer Zeit. Hamburg.
Die Weissen Blätter. Berlin and Leipzig.
Zeitschrift für Politik. Berlin.
Die Zukunft. Berlin.

PRIMARY SOURCES

Abeles, Otto. *Begegnung mit Juden.* Vienna and Jerusalem. 1936.
Agnon, Sh. Y. "Ad hena." In *Kol sipurav shel Sh. Y. Agnon.* Vol. 7. 11th ed., rev. Jerusalem and Tel Aviv, 1966.
Agnon, Sh. Y. *Behanuto shel Mar Lublin.* Jerusalem and Tel Aviv, 1974.
Andree, Richard. *Zur Volkskunde der Juden.* Bielefeld and Leipzig: Velhagen & Klasing, 1881.

Antin, Mary. *The Promised Land: With Illustrations from Photographs.* Boston and New York: Houghton Mifflin Co., 1912.

Auerbach, Berthold. *Gesammelte Schriften.* Stuttgart: Cotta 18, 1863–64.

Auerbach, Elias. *Pionier der Verwirklichung: Ein Arzt aus Deutschland erzählt vom Beginn der zionistischen Bewegung in Palästina kurz nach der Jahrhundertwende.* Stuttgart: Deutsche Verlags-Anstalt, 1969.

Bartels, Adolf. *Die Berechtigung des Antisemitismus.* Berlin, n.d.

Bartels, Adolf. *Rasse und Volkstum: Gesammelte Aufsätze zur nationalen Weltanschauung.* Weimar, 1920.

Bauer, Bruno. *Die Judenfrage.* Braunschweig, 1843.

Bernfeld, Siegfried. *Kinderheim Baumgarten: Bericht über einen ernsthaften Versuch mit neuer Erziehung.* Berlin, 1921.

Bernstein, Aaron David. *Mendel Gibbor: Eine Novelle.* Berlin: Schocken Verlag, 1935.

Bernstein, Aaron David. *Vogele der Maggid: Eine Novelle.* Berlin: Schocken Verlag, 1936.

Bertram, Rudolf. *Die Ostjuden in Deutschland.* Berlin, 1924.

Bialik, Hayyim Nahman. *Essays.* Autorisierte Übertragung aus dem Hebräischen von Viktor Kellner. Berlin: Jüdischer Verlag, 1925.

Bieber, Hugo, *Heinrich Heine: Jüdisches Manifest.* New York: Mary S. Rosenberg, 1946.

Bin Gorion, Micha Joseph [Berdichevsky]. *Mimekor Yisrael: Classical Jewish Folktales.* Vols. 1–5. Edited by E. Bin Gorion. Translated by I. M. Lask. Bloomington and London: Indiana University Press, 1976.

Bin Gorion, Micha Joseph [Berdichevsky]. *Die Sagen der Juden: Mythen, Legenden, Auslegungen.* Berlin: Schocken, 1935.

Bin Gorion, Micha Joseph [Berdichevsky]. *Vom Östlichen Judentum: Religiöses, Literarisches, Politisches.* Berlin: R. Lowitt, 1918.

Bin Gorion, Micha Joseph [Berdichevsky]. *Vor dem Sturm: Ostjüdische Geschichten.* Vienna: R. Lowitt, 1919.

Birnbaum, Nathan. *Ausgewählte Schriften zur jüdischen Frage.* Vols. 1–2. Czernowitz: Verlag der Buchhandlung Birnbaum & Kohut, 1910.

Birnbaum, Nathan. *Gottes Volk.* Vienna and Berlin: R. Lowitt, 1918.

Bischoff, Erich. *Klarheit in der Ostjudenfrage: Tatsachen, Gedanken und Grundsätze.* Dresden and Leipzig, 1916.

Blach, Friedrich. *Die Juden in Deutschland: Von einem jüdischen Deutschen.* Berlin: K. Curtius, 1911.

Blei, Franz. *Menschliche Betrachtungen zur Politik.* Munich, 1916.

Bloch, Ernst. *Durch die Wüste: Frühe kritische Aufsätze.* Frankfurt am Main: Suhrkamp, 1964.

Blumenfeld, Kurt. *Erlebte Judenfrage: Ein Vierteljahrhundert deutscher Zionismus.* Stuttgart: Deutsche Verlags-Anstalt, 1962.

Bodenheimer, Max Isidor. *Prelude to Israel: The Memoirs of M. I. Bodenheimer.* Edited by H. H. Bodenheimer. Translated by I. Cohen. New York: T. Yoseloff, 1963.

Bodenheimer, Max Isidor. *Wohin mit den russischen Juden?* Hamburg: Verlag des Deutsch-Israelitschen Familienblattes, 1891.

Boehlich, Walter, ed. *Der Berliner Antisemitismusstreit.* Frankfurt am Main: Insel-Verlag, 1965.

Borchardt, Georg Hermann [Georg Hermann]. *Hetty Geybert.* Translated by A. Barwell. New York: H. Doran Co., 1924.

Brunner, Constantin. *Der Judenhass und die Juden.* Berlin, 1919.

Brunner, Constantin. *Vom Einsiedler Constantin Brunner: Mein Leben und Schaffen: Unsre scholastische Bildung: Das Unglück unsres deutschen Volkes und unsre "Völkischen."* Potsdam: G. Kiepenheuer, 1924.

Brunner, Constantin. *Von den Pflichten der Juden und von den Pflichten des Staates.* Berlin: G. Kiepenheuer, 1930.

Buber, Martin. *Briefwechsel aus sieben Jahrzehnten.* Vols. 1–2. Edited by Grete Schaeder. Heidelberg: Schneider, 1972–73.

Buber, Martin. *Daniel: Dialogues on Realization.* Translated by M. Friedman. New York: Rinehart & Winston, 1964.

Buber, Martin. *Die Geschichten des Rabbi Nachman.* Frankfurt am Main: Rüttent Loening, 1906.

Buber, Martin. *Hasidism and Modern Man.* Edited and translated by M. Friedman. New York: Horizon Press, 1958.

Buber, Martin. *On Judaism.* Edited by N. N. Glatzer. New York: Schocken Books, 1967.

Buber, Martin. *Der Jude und sein Judentum: Gesammelte Aufsätze und Reden.* Cologne: J. Melzer, 1963.

Buber, Martin. *The Legend of the Baal Shem.* Translated by M. Friedman. New York: Harper, 1955.

Buber, Martin. *Werke: Schriften zum Chassidismus.* Vol. 3. Munich: Kösel-Verlag, 1962.

Busch, Moritz. *Israel und die Gojim: Beiträge zur Beurtheilung der Judenfrage.* Leipzig, 1880.

Carlebach, Solomon. *Der Zionismus in seiner jetzigen Gestalt und in der heutigen Zeit: Eine Gefahr der Judenheit.* Lübeck, 1917.

Cohen, Arthur, ed. *The Jew: Essays from Martin Buber's Journal "Der Jude," 1916–1928.* Translated by J. Neugroschel. Alabama: University of Alabama Press, 1980.

Cohen, Hermann. *Deutschtum und Judentum: Mit grundlegenden Betrachtungen über Staat und Internationalismus.* Giessen: A. Topelmann, 1916.

Dehmel, Richard. *Zwischen Volk und Menschheit: Kriegstagebuch.* Berlin, 1919.

Döblin, Alfred. *Flucht und Sammlung des Judenvolks: Aufsätze und Erzählungen.* Amsterdam: Querido Verlag, 1935.

Döblin, Alfred. *Jüdische Erneuerung.* Amsterdam: Querido, 1933.

Döblin, Alfred. *Reise in Polen.* Olten: Freiburg im Breisgau, 1968.

Dohm, Christian Wilhelm. *Ueber die bürgerliche Verbesserung der Juden.* Berlin, 1781.

Ehrlich, Eugen. *Die Aufgaben der Sozialpolitik im österreichischen Osten: Juden und Bauernfrage.* Munich and Leipzig, 1916.

Eliasberg, Alexander. *Jüdisches Theater: Eine dramatische Anthologie ostjüdischer Dichter.* Munich, 1919.

Eliasberg, Alexander. *Ostjüdische Novellen.* Munich, 1918.

Eliasberg, Alexander. *Ostjüdische Volkslieder.* Munich, 1918.

Eliasberg, Alexander. *Sagen polnischer Juden: Ausgewählt und übertragen von Alexander Eliasberg.* Munich: Gl Müller, 1916.

Feuchtwanger, Siegberg. *Die Judenfrage als wissenschaftliches und politisches Problem.* Berlin, 1916.

Fischer, Hans [Kurt Aram]. *Der Zar und seine Juden.* Berlin: K. Curtius, 1914.

Fraenkel, Abraham A. *Lebenskreise: Aus den Erinnerungen eines jüdischen Mathematikers.* Stuttgart: Deutsche Verlags-Anstalt, 1967.

Franzos, Karl Emil. *Halb-Asien: Land und Leute des östlichen Europa.* 6 vols. in 3. Stuttgart and Berlin: J. G. Cotta'sche Buchhandlung, 1912–14. Vols. 1, 2: *Aus Halb-Asien,* 5th ed., 1914. Vols. 3, 4: *Vom Don zur Donau,* 3rd ed., 1912. Vols. 5, 6: *Aus der grossen Ebene,* 2nd ed., n.d.

Franzos, Karl Emil. *The Jews of Barnow.* Translated by M. W. Macdowall. New York, 1883.

Franzos, Karl Emil. *Der Pojaz.* 1905. Königstein, 1979.

Freud, Sigmund. *Jokes and Their Relation to the Unconscious.* Translated by James Strachey. New York: W. W. Norton and Company, 1963.

Freud, Sigmund, and Arnold Zweig. *The Letters of Sigmund Freud and Arnold Zweig.* Edited by Ernest L. Freud. New York: Harcourt, Brace & World, 1970.

Freytag, Gustav. *Debit and Credit.* Translated by Mrs. Malcolm. London: R. Bentley, 1858.

Friedländer, David. *Ueber die Verbesserung der Israeliten im Königreich Pohlen: Ein von der Regierung daselbst im Jahr 1816 abgefordertes Gutachten.* Berlin, 1819.

Friedländer, Moriz. *Die drei Belfer: Culturbilder aus Galizien.* Vienna, 1894.

Friedländer, Moriz. *Vom Cheder zur Werkstätte: Eine Erzählung aus dem Leben in Galizien.* Vienna, 1885.

Friedmann, Lazarus. *Die Emanzipation der Ostjuden und ihr Einfluss auf die Westjuden: Ein Wort zur rechten Zeit.* Frankfurt am Main, 1917.

Fritsch, Theodor. *Handbuch der Judenfrage: Die wichtigsten Tatsachen zur Beurteilung des jüdischen Volkes.* Edited by Theodor Fritsch. 43rd ed., rev. Leipzig: Hammer-Verlag, 1934.

Fritz, Georg. *Die Ostjudenfrage: Zionismus und Grenzschluss.* Munich, 1915.

Fromer, Jakob. *Vom Ghetto zur modernen Kultur: Eine Lebensgeschichte.* Heidelberg: Im Verlage des Verfassers, 1906.

Fromer, Jakob. *Das Wesen des Judentums.* Berlin: Hupeden & Merzyn, 1905.

Fuchs, Eduard. *Die Juden in der Karikatur: Ein Beitrag zur Kulturgeschichte.* Munich: A. Langen, 1921.

Fuchs, Eugen. *Um Deutschtum und Judentum: Gesammelte Reden und Aufsätze (1894–1919)*. Im Auftrage des Centralvereins deutscher Staatsbürger jüdischen Glaubens. Edited by Leo Hirschfeld. Frankfurt am Main: J. Kaufmann, 1919.

Ganz, Hugo. *Vor der Katastrophe*. Frankfurt am Main, 1904.

Geiger, Abraham. *Abraham Geiger and Liberal Judaism: The Challenge of the Nineteenth Century*. Compiled by Max Wiener. Translated by D. J. Schlochauer. Philadelphia: Jewish Publication Society of America, 1962.

Geiger, Abraham. *Abraham Geigers nachgelassene Schriften*. Edited by Ludwig Geiger. Berlin: L. Gerschel, 1875–78.

Gellert, Christian. *Sämtliche Schriften*. Vol. 5. M. G. Weidmann and Caspar Fritsch: Leipzig, 1775.

Ginsberg, Asher Zvi [Achad Ha'am]. *Selected Essays of Achad Ha'am*. Edited and translated by Leon Simon. Cleveland: World Press, 1962.

Glatzer, Nahum N., ed. *Leopold Zunz: Jude, Deutscher, Europäer: Ein jüdisches Gelehrtenschicksal des 19. Jahrhunderts in Briefen an Freunde*. Tübingen: J. C. B. Mohr, 1964.

Goldman, Felix. *Polnische Juden*. Berlin, n.d.

Goldman, Felix. *Die Stellung des deutschen Rabbiners zur Ostjudenfrage*. Frankfurt am Main, 1916.

Goldmann, Nahum. *The Autobiography of Nahum Goldmann: Sixty Years of Jewish Life*. Translated by H. Sebba. New York: Holt, Rinehart & Winston, 1969.

Grabowsky, Adolf. *Die polnische Frage*. Berlin, 1916.

Grattenauer, C. W. F. *Ueber die physische und moralische Verfassung der heutigen Juden*. Berlin, 1791.

Grattenauer, C. W. F. *Wider die Juden*. Berlin, 1802.

Grätz, Heinrich. *History of the Jews: From the Chmielnicki Persecution of the Jews in Poland to the Period of Emancipation in Central Europe*. Vol. 5. Philadelphia: Jewish Publication Society of America, 1895.

Gronemann, Sammy. *Howdoloh und Zapfenstreich: Erinnerungen an die ostjüdische Etappe: 1916–18*. Berlin: Jüdischer Verlag, 1924.

Gronemann, Sammy. *Tohuwabohu*. Berlin, 1920.

Günther, Hans F. *Rassenkunde des jüdischen Volkes*. Munich: J. F. Lehmann, 1930.

Hardt, Fred B., ed. *Die deutschen Schützengraben- und Soldatenzeitungen*. Munich: R. Piper & Co., 1917.

Heimer, Ernst. *Der Giftpilz: Ein Stürmerbuch für jung und alt*. Bilder von Fips. Nuremberg: Der Stürmer, 1938.

Heine, Heinrich. *The Poetry and Prose of Heinrich Heine*. Edited by F. Ewen. New York: Citadel Press, 1948.

Herzberg-Fränkel, Leo. *Polnische Juden: Geschichten und Bilder*. Stuttgart, 1888.

Herzl, Theodor. *Zionist Writings: Essays and Addresses*. Translated by H. Zohn. New York: Herzl Press, 1973–75.

Hess, Moses. *Rome and Jerusalem*. Translated by M. J. Bloom. New York: Philosophical Library, 1958.

His, Wilhelm. *A German Doctor at the Front*. Translated by G. M. Blech and J. R. Kean. Washington, D.C.: The National Service Publishing Co., 1933.

Hitler, Adolf. *Mein Kampf*. Translated by R. Manheim. Boston: Houghton Mifflin Co., 1971.

Holdheim, Gerhard, and Walter Preuss, *Die theoretischen Grundlagen des Zionismus*. Berlin: Welt-Verlag, 1919.

Jacobowski, Ludwig. *Werther, der Jude*. Dresden and Leipzig, 1903.

Jost, Markus. *Geschichte der Israeliten seit der Zeit der Maccabäer bis auf unsere Tage*. Vol. 9. Berlin, 1828.

Kafka, Franz. *The Diaries of Franz Kafka*. 2 vols. New York: Schocken Books, 1965. Vol. 1: *1910–1913*. Edited by Max Brod. Translated by Joseph Kresh. Vol. 2: *1914–1923*. Edited by Max Brod. Translated by Martin Greenberg with the cooperation of Hannah Arendt.

Kafka, Franz. *I am a Memory Come Alive: Autobiographical Writings*. Edited by N. N. Glatzer. New York: Schocken Books, 1974.

Kafka, Franz. *Letters to Felice*. Edited by E. Heller and J. Born. Translated by J. Stem and E. Duckworth. Middlesex: Secker & Warburg, 1974.

Kafka, Franz. *Letters to Friends, Family and Editors*. Translated by R. and C. Winston. New York: Schocken Books, 1977.

Kafka, Franz. *Letter to His Father*. Translated by E. Kaiser and E. Wilkins. New York: Schocken Books, 1966.

Kaplun-Kogan, Wlad. *Die Juden in Polen: Ein geschichtlicher Überlick*. Berlin, 1915.

Kaplun-Kogan, Wlad. *Die jüdische Sprach- und Kulturgemeinschaft in Polen: Eine statistische Studie: Verfasst im Augtrage des "Komitees für den Osten"*. Berlin and Vienna: R. Lowitt, 1917.

Kaplun-Kogan, Wlad. *Der Krieg: Eine Schicksalsstunde des jüdischen Volkes*. Bonn: A. Marcus & E. Weber, 1915.

Kaufmann, Fritz Mordechai. *Gesammelte Schriften*. Berlin, 1923.

Kaufmann, Fritz Mordechai, and Werner Senator. *Die Einwanderung der Ostjuden: Eine Gefahr oder ein sozial-politisches Problem? Vier Aufsätze. Schriften des Arbeiterfürsorgeamtes der jüdischen Organisationen Deutschlands*. Berlin 1920.

Kaufmann, Walter, ed. and trans. *The Portable Nietzsche*. New York: Viking Press, 1968.

Kautsky, Karl. *Are the Jews a Race?* 2nd ed., rev. Westport, Connecticut: Greenwood Press, 1972.

Klatzkin, Jakob. *Hermann Cohen*. 2nd ed., rev. Berlin: Jüdischer Verlag, 1921.

Klatzkin, Jakob. *Probleme des modernen Judentums*. Berlin: Jüdischer Verlag, 1918.

Kompert, Leopold. *Sämtliche Werke*. Edited by S. Hock. Leipzig, n.d. [1906].

Langbehn, Julius. *Rembrandt als Erzieher: Von einem Deutschen*. 3rd ed., rev. Leipzig: C. L. Hirschfeld, 1896.

Langer, Jiri. *Die Erotik der Kabbala*. Prague, 1923.

Langer, Jiri. *Nine Gates to the Chassidic Mysteries.* Translated by S. Jolly. New York: Behrman House, 1976.

Lehmann, Alfred [Lemm]. *Der Weg der Deutschjuden: Eine Skizzierung.* Leipzig: Der Neue Geist-Verlag, 1919.

Lehmann, Siegfried. *Idee der jüdischen Siedlung und des Volksheims.* n.p., n.d.

Lehmann, Siegfried. *Das jüdische Volksheim: Erster Bericht.* Berlin, 1916.

Lehmann, Siegfried. *Von der Strassenhorde zur Gemeinschaft: Aus dem Leben des jüdischen Kinderhauses in Kowno.* n.p., 1926.

Lessing, Theodor. *Einmal und nie wieder: Lebenserinnerungen.* Gütersloh: Bertelsmann Sachbuchverlag, 1969.

Lessing, Theodor. *Der jüdische Selbsthass.* Berlin, 1930.

Lichtheim, Richard. *Rückkehr: Lebenserinnerungen aus der Frühzeit des deutschen Zionismus.* Stuttgart: Deutsche Verlags-Anstalt, 1970.

Liebermann, Mischket. *Aus dem Ghetto in die Welt: Autobiographie.* Berlin: Verlag der Nation, 1977.

Loewenberg, Jakob. *Aus zwei Quellen.* Berlin: E. Fleischel & Co., 1914.

Lubarsch, Otto. *Ein bewegtes Gelehrtenleben: Erinnerungen und Erleb-nisse. Kämpfe und Gedanken.* Berlin: J. Springer, 1931.

Maimon, Solomon. *Lebensgeschichte.* Edited by Jakob Fromer. Munich, 1911.

Marcus, Ahron. *Der Chassidismus.* Pleschen, 1901.

Marcus, Ahron. *Hartmanns inductive Philosophie im Chassidismus.* Vienna: M. Walzner, 1888.

Marx, Julius. *Kriegstagebuch eines Juden.* Zurich, 1939.

Mendelssohn, Moses. *Gesammelte Schriften.* Vol. 5. Edited by Dr. G. B. Mendelssohn. Leipzig, 1844.

Moser, Otto von. *Feldzugsaufzeichnungen, 1914–1918.* Stuttgart, 1928.

Nathan, Paul. *Die Ostjuden in Deutschland und die antisemitische Reak-tion: Zeit- und Streitfragen: Heft 5.* Berlin, 1922.

Naumann, Max. *Von mosaischen und nichtmosaischen Juden.* Berlin, 1921.

Naumann, Max. *Von nationaldeutschen Juden.* Berlin, 1920.

Neumann, Salomon. *Die Fabel von der jüdischen Masseneinwanderung.* Berlin: L. Simon, 1881.

Nietzsche, Friedrich. *Beyond Good and Evil: Prelude to a Philosophy of the Future.* Translated by Walter Kaufmann. New York: Vintage Books, 1966.

Nordau, Max Simon. *Degeneration.* New York: H. Fertig, 1968.

Nordau, Max Simon. *Zionistische Schriften.* Cologne and Leipzig, 1909.

Oppeln-Bronikowski, Friedrich von. *Antisemitismus? Eine unparteiische Prüfung des Problems.* Charlottenburg, 1920.

Oppeln-Bronikowski, Friedrich von. *Gerechtigkeit! Zur Lösung der Juden-frage.* Berlin and Wilmersdorf, 1932.

Oppenheimer, Franz. *Erlebtes, Erstrebtes, Erreichtes: Lebenserinnerun-gen.* Düsseldorf: J. Melzer, 1964.

Peyser, Alfred. *Nationaldeutsche Juden und ihre Lästerer: Eine Streit-schrift.* Berlin, n.d.

Piscator, Erwin. *The Political Theatre: A History 1914–1929.* Translated with chapter introductions by Hugh Rorrison. New York: Avon Books, 1978.

Raabe, Wilhelm. *Der Hungerpastor.* Berlin: O. Janke. 1899.

Rathhaus, Samuel. *Der Zurückgang der israelitischen Religionsgesellschaft.* Frankfurt am Main, 1914.

Rée, Anton. *Die Sprachverhältnisse der heutigen Juden im Interesse der Gegenwart und mit besonderer Rücksicht auf Volkserziehung.* Hamburg, 1844.

Rosenheim, Jacob. *Ausgewählte Aufsätze und Ansprachen.* Vol. 1. Frankfurt am Main, 1930.

Rosenzweig, Franz. *Briefe.* Edited by Edith Rosenzweig. Berlin: Schocken Verlag, 1935.

Rosenzweig, Franz. *Franz Rosenzweig: His Life and Thought.* Edited by Nahum N. Glatzer. New York: Schocken Books, 1961.

Rosenzweig, Franz. *The Star of Redemption.* 2nd ed., rev. Translated by W. W. Hallo. Boston: Beacon Press, 1971.

Roth, Alfred. *Judentum und Bolschewismus: Enthüllungen aus jüdischen Geheimakten: Ein Mahn- und Warnruf in letzter Stunde.* Hamburg, 1920.

Roth, Joseph. "Juden auf Wanderschaft" In *Werke,* vol. 3. Berlin: Kiepenheuer, 1956.

Sacher-Masoch, Leopold. *Ausgewählte Ghetto-Geschichten.* Leipzig, 1918.

Scheinhaus, Leon. *Ein deutscher Pionier: Dr. Lilienthals Kulturversuch in Russland.* Berlin, 1911.

Schiff, Hermann. *Hundert und ein Sabbath oder Geschichten und Sagen des israelitischen Volkes.* Leipzig, 1842.

Schiff, Hermann. *Schief Levinche mit seiner Kalle oder polnische Wirtschaft.* 2nd ed., rev. Hamburg and Berlin, 1919.

Schoeps, Hans-Joachim. *"Bereit für Deutschland!" Der Patriotismus deutscher Juden und der Nationalsozialismus: Frühe Schriften 1930 bis 1939: Eine historische Dokumentation.* Berlin: Haude & Spener, 1970.

Scholem, Gershom. *From Berlin to Jerusalem: Memories of My Youth.* New York: Schocken Books, 1980.

Sebottendorf, Rudolf von. *Bevor Hitler kam: Urkundliches aus der Frühzeit der nationalsozialistischen Bewegung.* Munich: Grassinger, 1933.

Segel, Binjamin Wolf. *Die Entdeckungsreise des Herrn Dr. Theodor Lessing zu den Ostjuden.* Lemberg, 1910.

Segel, Binjamin Wolf. *Die polnische Judenfrage.* Berlin: G. Stilke, 1916.

Segel, Binjamin Wolf. *Der Weltkrieg und das Schicksal der Juden: Stimme eines galizischen Juden an seine Glaubensgenossen in den neutralen Ländern insbesondere in Amerika.* Berlin: G. Stilke, 1916.

Sessa, Karl Alexander. *Unser Verkehr: Eine Posse in einem Aufzug.* Leipzig, 1815.

Simon, Max. *Der Weltkrieg und die Judenfrage.* Leipzig and Berlin, 1916.

Sombart, Werner. *The Jews and Modern Capitalism.* Translated by M. Epstein. New York: Burt Franklin, 1969.

Sombart, Werner, ed. *Judentaufen.* Munich: Georg Müller Verlag, 1912.

Spengler, Oswald. *The Decline of the West.* Vol. 2, *Perspectives of World History.* Authorized translation by Charles Francis Atkinson. New York: Alfred A. Knopf, 1980.

Strauss, Ludwig. *Ostjüdische Liebeslieder.* Berlin, 1920.

Susman, Margarete. *Ich habe viele Leben gelebt. Erinnerungen.* Stuttgart, 1966.

Tannenbaum, Eugen, ed. *Kriegsbriefe deutscher und österreichischer Juden.* Berlin, 1915.

Trebitsch, Arthur. *Deutscher Geist—oder Judentum! Der Weg der Befreiung.* Berlin, 1921.

Trebitsch, Arthur. *Geist und Judentum.* Vienna and Leipzig, 1919.

Treitschke, Heinrich von. *Treitschke's History of Germany in the Nineteenth Century.* Vol. 7. Translated by E. and C. Paul. London: Jarrold & Sons, 1919.

Tucholsky, Kurt. *Ausgewählte Werke.* Hamburg: Rowohlt, 1965.

Tucholsky, Kurt. *Gesammelte Werke.* Vol. 1. Hamburg: Rowohlt, 1960.

Viertel, Berthold. *Karl Kraus: Ein Charakter und die Zeit.* Dresden, 1921.

Vom Judentum: Ein Sammelbuch: Herausgegeben vom Verein jüdischer Hochschüler Bar Kochba in Prag. Leipzig: Kurt Wolff Verlag, 1913.

Voss, Julius von. *Die Griechheit: Originallustspiel in 5 Akten.* Berlin, 1807.

Wagner, Richard. *Richard Wagner's Prose Works.* Vol. 7, *The Theatre.* Translated by W. A. Ellis. London: K. Paul, Trench, Trubner & Co., 1907.

Wassermann, Jakob. *My Life as German and Jew.* Translated by S. N. Brainin. New York: Conrad-McCann, 1933.

Wedd, A. F., ed. *German Students' War Letters.* New York, 1929.

Weininger, Otto. *Sex and Character.* Authorized translation from the 6th German ed. New York: G. P. Putnam's Sons, 1906.

Weizmann, Chaim. *The Letters and Papers of Chaim Weizmann.* Vols. 1–6. General editor, M. W. Weisgal. London: Oxford University Press, 1968–74.

Weizmann, Chaim. *Trial and Error: The Autobiography of Chaim Weizmann.* Philadelphia, 1949.

Winninger, Salomon. *Grosse jüdische Nationalbiographie: Mit mehr als 8000 Lebensbeschreibungen namhafter jüdischer Männer und Frauen aller Zeiten und Länder: Ein Nachschlagewerk für das jüdische Volk and dessen Freunde.* Czernowitz: Druck "Orient," 1925–36.

World Zionist Organization, General Council. *The Minutes of the Zionist General Council: the Uganda Controversy.* Edited by M. Heymann. Jerusalem: Israel Unversities Press, 1970.

Zivier, Ezechiel. *Zur Rassen- und Ostjudenfrage.* Posen, 1916.

Zunz, Leopold. *Die gottesdienstlichen Vorträge der Juden historisch entwickelt: Ein Beitrag zur Altertumskunde und biblischen Kritik, zur Literatur und Religionsgeschichte.* Frankfurt am Main, 1892.

Zweig, Arnold. *Das Los der Geflüchteten.* Berlin, 1929.

Zweig, Arnold. "Das ostjüdische Antlitz" in *Herkunft und Zukunft: Zwei Essays zum Schicksal eines Volkes.* Vienna: Phaidon Verlag, 1929.

SECONDARY SOURCES

Adler-Rudel, Shalom. *Ostjuden in Deutschland 1880–1940: Schriftenreihe wissenschaftlicher Abhandlungen des Leo Baeck Instituts.* Tübingen: J. C. B. Mohr, 1959.

Altmann, Alexander. *Moses Mendelssohn: A Biographical Study.* Philadelphia: The Jewish Publication Society of America, 1973.

Arendt, Hannah. *The Origins of Totalitarianism.* New ed. 2nd ed. New York: Harcourt Brace, 1966.

Beck, Evelyn Tornton. *Kafka and the Yiddish Theater: Its Impact on His Work.* Madison, Wis.: University of Wisconsin Press, 1971.

Berger, Peter, Brigitte Berger, and Hansfried Kellner. *The Homeless Mind: Modernization and Consciousness.* New York: Vintage Books, 1974.

Berghahn, Volker R., and Martin Kitchen, eds. *Germany in the Age of Total War.* London: Croom Helm, 1981.

Biale, David. *Gershom Scholem: Kabbalah and Counter History.* Cambridge: Harvard University Press, 1979.

Bolkosky, Sidney M. *The Distorted Image: German Jewish Perceptions of Germans and Germany, 1918–1935.* New York: Elsevier, 1975.

Bronsen, David, ed. *Jews and Germans from 1860–1933.* Heidelberg, 1979.

Bruford, W. H. *Culture and Society in Classical Weimar, 1775–1806.* Cambridge: at the University Press, 1962.

Bruford, W. H. *The German Tradition of Self-Cultivation: "Bildung" from Humboldt to Thomas Mann.* Cambridge: Cambridge University Press, 1975.

Calebach, Alexander. *Adas Yeschurun of Cologne: The Life and Death of a Kehilla.* Belfast: Mullan, 1964.

Carsten, Francis L. *Fascist Movements in Austria: From Schönerer to Hitler.* London: Sage Publications, 1977.

Chazan, Robert, and Marc Lee Raphael, eds. *Modern Jewish History: A Source Reader.* New York: Schocken Books, 1974.

Conze, Werner. *Polnische Nation und deutsche Politik im Ersten Weltkrieg.* Cologne: Böhlau, 1958.

Cuddihy, John Murray. *The Ordeal of Civility: Freud, Marx, Levi-Strauss and the Jewish Struggle with Modernity.* New York: Basic Books, 1974.

Dawidowicz, Lucy S., ed. *The Golden Tradition: Jewish Life and Thought in Eastern Europe.* Boston: Beacon Press, 1967.

Dobois, E. X. *Sexual Life during the World War.* London, 1937.

Dobroszycki, Lucjan, and Barbara Kirschenblatt-Gimblett. *Image before My Eyes: A Photographic History of Jewish Life in Poland, 1864–1939.* New York: Schocken Books, 1977. Published in cooperation with YIVO Institute for Jewish Research.

Dunker, Ulrich. *Der Reichsbund jüdischer Frontsoldaten 1919–1938: Geschichte eines jüdischen Abwehrvereins.* Düsseldorf: Droste, 1977.

Elon, Amos. *Herzl.* New York: Holt, Rinehart & Winston, 1975.

Feder, Ernst. *Politik und Humanität: Paul Nathan. Ein Lebensbild.* Berlin, 1929.

Frenzel, Elizabeth. *Judengestalten auf der deutschen Bühne: Ein notwendiger Querschnitt durch 700 Jahre Rollengeschichte.* Munich: Deutscher Volksverlag, 1940.

Friedländer, Saul. *When Memory Comes.* New York: Farrar, Straus, Giroux, 1979.

Friedman, Isaiah. *Germany, Turkey and Zionism, 1897–1918.* Oxford: Clarendon Press, 1977.

Gay, Peter. *Freud, Jews and Other Germans: Masters and Victims in Modernist Culture.* New York: Oxford University Press, 1978.

Gay, Peter. *Weimar Culture: The Outsider as Insider.* New York: Harper & Row, 1970.

Goldsmith, Emanuel. *Architects of Yiddishism at the Beginning of the Twentieth Century: A Study in Jewish Cultural History.* Rutherford, N.J.: Fairleigh Dickinson University Press, 1976.

Greenberg, Louis. *The Jews in Russia: The Struggle for Emancipation.* Vol. 1, *1772–1880.* Vol. 2, *1881–1917.* Edited by M. Wischnitzer. New York: Schocken Books, 1976.

Grunfeld, Fredric. *Prophets without Honour: A Background of Freud, Kafka, Einstein and Their World.* New York: McGraw Hill, 1980.

Heer, Friedrich. *Land im Strom der Zeit: Österreich gestern, heute, morgen.* Vienna: Herold, 1958.

Hermann, Klaus J. *Das Dritte Reich und die deutsch-jüdischen Organisationen 1933–1934.* Cologne, 1969.

Hertzberg, Arthur, ed. *The Zionist Idea: A Historical Analysis and Reader.* Garden City, N.J.: Doubleday, 1959.

Hirschfeld, Magnus, and Andreas Gaspar, eds. *Sittengeschichte des Weltkrieges.* Hanau am Main, 1929.

Iggers, Wilma Abeles. *Karl Kraus: A Viennese Critic of the Twentieth Century.* The Hague: Martinus Nijoff, 1967.

Janik, Allan, and Steven Toulmin. *Wittgenstein's Vienna.* New York: Simon and Schuster, 1973.

Joll, James. *Intellectuals in Politics: Three Biographical Essays.* London: Weidenfeld & Nicholson, 1960.

Kahler, Erich. *The Jews Among the Nations.* New York: Frederick Ungar Publishing Co., 1967.

Kallner, Rudolf. *Herzl und Rathenau: Wege jüdischer Existenz an der Wende des 20. Jahrhunderts.* Stuttgart: Klett, 1976.

Kaplan, Marion A. *The Jewish Feminist Movement in Germany: The Campaigns of the Jüdischer Frauenbund, 1904–1938.* Westport, Connecticut: Greenwood Press, 1979.

Katz, Jacob. *Emancipation and Assimilation: Studies in Modern Jewish History.* Farnborough: Greggs, 1972.

Katz, Jacob. *From Prejudice to Destruction: Anti-Semitism, 1700–1933.* Cambridge, Mass.: Harvard University Press, 1980.

Katz, Jacob. *Out of the Ghetto: The Social Background of Emancipation.* New York: Schocken Books, 1978.

Katz, Jacob. *Tradition and Crisis: Jewish Society at the End of the Middle Ages.* New York: Schocken Books, 1971.

Kern, Stephen. *Anatomy and Destiny: A Cultural History of the Human Body.* Indianapolis: Bobbs Merrill, 1975.

Kobler, Franz. *Jüdische Geschichte in Briefen aus Ost and West: Das Zeitalter der Emanzipation.* Vienna: Saturn-Verlag, 1938.

Koestler, Arthur. *The Thirteenth Tribe: The Khazar Empire and Its Heritage.* London: Pan Books, 1977.

Kohn, Hans. *Martin Buber: Sein Werk und seine Zeit: Ein Beitrag zur Geistesgeschichte Mitteleuropas, 1880–1930.* 2nd ed., rev. Cologne: J. Melzer, 1961.

Krojanker, Gustav, ed. *Juden in der deutschen Literatur: Essays über zeitgenössische Schriftsteller.* Berlin: Welt-Verlag, 1922.

Kupferberg, Herbert. *The Mendelssohns: Three Generations of Genius.* New York: Charles Scribner's Sons, 1972.

Lamm, Hans, ed. *Von Juden in München: Ein Gedenkbuch.* Munich: Ner-Tamid Verlag, 1959.

Lewin, Kurt. *Resolving Social Conflicts: Selected Papers on Group Dynamics, 1935–1946.* New York: Harper & Row, 1958.

Liptzin, Solomon. *Germany's Stepchildren.* Philadelphia: Jewish Publication Society of America, 1944.

Lunn, Eugene. *Prophet of Community: The Romantic Socialism of Gustav Landauer.* Berkeley: University of California Press, 1973.

Magris, Claudio. *Weit von wo: Verlorene Welt des Ostjudentums.* Translated by Jutta Prasse. Vienna: Europaverlag, 1974.

Marcus, Markus. *Ahron Marcus: Die Lebensgeschichte eines Chossid.* Basel: Jüdische Rundschau Maccabi, 1966.

Martin, Mary Lynne. "Karl Emil Franzos: His Views on Jewry as Reflected in His Writings on the Ghetto." Ph.D. dissertation, University of Wisconsin, 1968.

Massing, Paul. *Rehearsal for Destruction: A Study of Political Anti-Semitism in Imperial Germany.* New York: Harper & Brothers, 1949.

Mendes-Flohr, Paul R., and Jehuda Reinharz, eds. *The Jew in the Modern World: A Documentary History.* New York: Oxford University Press, 1980.

Meyer, Michael. *The Origins of the Modern Jew.* Detroit: Wayne State University Press, 1967.

Mosse, George L. *The Crisis of German Ideology: Intellectual Origins of the Third Reich.* New York: Grosset & Dunlap, 1964.

Mosse, George L. *Germans and Jews: The Right, the Left and the Search for a "Third Force" in pre-Nazi Germany.* New York: Grosset & Dunlap, 1971.

Mosse, George L. *Masses and Man: Nationalist and Fascist Perceptions of Reality.* New York: Howard Fertig, 1980.

Mosse, George L. *Nazism: An Historical and Comparative Analysis of National Socialism*. New Brunswick: Transaction Books, 1978.

Mosse, Werner E., ed. *Deutsches Judentum in Krieg und Revolution 1916–1923*. Schriftenreihe wissenschaftlicher Abhandlungen des Leo Baecks Instituts, Bd. 25. Tübingen: J. C. B. Mohr, 1971.

Mosse, Werner E. *Juden im Wilhelminischen Deutschland 1890–1914*. Schriftenreihe wissenschaftlicher Abhandlungen des Leo Baecks Instituts, vol. 33. Tübingen: J. C. B. Mohr, 1976.

Neubach, Helmut. *Die Ausweisungen von Polen und Juden aus Preussen 1885–1886*. Wiesbaden, 1967.

Niewyk, Donald L. *The Jews in Weimar Germany*. Baton Rouge: Louisiana State University Press, 1980.

Niewyk, Donald L. *Socialist, Anti-Semite, and Jew: German Social Democracy Confronts the Problem of Anti-Semitism, 1918–1933*. Baton Rouge: Louisiana State University Press, 1971.

Patai, Raphael. *The Vanished World of Jewry*. Picture research by Eugene Rosow with Vivian Kleiman. New York: Macmillan Publishing Co., 1980.

Pierson, Ruth Louise. "German Jewish Identity in the Weimar Republic." Ph.D. dissertation, Yale University, 1970.

Poliakov, Leon. *Harvest of Hate: The Nazi Program for the Destruction of the Jews of Europe*. New York: Holocaust Library, 1979.

Poppel, Stephen M. *Zionism in Germany 1897–1933: The Shaping of a Jewish Identity*. Philadelphia: Jewish Publication Society of America, 1977.

Pulzer, Peter G. J. *The Rise of Political Anti-Semitism in Germany and Austria*. New York and London: John Wiley & Sons, 1964.

Reinharz, Jehuda. *Fatherland or Promised Land: The Dilemma of the German Jew 1893–1914*. Ann Arbor: University of Michigan Press, 1975.

Roshwald, Miriam. "The Stetl in the Works of Kark Emil Franzos, Shalom Aleichem and Shmuel Yosef Agnon." Ph.D. dissertation, University of Minnesota, 1972.

Rühle, Günther. *Theater für die Republik 1917–1933: Im Spiegel der Kritik*. Frankfurt am Main: S. Fischer, 1967.

Rühle, Günther. *Zeit und Theater: Von der Republik zur Diktatur 1925–1933*. Vol. 2. Berlin: Propyläen, 1972.

Ruppin, Arthur. *The Jews in the Modern World*. London: Macmillan & Co., 1934.

Sachar, Howard Morely. *The Course of Modern Jewish History*. Cleveland: World Publishing Co., 1958.

Schaeder, Grete. *The Hebrew Humanism of Martin Buber*. Translated by N. J. Jacobs. Detroit: Wayne State University Press, 1973.

Scholem, Gershom. *The Messianic Idea in Judaism and Other Essays on Jewish Spirituality*. New York: Schocken Books, 1971.

Scholem, Gershom. *On Jews and Judaism in Crisis: Selected Essays*. Edited by Werner J. Dannhauser. New York: Schoken Books, 1976.

Schorsch, Ismar. *Jewish Reactions to German Anti-Semitism 1870–1914*.

New York and Philadelphia: Columbia University Press and Jewish Publication Society of America, 1972.

Schorske, Carl. *Fin-de-Siecle Vienna: Politics and Culture.* New York: Knopf, 1980.

Selig, Wolfram. *Paul Nikolaus Cossmann und die Süddeutschen Monatshefte von 1914–1918: Ein Beitrag zur Geschichte der nationalen Publizistik im Ersten Weltkrieg.* Osnabrück: Fromm, 1967.

Selzer, Michael, ed. *Zionism Reconsidered; The Rejection of Jewish Normalcy.* New York: Macmillan, 1970.

Shulvass, Moses A. *From East to West: The Westward Migrations of Jews from Eastern Europe during the Seventeenth and Eighteenth Centuries.* Detroit: Wayne State University Press, 1971.

Stern, Fritz. *Gold and Iron: Bismarck, Bleichröder and the Building of the German Empire.* New York: Knopf, 1977.

Stern, Fritz. *The Politics of Cultural Despair: A Study in the Rise of Germanic Ideology.* Berkeley: University of California Press, 1974.

Stoffers, Wilhelm. *Juden und Ghetto in der deutschen Literatur bis zum Ausgang des Weltkrieges.* Graz: H. Stiasnys Söhne, 1939.

Tal, Uriel. *Christians and Jews in Germany: Religion, Politics and Ideology in the Second Reich, 1870–1914.* Translated by Noah Jonathan Jacobs. Ithaca and London: Cornell University Press, 1975.

Toury, Jacob. *Soziale und politische Geschichte der Juden in Deutschland 1847–1871: Zwischen Revolution, Reaktion und Emanzipation.* Düsseldorf: Droste, 1977.

Vital, David. *The Origins of Zionism.* Oxford: Clarendon Press, 1975.

Weltsch, Felix, ed. *Prag v'Yerushalayim: Sefer Lezekher Leo Hermann.* Jerusalem: Karen Hayessod Publications, 1954.

Weltsch, Robert. *An der Wende des modernen Judentums: Betrachtungen aus fünf Jahrzehnten.* Tübingen: Mohr, 1972.

Wertheimer, Jack L. "German Policy and Jewish Politics: The Absorption of East European Jews in Germany (1868–1914)." Ph.D. dissertation, Columbia University, 1978.

Williams, Robert C. *Culture in Exile: Russian Emigrés in Germany, 1881–1941.* Ithaca: Cornell University Press, 1972.

Zechlin, Egmont. *Die deutsche Politik und die Juden im Ersten Weltkrieg.* Göttingen: Vandenhoeck und Ruprecht, 1969.

INDEX

DESIGNED BY IRVING PERKINS ASSOCIATES
COMPOSED BY BYRD PREPRESS, SPRINGFIELD, VIRGINIA
MANUFACTURED BY CUSHING-MALLOY, INC., ANN ARBOR, MICHIGAN
TEXT IS SET IN BODONI, DISPLAY LINES IN BODONI AND CITY MEDIUM

Library of Congress Cataloging in Publication Data
Aschheim, Steven E., 1942–
Brothers and strangers.
Bibliography: pp. 307–323.
Includes index.
1. Jews, East European—Germany. 2. Jews—
Germany—Intellectual life. 3. Germany—Ethnic
relations. I. Title.
DS135.G33A76 1982   306'.089924043   81-69812
ISBN 0-299-09110-4